T0202877

Lecture Notes in Computer Science 13908

Founding Editors

Gerhard Goos
Juris Hartmanis

Editorial Board Members

The series Lecture Notes in Computer Science (LNCS), including its subseries Lecture Notes in Artificial Intelligence (LNAI) and Lecture Notes in Bioinformatics (LNBI), has established itself as a medium for the publication of new developments in computer science and information technology research, teaching, and education.

LNCS enjoys close cooperation with the computer science R & D community, the series counts many renowned academics among its volume editors and paper authors, and collaborates with prestigious societies. Its mission is to serve this international community by providing an invaluable service, mainly focused on the publication of conference and workshop proceedings and postproceedings. LNCS commenced publication in 1973.

Sung-Shik Jongmans · Antónia Lopes
Editors

Coordination Models and Languages

25th IFIP WG 6.1 International Conference, COORDINATION 2023
Held as Part of the 18th International Federated Conference
on Distributed Computing Techniques, DisCoTec 2023
Lisbon, Portugal, June 19–23, 2023
Proceedings

 Springer

Editors
Sung-Shik Jongmans 🆔
Open University of The Netherlands
Amsterdam, The Netherlands

Antónia Lopes 🆔
University of Lisbon
Lisbon, Portugal

ISSN 0302-9743   ISSN 1611-3349 (electronic)
Lecture Notes in Computer Science
ISBN 978-3-031-35360-4   ISBN 978-3-031-35361-1 (eBook)
https://doi.org/10.1007/978-3-031-35361-1

This Springer imprint is published by the registered company Springer Nature Switzerland AG
The registered company address is: Gewerbestrasse 11, 6330 Cham, Switzerland

Foreword

The 18th International Federated Conference on Distributed Computing Techniques (DisCoTec) took place in Lisbon, Portugal, from June 19 to June 23, 2023. It was organized by the Department of Computer Science of NOVA School of Science and Technology, NOVA University Lisbon. The DisCoTec series is one of the major events sponsored by the International Federation for Information Processing (IFIP). It comprises three conferences:

- COORDINATION, the IFIP WG 6.1 25th International Conference on Coordination Models and Languages
- DAIS, the IFIP WG 6.1 23rd International Conference on Distributed Applications and Interoperable Systems
- FORTE, the IFIP WG 6.1 43rd International Conference on Formal Techniques for Distributed Objects, Components and Systems

Together, these conferences cover a broad spectrum of distributed computing subjects, ranging from theoretical foundations and formal description techniques to systems research issues. In addition to the individual sessions of each conference, the event also included plenary sessions that gathered attendees from the three conferences. These included joint invited speaker sessions and a joint session for the best papers and artefacts from the three conferences. The keynote speakers of DisCoTec 2023 are listed below:

- Azalea Raad, Imperial College London, UK
- Frank Pfenning, Carnegie Mellon University, USA
- Peter Pietzuch, Imperial College London, UK

Associated with the federated event were also the following satellite events:

- ICE, the 16th Interaction and Concurrency Experience
- BehAPI Tutorial Day, a series of three tutorials covering results from the BehAPI project

in addition to other short tutorials on relevant topics to DisCoTec.

I would like to thank the Program Committee chairs of the different events for their help and cooperation during the preparation of the conference, and the Steering Committee and Advisory Boards of DisCoTec for their guidance, patience, and support. The organization of DisCoTec 2023 was only possible thanks to the work of the Organizing Committee, including João Costa Seco, João Leitão, Mário Pereira, Carlos Baquero (publicity chair), Simão Melo de Sousa (workshops and tutorials chair), Joana Dâmaso (logistics and finances), as well as all the students who volunteered their time to help. Finally, I would like to thank IFIP WG 6.1 and NOVA LINCS for sponsoring this event,

Springer's Lecture Notes in Computer Science team for their support and sponsorship, and EasyChair for providing the reviewing infrastructure.

June 2023   Carla Ferreira

Preface

This volume contains the proceedings of the 25th International Conference on Coordination Models and Languages (COORDINATION 2023), held during June 19–23, 2023, at NOVA University Lisbon, in Lisbon, Portugal, as part of the 18th International Federated Conference on Distributed Computing Techniques (DisCoTec 2023).

Modern information systems rely increasingly on combining concurrent, distributed, mobile, adaptive, reconfigurable, and heterogeneous components. New models, architectures, languages, and verification techniques are necessary to cope with the complexity induced by the demands of today's software development. Coordination languages have emerged as a successful approach, in that they provide abstractions that cleanly separate behavior from communication, thereby increasing modularity, simplifying reasoning, and ultimately enhancing software development. COORDINATION provides a well-established forum for the community of researchers interested in models, languages, architectures, and implementation techniques for coordination.

COORDINATION 2023 solicited contributions in five different categories: (1) long regular papers describing thorough and complete research results and experience reports; (2) short regular papers describing research in progress or opinion papers on past *coordination* research, on the current state of the art, or on prospects for the years to come; (3) short tool papers describing technological artefacts in the scope of the research topics of *coordination*; (4) long tool papers describing technological artefacts in the scope of the research topics of *coordination*; and (5) survey papers describing important results and success stories that originated in the context of *coordination*.

There were 27 paper submissions distributed over the different categories: 14 long regular papers, seven long tool papers, four short regular papers, and two short tool papers. The selection of the papers was entrusted to the Program Committee (PC), with 29 members from 15 different countries. The selection of the papers was done electronically, in two phases. In the first phase, which lasted three weeks, each submission was single-blind reviewed by at least three program committee members, in some cases with the help of external reviewers. During the second phase, which lasted slightly less than one week, the papers were throughly discussed. The decision to accept or reject a paper was based not only on the review reports and scores but also on these in-depth discussions. In the end, 14 papers were selected to be presented at the conference: eight long regular papers, four long tool papers and two short tool papers.

The authors of the accepted papers were subsequently invited to participate in the EAPLS artefact badging. The 11 members of the Artefact Evaluation Committee (AEC), chaired by Alceste Scalas, awarded the available badge to eight artefacts, the reusable badge to five artefacts, and the functional badge to three artefacts.

In addition to the selected papers, these proceedings contain a paper that accompanies the excellent invited talk by Frank Pfenning from Carnegie Mellon University, USA, entitled "Relating Message Passing and Shared Memory, Proof-Theoretically". This paper was subject to a different review process, carried out by the PC chairs.

We are grateful to all involved in COORDINATION 2023. In particular, to the authors for their submissions, the attendees of the conference for their participation, the PC members and external reviewers for their work in reviewing submissions and participating in the discussions, the AEC members for their effort in the evaluation of the artefacts, and the Steering Committee, chaired by Mieke Massink, for their guidance and support. We are also grateful to the Organizing Committee, chaired by Carla Ferreira, for their excellent job. We also thank the providers of EasyChair Conference Management System, which was a great help in organizing the submission and reviewing process and in the preparation of the proceedings. We would also like to acknowledge the prompt and professional support from Springer, who published these proceedings in printed and electronic volumes as part of their LNCS and LNPSE book series.

June 2023

Sung-Shik Jongmans
Antónia Lopes

Organization

General Chair

Carla Ferreira   NOVA University Lisbon, Portugal

Program Committee Chairs

Sung-Shik Jongmans   Open University of the Netherlands,
                                       The Netherlands
Antónia Lopes   University of Lisbon, Portugal

Program Committee

Giorgio Audrito   University of Turin, Italy
Marco Autili   Università dell'Aquila, Italy
Massimo Bartoletti   Università degli Studi di Cagliari, Italy
Laura Bocchi   University of Kent, UK
Marcello Bonsangue   Leiden University, The Netherlands
Javier Cámara   University of Malaga, Spain
Ilaria Castellani   Inria, France
Adrian Francalanza   University of Malta, Malta
Vashti Galpin   University of Edinburgh, UK
Eva Kühn   Vienna University of Technology, Austria
Narges Khakpour   Newcastle University, UK
Alberto Lluch Lafuente   Technical University of Denmark, Denmark
Michele Loreti   University of Camerino, Italy
Mieke Massink   CNR-ISTI, Italy
Sung Meng   Peking University, China
Hernán Melgratti   University of Buenos Aires, Argentina
Fabrizio Montesi   University of Southern Denmark, Denmark
Rumyana Neykova   Brunel University London, UK
Anna Philippou   University of Cyprus, Cyprus
José Proença   Polytechnic Institute of Porto, Portugal
Rosario Pugliese   University of Florence, Italy
Marjan Sirjani   Mälardalen University, Sweden

Violet Ka I Pun	Western Norway University of Applied Sciences, Norway
Carolyn Talcott	SRI International, USA
Silvia Tapia Tarifa	University of Oslo, Norway
Maurice ter Beek	CNR-ISTI, Italy
Peter Thiemann	Universität Freiburg, Germany
Emilio Tuosto	Gran Sasso Science Institute, Italy
Mirko Viroli	University of Bologna, Italy

Artefact Evaluation Committee

Lorenzo Bacchiani	University of Bologna, Italy
Manel Barkallah	University of Namur, Belgium
Christian B. Burlò	Gran Sasso Science Institute, Italy
Luca Di Stefano	University of Gothenburg, Sweden
Marco Giunti	NOVA University Lisbon, Portugal
Stefano Mariani	Università degli Studi di Modena e Reggio Emilia, Italy
Florian Rademacher	University of Applied Sciences and Arts Dortmund, Germany
Aniqa Rehman	University of Camerino, Italy
Neea Rusch	Augusta University, USA
Larisa Safina	Inria - Lille Nord Europe, France
Alceste Scalas (Chair)	Technical University of Denmark, Denmark

Steering Committee

Gul Agha	University of Illinois Urbana-Champaign, USA
Farhad Arbab	CWI and Leiden University, The Netherlands
Simon Bliudze	Inria Lille, France
Laura Bocchi	University of Kent, UK
Ferruccio Damiani	University of Turin, Italy
Ornela Dardha	University of Glasgow, UK
Wolfgang De Meuter	Vrije Universiteit Brussels, Belgium
Rocco De Nicola	IMT School for Advanced Studies Lucca, Italy
Giovanna di Marzo Serugendo	Université de Genève, Switzerland
Tom Holvoet	KU Leuven, Belgium
Jean-Marie Jacquet	University of Namur, Belgium
Christine Julien	University of Texas at Austin, USA
Eva Kühn	Vienna University of Technology, Austria

Alberto Lluch Lafuente	Technical University of Denmark, Denmark
Michele Loreti	Università di Camerino, Italy
Mieke Massink (Chair)	ISTI-CNR, Pisa, Italy
José Proença	CISTER, ISEP, Portugal
Rosario Pugliese	Università di Firenze, Italy
Hanne Riis Nielson	Technical University of Denmark, Denmark
Marjan Sirjani	Mälardalen University, Sweden
Carolyn Talcott	SRI International, USA
Maurice ter Beek	CNR-ISTI, Italy
Emilio Tuosto	Gran Sasso Science Institute, Italy
Vasco T. Vasconcelos	University of Lisbon, Portugal
Mirko Viroli	Università di Bologna, Italy
Gianluigi Zavattaro	Università di Bologna, Italy

Organizing Committee

Carla Ferreira (General Chair)	NOVA University Lisbon, Portugal
João Costa Seco	NOVA University Lisbon, Portugal
João Leitão	NOVA University Lisbon, Portugal
Mário Pereira	NOVA University Lisbon, Portugal
Carlos Baquero (Publicity Chair)	University of Porto, Portugal
Simão Melo de Sousa (Workshops and Tutorials Chair)	University of Beira Interior, Portugal

Additional Reviewers

Peter Ahn
Gianluca Aguzzi
Sara Abbaspour Asadollah
Henning Basold
Roberto Casadei
Erik De Vink
Dimitrios Kouzapas
Zahra Moezkarimi
Maghsood Salimi
Volker Stolz
Jasmine Xuereb

Contents

Keynote

Relating Message Passing and Shared Memory, Proof-Theoretically

Frank Pfenning[1(✉)] and Klaas Pruiksma[2]

[1] Carnegie Mellon University, Pittsburgh, PA, USA
fp@cs.cmu.edu
[2] University of Stuttgart, Stuttgart, Germany
klaas.pruiksma@sec.uni-stuttgart.de

Abstract. We exhibit a strong bisimulation between asynchronous message passing concurrency with session types and shared memory concurrency with futures. A key observation is that both arise from closely related interpretations of the semi-axiomatic sequent calculus with recursive definitions, which provides a unifying framework. As a further result we show that the bisimulation applies to both linear and nonlinear versions of the two languages.

Keywords: Session types · futures · bisimulation

1 Introduction

At first sight, message passing concurrency is quite different from shared memory concurrency. Then we remember the well-known encoding of shared memory cells in the π-calculus [25] and also implementations of message passing abstractions using shared memory [20]. Such mutual encodings are significant, but far from straightforward and difficult to reason about rigorously.

This paper is an attempt to reduce the relationship to its essence in the typed setting. On one side we have a language for asynchronous message passing using session types [14]. On the other side we have typed futures [13,23]. The key conceptual tools in understanding their relationship are the *semi-axiomatic sequent calculus* [10] (SAX) and the *polarities* of the connectives [1,18]. We introduce the relevant aspects of these tools one by one. At the end, we arrive at two *strong bisimulations* between the two sides, one each for linear and nonlinear versions of message passing and shared memory. This is the closest connection we could reasonably hope for.

2 Proof Reduction as Communication

The so-called *Curry-Howard correspondence* [8,16] is often summarized as saying that propositions are types and proofs are programs. This neglects an even deeper

---

Notes to an invited talk by the first author.

© IFIP International Federation for Information Processing 2023
S.-S. Jongmans and A. Lopes (Eds.): COORDINATION 2023, LNCS 13908, pp. 3–27, 2023.
https://doi.org/10.1007/978-3-031-35361-1_1

aspect of the relationship between logic and computation: *proof reduction is computation.* In natural deduction, the fundamental engine of proof reduction is substitution; in Hilbert-style calculi it is combinatory reduction. What about sequent calculus? At the logical level, we write a sequent as

$$A_1, \ldots, A_n \vdash C$$

where propositions A_i are the *antecedents* and C is the *succedent.* In our investigation, the succedent will always be a singleton since we restrict ourselves to *intuitionistic logic.*

We examine the computational interpretation first in the context of a *purely linear calculus,* that is, we take exchange between antecedents for granted, but we allow neither weakening nor contraction. We write

$$\begin{array}{c} P \\ a_1 : A_1, \ldots, a_n : A_n \vdash c : C \end{array}$$

where the a_i and c stand for *means of communication* for the proof (= process) P. Under a message passing interpretation names a_i and c stand for *channels;* under a shared memory interpretation, they stand for *addresses.* We use Γ and Δ to stand for a collection of antecedents, always presupposing that all names a_i and c are distinct.

For the moment, we stick with the message passing interpretation. Then *cut* represents two processes P and Q that are connected via a private communication channel x.

$$\frac{\begin{array}{cc} P(x) & Q(x) \\ \Gamma_1 \vdash x : A & \Gamma_2, x : A \vdash c : C \end{array}}{\Gamma_1, \Gamma_2 \vdash c : C} \text{ cut}$$

It is a *private* communication channel because by our general presupposition x must be different from c and must not already occur in Γ_1 or Γ_2.

The *propositions* A are interpreted as *session types* that govern the particular kinds of messages that are exchanged along a private channel $x : A$. As an example we consider $A \oplus B$, which is the linear rendering of disjunction $A \vee B$. Here is a *principal cut reduction* for this proposition/type.

$$\frac{\dfrac{\begin{array}{c} P'(x') \\ \Gamma_1 \vdash x' : A \end{array}}{\Gamma_1 \vdash x : A \oplus B} \oplus R_1 \quad \dfrac{\begin{array}{cc} Q_1(x') & Q_2(x') \\ \Gamma_2, x' : A \vdash c : C & \Gamma_2, x' : B \vdash c : C \end{array}}{\Gamma_2, x : A \oplus B \vdash c : C} \oplus L}{\Gamma_1, \Gamma_2 \vdash c : C} \text{ cut}$$

$$\longrightarrow \qquad \frac{\begin{array}{cc} P'(x') & Q_1(x') \\ \Gamma_1 \vdash x' : A & \Gamma_2, x' : A \vdash c : C \end{array}}{\Gamma_1, \Gamma_2 \vdash c : C} \text{ cut}$$

We see that the first premise of the cut (rule $\oplus R_1$) has a single premise, while the second premise of the cut (rule $\oplus L$) has two branches (Q_1 and Q_2). In essence, the proof of the first premise (either $\oplus R_1$ or $\oplus R_2$) selects one of the two branches of the second premise. So the information flows along the channel x from left to right. The message itself therefore should be one bit to indicate whether the first or second branch was chosen.

In this example, the communication between processes P and Q (the two premises of the cut) is *synchronous* because P evolves to P' and Q evolves to Q_1. Other connectives of linear logic follow the same pattern and we conclude [4,5]:

> *Principal cut reduction in the linear sequent calculus corresponds to synchronous message passing communication.*

3   Asynchronous Communication

In order to model *asynchronous* communication proof-theoretically we should have a proof that corresponds to a *message*. The salient aspects of a message are that (a) it carries relevant information, and (b) it does not have a continuation. We can achieve both if we represent *messages as axioms*.

Continuing the example from the previous section, we have two axioms for disjunction, where we write X for axiom instead of R for right rule.

$$\overline{a : A \vdash c : A \oplus B}\ \oplus X_1 \qquad \overline{b : B \vdash c : A \oplus B}\ \oplus X_2$$

The principal case of cut then becomes

$$\dfrac{\dfrac{}{a : A \vdash x : A \oplus B}\ \oplus X_1 \quad \dfrac{\begin{array}{cc} Q_1(x') & Q_2(x') \\ \Gamma_2, x' : A \vdash c : C & \Gamma_2, x' : B \vdash c : C \end{array}}{\Gamma_2, x : A \oplus B \vdash c : C}\ \oplus L}{\Gamma_2, a : A \vdash c : C}\ \text{cut}$$

$$\longrightarrow \qquad \dfrac{Q_1(a)}{\Gamma_2, a : A \vdash c : C}$$

We see that the reduction corresponds to the message represented by the first premise being received by the second premise (process Q that ends in $\oplus L$). The message "disappears" and process Q continues as $[a/x']Q_1(x')$ which we write just as $Q_1(a)$. And while we have changed the two conventional $\oplus R$ rules into axioms, the $\oplus L$ rules remains the same.

We also observe that the message contains not only the bit to choose the first or second branch, it also contains a *continuation channel* a. This would be either of type A or B, depending on whether it is an instance of $\oplus X_1$ or $\oplus X_2$.

We can continue this pattern. For each connective of (purely) linear logic, either the right or left rule is invertible and the other one is noninvertible. Intuitively, the invertible rule carries no specific information (after all, the premise(s) are derivable iff the conclusion is) while the noninvertible rule makes a choice. Therefore, we turn all noninvertible rules into axioms and keep the invertible rules as they are. The result is the linear semi-axiomatic sequent calculus [9,10] (Semi-axiomatic since half the usual rules are now axioms.) We conclude:

> *Principal cut reduction in the semi-axiomatic sequent calculus corresponds to asynchronous message passing communication.*

The reader might wonder how we send a message, now that, for example, the $\oplus R_1$ and $\oplus R_2$ processes are no longer available. The solution is actually the same as in the asynchronous π-calculus: we use cut ($=$ parallel composition) itself. For example,

$$\cfrac{\begin{array}{c} P(x) \\ \Gamma_1 \vdash x : A \end{array} \quad \cfrac{}{x : A \vdash c : A \oplus B}\ \oplus X_1}{\Gamma_1 \vdash c : A \oplus B}\ \text{cut}$$

sends the message "*choose the first branch and continue with channel x*" along the channel c. We retain our connection to the receiving process via the new continuation channel x. This technique is made explicit by Kobayashi et al. [17] and can also be identified in other examples for the π-calculus [19,25].

4   A Language for Asynchronous Communication

Following the motifs in the previous section, we now present a complete language for asynchronous message passing communication. We also specify the typing rules and how processes behave dynamically. For the purpose of more readable examples, we generalize binary sums to $\oplus_{\ell \in L}(\ell : A_\ell)$ for a finite set L of labels and, correspondingly, binary additive conjunction to $\&_{\ell \in L}(\ell : A_\ell)$.

$$
\begin{array}{llll}
\text{Types} & A, B, C ::= & A \otimes B \mid 1 \mid \oplus_{\ell \in L}(\ell : A_\ell) & \text{(positive)} \\
& \mid & A \multimap B \mid \&_{\ell \in L}(\ell : A_\ell) & \text{(negative)} \\
& \mid & t & \text{(type names)} \\
\text{Contexts } \Gamma & ::= & \cdot \mid \Gamma, x : A \mid \Gamma, a : A &
\end{array}
$$

Type names represent *equirecursive* types whose definitions are collected in a global signature Σ. Correspondingly, we allow mutually recursive process definitions, collected in the same signature. We use a, b, and c for *channels* (which are runtime objects) and x, y, and z for *variables* occurring in a process that stand for channels. Strictly speaking, we should introduce a category of *symbol* which may either be a variable or a channel, but since the rules do not need to distinguish between them we just follow the convention that we use x, y, and z for variables that are bound in a process expression and a, b, and c for channels or variables that are free. At runtime, a process will have only free channels and internally bound variables.

Processes are typed with

$$\underbrace{a_1 : A_1, \ldots, a_n : A_n}_{\text{use}} \vdash P :: \underbrace{(c : C)}_{\text{provide}}$$

where we say process P *provides* channel c and *uses* channels a_i. We also refer to P as a *client* of a_i and a *provider* of c.

Channels carry messages with *small values* V, which are either pairs of channels $\langle a, b \rangle$, a unit message $\langle \rangle$, or tagged channels $k(a)$ for labels k. The direction of the message depends on the *polarity* of the types. For a channel of *positive* type C the provider will send a message and the client will receive it. For a *negative* type the client will send a message and the provider will receive it.

4.1 The Dynamics of Process Configurations

We describe the state of the computation by a multiset of *semantic objects* we call a *configuration*. The possible state transitions are defined by *multiset rewriting rules* [7]. The left-hand side of a rule is matched against some objects in the configuration which are then replaced by the right-hand side. Later, we will refine this point of view slightly to allow *persistent objects* that always remain in a configuration.

As a first example, consider the construct $x \leftarrow P(x) \,;\, Q(x)$. A process of this form will allocate a new private channel a that is provided by $P(a)$ and used by $Q(a)$. Logically, it is a cut.

$$\frac{\Gamma_1 \vdash A \quad \Gamma_2, A \vdash C}{\Gamma_1, \Gamma_2 \vdash C} \text{ cut} \qquad \frac{\Gamma_1 \vdash P(x) :: (x : A) \quad \Gamma_2, x : A \vdash Q(x) :: (c : C)}{\Gamma_1, \Gamma_2 \vdash (x \leftarrow P(x) \,;\, Q(x)) :: (c : C)} \text{ cut}$$

Our first semantic object is $\mathsf{proc}\ P$ that represents a running process P. In the dynamics, a cut process evolves into two.

$$\mathsf{proc}\ (x \leftarrow P(x) \,;\, Q(x)) \quad \mapsto \quad \mathsf{proc}\ P(a), \mathsf{proc}\ Q(a) \qquad (a \text{ a fresh channel})$$

We now dive into the meaning of each of the logical connectives, extracting their computational meaning.

4.2 Positive Connectives

Internal choice $\oplus_{\ell \in L}(\ell : A_\ell)$. As motivated in the preceding section, the right rules for sums are replaced by axioms. At the same time, we generalize from binary disjunction to finite sums, indexed by a label set L. This is a strict generalization under the definition $A \oplus B \triangleq (\mathtt{inl} : A) \oplus (\mathtt{inr} : B)$

$$\frac{}{A \vdash A \oplus B} \oplus X_1 \qquad \frac{}{B \vdash A \oplus B} \oplus X_2$$

$$\frac{(k \in L)}{b : A_k \vdash \mathbf{send}^+ a\ k(b) :: (a : \oplus_{\ell \in L}(\ell : A_\ell))} \oplus X$$

The intent is for the process $\mathbf{send}^+$ a $k(b)$ to send the tagged channel $k(b)$ along channel a. The polarity annotation of the **send** construct is not syntactically necessary, but the redundant information will be helpful later in formulating the connection between message passing and futures. In order to express the dynamics, we use a second kind of semantic object msg a V, representing the value V as a message on channel a. Computationally, a sending process "becomes" a message.

$$\mathsf{proc}\ (\mathbf{send}^+\ a\ k(b))\quad \mapsto \quad \mathsf{msg}^+\ a\ k(b)$$

The left rule for sums branches on the label received.

$$\frac{\Gamma, A \vdash C \quad \Gamma, B \vdash C}{\Gamma, A \oplus B \vdash C}\ \oplus L$$

$$\frac{\Gamma, x : A_\ell \vdash P_\ell(x) :: (d : C) \quad (\forall \ell \in L)}{\Gamma, c : \oplus_{\ell \in L}(\ell : A_\ell) \vdash \mathbf{recv}^+\ c\ (\ell(x) \Rightarrow P_\ell(x))_{\ell \in L} :: (d : C)}\ \oplus L$$

A receiving process *blocks* until a message arrives. In the dynamics we represent a process blocked on channel a as a continuation object $\mathsf{cont}\ a\ K$. Here K is the continuation to invoke once a message has arrived. In the case of sums, this is the branching construct.

$$\mathsf{proc}\ (\mathbf{recv}^+\ a\ (\ell(x) \Rightarrow P_\ell(x))_{\ell \in L})\quad \mapsto \quad \mathsf{cont}^+\ a\ (\ell(x) \Rightarrow P_\ell(x))_{\ell \in L}$$

Messages always interact with continuations. Here, the message selects one of the branches and also carries the continuation channel for subsequent communication.

$$\mathsf{msg}^+\ a\ k(b), \mathsf{cont}^+\ a\ (\ell(x) \Rightarrow P_\ell(x))_{\ell \in L}\quad \mapsto \quad \mathsf{proc}\ P_k(b)$$

Pairs $A \otimes B$. Because $A \otimes B$ is a positive type, we turn the usual right rule of the sequent calculus into an axiom.

$$\frac{}{A, B \vdash A \otimes B}\ \otimes X \qquad \frac{}{a : A, b : B \vdash \mathbf{send}^+\ c\ \langle a, b \rangle :: (c : A \otimes B)}\ \otimes X$$

As for sums, a sending process simply becomes a message.

$$\mathsf{proc}\ (\mathbf{send}^+\ a\ \langle b, c \rangle)\quad \mapsto \quad \mathsf{msg}^+\ a\ \langle b, c \rangle$$

The left rule of the sequent calculus corresponds to the receipt of a message.

$$\frac{\Gamma, A, B \vdash C}{\Gamma, A \otimes B \vdash C}\ \otimes L \qquad \frac{\Gamma, x : A, y : B \vdash P(x, y) :: (d : C)}{\Gamma, c : A \otimes B \vdash \mathbf{recv}^+\ c\ (\langle x, y \rangle \Rightarrow P(x, y)) :; (d : C)}\ \otimes L$$

Again, just as for sums, a process receiving along a channel c will block until the message arrives. This is modeled by turning it into a continuation, which can then interact with a message.

$$\mathsf{proc}\ (\mathbf{recv}^+\ c\ (\langle x, y \rangle \Rightarrow P(x, y)))\quad \mapsto \quad \mathsf{cont}^+\ c\ (\langle x, y \rangle \Rightarrow P(x, y))$$
$$\mathsf{msg}^+\ c\ \langle a, b \rangle, \mathsf{cont}^+\ c\ (\langle x, y \rangle \Rightarrow P(x, y))\quad \mapsto \quad \mathsf{proc}\ P(a, b)$$

Unit 1. The (multiplicative) unit type 1 is also positive. Instead of a pair of channels, messages of unit type are just $\langle\rangle$ and carry no information, except that there is a message. The rules are the nullary versions of the rules for $A \otimes B$.

$$\frac{}{\cdot \vdash 1} \; 1X \qquad \frac{}{\cdot \vdash \mathbf{send}^+ \, c \, \langle\rangle :: (c : 1)} \; {\otimes}X$$

$$\frac{\Gamma \vdash C}{\Gamma, 1 \vdash C} \; 1L \qquad \frac{\Gamma \vdash P :: (d : C)}{\Gamma, c : 1 \vdash \mathbf{recv}^+ \, c \, (\langle\rangle \Rightarrow P) :: (d : C)} \; 1L$$

$$
\begin{array}{rcl}
\mathsf{proc} \, (\mathbf{send}^+ \, c \, \langle\rangle) & \mapsto & \mathsf{msg}^+ \, c \, \langle\rangle \\
\mathsf{proc} \, (\mathbf{recv}^+ \, c \, (\langle\rangle \Rightarrow P)) & \mapsto & \mathsf{cont}^+ \, c \, (\langle\rangle \Rightarrow P) \\
\mathsf{msg}^+ \, c \, \langle\rangle, \mathsf{cont}^+ \, c \, (\langle\rangle \Rightarrow P) & \mapsto & \mathsf{proc} \, P
\end{array}
$$

4.3   Refactoring the Rules of Computation

At this point we reflect on the dynamic rules and we see that we can refactor them, since both sending and receiving processes always turn into messages or continuations, respectively.

$$
\begin{array}{rcl}
\mathsf{proc} \, (x \leftarrow P(x) \, ; \, Q(x)) & \mapsto & \mathsf{proc} \, P(a), \mathsf{proc} \, Q(a) \quad (a \text{ fresh}) \\
\mathsf{proc} \, (\mathbf{send}^+ \, c \, V) & \mapsto & \mathsf{msg}^+ \, c \, V \\
\mathsf{proc} \, (\mathbf{recv}^+ \, c \, K) & \mapsto & \mathsf{cont}^+ \, c \, K \\
\mathsf{msg}^+ \, c \, V, \mathsf{cont}^+ \, c \, K & \mapsto & \mathsf{proc} \, (V \triangleright K)
\end{array}
$$

Passing a value to a continuation is handled as a separate operation.

$$
\begin{array}{rcll}
k(a) & \triangleright \, (\ell(x) \Rightarrow P_\ell(x))_{\ell \in L} & = P_k(a) & (\oplus) \\
\langle a, b \rangle & \triangleright \, (\langle x, y \rangle \Rightarrow P(x,y)) & = P(a,b) & (\otimes) \\
\langle\rangle & \triangleright \, (\langle\rangle \Rightarrow P) & = P & (1)
\end{array}
$$

4.4   Process Definitions

Recall that all process definitions are collected in a global signature. At a call site we just check that the types of the channel used and provided match those described in the type declaration for a process.

$$\frac{(x_1 : A_1, \ldots, x_n : A_n \vdash f :: (z : C)) \in \Sigma}{a_1 : A_1, \ldots, a_n : A_n \vdash f \, c \, [a_1, \ldots, a_n] :: (c : C)} \; \text{call}$$

In the first position after f is always the channel provided by the definition followed by a the list of channels used.

$$
\begin{array}{rcl}
\mathsf{proc} \, (\mathbf{call} \, f \, c \, [a_1, \ldots, a_n]) & \mapsto & \mathsf{proc} \, P(c, a_1, \ldots, a_n) \\
\text{for} \, (f \, z \, [x_1, \ldots, x_n] = P(z, x_1, \ldots, x_n)) \in \Sigma
\end{array}
$$

4.5   Some Examples

Even though our language is quite incomplete, we can already give some small examples. First, a process that flips a bit. We do not give an an explicit type declaration of the process *flip*, but show the type of the channel it provides (always first, here y) and the types of the channels it uses (here just x) in the left-hand side of the definition. We use sans serif for type names, fixed width for labels, **bold** for language keywords, and *italics* for process names.

bit $= (\text{b0} : 1) \oplus (\text{b1} : 1)$
flip $(y : \text{bit})\, [x : \text{bit}] =$
   recv $x\ (\text{b0}(u) \Rightarrow \textbf{send}\ y\ \text{b1}(u)$
         $|\ \text{b1}(u) \Rightarrow \textbf{send}\ y\ \text{b0}(u))$

Slightly more interesting is a recursive type that models an infinite stream of bits, and a process that flips them in turn.

bits $= (\text{b0} : \text{bits}) \oplus (\text{b1} : \text{bits})$
flips $(ys : \text{bits})\, [xs : \text{bits}] =$
   recv $xs\ (\text{b0}(xs') \Rightarrow ys' \leftarrow \textbf{call}\ \textit{flips}\ ys'\ [xs']\ ;$
                      $\textbf{send}\ ys\ \text{b1}(ys')$
        $|\ \text{b1}(xs') \Rightarrow ys' \leftarrow \textbf{call}\ \textit{flips}\ ys'\ [xs']\ ;$
                      $\textbf{send}\ ys\ \text{b0}(ys'))$

Next, a simple pipeline of two bit-flipping processes which should be the identity, with some delay between incoming and outgoing messages.

bits $= (\text{b0} : \text{bits}) \oplus (\text{b1} : \text{bits})$
flip2 $(zs : \text{bits})\, [xs : \text{bits}] =$
   $ys \leftarrow \textbf{call}\ \textit{flips}\ ys\ [xs]\ ;$
   $\textbf{call}\ \textit{flips}\ zs\ [ys]$

A very similar type is that of a binary number, where zero is represented by the label e followed by the unit. We start programming processes representing zero and computing the successor of a given stream (assuming the least significant bit arrives first).

bin $= (\text{b0} : \text{bits}) \oplus (\text{b1} : \text{bits}) \oplus (\text{e} : 1)$

zero $(y : \text{bin})\, [\,] =$
   $u \leftarrow \textbf{send}\ u\ \langle\,\rangle\ ;$
   $\textbf{send}\ y\ \text{e}(u)$

succ $(y : \text{bin})\, [x : \text{bin}] =$
   recv $x\ (\text{b0}(x') \Rightarrow \textbf{send}\ y\ \text{b1}(x')$
           $|\ \text{b1}(x') \Rightarrow y' \leftarrow \textbf{call}\ \textit{succ}\ y'\ [x']\ ;$
                   $\textbf{send}\ y\ \text{b0}(y')$
           $|\ \text{e}(u) \Rightarrow y' \leftarrow \textbf{send}\ y'\ \text{e}(u)\ ;$
                 $\textbf{send}\ y\ \text{b1}(y'))$

4.6 Negative Connectives

The negative connectives communicate in the opposite direction: the provider receives while the client sends. This is often the initial state of a provider/client system. In our language there are two such connectives: external choice $A \,\&\, B$ and linear implication $A \multimap B$. There could also be $\bot$ (dual to 1), but it would require an empty succedent, representing a process without a client. We choose to avoid this syntactic complication.

External choice $A \,\&\, B$. The right rule of *additive conjunction* or *external choice* of linear logic has two premises, and these remain the same in SAX since it is a negative connective. For programming convenience, we generalize from the binary to a finitary choice, where $A \,\&\, B \triangleq (\texttt{fst} : A) \,\&\, (\texttt{snd} : B)$.

$$\frac{\Gamma \vdash A \quad \Gamma \vdash B}{\Gamma \vdash A \,\&\, B} \; \&R \qquad \frac{\Gamma \vdash P_\ell(x) :: (x : A_\ell) \quad (\forall \ell \in L)}{\Gamma \vdash \textbf{recv}^- \; c \; (\ell(x) \Rightarrow P_\ell(x))_{\ell \in L} :: (c : \&_{\ell \in L}(\ell : A_\ell))} \; \&R$$

Symmetrically to the internal choice, the client now picks among the alternatives by sending a suitable message. In this way, a process providing an external choice represents an *object*, where each alternative is a *method*. This view of communication was already present in the original work on session types [14,15].

$$\frac{}{A \,\&\, B \vdash A} \; \&X_1 \qquad \frac{}{A \,\&\, B \vdash B} \; \&X_2$$

$$\frac{}{c : \&_{\ell \in L}(\ell : A_\ell) \vdash \textbf{send}^- \; c \; k(a) :: (a : A_k)} \; \&X$$

It turns out that *dynamically* there is nothing new: the receiving process suspends, and the sending process becomes a message. We repeat the relevant prior rules only to note the different polarities.

$$
\begin{aligned}
\text{proc} \, (\textbf{recv}^- \; c \; K) \quad &\mapsto \quad \text{cont}^- \; c \; K \\
\text{proc} \, (\textbf{send}^- \; c \; V) \quad &\mapsto \quad \text{msg}^- \; c \; V \\
\text{cont}^- \; c \; K, \text{msg}^- \; c \; V \quad &\mapsto \quad \text{proc} \, (V \rhd K)
\end{aligned}
$$

$$k(a) \rhd (\ell(x) \Rightarrow P_\ell(x))_{\ell \in L} = P_k(a) \quad (\&)$$

The constructs exhibit a remarkable symmetry in SAX, usually associated with classical linear logic [11]. While it is possible to give a message passing interpretation for classical linear logic [5,28], we stick with the intuitionistic version because of its conceptual and syntactic proximity to functional programming [12]. In particular, it helps to elucidate the connection to futures which have their origin in functional languages.

As an example of negative types, consider a binary counter that can receive a message to increment its value (inc) and to return its value (val). It maintains local state through a channel x that holds the current value as a binary number. In the case of a value request, we would like to "return" just that number. The way we can accomplish that is a *forwarding* construct **fwd** c a that forwards messages from a to c. It turns out to be a process assignment for the identity rule of the sequent calculus, which we explain in Sect. 4.7.

ctr = (inc : ctr) & (val : bin)

$counter$ $(c : ctr)$ $[x : bin]$ =
 recv c (inc(c') $\Rightarrow$ $y \leftarrow$ **call** $succ$ y $[x]$;
       call $counter$ c' $[y]$
  | val(x') $\Rightarrow$ **fwd** x' x

$init$ $(c : ctr)$ $[]$ =
 $z \leftarrow$ **call** $zero$ z $[]$;
 call $counter$ c $[z]$)

two $(x : bin)$ $[]$ =
 $c_0 \leftarrow$ **call** $init$ c_0 $[]$;
 $c_1 \leftarrow$ **send** c_0 inc(c_1) ;
 $c_2 \leftarrow$ **send** c_1 inc(c_2) ;
 send c_2 val(x)

Linear Implication $A \multimap B$. Linear implication $A \multimap B$ is the type of a process that receives a channel of type A together with a continuation channel of type B.

$$\frac{\Gamma, A \vdash B}{\Gamma \vdash A \multimap B} \; {\multimap}R \qquad \frac{\Gamma, x : A \vdash P :: (y : B)}{\Gamma \vdash \textbf{recv}^- \; c \, (\langle x, y \rangle \Rightarrow P(x, y)) :: (c : A \multimap B)} \; {\multimap}R$$

Sending, as for all other constructs, is asynchronous.

$$\frac{}{A, A \multimap B \vdash B} \; {\multimap}X \qquad \frac{}{a : A, c : A \multimap B \vdash \textbf{send}^- \; c \, \langle a, b \rangle :: (b : B)} \; {\multimap}X$$

The dynamics once again does not change. We just recall

$$\langle a, b \rangle \rhd (\langle x, y \rangle \Rightarrow P(x, y)) = P(a, b)$$

As an example, consider a stack with push and pop methods. When the stack is empty, the response to pop will be none after which the stack process terminates. We don't treat first-class polymorphism here, so we think of stack$_A$ as a family of types indexed by A.

stack$_A$ = (push : $A \multimap$ stack$_A$)
   & (pop : (some : $A \otimes$ stack$_A$) $\oplus$ (none : 1))

$empty$ $(s : \text{stack}_A)$ $[]$ =

recv s (push$(s') \Rightarrow$ **recv** s' ($\langle x, s'' \rangle \Rightarrow$
$t \leftarrow$ **call** $empty\ t\ [\ ]$;
call $elem\ s''\ [x, t]$)
$|\ \mathrm{pop}(s') \Rightarrow u \leftarrow$ **send** $u\ \langle\ \rangle$;
send $s'\ \mathrm{none}(u)$)

$elem\ (s : \mathsf{stack}_A)\ [x : A, t : \mathsf{stack}_A] =$
recv s (push$(s') \Rightarrow$ **recv** s' ($\langle y, s'' \rangle \Rightarrow$
$t' \leftarrow$ **call** $elem\ t'\ [x, t]$;
call $elem\ s''\ [y, t']$)
$|\ \mathrm{pop}(s') \Rightarrow p \leftarrow$ **send** $p\ \langle x, t \rangle$;
send $s'\ \mathrm{some}(p)$)

$stack10\ (s_{10} : \mathsf{stack}_{\mathsf{bin}})\ [\ ] =$
$n_0 \leftarrow$ **call** $zero\ [\ ]$;
$s_0 \leftarrow$ **call** $empty\ [\ ]$;
$s_0' \leftarrow$ **send** $s_0\ \mathrm{push}(s_0')$;
$s_1 \leftarrow$ **send** $s_0'\ \langle n_0, s_1 \rangle$;
$n_0 \leftarrow$ **call** $zero\ [\ ]$;   % necssary for linearity
$n_1 \leftarrow$ **call** $succ\ [n_0]$;
$s_1' \leftarrow$ **send** $s_1\ \mathrm{push}(s_1')$;
send $s_1'\ \langle n_1, s_{10} \rangle$

4.7   Identity as Forwarding

The sequent calculus rule of identity essentially equates two channels. The way we define this in our dynamics is for the identity to become a form of continuation, waiting to forward a message on one channel to the other.

$$\frac{}{A \vdash A}\ \mathrm{id} \qquad \frac{}{a : A \vdash \mathbf{fwd}^{\pm}\ c\ a :: (c : A)}\ \mathrm{id}$$

The direction of the messages is prescribed by the polarity of the type, so we split the dynamics into two rules, forwarding message on one channel to another.

$$\begin{aligned} \mathrm{proc}\ (\mathbf{fwd}^+\ c\ a) &\longmapsto \mathrm{cont}^+\ a\ c \\ \mathrm{msg}^+\ a\ V, \mathrm{cont}^+\ a\ c &\longmapsto \mathrm{msg}^+\ c\ V \end{aligned}$$

$$\begin{aligned} \mathrm{proc}\ (\mathbf{fwd}^-\ c\ a) &\longmapsto \mathrm{msg}^-\ a\ c \\ \mathrm{cont}^-\ a\ K, \mathrm{msg}^-\ a\ c &\longmapsto \mathrm{cont}^-\ c\ K \end{aligned}$$

This means a channel is another form of extended value or continuation. We write $\hat{V}$ and $\hat{K}$ when we need to include channels as values or continuations, respectively.

5   Preservation and Progress

The recursion-free fragment of SAX satisfies a variant of the cut elimination theorem that guarantees a subformula property [10]. In the presence of recursion, we are more interested in *preservation* and *progress*. These are properties of *configurations*, so we need to provide typing rules for configurations. Even though configurations are unordered collection of semantic objects, the typing rules impose a partial order where the provider of a channel always precedes its client. We treat the join as an associative operation, with the empty configuration as its unit. Globally, in a configuration, each channel must be provided and used at most once.

It is convenient for the typing of messages and continuations objects to refer to a corresponding process for its typing to avoid a proliferation of typing rules.

$$\frac{}{\Delta \vdash (\cdot) :: \Delta} \text{ empty} \qquad \frac{\Delta_1 \vdash \mathcal{C}_1 :: \Delta_2 \quad \Delta_2 \vdash \mathcal{C}_2 :: \Delta_3}{\Delta_1 \vdash \mathcal{C}_1, \mathcal{C}_2 :: \Delta_3} \text{ join}$$

$$\frac{\Gamma \vdash P :: (a : A)}{\Delta, \Gamma \vdash \mathsf{proc}\ P :: (\Delta, a : A)} \text{ proc}$$

$$\frac{\Gamma \vdash \mathbf{send}^+\ a\ V :: (a : A)}{\Delta, \Gamma \vdash \mathsf{msg}^+\ a\ V :: (\Delta, a : A)} \text{ msg}^+ \qquad \frac{\Gamma \vdash \mathbf{recv}^+\ a\ K :: (c : C)}{\Delta, \Gamma \vdash \mathsf{cont}^+\ a\ K :: (\Delta, c : C)} \text{ cont}^+$$

$$\frac{\Gamma \vdash \mathbf{send}^-\ a\ V :: (c : C)}{\Delta, \Gamma \vdash \mathsf{msg}^-\ a\ V :: (\Delta, c : C)} \text{ msg}^- \qquad \frac{\Gamma \vdash \mathbf{recv}^-\ a\ K :: (a : A)}{\Delta, \Gamma \vdash \mathsf{cont}^-\ a\ K :: (\Delta, a : A)} \text{ cont}^-$$

$$\frac{}{\Delta, a : A \vdash \mathsf{cont}^+\ a\ c :: (\Delta, c : A)} \text{ fwd}^+ \qquad \frac{}{\Delta, a : A \vdash \mathsf{msg}^-\ a\ c :: (\Delta, c : A)} \text{ fwd}^-$$

With this bit of bureaucracy settled, we can now state the preservation theorem. Even though *internally* new channels might be created or closed, *externally* the interface to a configuration remains constant. For reference, the language and its operational semantics can be found in Fig. 1, the typing rules are collected in Fig. 2.

Theorem 1 (Preservation for Linear Message Passing). *If* $\Delta_1 \vdash \mathcal{C} :: \Delta_2$ *and* $\mathcal{C} \mapsto \mathcal{D}$ *then* $\Delta_1 \vdash \mathcal{D} :: \Delta_2$.

Proof. By induction on the typing of a configuration, using inversion on the typing of the semantic objects to observe that the endpoints of each channel perform complementary actions and that the continuation channels once again have matching types.

For the progress theorem, it is convenient to assume that we are executing a closed configuration, providing a finite collection Δ of channels. Such a configuration is *terminal* if all semantic objects are *positive messages* or *negative continuations*.

Theorem 2 (Progress for Linear Message Passing). *If* $\cdot \vdash \mathcal{C} :: \Delta$ *then either* $\mathcal{C} \mapsto \mathcal{D}$ *for some* $\mathcal{D}$, *or* $\mathcal{C}$ *is terminal.*

Proof. We proceed by right-to-left induction over the typing derivation of a configuration, analyzing the rightmost semantic object. We observe that $\mathcal{C} = (\mathcal{C}_1, \phi)$ for a semantic object ϕ can make a transition if $\mathcal{C}_1$ can. So we may assume $\mathcal{C}_1$ is terminal. We distinguish cases based on the shape of ϕ.

(i) proc P can always make a transition.

(ii) $\mathsf{msg}^+\ a\ V$ is terminal, and therefore $\mathcal{C}$ is.

(iii) $\mathsf{cont}^-\ a\ K$ is terminal, and therefore $\mathcal{C}$ is.

(iv) For $\mathsf{msg}^-\ a\ \hat{V}$ there must be a continuation $\mathsf{cont}^-\ a\ K$ in $\mathcal{C}_1$. By inversion on typing, the two can interact.

(v) For $\mathsf{cont}^+\ a\ \hat{K}$ there must be a message $\mathsf{msg}^+\ a\ V$ in $\mathcal{C}_1$. By inversion on typing, the two can interact.

Summary. A summary of the asynchronous linear message passing language using session types can be found in Figs. 1 and 2. Here is a summary of the salient aspects of the language. We show the actions from the provider's perspective; the client will take the matching opposite reaction.

cut	Channel allocation and process spawn
id	Message forwarding
call	Invoking defined process
$\oplus_{\ell \in L}(\ell : A_\ell)$	sending a label with continuation channel
$A \otimes B$	sending a pair of channels
1	sending unit
$\&_{\ell \in L}(\ell : A_\ell)$	receiving and branching on a label with continuation channel
$A \multimap B$	receiving a pair of channels

6 Linear Futures

We stay with the SAX system of logical inference, giving a new interpretation to sequents and proofs. Instead of *channels*, variables now stand for *addresses* of memory cells. A sequent is read as follows:

$$\underbrace{a_1 : A_1, \ldots, a_n : A_n}_{\text{read from}} \vdash P :: \underbrace{(c : C)}_{\text{write to}}$$

Cut allocates a new memory cell a and spawns a process to write to a. As for *futures* [13], every cell has exactly one writer. Because futures are *linear* for now, every cell also has exactly one reader, a discipline sketched by Blelloch and Reid-Miller [3].

6.1 Statics and Dynamics of Futures

In our message passing interpretation, the type of a channel specifies a communication protocol. Here, the type of a cell specifies the shape of its contents.

Language

Types $A, B, C ::= A \otimes B \mid 1 \mid \oplus_{\ell \in L}(\ell : A_\ell)$ (positive)
$\mid\ A \multimap B \mid \&_{\ell \in L}(\ell : A_\ell)$ (negative)
$\mid\ t$ (type names)

Contexts Γ $::= \cdot \mid \Gamma, x : A \mid \Gamma, a : A$

Processes P, Q $::= x \leftarrow P(x) \,;\, Q(x)$ (spawn $P(a)$, continue as $Q(a)$, a fresh)
$\mid\ \mathbf{fwd}^{\pm}\ a\ b$ (forward between a and b)
$\mid\ \mathbf{send}^{\pm}\ c\ V$ (send value V on c)
$\mid\ \mathbf{recv}^{\pm}\ c\ K$ (receive a value on c and pass it to K)
$\mid\ \mathbf{call}\ f\ c\ [a_1, \ldots, a_n]$ (call f to provide c, using $a_1, \ldots, a_n$)

Values V $::= \langle a, b \rangle$ $(\otimes, \multimap)$
$\mid\ \langle \rangle$ (1)
$\mid\ k(a)$ $(\oplus, \&)$

Continuations K $::= \langle x, y \rangle \Rightarrow P(x, y)$ $(\otimes, \multimap)$
$\mid\ \langle \rangle \Rightarrow P$ (1)
$\mid\ (\ell(x) \Rightarrow P(x))_{\ell \in L}$ $(\oplus, \&)$

Signature Σ $::= \cdot$
$\mid\ \Sigma, t = A$ (type definition)
$\mid\ \Sigma, (\Gamma \vdash f :: (z : C))$ (process declaration)
$\mid\ \Sigma, f\ z\ [x_1, \ldots, x_n] = P$ (process definition)

Dynamics

$$
\begin{aligned}
\mathsf{proc}\ (x \leftarrow P(x) \,;\, Q(x)) &\mapsto \mathsf{proc}\ P(a), \mathsf{proc}\ Q(a) \quad (a\ \text{fresh}) \\
\mathsf{proc}\ (\mathbf{send}^{\pm}\ c\ V) &\mapsto \mathsf{msg}^{\pm}\ c\ V \\
\mathsf{proc}\ (\mathbf{recv}^{\pm}\ c\ K) &\mapsto \mathsf{cont}^{\pm}\ c\ K \\
\mathsf{msg}^{\pm}\ c\ V, \mathsf{cont}^{\pm}\ c\ K &\mapsto \mathsf{proc}\ (V \rhd K)
\end{aligned}
$$

$$
\mathsf{proc}\ (\mathbf{call}\ f\ c\ [a_1, \ldots, a_n]) \mapsto \mathsf{proc}\ (P(c, a_1, \ldots, a_n))
$$
$$
\text{for}\ (f\ z\ [x_1, \ldots, x_n] = P(z, x_1, \ldots, x_n)) \in \Sigma
$$

$$
\begin{aligned}
\mathsf{proc}\ (\mathbf{fwd}^+\ c\ a) &\mapsto \mathsf{cont}^+\ a\ c \\
\mathsf{msg}^+\ a\ V, \mathsf{cont}^+\ a\ c &\mapsto \mathsf{msg}^+\ c\ V
\end{aligned}
$$

$$
\begin{aligned}
\mathsf{proc}\ (\mathbf{fwd}^-\ c\ a) &\mapsto \mathsf{msg}^-\ a\ c \\
\mathsf{cont}^-\ a\ K, \mathsf{msg}^-\ a\ c &\mapsto \mathsf{cont}^-\ c\ K
\end{aligned}
$$

Passing a value to a continuation

$$
\begin{aligned}
k(a) &\rhd (\ell(x) \Rightarrow P_\ell(x))_{\ell \in L} = P_k(a) \quad (\oplus, \&) \\
\langle a, b \rangle &\rhd (\langle x, y \rangle \Rightarrow P(x, y)) = P(a, b) \quad (\otimes, \multimap) \\
\langle \rangle &\rhd (\langle \rangle \Rightarrow P) \qquad\qquad = P \qquad (1)
\end{aligned}
$$

Fig. 1. Language for asynchronous message passing

This approach leads to the following correspondences. We refer to antecedents in a sequent as "left" and succedents as "right".

	Logic	Message Passing	Shared Memory
Positive/Right	Axiom	send value V	write value V
Positive/Left	Rule	receive value V	read value V
Negative/Right	Rule	receive value V	write continuation K
Negative/Left	Axiom	send value V	read continuation K

The language of types and values does not change, and continuations only change to the extent that the embedded processes now have a different syntax.

Storable S $::= V \mid K$

$$
\begin{array}{lll}
\text{Processes } P, Q ::= & x \leftarrow P(x) \,; Q(x) & \text{(spawn } P(a), \text{ continue as } Q(a), a \text{ fresh)} \\
& \mid \ \textbf{move}^{\pm} \, c \, a & \text{(move storable from } a \text{ to } c) \\
& \mid \ \textbf{write}^{\pm} \, c \, S & \text{(write storable } S \text{ to } c) \\
& \mid \ \textbf{read}^{\pm} \, c \, S & \text{(read storable from } c \text{ and pass to } S) \\
& \mid \ \textbf{call} \, f \, c \, [a_1, \ldots, a_n] & \text{(call } f \text{ with dest. } c, \text{ reading } a_1, \ldots, a_n)
\end{array}
$$

Note that defined processes f are always called with a *destination* [27]. Remarkably, we do not need any new typing rules! Instead we define

$$
\begin{array}{lll}
\textbf{move}^{\pm} \, c \, a & \triangleq & \textbf{fwd}^{\pm} \, c \, a \\
\textbf{write}^{+} \, c \, V & \triangleq & \textbf{send}^{+} \, c \, V \\
\textbf{read}^{+} \, c \, K & \triangleq & \textbf{recv}^{+} \, c \, K \\
\textbf{write}^{-} \, c \, K & \triangleq & \textbf{recv}^{-} \, c \, K \\
\textbf{read}^{-} \, c \, V & \triangleq & \textbf{send}^{-} \, c \, V
\end{array}
$$

and the previous set of rules apply!

The dynamics can be similarly derived. Instead of messages and continuations we have *memory cells* $\mathsf{cell}^{\pm} \, c \, S$ and *suspensions* $\mathsf{susp}^{\pm} \, c \, S$. A suspension may block because the corresponding cell may not have been written yet. These can be defined from the message passing dynamics.

$$
\begin{array}{lll}
\mathsf{cell}^{+} \, c \, V & \triangleq & \mathsf{msg}^{+} \, c \, V \\
\mathsf{susp}^{+} \, c \, \hat{K} & \triangleq & \mathsf{cont}^{+} \, c \, \hat{K} \\
\mathsf{cell}^{-} \, c \, K & \triangleq & \mathsf{cont}^{-} \, c \, K \\
\mathsf{susp}^{-} \, c \, \hat{V} & \triangleq & \mathsf{msg}^{-} \, c \, \hat{V}
\end{array}
$$

Under the shared memory semantics, forwarding becomes a move from one cell to another—simpler than in the message passing semantics. The correspondences continue to hold if we generalize suspensions to allow the form $\mathsf{susp}^{\pm} \, a \, c$ where a is a channel to read a storable S from, and c is the destination write S to.

The table below visualizes the correspondences.

Shared Memory		Message Passing	
proc ($\mathbf{move}^+$ c a)	$\mapsto$ susp$^+$ a c	proc ($\mathbf{fwd}^+$ c a)	$\mapsto$ cont$^+$ a c
proc ($\mathbf{move}^-$ c a)	$\mapsto$ susp$^-$ a c	proc ($\mathbf{fwd}^-$ c a)	$\mapsto$ msg$^-$ a c
cell$^+$ a V, susp$^+$ a c	$\mapsto$ cell$^+$ c V	msg$^+$ a V, cont$^+$ a c	$\mapsto$ msg$^+$ c V
cell$^-$ a K, susp$^-$ a c	$\mapsto$ cell$^-$ c K	cont$^-$ a K, msg$^-$ a c	$\mapsto$ cont$^-$ c K

Theorem 3 (Bisimulation). *There is a strong bisimulation between the shared memory and the message passing semantics on well-typed processes.*

Proof. Under the correspondences shown above, the steps of the two operational semantics rules correspond exactly, by definition.

Corollaries of this bisimulation are analogues of preservation, terminal configurations, and progress. We say a configuration is *final* if it consists only of objects cell$^{\pm}$ a S.

Corollary 1 (Preservation and Progress for Linear Futures).

1. *If $\Delta_1 \vdash \mathcal{C} :: \Delta_2$ and $\mathcal{C} \mapsto \mathcal{D}$ then $\Delta_1 \vdash \mathcal{D} :: \Delta_2$.*
2. *If $\cdot \vdash \mathcal{C} :: \Delta$ then either $\mathcal{C} \mapsto \mathcal{D}$ for some $\mathcal{D}$, or $\mathcal{C}$ is final.*

Proof. By the correspondence with the message passing semantics and Theorems 1 and 2.

6.2   Shared Memory Examples

We can transliterate the earlier examples. Here is just one.

bin $=$ (b0 : bin) $\oplus$ (b1 : bin) $\oplus$ (e : 1)

zero $(y : \mathsf{bin})\ [] =$
  $u \leftarrow$ **write** $u\ \langle\ \rangle$;
  write y e(u)

succ $(y : \mathsf{bin})\ [x : \mathsf{bin}] =$
  read x (b0(x') $\Rightarrow$ **write** y b1(x')
       | b1(x') $\Rightarrow y' \leftarrow$ **call** *succ* y' $[x']$;
             write y b0(y')
       | e(u) $\Rightarrow y' \leftarrow$ **write** y' e(u) ;
             write y b1(y'))

As an example that uses two negative types (external choice and linear implication), we revisit the stack data structure. The *empty* and *elem* processes, for example, *write* a continuation to memory and thereby terminate immediately.

A client *reads* this continuation and passes it either a push or pop label together with a *destination* for the results. In general, all functions and objects are written in destination-passing style [27]. Processes never return a value; instead they are given a destination where to write the result.

$$\mathsf{stack}_A = (\mathrm{push} : A \multimap \mathsf{stack}_A)$$
$$\& \ (\mathrm{pop} : (\mathrm{some} : A \otimes \mathsf{stack}_A) \oplus (\mathrm{none} : 1))$$

$empty\ (s : \mathsf{stack}_A)\ [\,] =$
   write s ($\mathrm{push}(s') \Rightarrow$ **write** s' ($\langle x, s'' \rangle \Rightarrow$
                           $t \leftarrow$ **call** $empty\ t\ [\,]$;
                           call $elem\ s''\ [x, t]$)
           $|\ \mathrm{pop}(s') \Rightarrow u \leftarrow$ **write** $u\ \langle\rangle$;
                      write $s'\ \mathrm{none}(u)$)

$elem\ (s : \mathsf{stack}_A)\ [x : A, t : \mathsf{stack}_A] =$
   write s ($\mathrm{push}(s') \Rightarrow$ **write** s' ($\langle y, s'' \rangle \Rightarrow$
                           $t' \leftarrow$ **call** $elem\ t'\ [x, t]$;
                           call $elem\ s''\ [y, t']$)
           $|\ \mathrm{pop}(s') \Rightarrow p \leftarrow$ **write** $p\ \langle x, t \rangle$;
                      write $s'\ \mathrm{some}(p)$)

$stack10\ (s_{10} : \mathsf{stack}_{\mathsf{bin}})\ [\,] =$
   $n_0 \leftarrow$ **call** $zero\ [\,]$;
   $s_0 \leftarrow$ **call** $empty\ [\,]$;
   $s_0' \leftarrow$ **read** $s_0\ \mathrm{push}(s_0')$;
   $s_1 \leftarrow$ **read** $s_0'\ \langle n_0, s_1 \rangle$;
   $n_0 \leftarrow$ **call** $zero\ [\,]$;
   $n_1 \leftarrow$ **call** $succ\ [n_0]$;
   $s_1' \leftarrow$ **read** $s_1\ \mathrm{push}(s_1')$;
   read $s_1'\ \langle n_1, s_{10} \rangle$

This program highlights that there is a rather immediate *sequential* interpretation of parallel composition $x \leftarrow P(x)\ ;\ Q(x)$. As usual, we allocate a fresh memory cell a for x, but rather than executing $P(a)$ and $Q(a)$ in parallel, we first complete the execution of $P(a)$ (which will write to cell a), and then proceed with $Q(a)$. This corresponds to an eager (by-value) strategy. We can also pursue a lazy (by-need) strategy: postpone computation of $P(a)$ and start with $Q(a)$. When $Q(a)$ attempts to read from a, $P(a)$ is awakened and will run to completion (writing to a), after which $Q(a)$ continues by reading from a. This embodies call-by-need and not call-by-name because other readers of a now directly access the value stored in the cell.

Such simple sequential interpretations of computations are not immediately available in the message passing setting, but are quite clear here. In particular, in our language all memory allocation is for futures. In a more realistic language we would have both parallel composition, and maybe two forms of sequential composition: one eager and one lazy.

7 From Linear to Nonlinear Futures

So far all constructs, whether message passing or shared memory, have been strictly linear. It is easy to imagine how we can take the shared memory interpretation and make it nonlinear. We add two rules, one for weakening and one for contraction.

$$\frac{\Gamma \vdash P :: (c : C)}{\Gamma, a : A \vdash P :: (c : C)} \text{ weaken} \qquad \frac{\Gamma, a : A, a : A \vdash P :: (c : C)}{\Gamma, a : A \vdash P :: (c : C)} \text{ contract}$$

At this point an object cell $a\ S$ may have multiple readers. This means when it is read, it cannot be immediately deallocated but has to be left for eventual garbage collection. Therefore memory cells in the operational semantics are now *persistent*. In multiset rewriting we indicate this by prefixing a semantic object with an exclamation mark "!" (the exponential of linear logic). Such objects, when matched on the left of a rule are carried over implicitly and remain in the configuration. We call the others *ephemeral*.

In our semantics, now formulated using the syntax of shared memory, cells are persistent and processes as well as suspensions remain linear. That must be the case so that they can change state. A "persistent process" !proc P could transition over and over again and, for example, allocate an unbounded amount of memory without ever making progress. Parallel composition (cut) and **call** (definitions) remain unchanged.

$$
\begin{aligned}
\text{proc } (\textbf{write}^{\pm} c\ S) &\mapsto \ !\text{cell}^{\pm} c\ S \\
\text{proc } (\textbf{read}^{\pm} c\ S) &\mapsto \ \text{susp}^{\pm} c\ S \\[4pt]
!\text{cell}^{+} a\ V, \text{susp}^{+} a\ K &\mapsto \ \text{proc } (V \rhd K) \\
!\text{cell}^{-} a\ K, \text{susp}^{-} a\ V &\mapsto \ \text{proc } (V \rhd K) \\[4pt]
\text{proc } (\textbf{move}^{\pm} c\ a) &\mapsto \ \text{susp}^{\pm} a\ c \\
!\text{cell}^{\pm} a\ S, \text{susp}^{\pm} a\ c &\mapsto \ !\text{cell}^{\pm} c\ S
\end{aligned}
$$

The **move** process now *copies* from one cell to another. We postpone the metatheory of the nonlinear version of future to Corollary 2.

Now we consider a binary trie as a data structure for maintaining sets of binary numbers (and other data that can be interpreted in this form). We take the liberty of writing an underscore (_) for an anonymous variable and combining consecutive pattern matches and consecutive writes. The interface to this data structure would construct empty and singleton tries, as well as union, intersection and difference. We show only empty, singleton, and difference.

First, the straightforward setup of the booleans with the operation of $b \wedge \neg c$. If we were to show the definitions of union and intersection we would also need conjunction and disjunction.

bool $= (\texttt{true} : 1) \oplus (\texttt{false} : 1)$

true $(b : \textbf{bool})\ [] = u \leftarrow \textbf{write } u\ \langle \rangle \ ; \textbf{write } b\ \texttt{true}(u)$
false $(b : \textbf{bool})\ [] = u \leftarrow \textbf{write } u\ \langle \rangle \ ; \textbf{write } b\ \texttt{false}(u)$

$andnot\ (d : \mathsf{bool})\ [b : \mathsf{bool}, c : \mathsf{bool}] =$
 $\mathbf{read}\ b\ (\,\mathtt{true(\_)} \Rightarrow \mathbf{read}\ c\ (\,\mathtt{true(\_)} \Rightarrow \mathbf{call}\ \mathit{false}\ d\ [\,]$
             $|\ \mathtt{false(\_)} \Rightarrow \mathbf{call}\ \mathit{true}\ d\ [\,]\,)$
   $|\ \mathtt{false(\_)} \Rightarrow \mathbf{call}\ \mathit{false}\ d\ [\,]\,)$

We reuse the binary numbers and define tries as being either a leaf or a node containing three addresses: the left subtrie selected for the bit 0, the boolean b which is true if the sequence of bits which led to this node is in the trie, and the right subtrie selected for the bit 1.

 The process $empty$ constructs a leaf (the empty trie), while $singleton$ traverses a binary number, constructing a trie with exactly one node marked true.

$\mathsf{trie} = (\mathtt{leaf} : 1) \oplus (\mathtt{node} : \mathsf{trie} \otimes \mathsf{bool} \otimes \mathsf{trie})$

$empty\ (r : \mathsf{trie})\ [\,] =$
 $u \leftarrow \mathbf{write}\ u\ \langle\,\rangle\ ;\ \mathbf{write}\ r\ \mathtt{leaf}(u)$

$singleton\ (r : \mathsf{trie})\ [x : \mathsf{bin}] =$
 $\mathbf{read}\ x\ (\,\mathtt{b0}(x') \Rightarrow r_0 \leftarrow \mathbf{call}\ singleton\ r_0\ [x']\ ;$
        $b \leftarrow \mathbf{call}\ \mathit{false}\ [\,]\ ;$
        $r_1 \leftarrow \mathbf{call}\ empty\ [\,]\ ;$
        $\mathbf{write}\ r\ \mathtt{node}\langle r_0, b, r_1\rangle$
    $|\ \mathtt{b1}(x') \Rightarrow r_0 \leftarrow \mathbf{call}\ empty\ [\,]\ ;$
        $b \leftarrow \mathbf{call}\ \mathit{false}\ [\,]\ ;$
        $r_1 \leftarrow \mathbf{call}\ singleton\ r_1\ [x']\ ;$
        $\mathbf{write}\ r\ \mathtt{node}\langle r_0, b, r_1\rangle$
    $|\ \mathtt{e(\_)} \Rightarrow r' \leftarrow \mathbf{call}\ empty\ r'\ [\,]\ ;$
       $b \leftarrow \mathbf{call}\ \mathit{true}\ b\ [\,]\ ;$
       $\mathbf{write}\ r\ \mathtt{node}\langle r', b, r'\rangle\,)$

Finally, the $diff$ process traverses the two tries in parallel, short-circuiting if one is a leaf. If not, it applies the $andnot$ operation to decide if the resulting node should be true. While $singleton$ can easily be made linear, this would take significant effort here. For example, when s is empty, t is ignored entirely. The $remove$ process just computes the difference with a singleton.

$diff\ (r : \mathsf{trie})\ [s : \mathsf{trie}, t : \mathsf{trie}] =$
 $\mathbf{read}\ s\ (\,\mathtt{leaf}\langle\,\rangle \Rightarrow \mathbf{call}\ empty\ r\ [\,]$
    $|\ \mathtt{node}\langle s_0, b, s_1\rangle \Rightarrow$
 $\mathbf{read}\ t\ (\,\mathtt{leaf}\langle\,\rangle \Rightarrow \mathbf{move}\ r\ s$
    $|\ \mathtt{node}\langle t_0, c, t_1\rangle \Rightarrow$
    $r_0 \leftarrow \mathbf{call}\ diff\ r_0\ [s_0, t_0]\ ;$
    $d \leftarrow \mathbf{call}\ andnot\ d\ [b, c]\ ;$
    $r_1 \leftarrow \mathbf{call}\ diff\ r_1\ [s_1, t_1]\ ;$
    $\mathbf{write}\ r\ \mathtt{node}\langle r_0, d, r_1\rangle\,))$

$remove\ (r : \mathsf{trie})\ [s : \mathsf{trie}, x : \mathsf{bin}] =$
 $t \leftarrow \mathbf{call}\ singleton\ t\ [x]\ ;$
 $\mathbf{call}\ diff\ r\ [s, t]$

8   Backporting Persistence to Message Passing

Persistent cells are quite easy to understand from the shared memory perspective. Now we can use our correspondences in the opposite direction to obtain a bisimilar version of message passing in which certain messages and suspensions are persistent! The language of programs itself does not change, but as defined above the client can use weakening and contraction on channels it uses.

A positive message, flowing from the provider to the client, may then have multiple recipients. We therefore make such messages *persistent* in the dynamic rules. The recipient of such a message only reacts once, so it will not be persistent. Conversely, a negative suspension may be waiting for messages from multiple clients and therefore should be *persistent*, but each such message should be processed only once.

$$\begin{aligned}
\mathsf{!cell^+}\ c\ V &\triangleq \mathsf{!msg^+}\ c\ V \\
\mathsf{susp^+}\ c\ K &\triangleq \mathsf{cont^+}\ c\ K \\
\mathsf{!cell^-}\ c\ K &\triangleq \mathsf{!cont^-}\ c\ K \\
\mathsf{susp^-}\ c\ V &\triangleq \mathsf{msg^-}\ c\ V \\[6pt]
\mathsf{susp^+}\ a\ c &\triangleq \mathsf{cont^+}\ c\ a \\
\mathsf{susp^-}\ a\ c &\triangleq \mathsf{msg^-}\ c\ a
\end{aligned}$$

8.1   Examples

As example we start with *nor* which takes two bits x and y and produces the negation of the disjunction of x and y on the output channel z.

$\mathsf{bit} = (\mathsf{b0} : 1) \oplus (\mathsf{b1} : 1)$

$nor\ (z : \mathsf{bit})\ [x : \mathsf{bit}, y : \mathsf{bit}] =$
  recv x ($\mathsf{b0}(\_) \Rightarrow$ **recv** y ($\mathsf{b0}(u) \Rightarrow$ **send** $z\ \mathsf{b1}(u)$
             $\mid \mathsf{b1}(u) \Rightarrow$ **send** $z\ \mathsf{b0}(u)$)
        $\mid \mathsf{b1}(\_) \Rightarrow$ **recv** y ($\mathsf{b0}(u) \Rightarrow$ **send** $z\ \mathsf{b0}(u)$
             $\mid \mathsf{b1}(u) \Rightarrow$ **send** $z\ \mathsf{b0}(u)$))

We now use this in the construction of a latch which uses a feedback loop and recursion.

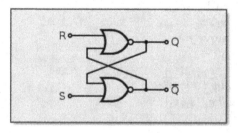

In the code below the stream of pairs of signals R and S is represented by channel in : bits2 and the pair of signals Q and $\overline{Q}$ is represented by out : bits2. The initial (and in later calls, previous) value of Q and $\overline{Q}$ is provided on the channels q and $\overline{q}$. We have combined two consecutive receives and sends for readability.

$\mathsf{bits2} = (\mathsf{bit} \otimes \mathsf{bit}) \otimes \mathsf{bits2}$

$latch\ (out : \mathsf{bits2})\ [q : \mathsf{bit}, \overline{q} : \mathsf{bit}, in : \mathsf{bits2}] =$
 $\quad \mathbf{recv}\ in\ (\langle\langle r, s\rangle, in'\rangle \Rightarrow$
 $\quad\quad q' \leftarrow \mathbf{call}\ nor\ q'\ [r, \overline{q}]\ ;$
 $\quad\quad \overline{q}' \leftarrow \mathbf{call}\ nor\ \overline{q}'\ [s, q]\ ;$
 $\quad\quad out' \leftarrow \mathbf{call}\ latch\ out'\ [q', \overline{q}', in']\ ;$
 $\quad\quad \mathbf{send}\ out\ \langle\langle q', \overline{q}'\rangle, out'\rangle\ )$

8.2 Metatheory

The metatheory for nonlinear message passing changes systematically from the linear case, reflecting persistence of positive messages and negative suspensions. Instead of splitting the context to check the processes, messages, and continuations embedded in them, we pass all channels in all configuration typing rules.

$$\frac{}{\Delta \vdash (\cdot) :: \Delta}\ \mathsf{empty} \qquad \frac{\Delta_1 \vdash \mathcal{C}_1 :: \Delta_2 \quad \Delta_2 \vdash \mathcal{C}_2 :: \Delta_3}{\Delta_1 \vdash \mathcal{C}_1, \mathcal{C}_2 :: \Delta_3}\ \mathsf{join}$$

$$\frac{\Delta \vdash P :: (a : A)}{\Delta \vdash \mathsf{proc}\ P :: (\Delta, a : A)}\ \mathsf{proc}$$

$$\frac{\Delta \vdash \mathbf{send}^+\ a\ V :: (a : A)}{\Delta \vdash \mathsf{msg}^+\ a\ V :: (\Delta, a : A)}\ \mathsf{msg}^+ \qquad \frac{\Delta \vdash \mathbf{recv}^+\ a\ K :: (c : C)}{\Delta \vdash \mathsf{cont}^+\ a\ K :: (\Delta, c : C)}\ \mathsf{cont}^+$$

$$\frac{\Delta \vdash \mathbf{send}^-\ a\ V :: (c : C)}{\Delta \vdash \mathsf{msg}^-\ a\ V :: (\Delta, c : C)}\ \mathsf{msg}^- \qquad \frac{\Delta \vdash \mathbf{recv}^-\ a\ K :: (a : A)}{\Delta \vdash \mathsf{cont}^-\ a\ K :: (\Delta, a : A)}\ \mathsf{cont}^-$$

$$\frac{a : A \in \Delta}{\Delta \vdash \mathsf{cont}^+\ a\ c :: (\Delta, c : A)}\ \mathsf{fwd}^+ \qquad \frac{a : A \in \Delta}{\Delta \vdash \mathsf{msg}^-\ a\ c :: (\Delta, c : A)}\ \mathsf{fwd}^-$$

In the statement of preservation we now have to account for a freshly allocated channel to become visible at the external interface to the configuration.

Theorem 4 (Preservation for Nonlinear Message Passing).
If $\Delta_1 \vdash \mathcal{C} :: \Delta_2$ and $\mathcal{C} \mapsto \mathcal{D}$ then $\Delta_1 \vdash \mathcal{D} :: \Delta_2'$ for some $\Delta_2' \supseteq \Delta_2$.

Proof. By induction on the typing of a configuration as before. In the case the step is a spawn which allocates a fresh channel $a : A$, we have $\Delta_2' = (\Delta_2, a : A)$.

Recall that a configuration was defined to be *terminal* if all semantics objects are *positive messages* or *negative continuations*. These objects are precisely those that become persistent, so terminal configurations now consist entirely of persistent objects.

Theorem 5 (Progress for Nonlinear Message Passing). *If $\cdot \vdash \mathcal{C} :: \Delta$ then either $\mathcal{C} \mapsto \mathcal{D}$ for some $\mathcal{D}$, or $\mathcal{C}$ is terminal.*

Judgmental Rules

$$\frac{\Gamma_1 \vdash P(x) :: (x : A) \quad \Gamma_2, x : A \vdash Q(x) :: (c : C)}{\Gamma_1, \Gamma_2 \vdash (x \leftarrow P(x) \,;\, Q(x)) :: (c : C)} \; \text{cut} \qquad \frac{}{a : A \vdash \mathbf{fwd}\ \mathbf{c}\ \mathbf{a} :: (c : A)} \; \text{id}$$

Positives

$$\frac{(k \in L)}{b : A_k \vdash \mathbf{send}\ a\ k(b) :: (a : \oplus_{\ell \in L}(\ell : A_\ell))} \; \oplus X$$

$$\frac{\Gamma, x : A_\ell \vdash P_\ell(x) :: (d : C) \quad (\forall \ell \in L)}{\Gamma, c : \oplus_{\ell \in L}(\ell : A_\ell) \vdash \mathbf{recv}\ c\ (\ell(x) \Rightarrow P_\ell(x))_{\ell \in L} :: (d : C)} \; \oplus L$$

$$\frac{}{a : A, b : B \vdash \mathbf{send}\ c\ \langle a, b \rangle :: (c : A \otimes B)} \; \otimes X$$

$$\frac{\Gamma, x : A, y : B \vdash P(x, y) :: (d : C)}{\Gamma, c : A \otimes B \vdash \mathbf{recv}\ c\ (\langle x, y \rangle \Rightarrow P(x, y)) :; (d : C)} \; \otimes L$$

$$\frac{}{\cdot \vdash \mathbf{send}\ c\ \langle\,\rangle :: (c : 1)} \; \otimes X \qquad \frac{\Gamma \vdash P :: (d : C)}{\Gamma, c : 1 \vdash \mathbf{recv}\ c\ (\langle\,\rangle \Rightarrow P) :; (d : C)} \; 1L$$

Negatives

$$\frac{\Gamma \vdash P_\ell(x) :: (x : A_\ell) \quad (\forall \ell \in L)}{\Gamma \vdash \mathbf{recv}\ c\ (\ell(x) \Rightarrow P_\ell(x))_{\ell \in L} :: (c : \&_{\ell \in L}(\ell : A_\ell))} \; \&R$$

$$\frac{}{c : \&_{\ell \in L}(\ell : A_\ell) \vdash \mathbf{send}\ c\ k(a) :: (a : A_k)} \; \&X$$

$$\frac{\Gamma, x : A \vdash P :: (y : B)}{\Gamma \vdash \mathbf{recv}\ c\ (\langle x, y \rangle \Rightarrow P(x, y)) :: (c : A \multimap B)} \; \multimap R$$

$$\frac{}{a : A, c : A \multimap B \vdash \mathbf{send}\ c\ \langle a, b \rangle :: (b : B)} \; \multimap X$$

Definitions

$$\frac{(x_1 : A_1, \ldots, x_n : A_n \vdash f :: (z : C)) \in \Sigma}{a_1 : A_1, \ldots, a_n : A_n \vdash f\ c\ [a_1, \ldots, a_n] :: (c : C)} \; \text{call}$$

Fig. 2. Typing for Message Passing

Proof. As before, by right-to-left induction over the typing derivation of the given configuration.

Now we can transport this result to nonlinear futures as before.

Corollary 2 (Preservation and Progress for Nonlinear Futures).

1. *If* $\Delta_1 \vdash \mathcal{C} :: \Delta_2$ *and* $\mathcal{C} \mapsto \mathcal{D}$ *then* $\Delta_1 \vdash \mathcal{D} :: \Delta_2'$ *for some* $\Delta_2' \supseteq \Delta_2$.
2. *If* $\cdot \vdash \mathcal{C} :: \Delta$ *then either* $\mathcal{C} \mapsto \mathcal{D}$ *for some* $\mathcal{D}$, *or* $\mathcal{C}$ *is final.*

Proof. By the correspondence with the message passing semantics and Theorems 4 and 5.

9   Conclusion

We have taken the journey from linear asynchronous message passing through linear futures and nonlinear futures back to nonlinear asynchronous message passing. In each layer, the operational semantics of message passing and futures are (strongly) bisimilar. This tight relationship is possible because all formalisms are based on the semi-axiomatic sequent calculus. The two kinds of interpretations have different characteristics: message passing exchanges only small messages ($\langle\rangle$, $\langle a, b \rangle$, and $k(a)$ for channels a, b, and labels k), while futures allow two natural sequential interpretations (eager and lazy) in addition to the parallel one.

We have not discussed type checking for the languages here, but standard techniques, including input/output contexts [6] apply. We can also use standard translations from natural deduction to sequent calculi to map a more familiar functional syntax to either message passing or futures (see, for example, [26]).

An alternative operational semantics for the language with weakening and contraction tracks multiple clients precisely, which can then be deallocated eagerly, avoiding the need for a general garbage collector [22]. This dynamics is significantly more complex than the model we have presented here, so we have not yet attempted to relate message passing and futures when both use explicit deallocation.

We can easily extend our bisimulation further by following the blueprint of mixed linear/nonlinear logic [2] and its generalization in adjoint logic [21,24]. In brief, we can extend the type systems of this paper by introducing multiple *modes* of types, potentially with different structural properties (e.g., linear/nonlinear, or message passing/futures), and then combine them using adjoint pairs of modalities. We have already investigated adjoint types separately for message passing [22] and futures [23]. These prior formulations are incompatible with each other, and the present paper recasts them into a single unifying framework of SAX.

Acknowledgments. We would like to thank Henry DeYoung, Luiz de Sa, and Siva Somayyajula for helpful discussions regarding the subject of this paper and comments on an earlier draft.

References

1. Andreoli, J.M.: Logic programming with focusing proofs in linear logic. J. Log. Comput. **2**(3), 197–347 (1992)
2. Benton, P.N.: A mixed linear and non-linear logic: Proofs, terms and models. In: Pacholski, L., Tiuryn, J. (eds.) CSL 1994. LNCS, vol. 933, pp. 121–135. Springer, Heidelberg (1995). https://doi.org/10.1007/BFb0022251
3. Blelloch, G.E., Reid-Miller, M.: Pipeling with futures. Theory Comput. Syst. **32**, 213–239 (1999)
4. Caires, L., Pfenning, F.: Session types as intuitionistic linear propositions. In: Gastin, P., Laroussinie, F. (eds.) CONCUR 2010. LNCS, vol. 6269, pp. 222–236. Springer, Heidelberg (2010). https://doi.org/10.1007/978-3-642-15375-4_16
5. Caires, L., Pfenning, F., Toninho, B.: Linear logic propositions as session types. Math. Struct. Comput. Sci. **26**(3), 367–423 (2016). Special Issue on Behavioural Types
6. Cervesato, I., Hodas, J.S., Pfenning, F.: Efficient resource management for linear logic proof search. Theoret. Comput. Sci. **232**(1–2), 133–163 (2000). Special issue on Proof Search in Type-Theoretic Languages
7. Cervesato, I., Scedrov, A.: Relating state-based and process-based concurrency through linear logic. Inf. Comput. **207**(10), 1044–1077 (2009)
8. Curry, H.B.: Functionality in combinatory logic. Proceed. Nat. Acad. Sci. U.S.A. **20**, 584–590 (1934)
9. DeYoung, H., Pfenning, F.: Data layout from a type-theoretic perspective. In: Proceedings of the 38th Conference on the Mathematical Foundations of Programming Semantics (MFPS 2022). Electronic Notes in Theoretical Informatics and Computer Science, vol. 1 (2022). https://arxiv.org/abs/2212.06321v6
10. DeYoung, H., Pfenning, F., Pruiksma, K.: Semi-axiomatic sequent calculus. In: Ariola, Z. (ed.) 5th International Conference on Formal Structures for Computation and Deduction (FSCD 2020), pp. 1–22. LIPIcs 167, Paris, France (2020)
11. Girard, J.Y.: Linear logic. Theoret. Comput. Sci. **50**, 1–102 (1987)
12. Girard, J.Y., Lafont, Y.: Linear logic and lazy computation. In: Ehrig, H., Kowalski, R., Levi, G., Montanari, U. (eds.) TAPSOFT 1987. LNCS, vol. 250, pp. 52–66. Springer, Heidelberg (1987). https://doi.org/10.1007/BFb0014972
13. Halstead, R.H.: MultiLisp: a language for parallel symbolic computation. ACM Trans. Program. Lang. Syst. **7**(4), 501–539 (1985)
14. Honda, K.: Types for dyadic interaction. In: Best, E. (ed.) CONCUR 1993. LNCS, vol. 715, pp. 509–523. Springer, Heidelberg (1993). https://doi.org/10.1007/3-540-57208-2_35
15. Honda, K., Tokoro, M.: An object calculus for asynchronous communication. In: America, P. (ed.) ECOOP 1991. LNCS, vol. 512, pp. 133–147. Springer, Heidelberg (1991). https://doi.org/10.1007/BFb0057019
16. Howard, W.A.: The formulae-as-types notion of construction (1969), unpublished note. An annotated version appeared. In: To H.B. Curry: Essays on Combinatory Logic, Lambda Calculus and Formalism, 479–490, Academic Press (1980)
17. Kobayashi, N., Pierce, B.C., Turner, D.N.: Linearity and the pi-calculus. In: Boehm, H.J., Steele, G. (eds.) Proceedings of the 23rd Symposium on Principles of Programming Languages (POPL1996), pp. 358–371. ACM, St. Petersburg Beach, Florida, USA (1996)
18. Laurent, O.: Syntax vs. semantics: a polarized approach. Theoret. Comput. Sci. **343**(1–2), 177–206 (2005)

19. Milner, R.: Communicating and Mobile Systems: the π-Calculus. Cambridge University Press (1999)
20. OpenMP. http://openmp.org
21. Pruiksma, K., Chargin, W., Pfenning, F., Reed, J.: Adjoint logic (2018). http://www.cs.cmu.edu/~fp/papers/adjoint18b.pdf
22. Pruiksma, K., Pfenning, F.: A message-passing interpretation of Adjoint logic. J. Logical Algebr. Methods Programm. **120**, 100637 (2021)
23. Pruiksma, K., Pfenning, F.: Back to futures. J. Funct. Program. **32**, e6 (2022)
24. Reed, J.: A judgmental deconstruction of modal logic (2009). http://www.cs.cmu.edu/~jcreed/papers/jdml2.pdf
25. Sangiorgi, D., Walker, D.: The π-Calculus: a Theory of Mobile Processes. Cambridge University Press (2001)
26. Toninho, B., Caires, L., Pfenning, F.: Functions as session-typed processes. In: Birkedal, L. (ed.) FoSSaCS 2012. LNCS, vol. 7213, pp. 346–360. Springer, Heidelberg (2012). https://doi.org/10.1007/978-3-642-28729-9_23
27. Wadler, P.: Listlessness is better than laziness: lazy evaluation and garbage collection at compile-time. In: Conference on Lisp and Functional Programming (LFP 1984), pp. 45–52. ACM, Austin, Texas (1984)
28. Wadler, P.: Propositions as sessions. In: Proceedings of the 17th International Conference on Functional Programming (ICFP 2012), pp. 273–286. ACM Press, Copenhagen, Denmark (2012)

Collective Adaptive Systems
and Aggregate Computing

MacroSwarm: A Field-Based Compositional Framework for Swarm Programming

Gianluca Aguzzi$^{(\boxtimes)}$ ⓘ, Roberto Casadei ⓘ, and Mirko Viroli ⓘ

Alma Mater Studiorum – Università di Bologna, Cesena, Italy
{gianluca.aguzzi,roby.casadei,mirko.viroli}@unibo.it

Abstract. Swarm behaviour engineering is an area of research that seeks to investigate methods for coordinating computation and action within groups of simple agents to achieve complex global goals like collective movement, clustering, and distributed sensing. Despite recent progress in the study and engineering of swarms (of drones, robots, vehicles), there is still need for general design and implementation methods that can be used to define complex swarm coordination in a principled way. To face this need, this paper proposes a new field-based coordination approach, called MacroSwarm, to design fully composable and reusable blocks of swarm behaviour. Based on the macroprogramming approach of aggregate computing, it roots on the idea of modelling each block of swarm behaviour by a purely functional transformation of sensing fields into actuation description fields, typically including movement vectors. We showcase the potential of MacroSwarm as a framework for collective intelligence by simulation, in a variety of scenarios including flocking, morphogenesis, and collective decision-making.

Keywords: Swarm Behaviours · Field-based Coordination · Aggregate Computing · Collective Intelligence · Distributed Computing · DSLs

1 Introduction

Recent technological advances foster a vision of *swarms* of mobile cyber-physical agents able to compute, coordinate with neighbours, and interact with the environment according to increasingly complex patterns, plans, and goals. Notable examples include swarms of drones and robots [44], fleets of vehicles [45], and crowds of wearable-augmented people [24]. In these domains, a prominent research problem is how to effectively engineer *swarm behaviour* [13], i.e., how to promote the emergence of desired global-level outcomes with inherent robustness and resiliency to changes and faults in the swarm or the environment. Complex patterns can emerge through the interaction of simple agents [12], and centralised approaches can suffer from scalability and dependability issues: as such, we seek for an approach based on suitable distributed coordination models and languages to steer the micro-level activity of a possibly large set of

S.-S. Jongmans and A. Lopes (Eds.): COORDINATION 2023, LNCS 13908, pp. 31–51, 2023.
https://doi.org/10.1007/978-3-031-35361-1_2

agents. This direction has been explored by various research threads related to coordination like *macroprogramming* [16,35], *spatial computing* [10], *ensemble languages* [1,21], *field-based coordination* [31,33], and *aggregate computing* [50].

Though a number of approaches and languages have been proposed for specifying or programming swarm behaviour [4,15,22,28–30,34,41,51], a key feature that is generally missing or provided only to a limited extent is *compositionality*, namely the ability of combining blocks of simple swarm behaviour to construct swarm systems of increasing complexity in a controlled/engineered way. Additionally, most of existing approaches tend to be pragmatic, not formally-founded and quite ad-hoc: they enable construction of certain types of swarm applications but with limited support for analysis and principled design of complex applications (e.g. [15,22,30,41]). Exceptions that provide a formal approach exist but they are typically overly abstract, requiring additional effort to actually code and execute swarm control programs [32].

The goal of this work is to introduce a formally-grounded Application Program Interface (API), expressive and practical enough to concisely and elegantly encode a wide array of swarm behaviours. This is based on the field-based coordination paradigm [50] and the field calculus [9]: each block of swarm behaviour is captured by a purely functional transformation of sensing fields into actuation fields including movement vectors, and such a transformation declaratively captures the state/computation/interaction mechanisms necessary to achieve that behaviour. Practically, such specifications can be programmed as Scala scripts in the SCAFI framework [8,18], a reference implementation for field-based coordination and aggregate computing. Accordingly, we present MACROSWARM, a SCAFI-based framework to help programming with swarm behaviours by providing a set of blocks covering key swarming patterns as identified in literature [13]: flocking, leader-follower behaviours, morphogenesis, and team formation. To evaluate MACROSWARM, we show a use case that leverage our API in a simulated environment based on the Alchemist multi-agent system simulator [40].

The remainder of this paper is organised as follows. Section 2 provides context and motivation. Section 3 reviews background on aggregate computing. Section 4 presents the main contribution of the paper, MACROSWARM. Section 5 provides a simulation-based evaluation of the approach. Section 6 reviews related works on swarm programming. Finally, Sect. 7 provides a conclusion and future work.

2   Context and Motivation

Engineering the collective behaviour of swarms is a significant research challenge [13]. Two main kinds of design methods can be identified [13]: *automatic* design methods like evolutionary robotics [46] or multi-agent reinforcement learning [14], also called *behaviour-based* design, involving manually-implemented algorithms expressed via general-purpose or domain-specific languages (DSLs). Our focus is on the latter category of methods and especially on DSLs for expressing swarm behaviour (which are reviewed in Sect. 6).

Another main distinction is between *centralised* (*orchestration-based*) and *decentralised* (*choreographical*) approaches. In the former category, programs generally specify tasks and relationships between tasks, and these descriptions are used by a centralised entity to command the behaviour of the individual entities of the swarm. By contrast, decentralised approaches do not rely on any centralised entity: each robot is driven by a control program and the resulting execution is decentralised (e.g., based on interaction with neighbours, like in Meld [4]). In this work, we focus on *decentralised* solutions, for they support resilience and scalability by avoiding single-points-of-failure and bottlenecks.

In the general context of behaviour-based swarm design, researchers have pointed out various issues [13,23] like a general lack of *top-down* design methods of collective behaviours (cf. the scientific issue of "emergence programming" [47] and "self-organisation steering" [25]), the problem of formal verification and validation [32], heterogeneity, and operational/maintenance issues (e.g., scalability, adaptation, and security).

To address top-down swarm programming, an approach should provide the means to define and compose blocks of high-level swarm behaviours. Regarding the kinds of blocks that can be provided, it is helpful to look at proposed taxonomies of collective/swarm behaviour. In a prominent survey on swarm engineering [13], collective behaviours are classified into (i) spatially-organising behaviours (e.g., pattern formation, morphogenesis), (ii) navigation behaviours (e.g., collective exploration, transport, and coordinated motion), (iii) collective decision-making (e.g., consensus achievement and task allocation), and (iv) others (e.g., human-swarm interaction and group size regulation).

Finally, we observe in the literature a rather sharp distinction between approaches leveraging formal methods for specifying swarm behaviour [32], also enabling verification, and more pragmatic approaches offering concrete DSLs that are more usable. In a recent survey on formal specification methods for swarm robotics [32] it is reported that a major limitation lies in (i) the tooling and (i) the formalisation of the "last step" of passing from a formal model to program code. Hence, we seek here for an approach that combines the benefits of formal methods and the pragmatism of concrete DSLs.

In summary, this work is motivated by the need of an approach for *formal-yet-practical top-down behaviour-based design of decentralised swarm behaviour*.

3   Background: Aggregate Computing

Aggregate computing [50] is a field-based coordination [33] and macroprogramming [16] approach especially suitable to express the collective adaptive [36] and self-organising behaviour of large groups of situated agents.

System Model. In aggregate computing, a system can be simply modelled as a logical set of computing *nodes* (also called *devices*), where each node is equipped with *sensors* and *actuators*, and is connected with other nodes according to some *neighbouring relationships*. This abstract logical model does not prescribe particular technological solutions; instead, it uses minimal assumptions on the capabilities of devices (e.g., regarding synchrony, connectivity, and computing power).

Execution Model. The approach is generally used to program long-running control tasks that need several sensing, communication, computation, and actuation steps to be carried out. Accordingly, the execution model is based on (or can be understood as) a repeated execution, by each device, of asynchronous sense–compute–interact *rounds*—fundamentally mimicking self-organisation in biological systems [12]. For simplicity, we can consider each round to atomically consist of three steps:

- **Sense** – the node's *local context* is assessed, by sampling sensors and gathering the most recent (and not expired) message from any neighbour;
- **Compute** – the so-called *aggregate program* is evaluated against the local context, producing an output (which can be used to describe actuations) and an internal output (invisible to programmers), called an *export*, that contains the message to be sent to neighbours for coordination purposes;
- **Interact** – the export is sent to neighbours (logically, as a broadcast), and potential actuations can be performed.

In general, programs define the logic for spreading information from neighbourhood to neighbourhood, and progressively compute results eventually reaching convergence once no more changes perturb the system. Interestingly, device failure, message loss, and the like are automatically tolerated as assessed by context updates at the beginning of rounds. In order to understand how an aggregate program executed in this fashion promotes collective adaptive behaviour, we briefly present the programming model.

Programming Model. Aggregate computing is based on the *(computational) field* abstraction [33]. A field is basically a function or map from devices to computational values. For instance, having a collection of devices query their temperature sensor would yield a field of real numbers denoting temperature readings, whereas a field of speed vectors could be use to denote the desired actuations to make a swarm move.

The *field calculus* [9] is the minimal core language at the basis of aggregate computing, which defines the primitives for expressing "space-time universal" [5] distributed computations in terms of field manipulations. Then, concrete languages like the Scala-internal DSL ScaFi (ScAla FIelds) [8,18] can be used to actually develop aggregate programs.

The reader can refer to [8] for a full presentation of programming with ScaFi. Here, we briefly introduce the main language constructs.

Construct rep: *stateful field evolution.* Consider the following example.

```
// def rep[T](init: T)(f: T => T): T
rep(0)(x => x+1) // type T=Int inferred
```

This purely local computation, when considered executed by all the devices in the system, yields a field of integers denoting the number of rounds executed by each device. This is obtained by applying function f to the value computed the previous round (or init, initially).

Construct foldhood/nbr: *interaction with neighbours.* Consider:

```
// def foldhood[A](init: => A)(acc: (A, A) => A)(expr: => A): A
// def nbr[A](expr: => A): A
foldhood[Set[ID]](Set.empty)(_++_){ Set(nbr(mid())) }
```

It yields, in each device, the set of identifiers of all its neighbours. This is achieved by a purely functional fold over the collection of the singleton sets of neighbour identifiers, starting from the empty set, and aggregating using the set union operator (++). mid() provides the local identifier. Within the foldhood, a nbr(e) expression has the twofold role of sending and gathering the local value of e to/from neighbours. Note that constructs rep and foldhood/nbr can be combined to support the diffusion of information beyond direct neighbours.

Functional Abstraction. New blocks can be defined with standard Scala functions:

```
def neighbouringField[T](f: => T): Set[T] =
  foldhood[Set[T]](Set.empty)(_++_){ Set(nbr(f)) }
def neighbourIDs(): Set[ID] = neighbouringField{ mid() }
```

Construct branch: *splitting computation domains.* Consider:

```
// def branch[A](cond: => Boolean)(th: => A)(el: => A)
branch(sense[Boolean]("hasTemperatureSensor")){
  val nearbyTemperatures: Set[Double] =
    neighbouringField{ sense[Double]("temperature") }
  // ...
}{ noOp }
```

Here, computation is split into separate subsets of devices. Notice that neighbourhoods are restricted in each computation branch. So, in the first branch, it is ensured that only the neighbours with a temperature sensor are folded over.

General Resilient Operators. It is possible to identify some general higher-level operators to account for common self-organisation patterns [49]. These will be leveraged in Sect. 4 and hence are briefly described.

- *Sparse choice (leader election)* [38]. Block S(grain:Double):Boolean can be used to yield a self-stabilising Boolean field which is true in a sparse set of devices located at a mean distance grain.
- *Gradient-cast   (distributed   propagation)*   [49].   Block G[T](source:Boolean,value:T,acc:T=>T):T is used to propagate value from source devices outwards along the gradient [49] of increasing distances from them, transforming the value through acc along the way.

– *C*ollect-cast (distributed collection) [6]. Block
  `C[T](sink:Boolean,value:T,acc(T,T)=>T):T` is used to summarise distributed information into `sink` devices, the `values` provided by devices around the system, while aggregating information through `acc` along the gradient directed towards the sinks.

Examples further showing the compositionality of the approach are in Sect. 4.

Aggregate Computing for Swarm Programming. To motivate why aggregate computing appears to be a good match for swarm programming, we briefly explain how it helps to address the challenges identified, as studied in previous papers (presented in Sect. 2).

– *Top-down behaviour-based design.* It is promoted by the *compositionality* and *collective stance* of aggregate computing, supported by the functional paradigm and the field abstraction [7,9].
– *Scalability.* Since execution is fully decentralised and asynchronous, the approach is scalable to hundreds, thousands, and even more devices [19].
– *Formal approach.* Aggregate computing and SCAFI are based on the field calculus [8,9], which enables formal analysis of programs and proofs of interesting properties like self-stabilisation [49], universality [5], and others [50].
– *Pragmatism.* Promoted by layers of abstractions, this is witnessed by open-source, maintained, concrete software artefacts like the SCAFI DSL [18], simulation platforms like Alchemist [40] and SCAFI-WEB [2][1], and the possibility to devise libraries of high-level functions [19].
– *Operational flexibility.* Concrete aggregate computing systems can be deployed and operated using different architectural styles [17] and execution policies [39], supporting different technological and resource requirements.

4   MACROSWARM

This section presents the MACROSWARM approach and API. In particular, we describe its overall architecture, and the main blocks exposed by the API (summarised in Fig. 1), which support the specification of a wide range of high-level swarm behaviours. The key idea in the design of MACROSWARM lies in the representation of a swarm behavioural unit as a function mapping sensing and parameter fields to actuation fields (often, velocity vectors). We have organised the API into multiple *modules*, capturing logically related sets of behaviours, and comprising more fundamental and reusable sets of behaviours as well as more application-specific sets (e.g., related to movement or team formation).

Movement Blocks. These blocks control the movement of individual agents within the swarm. The simplest movement expressible with MACROSWARM is a collective constant movement (Fig. 2a), described through a tuple like `Vector(x,y,z)` that devises the velocity vector of the swarm:

---

[1] https://scafi.github.io/web/.

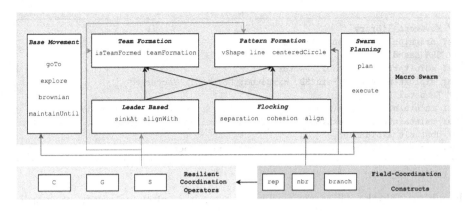

Fig. 1. MACROSWARM: architecture overview. The black boxes contained in the green rectangle represent the main modules of the library.

```
Vector(2.5, 0, 0) // a constant field which is the same for all the agents
```

This vector must then be appropriately mapped the right electrical stimulus for the underlying engine platform of the mobile robot of interest. On top of that, this module exposes several blocks to explore an environment. Particularly, the **brownian** block produces a random velocity vector for each evaluation of the program. In addition to that simple logic, there are movements based on GPS like goTo (produces a velocity vector that eventually moves the system to sink at one single point) and **explore** (produces a velocity vector that let the system explore a rectangle defined through minBound and maxBound). The last one is based on temporal blocks, like maintainTrajectory and maintainUntil. The former allows the systems to maintain a certain velocity for the time specified. At that moment, a new velocity is generated according to the given strategy. The latter, instead, is used to maintain a certain velocity until a condition is met (e.g., a target position is reached). This module also exposes an obstacleAvoidance block (Fig. 2d), which creates a vector pointing away from obstacles.

Even if these blocks are quite simple, it is still possible to combine them to create interesting behaviours. For instance, program

```
(maintainVelocity(browian()) + obstacleAvoidance(sense("obs"))).normalize
```

expresses a collective behaviour in which the nodes will explore the environment, while avoiding any obstacles perceived through a sensor. Notice how the composition is achieved by simply summing the computational fields produced by the sub-blocks. Expression v.normalize yields v as a unit vector (of length 1), while keeping the same direction—useful when combining several vectors together. A summary of the blocks exposed by this module is reported in the following listing:

```
// Movement library
def brownian(scale: Double): Vector
// GPS Based
def goTo(target: Point3D): Vector
def explore(minBound: Point3D, maxBound: Point3D): Vector
// Temporal Based
def maintainTrajectory(trajectory: => Vector)(time: FiniteDuration):Vector
def maintainUntil(direction: Vector)(condition: Boolean): Vector
// Obstacle Avoidance
def obstacleAvoidance(obstacles: List[Vector]): Vector
```

Flocking Blocks. In a swarm-like system, it is often necessary to coordinate the movement of the entire swarm, rather than just individual agents, to achieve emergent behaviours, and ensure that the nodes move cohesively, avoid collisions, and strive to be aligned in a common direction. Therefore, in this module, we have implemented the main blocks to support the *flocking* of agents. Several models are available in the literature for this purpose. Particularly, MACROSWARM exposes the Vicsek [48], Cucker-Smale [20], and Reynolds (Fig. 2e) [42] models. We have also exposed the individual blocks to implement Reynolds, which are `cohesion`, `separation`, and `alignment`. These blocks can be used individually by higher-level blocks to implement specific behaviours (e.g., following a leader while avoiding collisions).

Another essential aspect that emerges at this level is the concept of a *variable neighbourhood*. Indeed, it may happen that the logical neighbourhood model used by aggregate computing does not match the one used to coordinate the agents. Thus, the node's visibility can be more *restrictive* or *extensive* according to the neighbourhood model applied. In particular, in the case of Reynolds, it is typical for the separation range to be different from that of alignment. Therefore, the flocking blocks accept a "query" strategy towards a variable neighbourhood. The main implementation of these queries are:

- `OneHopNeighborhood`: the same as the aggregate computing model;
- `OneHopNeighborhoodWithinRange(radius: Double)`: it takes all the nodes in the neighbourhood within the given range.

The flocking models are typically described by an iterated function in which the velocity at time $t+1$ depends on the velocity at time t. Taking as an example the Vicsek rule, it is described as: $v_i(t+1) = \frac{\sum_{j \in \mathcal{N}} v_j(t)}{|\mathcal{N}|} + \eta_i(t)$ where $\mathcal{N}$ is the neighbourhood of the node i at time t, $v_i(t)$ is the velocity of the node i at time t, and $\eta_i(t)$ is a random vector that models the noise of the model. For this reason, each block receives the previous velocity field as a parameter, rather than encoding it internally within each block. This is because the previous velocities may be influenced by other factors, such as constant movements or a target position. Typical usage of this operator follows the following schema:

```
rep(initialVelocity) { oldVelocity => flockingOperator(oldVelocity, ..) }
```

For example, the following program describes a collective movement in which the nodes try to reach the position (x,y) while maintaining a distance of k meters from one another:

```
rep(Point2D.Zero) {
  v => (goTo(Point2D(x, y)) +
      separation(v, OneHopNeighbourhoodWithinRange(k))).normalize
}
```

Leader-Based Blocks. These blocks allow agents to follow a designated leader. The idea behind leadership in swarm systems is that a leader can act as a coordinator, influencing the followers that recognise it as such. In the context of aggregate computing, leaders are typically defined as Boolean fields holding **true** for leaders and **false** for non-leaders. Leaders can be predetermined (i.e., nodes with certain characteristics), virtual (i.e., nodes that do not actually exist in the system but are simulated for collective movement steering), or chosen in space (e.g., using the S block—see Sect. 3). A leader can be thought of as creating an *area of influence*, affecting the actions of its followers.

Currently, we have identified **alignWithLeader** and **sinkAt** (Fig. 2b) as essential blocks. The former propagates the leader's velocity throughout its area of influence (e.g., via G—see Sect. 3), with followers adjusting their velocity to it. However, sometimes it may also be desirable to create a sort of attraction towards the leader, so that the nodes remain cohesive with it. For this reason, the **sinkAt** block creates a computational field in which nodes tend to move towards the leader. These blocks are useful for higher-level blocks, such as those associated with the creation of teams or spatial formations.

Team Formation Blocks. These blocks allow agents to form *teams* or subgroups within the swarm, useful e.g. for work division or situations requiring intervention by few agents. In general, the formation of a team creates a "split" in the swarm logic, conceptually creating multiple swarms with potentially different goals (cf. Fig. 2c). One way to create teams is by using the branch construct (see Sect. 3). For example, the following program,

```
def alignVelocity(id: Int) =
  alighWithLeader(id == mid(), rep(browian())(x => x)
branch(mid() < 50) { alignVelocity(0) } { alignVelocity(50) }
```

creates two groups, each of which follows a certain velocity dictated by the leaders (0 and 50).

Other times, one needs to create teams based on the spatial structure of the network or when certain conditions are met. The **teamFormation** block supports this scenario. By internally using S, it allows for the creation of teams based on certain spatial constraints expressed through parameters **intraDistance** (i.e., the distance between team members) and **targetExtraDistance** (i.e., the size of the leader's area of influence). It is also possible to create teams based on

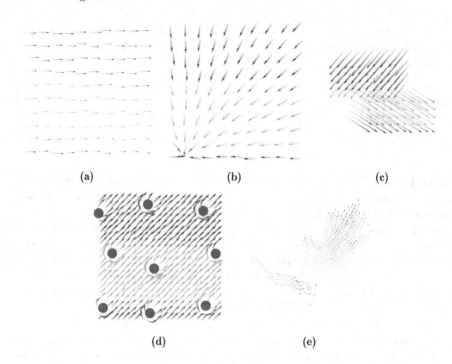

(a)   (b)   (c)

(d)   (e)

Fig. 2. Overview of swarm behaviours expressible with MACROSWARM.

predetermined leaders, denoted explicitly by Boolean fields. Moreover, since team formation may take time to complete, or require conditions to be met (e.g., that at least N members are present, or that the minimum distance between all nodes is less than a certain threshold), we also parameterise `teamFormation` by a `condition` predicate. An example of built-in predicate is `isTeamFormed`, which verifies that each node under the influence of the leader has a `necessary` a number of neighbours within a `targetDistance` radius. An example is as follows.

```
teamFormation(targetIntraDistance = 30, // separation
  targetExtraDistance = 300, // influence of the leader
  condition = leader => isTeamFormed(leader, targetDistance = 40)
).velocity // use the velocity vector to create the Team
```

Each team must refer to a single leader, who can coordinate the associated nodes (using the APIs exposed by the **Leader Based Block**). In particular, to execute a certain behaviour within a team, the `insideTeam` method must be used. Given the ID of the leader to which a node belongs, this method can define the movement logic relative to that leader. For instance, this code aligns the followers with a velocity generated by a leader,

```
team.insideTeam{leader => alignWithLeader(leader)(rep(brownian())(x => x))}
```

Fig. 3. Examples of the supported patterns. From left to right: line formation, v-like formation, and circular formation.

Pattern Formation Blocks. Team formation blocks can be used to create groups of agents with certain characteristics. However, sometimes we are also interested in the *spatial structure* of the group. In swarm behaviours, the spatial structures of the teams can be instrumental for performing certain tasks (e.g., coverage or transportation tasks). In MACROSWARM some of the most idiomatic spatial structures are available.

The implementation is as follows. First of all, the formation of structures is based on the presence of a leader that collects the hop-by-hop distances of their followers (leveraging G and C) and sends them a direction in which they should go to form the required structure (using G).

The structures currently supported (Fig. 3) are v-like shapes (vShape), lines (line), and circular formations (centeredCircle). These structures are *self-healing*: if there is a disturbance of the structure, the group tends to reconstruct itself and return to a stable structure. Additionally, it is assumed that the leader has his own speed logic. In this way, the group will follow the leader maintaining the chosen structure.

Swarm Planning Blocks. With the previous blocks available, there is a need for a handy mechanism to express a series of *plans* that change over time and move the swarm towards different targets. For this reason, MACROSWARM also exposes the concept of *swarm planning*. The idea is to express a series of plans (or missions) defined by a *behaviour* (i.e., the logic of production of a velocity vector) and a *goal* (defined as a boolean predicate condition). At any given time, the swarm will be executing a certain sub-plan, which will be considered complete only when the boolean condition is satisfied. At this point, the swarm will follow the next objective described by the overall plan. The exposed API allows for the creation of these collective plans in the following way:

```
execute.once {
  plan(goTo(goalOne).endWhen(isClose(goalOne)),
  plan(goTo(goalTwo).endWhen(isClose(goalTwo)),
}.run() // will trigger the execution of the plan
```

This snippet creates a plan in which the nodes will first go to goalOne, and once reached (isClose verifies that the node is close enough to the point passed), it will move on to the next objective goalTwo. Since it is specified that the mission is executed once, after the completion of the last plan, the group will stop moving. To make the group repeat the plan, the `repeat` method can be used instead of `once`. Note that there is no coordination between agents in the above code, but you can enforce it using lower-level blocks (e.g., flocking or team-based behaviours). For example, MACROSWARM enables describing a swarm behaviour where: (i) a group of nodes gather around a leader, (ii) the leader brings the entire group towards the `goalOne`, (iii) the leader brings the entire group towards the `goalTwo`. This can be described using the following code:

```
execute.once( // if it is repeated, you can use 'repeat'
  plan{sinkAt(leaderX)}.endWhen{isTeamFormed(leaderX, targetDistance=100)},
  plan(goTo(goalOne)).endWhen{ G(leaderX, isClose(goalOne), x => x)},
  plan(goTo(goalTwo)).endWhen{ G(leaderX, isClose(goalTwo), x => x)},
).run()
```

The use of `G` in this way is a recurrent pattern, and in SCAFI it is exposed through the `broadcast[T](center: Boolean, value: T): T` block.

5   Evaluation

To validate the proposed approach and API we define a simulated *find-and-rescue* case study, to show the ability of MACROSWARM to express complex swarm behaviours (Sect. 5.1). Then, we discuss the results of the case study and the applicability of the proposed approach in real-world scenarios (Sect. 5.2).

5.1   Case Study: Find and Rescue

In our scenario, we want a fleet of drones to patrol a spatial area. In the area, dangerous situations may arise (e.g., a fire breaks out, a person gets injured, etc.). In response to these, a drone designated as a *healer* must approach and resolve them. Exploration must be carried out in groups composed of *at least* one healer and several *explorers*, who will help the healer identify alarm situations.

Goal. The goal of the proposed case study is to demonstrate the effectiveness of the proposed API in terms of expressiveness (i.e., the ability to describe complex behaviours easily) and correctness (i.e., the described behaviour collectively does what is expressed). For the first point, since it is a qualitative metric, we will show the development process that led to the implementation of the produced code, demonstrating its ease of understanding. For the second point, since deploying a swarm of drones is costly, we will make use of simulations to verify that the program is functioning correctly both qualitatively (e.g., observing the graphical simulation) and quantitatively (i.e., extracting the necessary data and computing metrics that allow us to understand if the system behaves as it should).

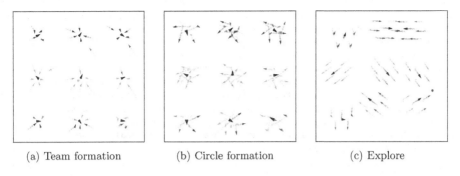

(a) Team formation   (b) Circle formation   (c) Explore

Fig. 4. The first phases of the scenario described in Sect. 5. At the beginning, the system is split into teams; afterwards, the teams assume a spatial formation (circular, in this case); finally, the teams start exploring the overall area.

Setup. Initially, 50 explorers and 5 healers are randomly positioned in an area of $1km^2$. Each drone has a maximum speed of approximately $20\,km/h$ and a communication range of $100\,m$. The alarm situations are randomly generated at different times within the spatial area in a $[0, 50]$ minutes time-frame. Each simulation run lasts $90\,min$, during which we expect the number of alarm situations to reach a minimum value. The node should form teams of at least one healer and several explorers, maintaining a distance of at least $50\,m$ between the node and the leader

Implementation Details. To structure the desired swarm behaviour, we break the problem into parts:

1. the swarm must split into teams regulated by a healer, who works as a *leader* (Fig. 4a);
2. teams must assume a spatial formation promoting the efficiency of the exploration (Fig. 4b);
3. the teams must explore the overall area (Fig. 4c);
4. when any node detects an alarm zone, it must point that to the healer;
5. the healer node approaches the dangerous situation to fix it;
6. then, the team should return to the exploration phase.

We now describe the implementation of each part, leveraging the MACROSWARM API. First of all, for creating teams, we can use the **Team Formation** blocks:

```
val teamFormedLogic =
  (leader: ID) => isTeamFormed(leader, minimumDistance + confidence)
def createTeam() =
  teamFormation(sense("healer"), minimumDistance, teamFormedLogic)
```

where `minimumDistance` is the minimum distance between nodes during the team formation phases and `confidence` is the confidence interval used to check if the team is formed through the `isTeamFormed` method. Each team then should follow the aforementioned steps, expressible using the **Swarm Planning** API:

```
def insideTeamPlanning(team: Team): Vector =
 team.insideTeam {
  healerId =>
   val leading = healerId == mid() // team leader
   execute.repeat(
    plan(formation(leading)).endWhen(circleIsFormed), // shape formation
    plan(wanderInFormation(leading)).endWhen(dangerFound), // exploration
    plan(goToHealInFormation(leading, inDanger)).endWhen(dangerReached),
    plan(heal(healerId, inDanger)).endWhen(healed(dangerFound)) // healing
    ).run() // repeat the plan
 }
```

The first step is the formation of the teams, based on method `formation` which internally uses `centeredCircle` to place the nodes in a circle around the leader node. Function `circleIsFormed` verifies whether the nodes are in a circle formation, i.e., that the distance between any node and the leader is less than `radius` (set to 50 m in this scenario). The second step is the exploration phase, implemented by method `wanderInFormation`, which uses the `explore` function to move the nodes to a random direction within given bounds while keeping the circle formation. This leverages `centeredCircle`, passing the movement logic of the healer (leader) to the block. Exploration will go on until someone finds a danger node, denoted by predicate `dangerFound`. This internally uses C and G to collect the danger nodes' psitions and share them within the team:

```
def dangerFound(healer: Boolean): Boolean = {
  val dangerNodes =
    C(sense("healer"), combinePosition, List(sense("danger")), List.empty)
  broadcast(healer, dangerNodes.nonEmpty)
}
```

The third step is the movement towards the danger node, which is implemented by the `goToHealInFormation` method, which uses again the `centeredCircle` function with a delta vector that moves the leader node towards the danger node. `inDanger` is computed similarly to `dangerFound`, but, in this case, the position will be shared instead. `dangerReached` is a Boolean field indicating if the healer node is close enough to the danger node. The last step is the healing of the danger node, which is modelled as an actuation of the healer. The rescue ends when the danger node is healed. As a final note, we also want the nodes to be able to avoid each other when they are too close, even if they are not in the same team. For this, we leverage the **Flocking** API the `separation` block outside the team logic. Then, the main program is as follows:

```
val team = createTeam()
rep(Vector.Zero) { v =>
  insideTeamPlanning(team) +
  separation(v, OneHopNeighbourhoodWithinRange(avoidDistance))
}.normalize
```

This program shows that the API is flexible enough to create complex behaviours handling various coordination aspects.

Results. We validated the results by effectively running simulations, publicly available at https://zenodo.org/badge/latestdoi/611692727. For this task, we used Alchemist [40], a general simulator for multi-agent and pervasive systems. We launched 64 simulation runs with different random seeds: Fig. 5 shows the average results obtained. We extracted the following data:

- *intra-team distance*: after an initial adjustment phase, the system should converge to an average distance of 50 m (Fig. 5a);
- *minimum distance between each node*: as we want to avoid collisions, the minimum distance between two nodes should always be greater than zero (Fig. 5b);
- *number of nodes in danger*: we expect the nodes in danger to increase up to 50 min and then decrease, tending towards zero (Fig. 5c).

The results (Fig. 5) show that the system can achieve the expected outcomes.

5.2   Discussion

Despite its simplicity, this use case allowed us to demonstrate the capability of MACROSWARM, both in qualitative terms (i.e., the produced code is simple and understandable) and quantitative terms (i.e., the data show that the swarm follows the given instructions correctly).

That being said, there are several things to consider when using the library in real-world contexts. Ours is a top-down approach, in which we have defined an evaluation and implementation system that is general enough to be executed in various multi-robot systems. Specifically, we require that at least: *i)* nodes can perceive and interact with neighbours and approximate a direction vector to each of them; *ii)* they can move in a specific direction with a certain velocity; and *iii)* they can perceive distance and direction for certain obstacles. As for point *i)*, this can be developed using specific local sensors (e.g., range and bearing systems [11]), by using GPS, by approximating distances using cameras mounted on each drone, or by using Bluetooth direction finding [43]. Concerning the point *ii)* the velocity vector can be mapped to the motors of the UAVs, or the motor's wheels of the ground robots [27], so it can be easily implemented in real case scenarios. Finally, concerning *iii)*, there are several solutions for perceiving the direction of obstacles by leveraging various sensors, like *Laser Imaging Detection And Ranging (LIDAR)* systems [37].

That being said, we know that the reality gap for real-world scenarios could introduce divergences from the behaviours shown, as the used simulator, although general, does not simulate many aspects of reality, such as communication delay, friction, and possible perception errors. We aim to test the API in more realistic simulators (like Gazebo [26]) or real systems as a future work.

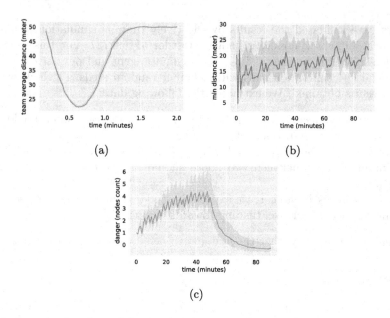

Fig. 5. Quantitative plots of the simulated scenario. Figure 5a shows the average team distance in the first two minutes. Figure 5b shows the minimum distance between nodes. Figure 5c shows the nodes in danger through time. Since we run several simulations, the lines show the average values, whereas the area around the lines shows the confidence interval throughout the simulations.

6   Related Work

Related programming approaches for swarms include Meld [4], Buzz [41], Voltron [34], TeCoLa [29], Dolphin [30], Maple-Swarm [28], PARoS [22], Resh [15], and [51]. In the following, we review the works that are more related to MACROSWARM, which are those for expressing *decentralised* behaviours.

Buzz [41] is a mixed imperative-functional language for programming swarms. In Buzz, swarms are first-class abstractions: they can be explicitly created, manipulated, joined (e.g., based on local conditions), and used as a way to address individual members (e.g., for tasking them). For individual robots, the language provides access to local features and the local set of neighbours, for interaction. For swarm-wide consensus, a notion of *virtual stigmergy* is leveraged, based on distributed tuple spaces. Buzz is designed to be an extensible language, since new primitives can be added. Indeed, Buzz is based on a set of quite effective but ad-hoc mechanisms. By contrast, MACROSWARM uses few general and expressive primitives, and supports swarm programming through a library of reusable, composable blocks. Additionally, MACROSWARM can leverage theoretical results from field calculi [49,50], making programs amenable for formal analysis.

Voltron [34] is a programming model for team-level design of drone systems. It represents a group of individual drones through a *team abstraction*, which is responsible for the overall task. The details of individual drone actions and their timing are delegated to the platform system during runtime. The programmer issues *action commands* to the drone team, along with *spatiotemporal constraints*. The tasks in Voltron are associated with spatial locations, and the team self-organises to populate *multisets of future values* that represent the task's eventual result at a specific location. However, Voltron is imperative in nature, limiting the compositionality of team-level behaviours.

Meld [4] is a logic-based language for programming modular ensembles, for systems where communication is limited to immediate neighbours. It leverages *facts with side-effects* to handle actuation, *production rules* to generate new facts from existing facts, and *aggregate rules* to combine multiple facts into one fact by folding (e.g., maximisation or summation). The runtime deals with communication of facts and removal of invalidated facts. The declarativity and logical foundation make Meld an interesting macroprogramming system; however, it is not clear how it can scale with the complexity of general swarm behaviour. Indeed, it is mainly adopted for shape formation and self-reconfiguring ensembles.

Finally, we mention another category of related works, which are *task orchestration languages* for swarms (e.g., TeCoLa [29], Dolphin [30], Maple-Swarm [28], PARoS [22], Resh [15], and [51]): they adopt quite a different approach that leverages centralised entities to control the activity of the swarm members based on the provided task descriptions.

7 Conclusion and Future Work

We presented MacroSwarm, a framework for top-down swarm programming that provides composable blocks capturing common decentralised swarm behaviours. It builds on aggregate computing, a formally-grounded field-based coordination paradigm, and is implemented on top of the ScaFi toolkit/DSL. We show through examples and a simulated case study that the approach is compositional, practical, and expressive.

As future work, we plan to make the API more comprehensive, by covering all the main patterns from notable taxonomies of swarm behaviour [13]. Additionally, it would be interesting to investigate approaches for synthesising compositions of MacroSwarm blocks, e.g., by following the reinforcement learning-based approach of [3]. Last but not least, we would like to deploy and test the framework on real testbeds.

Acknowledgements. This work was supported by the Italian PRIN project "CommonWears" (2020HCWWLP) and the EU/MUR FSE PON-R&I 2014-2020.

Data Availability Statement. The artifact is available in the Zenodo repository: doi:10.5281/zenodo.7829208

References

1. Abd Alrahman, Y., De Nicola, R., Loreti, M.: Programming interactions in collective adaptive systems by relying on attribute-based communication. Sci. Comput. Program. **192** (2020)

2. Aguzzi, G., Casadei, R., Maltoni, N., Pianini, D., Viroli, M.: SCAFI-WEB: a web-based application for field-based coordination programming. In: Damiani, F., Dardha, O. (eds.) COORDINATION 2021. LNCS, vol. 12717, pp. 285–299. Springer, Cham (2021). https://doi.org/10.1007/978-3-030-78142-2_18

3. Aguzzi, G., Casadei, R., Viroli, M.: Towards reinforcement learning-based aggregate computing. In: ter Beek, M.H., Sirjani, M. (eds.) DisCoTec 2022. LNCS, vol. 13271, pp. 72–91. Springer, Cham (2022). https://doi.org/10.1007/978-3-031-08143-9_5

4. Ashley-Rollman, M.P., Goldstein, S.C., Lee, P., Mowry, T.C., Pillai, P.: Meld: a declarative approach to programming ensembles. In: 2007 IEEE/RSJ International Conference on Intelligent Robots and Systems, pp. 2794–2800. IEEE (2007). https://doi.org/10.1109/IROS.2007.4399480

5. Audrito, G., Beal, J., Damiani, F., Viroli, M.: Space-time universality of field calculus. In: Serugendo, G.D.M., Loreti, M. (eds.) DisCoTec 2018. LNCS, vol. 10852, pp. 1–20. Springer, Cham (2018). https://doi.org/10.1007/978-3-319-92408-3_1

6. Audrito, G., Casadei, R., Damiani, F., Pianini, D., Viroli, M.: Optimal resilient distributed data collection in mobile edge environments. Comput. Electr. Eng. **96**(Part), 107580 (2021). https://doi.org/10.1016/j.compeleceng.2021.107580

7. Audrito, G., Casadei, R., Damiani, F., Salvaneschi, G., Viroli, M.: Functional programming for distributed systems with XC. In: Ali, K., Vitek, J. (eds.) 36th European Conference on Object-Oriented Programming, ECOOP 2022, 6–10 June 2022, Berlin, Germany. LIPIcs, vol. 222, pp. 20:1–20:28. Schloss Dagstuhl - Leibniz-Zentrum für Informatik (2022). https://doi.org/10.4230/LIPIcs.ECOOP.2022.20

8. Audrito, G., Casadei, R., Damiani, F., Viroli, M.: Computation against a neighbour: addressing large-scale distribution and adaptivity with functional programming and scala. Logical Methods Comput. Sci. **19**(1) (2023). https://lmcs.episciences.org/10826

9. Audrito, G., Viroli, M., Damiani, F., Pianini, D., Beal, J.: A higher-order calculus of computational fields. ACM Trans. Comput. Logic **20**(1), 5:1–5:55 (2019). http://doi.acm.org/10.1145/3285956

10. Beal, J., Dulman, S., Usbeck, K., Viroli, M., Correll, N.: Organizing the aggregate: languages for spatial computing. In: Formal and Practical Aspects of Domain-Specific Languages: Recent Developments, Chap. 16, pp. 436–501. IGI Global (2013). https://doi.org/10.4018/978-1-4666-2092-6.ch016

11. Bilaloglu, C., Sahin, M., Arvin, F., Sahin, E., Turgut, A.E.: A novel time-of-flight range and bearing sensor system for micro air vehicle swarms. In: Dorigo, M., et al. (eds.) ANTS 2022. LNCS, vol. 13491, pp. 248–256. Springer, Cham (2022). https://doi.org/10.1007/978-3-031-20176-9_20

12. Bonabeau, E., Dorigo, M., Théraulaz, G.: Swarm intelligence: from natural to artificial systems. Santa Fe Institute Studies in the Sciences of Complexity, Oxford University Press (1999)

13. Brambilla, M., Ferrante, E., Birattari, M., Dorigo, M.: Swarm robotics: a review from the swarm engineering perspective. Swarm Intell. **7**(1), 1–41 (2013). https://doi.org/10.1007/s11721-012-0075-2

14. Busoniu, L., Babuska, R., Schutter, B.D.: A comprehensive survey of multiagent reinforcement learning. IEEE Trans. Syst. Man Cybern. Part C **38**(2), 156–172 (2008). https://doi.org/10.1109/TSMCC.2007.913919
15. Carroll, M., Namjoshi, K.S., Segall, I.: The Resh programming language for multi-robot orchestration. In: IEEE International Conference on Robotics and Automation, ICRA 2021, Xi'an, China, 30 May–5 June 2021, pp. 4026–4032. IEEE (2021). https://doi.org/10.1109/ICRA48506.2021.9561133
16. Casadei, R.: Macroprogramming: concepts, state of the art, and opportunities of macroscopic behaviour modelling. ACM Comput. Surv. (2023). https://doi.org/10.1145/3579353
17. Casadei, R., Pianini, D., Placuzzi, A., Viroli, M., Weyns, D.: Pulverization in cyber-physical systems: Engineering the self-organizing logic separated from deployment. Future Internet **12**(11), 203 (2020). https://doi.org/10.3390/fi12110203
18. Casadei, R., Viroli, M., Aguzzi, G., Pianini, D.: ScaFi: a Scala DSL and toolkit for aggregate programming. SoftwareX **20**, 101248 (2022). https://doi.org/10.1016/j.softx.2022.101248
19. Casadei, R., Viroli, M., Audrito, G., Pianini, D., Damiani, F.: Engineering collective intelligence at the edge with aggregate processes. Eng. Appl. Artif. Intell. **97**, 104081 (2021). https://doi.org/10.1016/j.engappai.2020.104081
20. Cucker, F., Smale, S.: Emergent behavior in flocks. IEEE Trans. Autom. Control **52**(5), 852–862 (2007). https://doi.org/10.1109/TAC.2007.895842
21. De Nicola, R., Loreti, M., Pugliese, R., Tiezzi, F.: A formal approach to autonomic systems programming: The SCEL language. ACM Trans. Auton. Adapt. Syst. **9**(2), 7:1–7:29 (2014)
22. Dedousis, D., Kalogeraki, V.: A framework for programming a swarm of UAVs. In: 11th PErvasive Technologies Related to Assistive Environments Conference (PETRA'18), Proceedings, pp. 5–12. ACM (2018). https://doi.org/10.1145/3197768.3197772
23. Dorigo, M., Theraulaz, G., Trianni, V.: Reflections on the future of swarm robotics. Sci. Robot. **5**(49), 4385 (2020). https://doi.org/10.1126/scirobotics.abe4385
24. Galinina, O., Mikhaylov, K., Huang, K., Andreev, S., Koucheryavy, Y.: Wirelessly powered urban crowd sensing over wearables: trading energy for data. IEEE Wirel. Commun. **25**(2), 140–149 (2018). https://doi.org/10.1109/MWC.2018.1600468
25. Gershenson, C., Trianni, V., Werfel, J., Sayama, H.: Self-organization and artificial life. Artif. Life **26**(3), 391–408 (2020). https://doi.org/10.1162/artl_a_00324
26. Koenig, N.P., Howard, A.: Design and use paradigms for gazebo, an open-source multi-robot simulator. In: 2004 IEEE/RSJ International Conference on Intelligent Robots and Systems, Sendai, Japan, 28 September–2 October 2004, pp. 2149–2154. IEEE (2004). https://doi.org/10.1109/IROS.2004.1389727
27. Koren, Y., Borenstein, J.: Potential field methods and their inherent limitations for mobile robot navigation. In: Proceedings of the 1991 IEEE International Conference on Robotics and Automation, Sacramento, CA, USA, 9–11 April 1991, pp. 1398–1404. IEEE Computer Society (1991). https://doi.org/10.1109/ROBOT.1991.131810
28. Kosak, O., Huhn, L., Bohn, F., Wanninger, C., Hoffmann, A., Reif, W.: Maple-swarm: programming collective behavior for ensembles by extending HTN-planning. In: Margaria, T., Steffen, B. (eds.) ISoLA 2020, Part II. LNCS, vol. 12477, pp. 507–524. Springer, Cham (2020). https://doi.org/10.1007/978-3-030-61470-6_30

29. Koutsoubelias, M., Lalis, S.: Tecola: a programming framework for dynamic and heterogeneous robotic teams. In: Proceedings of the 13th International Conference on Mobile and Ubiquitous Systems: Computing, Networking and Services (MobiQuitous 2016), pp. 115–124. ACM (2016). https://doi.org/10.1145/2994374.2994397

30. Lima, K., Marques, E.R.B., Pinto, J., Sousa, J.B.: Dolphin: a task orchestration language for autonomous vehicle networks. In: 2018 IEEE/RSJ International Conference on Intelligent Robots and Systems, IROS 2018, Madrid, Spain, 1–5 October 2018, pp. 603–610. IEEE (2018). https://doi.org/10.1109/IROS.2018.8594059

31. Lluch-Lafuente, A., Loreti, M., Montanari, U.: Asynchronous distributed execution of fixpoint-based computational fields. Log. Methods Comput. Sci. **13**(1) (2017)

32. Luckcuck, M., Farrell, M., Dennis, L.A., Dixon, C., Fisher, M.: Formal specification and verification of autonomous robotic systems: a survey. ACM Comput. Surv. **52**(5), 100:1–100:41 (2019). https://doi.org/10.1145/3342355

33. Mamei, M., Zambonelli, F.: Programming pervasive and mobile computing applications with the TOTA middleware. In: Pervasive Computing and Communications, pp. 263–273. IEEE (2004)

34. Mottola, L., Moretta, M., Whitehouse, K., Ghezzi, C.: Team-level programming of drone sensor networks. In: Proceedings of the 12th ACM Conference on Embedded Network Sensor Systems (SenSys'14), pp. 177–190. ACM (2014). https://doi.org/10.1145/2668332.2668353

35. Newton, R., Welsh, M.: Region streams: functional macroprogramming for sensor networks. In: Workshop on Data Management for Sensor Networks, pp. 78–87 (2004)

36. De Nicola, R., Jähnichen, S., Wirsing, M.: Rigorous engineering of collective adaptive systems: special section. Int. J. Softw. Tools Technol. Transfer **22**(4), 389–397 (2020). https://doi.org/10.1007/s10009-020-00565-0

37. Peng, Y., Qu, D., Zhong, Y., Xie, S., Luo, J., Gu, J.: The obstacle detection and obstacle avoidance algorithm based on 2-d lidar. In: IEEE International Conference on Information and Automation, ICIA 2015, Lijiang, China, 8–10 August 2015, pp. 1648–1653. IEEE (2015). https://doi.org/10.1109/ICInfA.2015.7279550

38. Pianini, D., Casadei, R., Viroli, M.: Self-stabilising priority-based multi-leader election and network partitioning. In: Casadei, R., et al. (eds.) IEEE International Conference on Autonomic Computing and Self-Organizing Systems, ACSOS 2022, Virtual, CA, USA, 19–23 September 2022, pp. 81–90. IEEE (2022). https://doi.org/10.1109/ACSOS55765.2022.00026

39. Pianini, D., Casadei, R., Viroli, M., Mariani, S., Zambonelli, F.: Time-fluid field-based coordination through programmable distributed schedulers. Log. Methods Comput. Sci. **17**(4) (2021). https://doi.org/10.46298/lmcs-17(4:13)2021

40. Pianini, D., Montagna, S., Viroli, M.: Chemical-oriented simulation of computational systems with ALCHEMIST. J. Simulation **7**(3), 202–215 (2013). https://doi.org/10.1057/jos.2012.27

41. Pinciroli, C., Beltrame, G.: Buzz: an extensible programming language for heterogeneous swarm robotics. In: 2016 IEEE/RSJ International Conference on Intelligent Robots and Systems, IROS 2016, Daejeon, South Korea, 9–14 October 2016, pp. 3794–3800. IEEE (2016). https://doi.org/10.1109/IROS.2016.7759558

42. Reynolds, C.W.: Flocks, herds and schools: a distributed behavioral model. In: Stone, M.C. (ed.) Proceedings of the 14th Annual Conference on Computer Graphics and Interactive Techniques, SIGGRAPH 1987, Anaheim, California, USA, 27–31 July 1987, pp. 25–34. ACM (1987), https://doi.org/10.1145/37401.37406

43. Sambu, P., Won, M.: An experimental study on direction finding of bluetooth 5.1: Indoor vs outdoor. In: IEEE Wireless Communications and Networking Conference, WCNC 2022, Austin, TX, USA, 10–13 April 2022, pp. 1934–1939. IEEE (2022). https://doi.org/10.1109/WCNC51071.2022.9771930

44. Schranz, M., Umlauft, M., Sende, M., Elmenreich, W.: Swarm robotic behaviors and current applications. Front. Robot. AI **7**, 36 (2020). https://doi.org/10.3389/frobt.2020.00036

45. Tahir, A., Böling, J., Haghbayan, M.H., Toivonen, H.T., Plosila, J.: Swarms of unmanned aerial vehicles - a survey. J. Ind. Inf. Integr. **16**, 100106 (2019). https://doi.org/10.1016/j.jii.2019.100106

46. Trianni, V.: Evolutionary Swarm Robotics - Evolving Self-Organising Behaviours in Groups of Autonomous Robots. SCI, vol. 108. Springer, Cham (2008). https://doi.org/10.1007/978-3-540-77612-3

47. Varenne, F., Chaigneau, P., Petitot, J., Doursat, R.: Programming the emergence in morphogenetically architected complex systems. Acta. Biotheor. **63**(3), 295–308 (2015). https://doi.org/10.1007/s10441-015-9262-z

48. Vicsek, T., Czirók, A., Ben-Jacob, E., Cohen, I., Shochet, O.: Novel type of phase transition in a system of self-driven particles. Phys. Rev. Lett. **75**, 1226–1229 (1995). https://link.aps.org/doi/10.1103/PhysRevLett.75.1226

49. Viroli, M., Audrito, G., Beal, J., Damiani, F., Pianini, D.: Engineering resilient collective adaptive systems by self-stabilisation. ACM Trans. Model. Comput. Simul. **28**(2), 16:1–16:28 (2018). https://doi.org/10.1145/3177774

50. Viroli, M., Beal, J., Damiani, F., Audrito, G., Casadei, R., Pianini, D.: From distributed coordination to field calculus and aggregate computing. J. Log. Algebraic Methods Program. **109** (2019)

51. Yi, W., et al.: An actor-based programming framework for swarm robotic systems. In: IEEE/RSJ International Conference on Intelligent Robots and Systems, IROS 2020, Las Vegas, NV, USA, 24 October 2020–24 January 2021, pp. 8012–8019. IEEE (2020). https://doi.org/10.1109/IROS45743.2020.9341198

ScaRLib: A Framework for Cooperative Many Agent Deep Reinforcement Learning in Scala

Davide Domini⬥, Filippo Cavallari⬥, Gianluca Aguzzi$^{(\boxtimes)}$⬥,
and Mirko Viroli⬥

Alma Mater Studiorum – Università di Bologna, Cesena, Italy
filippo.cavallari2@studio.unibo.it,
{davide.domini2,gianluca.aguzzi,mirko.viroli}@unibo.it

Abstract. Multi Agent Reinforcement Learning (MARL) is an emerging field in machine learning where multiple agents learn, simultaneously and in a shared environment, how to optimise a global or local reward signal. MARL has gained significant interest in recent years due to its successful applications in various domains, such as robotics, IoT, and traffic control. Cooperative Many Agent Reinforcement Learning (CMARL) is a relevant subclass of MARL, where thousands of agents work together to achieve a common coordination goal.

In this paper, we introduce ScaRLib, a Scala framework relying on state-of-the-art deep learning libraries to support the development of CMARL systems. The framework supports the specification of centralised training and decentralised execution, and it is designed to be easily extensible, allowing to add new algorithms, new types of environments, and new coordination toolchains.

This paper describes the main structure and features of ScaRLib and includes basic demonstrations that showcase binding with one such toolchain: ScaFi programming framework and Alchemist simulator can be exploited to enable learning of field-based coordination policies for large-scale systems.

Keywords: Many Agent Reinforcement Learning · Deep Learning · Aggregate Computing

1 Introduction

Recent advances in machine learning have led to the development of Multi Agent Reinforcement Learning (MARL) [9], in which multiple agents learn simultaneously within a shared environment to optimise either a global or local reward signal. This area of research has gained significant interest in recent years due to its successful applications in various domains, such as robotics [21],

---

Supported by Department of Computer Science and Engineering @ Alma Mater Studiorum - University of Bologna.

S.-S. Jongmans and A. Lopes (Eds.): COORDINATION 2023, LNCS 13908, pp. 52–70, 2023.
https://doi.org/10.1007/978-3-031-35361-1_3

IoT [19], and traffic control [13]. MARL provides a powerful approach to tackling complex problems that cannot be easily solved by single-agent reinforcement learning. Most specifically, Cooperative Many Agent Reinforcement Learning (CMARL) [16,33] is a relevant subclass of MARL, where thousands of agents work together to achieve a common coordination goal. CMARL finds several applications in contexts like swarm robotics [17], wireless sensor networks, and smart grid management. CMARL offers significant opportunities in the design of large-scale systems requiring agents to coordinate and collaborate effectively, even in environments with partial observability and intrinsic unpredictability. Therefore, there is a need for effective frameworks (and tools) that can foster CMARL adoption.

However, although several frameworks exist both for describing and solving CMARL problems (Ray [24]) and for using and defining multi-agent environments (PettingZoo [31]) they generally lack the following aspects: *(i)* setting up complex environments (and hence simulation scenarios) is particularly difficult, and *(ii)* they are typically tailored for handling a limited number of agents, and for non-collaborative tasks. To start addressing these problems, in this work we present ScaRLib, a framework for the design of effective CMARL systems. ScaRLib offers several key features, including support for centralised training and decentralised execution, easy extensibility, and a Domain Specific Language (DSL) for expressing complex cooperative scenarios. Additionally, ScaRLib integrates with the Alchemist [25] simulator for large-scale pervasive computing systems and provides the ability to express field-based coordination problems through its integration with ScaFi [11]. The latter, in particular, provides a high-level language for distributed computing that provides a declarative and compositional ways of expressing complex coordination tasks.

The remainder of this paper is organised as follows: Sect. 2 provides key background in the context of learning and the Alchemist/Scafi toolchain, Sect. 3 presents the ScaRLib tool, Sect. 4 presents demos of ScaRLib, Sect. 5 discuss some state-of-the-art solutions, and finally Sect. 6 concludes and presents future works.

2   Background

2.1   Reinforcement Learning

Reinforcement Learning (RL) is a subfield of machine learning, other than supervised and unsupervised learning, that focuses on solving sequential decision problems: giving an *agent* that can interact with an *environment*, the RL goal is to *learn* a policy (i.e., the action to take in a certain *state* of the environment) that maximises a *reward* signal. Most specifically, the dynamics of these agent-environment interactions are modelled in discrete steps (i.e., $t = 0, 1, 2, \dots$). At each step, the agent receives an *observation* $S_t \in \mathcal{S}$ ($\mathcal{S}$ is the set of all the possible states) from the environment and takes an action $A_t \in \mathcal{A}(S_t)$ ($\mathcal{A}(S_t)$ is the action space from the state S_t). One time step later, the agent receives a reward $R_{t+1} \in \mathbb{R}$ and the new state S_{t+1}. The agent decisions are based on

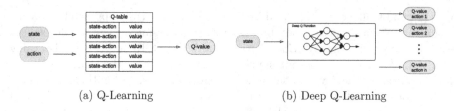

(a) Q-Learning   (b) Deep Q-Learning

Fig. 1. Q-Learning and Deep Q-Learning visual comparison

a *probabilistic policy* $\pi_t(a|s)$, which indicates the probability of choosing action *a* from the state *s* at time *t*. In order for RL to be effective, two conditions are fundamental: *(i)* all is meant by *goals/purposes/success* can be well thought of as the maximization of the expected value of the cumulative sum of the reward (i.e., a scalar signal) – called *the reward hypothesys*; and *(ii)* the environment state should summarise the past compactly so that future states only depend on the current state (and not on past states) – *the markov property*.

In literature, several algorithms can be used to solve RL problems. In this work, we will focus on two of them: the *Q-Learning* [32] algorithm and the *Deep Q-Learning* [22] algorithm. The core part of both of these algorithms is the *Q-function*, which maps each state-action pair to a value that represents the expected future reward of taking that action in that state. Using a modified Bellman equation update, the Q-function is iteratively updated based on the rewards received by the agent as it takes actions in the environment. From the Q-function, the agent can follow both an *exploration* policy during the training phase and a *behavioural* policy once the learning phase is complete. The *behavioural* policy is a greedy policy, in which the agent chooses the action with the highest Q-value in a given state. This policy ensures that the agent always chooses the best action to maximise its expected future reward. On the other hand, during the exploration phase, the agent uses an ϵ-greedy policy, where it chooses a random action with probability ϵ and the best action (according to the Q-table) with probability 1-ϵ. This allows the agent to explore the environment and learn from new experiences.

The main difference between the two algorithms is that in Q-Learning the Q-table is represented as a table, while in Deep Q-Learning it is approximated by a neural network. Therefore, the first approach works well for simple problems, but it struggles to scale to complex problems due to the explosion of the state space; the second approach, on the other hand, addresses large-scales but requires much data to train the neural network (Fig. 1).

2.2   Multi Agent Reinforcement Learning

MARL is an extension of RL where multiple agents interact with one another and with the environment. Usually, MARL is modelled as a *Markov Game* (or Stochastic Game $\mathcal{S}$) [20] in which we have:

- A tuple $\mathcal{S} = < N, S, \{A^i\}, P, \{R^i\} >$ with $i \in 1 \ldots N$
- The number of agents $N > 1$
- The action space of the i-th agent A^i. The global action space is defined as $\mathbb{A} = A^1 \times A^2 \times \cdots \times A^N$
- A function describing the transition dynamics $P : S \times \mathbb{A} \rightarrow \mathcal{P}(S)$
- The reward function $R^i : S \times \mathbb{A} \times S \rightarrow \mathbb{R}$ for each agent i

Based on the reward function used by the agents, MARL can be divided into two categories: i) *cooperative*, where all the agents trying to maximise the same reward function (e.g., a group of robots trying to clean a room); ii) *competitive*, where, potentially, each agent has its own reward function that is conflictual with the other (e.g., a rock-paper-scissor game). Cooperative MARL can be further divided into two additional categories (based on the policy), namely: i) *homogeneous*, where all the agents have the same capabilities, i.e., they use the same policy ii) *heterogeneous*, where each agent may have its own policy

In this work, we focus on a subset of MARL, namely: *Many Agent Reinforcement Learning* [33]. The only difference between the two approaches is in the number of agents involved. Typically, in Many Agent Reinforcement Learning the number of agents may range from a hundred to one or two thousand whereas, in Multi Agent Reinforcement Learning, there are only a few tens [6,28]. Moreover, we focus on cooperative homogeneous and heterogeneous learning.

2.3 Alchemist

Alchemist[1] [25] is meta-simulator mainly designed for simulating complex distributed systems in a rich variety of scenarios like swarm robotics [12], large-scale sensor networks [2], crowd simulation [7], path planning, and even morphogenesis of multi-cellular systems. The simulator is *meta* in nature, as it is based on general abstractions that can be mapped to specific use cases (i.e., *incarnations*). Inspired by biochemistry, the meta-model consists of a set of *nodes* that exist in an *environment* and are linked together by *relationship* rules. Each node contains a sequence of *molecules* and *reactions*. A *molecule* represents a variable, which acts as a container for data. *Reactions* instead are events that occur based on a set of *conditions*, and are fired according to a time distribution, producing an effect that is described as an action. This abstraction allows the simulator to be flexible and adaptable to a variety of use cases and node numbers (it could support thousands of nodes), while maintaining a consistent underlying structure.

The Alchemist simulator features four incarnations: biochemistry, Sapere, Protelis, and ScaFi, each with a different way of modelling molecules and actions. Moreover, the simulator offers an effortless method for loading simulations. The process requires a YAML file that includes essential parameters, such as the incarnation type, neighbour connection model, and node deployment. In Fig. 2, we have provided an example YAML file that creates a simulation using the ScaFi

---

[1] http://alchemistsimulator.github.io/.

incarnation (first row). It also defines the neighbourhood relationship based on fixed distances (0.5 in this case), placing nodes in a fixed grid of size 10×10 starting at -(5,5) and ending at (5,5), with a node-to-node distance of 0.25. Finally, it loads the ScaFi program called "program", which is evaluated at each node with a frequency 1 Hz.

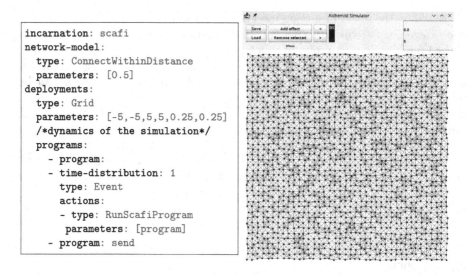

Fig. 2. An Alchemist simulation example. The simulation result on the right is obtained by running the simulation described on the left.

2.4   ScaFi

ScaFi (Scala Fields[2]) [11] is a scala framework for developing large-scale distributed applications and simulating systems of networked agents. ScaFi is designed for Aggregate Programming [7], which is a top-down global-to-local macro-programming [10] paradigm for distributed systems where the focus is on the collective behaviour of the system rather than on the individual agents that make up the system. One of the unique features of aggregate computing is its support for self-organising systems – that are systems that can adapt to changes in the environment and maintain their functionality without requiring centralised control.

In ScaFi, agents are represented as nodes in a logical network, and the interactions between agents are modelled as the exchange of messages over edges in the graph. ScaFi provides a set of primitives for expressing distributed algorithms, which can all be interpreted as field-based coordination policies, namely,

---

[2] https://scafi.github.io/.

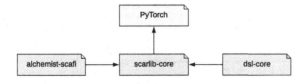

Fig. 3. ScaRLib main modules

distributed computations of maps from nodes to values (i.e. *fields*). These primitives are designed to be composable and reusable, allowing programmers to build complex distributed algorithms from simple building blocks.

3   ScaRLib

ScaRLib[3,4] is a research Scala framework designed to support the development of CMARL systems by JVM-based high-level specification, and with learning performed under the hood by PyTorch[5]. This project aims to provide a tool that allows easy and powerful system specification. To meet this purpose we have designed many abstractions, that model high-level aspects of the CMARL domain, without caring about low-level implementation details. Basically, ScaRLib is composed of three main modules (Fig. 3), namely: i) `scarlib-core` that implements the main abstractions over the CMARL domain, ii) `dsl-core` that provides a high-level language to specify the system, and iii) `alchemist-scafi` that provides bindings between ScaRLib and the two tools Alchemist and ScaFi. It is important to note that ScaRLib is not limited to the Alchemist-Scafi combination, since it is possible to implement other bindings to other tools (e.g., by replacing Alchemist with some other simulator, for example, FLAME GPU [27]).

3.1   Core Abstraction

The module `scarlib-core` implements the core functionalities and abstractions of the framework, such as the definition of the main data structures and the implementation of the main algorithms. All the abstractions (Fig. 4) are built around a bunch of concepts. The key element is the `System`, which is a collection of agents that interact within a shared environment and that are trained to optimise a reward signal expressed by a reward function. The tool comes with two types of systems already implemented that are very common in literature [14], i.e., centralised training and decentralised execution (`CTDESystem`) and decentralised training and execution (`DTDESystem`). Furthermore, an implementation of the DQN algorithm [23] is provided and used to train agents. The end-user

---

[3] Tool available on GitHub at https://github.com/ScaRLib-group/ScaRLib.

[4] Demo video at: https://github.com/ScaRLib-group/ScaRLib-demo-video.

[5] https://pytorch.org/.

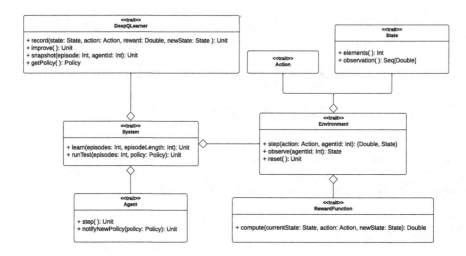

Fig. 4. ScaRLib core architecture

who wants to run a learning process only has to implement four elements to define his own system with the desired collective goal, which are: i) the environment, ii) the agent state space, iii) the action space and, iv) the reward function. Only by using this module, it is possible to run a simple learning process in a simulated environment based on our platform.

To better understand the dynamics of the system it is useful to explain some of the internals. Both systems utilise a training process that consists of multiple *epochs*, with each epoch comprising a set of *episodes*. During each episode, the agents receive the current state as input and execute an action based on that state. This collective action causes the environment to move to the next state, advancing the simulation to the next episode. At the end of an epoch, the environment is reset and the agents are trained using the collected experience. Most specifically, if the chosen system is a CTDESystem (Fig. 5a) the agents are trained in a centralised way, for that reason, there is a single central dataset, where the global experience of all the agents is stored, and a single central learner that is responsible for the training process and for the improvement of the policy neural network. The system is also responsible for the execution of all the agents and the notification of the updated policy. In this way, it is possible to easily extend the system in order to modify the execution flow, e.g., if a concurrent and distributed execution is needed. The DTDESystem (Fig. 5b) works similarly, the only difference is that every agent has its own dataset and learner.

Regarding the training process, since the tool aims to support neural-network-based RL algorithms (like DQN), we chose to use the current de facto standard framework for building neural networks, which is PyTorch—alternatives include DL4J[6], which could be subject of future investigation.

---

[6] https://deeplearning4j.konduit.ai/.

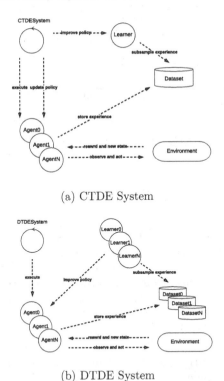

(a) CTDE System

(b) DTDE System

Fig. 5. Examples of developed System dynamics. On the left, there is the centralised system, where a learner with a global view of the system updates the policy shared with all agents. On the right, there is a decentralised system, where each agent has a local policy and a local policy.

One way to integrate this library into a JVM environment could be to rely on its native core (LibTorch) using JNI – as was done in `scala_torch`[7] project. In ScaRLib, we chose a convenient approach that allowed us not only to access PyTorch but also all the libraries connected to it (e.g., torch geometric [15], etc.), which is to use ScalaPy [18] to interact directly with the Python API of these libraries. This integration generally involves: i) setting up a Python environment in which the libraries of interest are instantiated, and ii) creating a Scala API that isolates what is necessary to access the Python ecosystem. In this case, we have isolated everything in DQN, which is, therefore, the entry point for accessing Torch.

---

[7] https://github.com/microsoft/scala_torch.

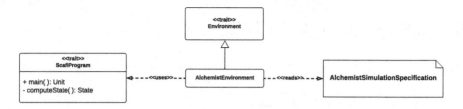

Fig. 6. ScaRLib `alchemist-scafi` architecture. A `ScafiProgram` should be passed to the `AlchemistEnvironment` in order to start the learning process.

3.2 ScaFi-Alchemist Integration:

In addition to the core, we have implemented another module called `alchemist-scafi` (Fig. 6) in which there is integration with the two tools: Alchemist [25] and ScaFi [11]. Such integration enables the possibility to run the learning process in an aggregate computing context. This is a key part of this contribution. In fact, although Alchemist has been used for CMARL with ScaFi in the past [3,5], ad-hoc solutions were always created that were difficult to *reuse, rigid, untested,* and had *interoperability issues* between Alchemist and the chosen native libraries. With this integration, we want to provide a usable system once and for all, to bring the Many-agent RL community closer to the use of this simulator and this paradigm, which has proven flexible in describing the most diverse environments – from robotic swarms [12] to data centres.

The specification of a learning system does not change, only two new elements are added: the specification of the Alchemist simulation and the implementation of the ScaFi-based logic. In particular, the Alchemist simulation will be defined as shown in Fig. 2, by passing a ScaFi class as a program, which contains aggregate programming code. In order to advance the training process, a molecule with the current action to be taken (a subtype of `Action` class) will be present in the ScaFi program. This will be injected by a learner that contains the RL policy. Moreover, the aggregate program will evaluate the environment state (which must be a subtype of `State`) using `computeState` and insert it into the `state` molecule, that will be used by the learner to update the policy.

3.3 DSL for Learning Configurations

The latest module developed is an internal DSL that allows for agile and flexible creation of CMARL training systems. We made this choice to bridge the gap between the MARL system designer's idea and the actual training system. Additionally, by using a system like Scala, creating a typed DSL allows for capturing errors during compilation, rather than waiting for the actual system runs to intercept simple configuration errors.

The exposed DSL is a simple facade to the abstractions shown in the `scarlib-core` module. Therefore, if a developer wants to start their simulation they must first define a reward function that indicates how good is the current state of a certain agent is compared to the current environmental condition.

```
class MyRewardFunction extends CollectiveRewardFunction:
    override def computeReward(
        state: State, action: Action, nextState: State
    ): Double = ...
```

Consequently, they must decide which actions are supported by the agents living in the chosen system. Since we are talking about CMARL systems, we suppose that each agent has the same action space. Thus, it is possible to define a set of actions as a product type:

```
sealed trait MyAction extends Action
object MyAction:
    case object A extends MyAction
    case object B extends MyAction
    case object C extends MyAction
    def all: Seq[MyAction] = Seq(A, B, C)
```

Final refinements required include: i) choosing the class of the Alchemist environment to instantiate, ii) defining the number of agents living in the chosen environment, and iii) defining the size of the buffer in which the memory will be stored, expressed as follows:

```
val system = learningSystem {
    rewardFunction { new MyRewardFunction() }
    actions { MyAction.all}
    dataset { ReplayBuffer[State, Action](10000) }
    agents { 50 } // select the number of agent
    environment {
        // select a specific environment
        "it.unibo.scarlib.experiments.myEnvironment"
    }
}
```

3.4 Tool Usage

The tool is published on Maven Central and it is possible to include it in your project, for example, through a build system. In the case of Gradle, for instance, you will need to add the following instructions:

```
implementation("io.github.davidedomini:scarlib-core:1.5.0")
implementation("io.github.davidedomini:dsl-core:1.5.0")
```

At this point, it will be possible to create your own training system as shown in the DSL section. To start the training, you will then need to write:

```
learningSystem.train(episodes = 1000, episodeLength = 100)
```

Of course, the system can also be used to verify a certain policy that has been learned during a training process. To do this, first, you will need to load the neural network extracted during training:

```
val network = PolicyNN(path, inputSize = ..., hiddenSize = ...)
```

Then you can execute the test in the following way:

```
system.runTest(episodeLength = 100, network)
```

For further details on how to specify simulations and environments, please refer to the repository README, the presentation video and the developed simulation (following section).

4   Experiments

4.1   Scenario Description

To test ScarLib's functionality, we develop an experiment[8] involving a relatively large number of agents and non-trivial coordination tasks. We aim to create a flock of drones that moves to avoid collisions with each others, by learning a policy by which each agents decide how to move based on neighbors relative position. This is a well-known problem, and various models and algorithms exist which we draw upon [26,36]. In this case, we assumed that agents position themselves in an unlimited 2D environment with a fixed neighborhood (the closest five, in our experiments, though this is a simulation parameter) and have the ability to perform movement steps in the 8 directions of a square grid (horizontally, vertically, or diagonally). The environment state, as perceived by the single agent, is the relative distance to the closest neighbors. Particularly, it was expressed through ScaFi as:

```
val state = foldhoodPlus(Seq.empty)(_ ++ _)(Set(nbrVector))
```

where `nbrVector` is the vector representing the relative position of the neighbor. `foldhoodPlus` is a ScaFi function that allows to fold over the neighborhood and `++` is the concatenation operator for sequences.

The crucial point for this task is the definition of the reward function. In this simulation, we based it on *collision* and *cohesion* factors. We aim to learn a policy by which agents, initially spread in a very sparse way in the environment, move toward each other until reaching approximate δ distance without colliding, ultimately forming one or many close groups.

The collision factor comes into play when the distance is less than δ, and exponentially weighs the distance d relative to its closest neighbour:

$$\text{collision} = \begin{cases} 0 & \text{if } d > \delta \\ \exp\left(-\frac{d}{\delta}\right) & \text{otherwise} \end{cases} \quad (1)$$

---

[8] Repository available at https://github.com/ScaRLib-group/ScaRLib-flock-demo.

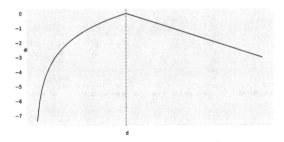

Fig. 7. Cohesion-Collision reward function: the red vertical line represents the target distance d. The portion of the graph to the right of the red line represents the influence of the cohesion term, while the left one represents the influence of the collision term. (Color figure online)

In this way, when the negative factor is taken into account: the system will tend to move nodes away from each other.

However, if only this factor were used, the system would be disorganised. This is where the cohesion factor comes in. Given the neighbor with the maximum distance D, it linearly adjusts the distance relative to the node being evaluated by function:

$$\text{cohesion} = \begin{cases} 0 & \text{if } d < \delta \\ -(D - \delta) & \text{otherwise} \end{cases} \tag{2}$$

The overall reward function is defined as the sum of these two factors (*cohesion* + *collision*) as shown in Fig. 7.

4.2   Results

To verify the functionality of the described simulation, we divided the evaluation into two parts. In the first part, we trained the system for a total of 1000 epochs, each consisting of 100 episodes (or steps). For each epoch, we randomly place 50 agents in a grid large 50×50 meters. We set the target distance δ at 2 m.

Given the flexibility of ScaRLib, we tested the training with both CDTE and DTDE processes to ensure that the system could produce policies capable of solving the described task in both cases. With the homogeneous policies found (i.e., the one extracted from the CTDE process), we verified that the system's behavior was consistent with what was learned by varying the initial seed in 16 simulations With the CDTE policy, since we considered the system homogeneous, we also verified the behavior as the number of nodes varied, expecting similar performance as the nodes increased.

The graphs shown in Fig. 8 demonstrate the multi-objective nature of the problem. In fact, cohesion and collision are two contrasting signals, and the system had to find a balance between these two values. The graphs show that DQN can generally optimise one signal at a time, with cohesion tending towards zero and collision increasing. Nonetheless, after 500 epochs in CTDE simulation,

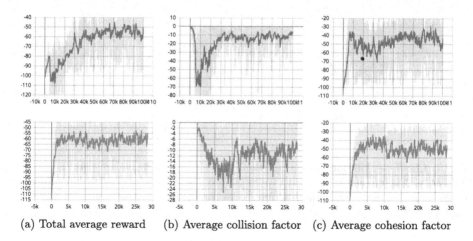

(a) Total average reward   (b) Average collision factor   (c) Average cohesion factor

Fig. 8. Cohesion and collision experiment results. The y-axis represents the reward value. The x-axis represents the total number of episodes. The first three graphs show the results of the CDTE learning process, while the last three show the results of the DTDE learning process.

we see that the system had already found a balance between these two factors. In the case of DTDE learning, we observe that convergence is achieved in fewer steps (50). This is because there is a greater number of policies and therefore greater overall complexity compared to a single homogeneous policy.

During the testing phase (Fig. 9 shows a series of snapshots of the learned policy), we observed that the system is capable of maintaining a distance of approximately δ, both in the CDTE and DTDE cases. Most specifically, we note that the homogeneous policy is generally a winning choice for homogeneous CMARL tasks. Increasing the number of agents (from 50 to 200), we can observe that collective performances are similar to those with few agents (Fig. 10).

5   Related Work

MARL has gained significant interest in the past decade, leading to the development of several frameworks for use in both research and industry communities. Here, we highlight current state-of-the-art solutions for MARL problems and compare them to the tools presented in this work.

Many Agent Simulators: Unlike supervised learning, where a large dataset is required to improve neural network performance, in RL, algorithms require a simulator to gain experience. One such comprehensive solution for MARL is PettingZoo [31], which provides both competitive and cooperative settings for simulations with multiple agents. Another option for many-agent scenarios is NeuralMMO [30], a GPU-optimised simulator for MMO-like games that is designed to handle large-scale simulations of thousands of agents. Vectorized

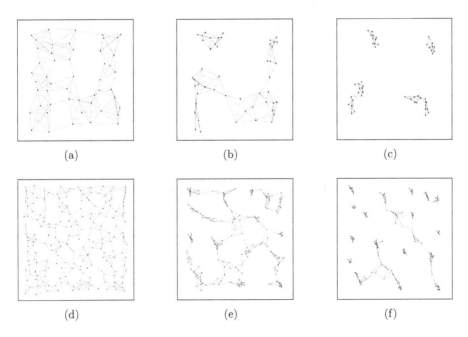

Fig. 9. Snapshots of the learned policy, the time flow is from left to right. In the first row, there are 50 agents, whereas in the second row, there are 200 agents. In the last step of the simulation, the agents converged to a distance of approximately δ.

Multi-agent Simulator [8] is another promising solution, as it is optimised for collective tasks through GPU computation, and it can be extended with additional environments. While ScarLib is not directly linked to any simulator, its main abstraction can be potentially linked to both JVM-based simulators and gym-based Python environments. Our choice of Alchemist was mainly due to its ability to express CMARL settings easily, but potentially it can be used with any of the above-described solutions.

Multi-Agent Deep RL Libraries: Since the importance of multi-agent settings several libraries have been developed in recent years. Ray [24] is one of the most comprehensive frameworks, originally designed for single-agent RL but now integrated with basic concepts for MARL solutions thanks to MALib. It offers various MARL algorithms, supports different gym-like environments, and is highly customizable through configuration files. PyMARL [29] is one of the first solutions in Python for MARL, though it is limited to specific algorithms (like VDN and QMIX), and it is not generalizable. ScaRLib is more similar to the first framework, even though it is primarily designed for cooperative applications. However, since it was developed specifically for CMARL, it includes some abstractions and configurations that are not present in Ray, such as the concept of a collective reward function and the configuration for CTDE. This reduces the time required to use ScarLib compared to Ray. Additionally, ScaRLib has a

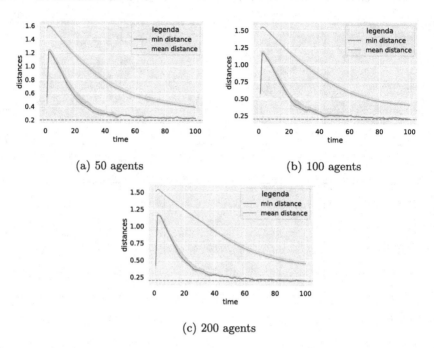

(a) 50 agents   (b) 100 agents

(c) 200 agents

Fig. 10. The performance of the learned policy. The y-axis represents the distance between the agents. The x-axis represents the time. The green line is equal to δ. In the charts, as the number of agents varies, the performance of the learned policy is similar. Moreover, the minimum (blue line) distance between the agents is always greater than δ. The average distance (orange line) stays close to $2 * \delta$ (after convergence). (Color figure online)

simple DSL that is easier to use than Ray's configuration system and is aided by the type system.

Finally, some innovative approaches aim to scale solutions to large populations of cooperative agents, such as mean-field RL. However, only a few implementations currently exist, and they are not considered to be general-purpose. ScarLib, on the other hand, offers a practical, simple implementation that can be leveraged in CMARL settings.

Overall, CMARL is a high-level framework that reduces the effort required for developers and practitioners to define and implement CMARL problems when compared to current state-of-the-art solutions.

Many-Agent Proof of Concept: The above RL library solutions are mainly created for multi-agent systems, so they generally do not scale well with large populations of agents. Novel approaches aim to scale the solution to potentially infinite populations of cooperative agents. In particular, mean-field RL [34] is probably one of the most interesting solutions in this context, as it abstracts over the entire agent population by considering only the average response of the neighborhood. Currently, however, only a few implementations exist[9] and they are not considered to be general-purpose. ScaRLib instead is practical and already provides a simple implementation that can be leveraged in CMARL settings.

6 Conclusion and Future Work

In this paper, we presented ScaRLib: a collaborative many-agent deep reinforcement learning framework that integrates the functionalities of ScaFi and Alchemist. The framework enables the definition of simulations of large-scale distributed scenarios and the creation of complex scenarios with ease through its exposed DSL. With ScaRlib, developers can effectively and efficiently simulate and experiment with different reinforcement learning algorithms, thereby providing a valuable tool for the advancement of coordination and multi-agent systems research. Looking forward, ScaRLib presents a promising solution for expressing collaborative multi-agent reinforcement learning applications – like hybrid aggregate computing solutions [1,3–5]. However, further development and integration is necessary for it to be more easily adopted by non-expert users. One area of improvement would be to integrate additional learning algorithms such as MAPPO [35] and mean field reinforcement learning [34], as DQN is only a baseline approach. Another aspect to be considered is the potential bottleneck that Alchemist may create during the learning phase since it is a JVM-based systems. To address this, we propose integrating a new environment, FLAME GPU [27], which has the ability to run entirely on GPU, thus providing faster learning and reducing the computational load. This integration would further enhance the capabilities of ScaRLib and make it a more practical and efficient tool for CMARL research.

Data Availability Statement

The artifact is available in the Zenodo repository:

doi:10.5281/zenodo.7831045

References

1. Aguzzi, G.: Research directions for aggregate computing with machine learning. In: 2021 IEEE International Conference on Autonomic Computing and Self-Organizing Systems Companion (ACSOS-C). IEEE (2021). https://doi.org/10.1109/acsos-c52956.2021.00078
2. Aguzzi, G., Casadei, R., Pianini, D., Viroli, M.: Dynamic decentralization domains for the internet of things. IEEE Internet Comput. **26**(6), 16–23 (2022). https://doi.org/10.1109/mic.2022.3216753

---

[9] https://github.com/mlii/mfrl.

3. Aguzzi, G., Casadei, R., Viroli, M.: Addressing collective computations efficiency: Towards a platform-level reinforcement learning approach. In: Casadei, R., et al. (eds.) IEEE International Conference on Autonomic Computing and Self-Organizing Systems, ACSOS 2022, Virtual, CA, USA, 19–23 September 2022, pp. 11–20. IEEE (2022). https://doi.org/10.1109/ACSOS55765.2022.00019
4. Aguzzi, G., Casadei, R., Viroli, M.: Machine learning for aggregate computing: a research roadmap. In: 2022 IEEE 42nd International Conference on Distributed Computing Systems Workshops (ICDCSW). IEEE (2022). https://doi.org/10.1109/icdcsw56584.2022.00032
5. Aguzzi, G., Casadei, R., Viroli, M.: Towards reinforcement learning-based aggregate computing. In: ter Beek, M.H., Sirjani, M. (eds) Coordination Models and Languages. COORDINATION 2022. IFIP Advances in Information and Communication Technology, vol. 13271, pp. 72–91. Springer, Cham (2022). https://doi.org/10.1007/978-3-031-08143-9_5
6. Baker, B., et al.: Emergent tool use from multi-agent autocurricula (2019). https://doi.org/10.48550/ARXIV.1909.07528. https://arxiv.org/abs/1909.07528
7. Beal, J., Pianini, D., Viroli, M.: Aggregate programming for the internet of things. Computer 48(9), 22–30 (2015). https://doi.org/10.1109/mc.2015.261
8. Bettini, M., Kortvelesy, R., Blumenkamp, J., Prorok, A.: VMAS: a vectorized multi-agent simulator for collective robot learning. The 16th International Symposium on Distributed Autonomous Robotic Systems (2022)
9. Busoniu, L., Babuska, R., Schutter, B.D.: A comprehensive survey of multiagent reinforcement learning. IEEE Trans. Syst. Man Cybern. Part C (Appl. Rev.) 38(2), 156–172 (2008). https://doi.org/10.1109/tsmcc.2007.913919
10. Casadei, R.: Macroprogramming: Concepts, state of the art, and opportunities of macroscopic behaviour modelling. ACM Computing Surveys (2023). https://doi.org/10.1145/3579353
11. Casadei, R., Viroli, M., Aguzzi, G., Pianini, D.: ScaFi: a scala DSL and toolkit for aggregate programming. SoftwareX 20, 101248 (2022). https://doi.org/10.1016/j.softx.2022.101248
12. Casadei, R., Viroli, M., Audrito, G., Pianini, D., Damiani, F.: Engineering collective intelligence at the edge with aggregate processes. Eng. Appl. Artif. Intell. 97, 104081 (2021). https://doi.org/10.1016/j.engappai.2020.104081
13. Chu, T., Wang, J., Codecà, L., Li, Z.: Multi-agent deep reinforcement learning for large-scale traffic signal control (2019). https://doi.org/10.48550/ARXIV.1903.04527. https://arxiv.org/abs/1903.04527
14. Du, W., Ding, S.: A survey on multi-agent deep reinforcement learning: from the perspective of challenges and applications. Artif. Intell. Rev. 54(5), 3215–3238 (2020). https://doi.org/10.1007/s10462-020-09938-y
15. Fey, M., Lenssen, J.E.: Fast graph representation learning with pyTorch geometric (2019)
16. He, K., Doshi, P., Banerjee, B.: Many agent reinforcement learning under partial observability (2021). https://doi.org/10.48550/ARXIV.2106.09825. https://arxiv.org/abs/2106.09825
17. Hüttenrauch, M., Adrian, S., Neumann, G., et al.: Deep reinforcement learning for swarm systems. J. Mach. Learn. Res. 20(54), 1–31 (2019)
18. Laddad, S., Sen, K.: ScalaPy: seamless python interoperability for cross-platform scala programs. In: Proceedings of the 11th ACM SIGPLAN International Symposium on Scala. ACM (2020). https://doi.org/10.1145/3426426.3428485

19. Lei, L., Tan, Y., Zheng, K., Liu, S., Zhang, K., Shen, X.: Deep reinforcement learning for autonomous internet of things: Model, applications and challenges. IEEE Commun. Surv. Tutorials **22**(3), 1722–1760 (2020). https://doi.org/10.1109/comst.2020.2988367

20. Littman, M.L.: Markov games as a framework for multi-agent reinforcement learning. In: Cohen, W.W., Hirsh, H. (eds.) Machine Learning Proceedings 1994, pp. 157–163. Morgan Kaufmann, San Francisco (CA) (1994). https://doi.org/10.1016/B978-1-55860-335-6.50027-1. https://www.sciencedirect.com/science/article/pii/B9781558603356500271

21. Long, P., Fanl, T., Liao, X., Liu, W., Zhang, H., Pan, J.: Towards optimally decentralized multi-robot collision avoidance via deep reinforcement learning. In: 2018 IEEE International Conference on Robotics and Automation (ICRA). IEEE (2018). https://doi.org/10.1109/icra.2018.8461113

22. Mnih, V., et al.: Playing Atari with deep reinforcement learning (2013). https://doi.org/10.48550/ARXIV.1312.5602. https://arxiv.org/abs/1312.5602

23. Mnih, V., et al.: Human-level control through deep reinforcement learning. Nature **518**(7540), 529–533 (2015). https://doi.org/10.1038/nature14236

24. Moritz, P., et al.: Ray: a distributed framework for emerging AI applications (2017). https://doi.org/10.48550/ARXIV.1712.05889. https://arxiv.org/abs/1712.05889

25. Pianini, D., Montagna, S., Viroli, M.: Chemical-oriented simulation of computational systems with ALCHEMIST. J. Simulation **7**(3), 202–215 (2013). https://doi.org/10.1057/jos.2012.27

26. Reynolds, C.W.: Flocks, herds and schools: a distributed behavioral model. In: Stone, M.C. (ed.) Proceedings of the 14th Annual Conference on Computer Graphics and Interactive Techniques, SIGGRAPH 1987, Anaheim, California, USA, 27–31 July 1987, pp. 25–34. ACM (1987). https://doi.org/10.1145/37401.37406

27. Richmond, P., Coakley, S., Romano, D.M.: A high performance agent based modelling framework on graphics card hardware with Cuda. In: Proceedings of The 8th International Conference on Autonomous Agents and Multiagent Systems - Volume 2, pp. 1125–1126. AAMAS 2009, International Foundation for Autonomous Agents and Multiagent Systems, Richland, SC (2009)

28. Samvelyan, M., et al.: The starcraft multi-agent challenge (2019). https://doi.org/10.48550/ARXIV.1902.04043. https://arxiv.org/abs/1902.04043

29. Samvelyan, M., et al.: The StarCraft Multi-Agent Challenge. CoRR abs/1902.04043 (2019)

30. Suarez, J., Du, Y., Isola, P., Mordatch, I.: Neural MMO: a massively multiagent game environment for training and evaluating intelligent agents (2019). https://doi.org/10.48550/ARXIV.1903.00784. https://arxiv.org/abs/1903.00784

31. Terry, J., et al.: PettingZoo: Gym for multi-agent reinforcement learning. In: Ranzato, M., Beygelzimer, A., Dauphin, Y., Liang, P., Vaughan, J.W. (eds.) Advances in Neural Information Processing Systems. vol. 34, pp. 15032–15043. Curran Associates, Inc. (2021). https://proceedings.neurips.cc/paper/2021/file/7ed2d3454c5eea71148b11d0c25104ff-Paper.pdf

32. Watkins, C.J.C.H., Dayan, P.: Q-learning. Mach. Learn. **8**(3-4), 279–292 (1992). https://doi.org/10.1007/bf00992698

33. Yang, Y.: Many-agent reinforcement learning, Ph. D. thesis, UCL (University College London) (2021)

34. Yang, Y., Luo, R., Li, M., Zhou, M., Zhang, W., Wang, J.: Mean field multi-agent reinforcement learning (2018). https://doi.org/10.48550/ARXIV.1802.05438. https://arxiv.org/abs/1802.05438

35. Yu, C., et al.: The surprising effectiveness of PPO in cooperative, multi-agent games (2021). https://doi.org/10.48550/ARXIV.2103.01955. https://arxiv.org/abs/2103.01955
36. Šošić, A., KhudaBukhsh, W.R., Zoubir, A.M., Koeppl, H.: Inverse reinforcement learning in swarm systems (2016). https://doi.org/10.48550/ARXIV.1602.05450. https://arxiv.org/abs/1602.05450

Programming Distributed Collective Processes for Dynamic Ensembles and Collective Tasks

Giorgio Audrito[1] , Roberto Casadei[2(✉)] , Ferruccio Damiani[1] ,
Gianluca Torta[1] , and Mirko Viroli[2]

[1] Università di Torino, Torino, Italy
{giorgio.audrito,ferruccio.damiani,gianluca.torta}@unito.it
[2] Università di Bologna, Cesena, Italy
{roby.casadei,mirko.viroli}@unibo.it

Abstract. Recent trends like the Internet of Things (IoT) suggest a vision of dense and multi-scale deployments of computing devices in nearly all kinds of environments. A prominent engineering challenge revolves around programming the collective adaptive behaviour of such computational ecosystems. This requires abstractions able to capture concepts like ensembles (dynamic groups of cooperating devices) and collective tasks (joint activities carried out by ensembles). In this work, we consider collections of devices interacting with neighbours and that execute in nearly-synchronised sense–compute–interact rounds, where the computation is given by a single control program. To support programming whole computational collectives, we propose the abstraction of a distributed collective process (DCP), which can be used to define at once the ensemble formation logic and its collective task. We implement the abstraction in the eXchange Calculus (XC), a core language based on neighbouring values (maps from neighbours to values) where state management and interaction is handled through a single primitive, **exchange**. Then, we discuss the features of the abstraction, its suitability for different kinds of distributed computing applications, and provide a proof-of-concept implementation of a wave-like process propagation.

Keywords: collective computing · collective processes · ensembles · formation control

1 Introduction

Programming the collective behaviour of large collections of computing and interacting devices is a major research challenge, promoted by recent trends

This publication is part of the project NODES which has received funding from the MUR - M4C2 1.5 of PNRR with grant agreement no. ECS00000036. The work was also partially supported by the Italian PRIN project "CommonWears" (2020HCWWLP) and the EU/MUR FSE PON-R&I 2014-2020.

S.-S. Jongmans and A. Lopes (Eds.): COORDINATION 2023, LNCS 13908, pp. 71–89, 2023.
https://doi.org/10.1007/978-3-031-35361-1_4

like the Internet of Things [6] and swarm robotics [15]. This challenge is investigated and addressed by several related research threads including *coordination* [24,42], *multi-agent systems* [14], *collective adaptive systems* [23], *macro-programming* [18,40], *spatial computing* [13], *field-based coordination* [36], *aggregate computing* [49], and *attribute-based communication* [1].

This activity can be supported by suitable *programming abstractions* supporting declarative specifications of collective behaviours. Examples of abstractions include ensembles [41], computational fields [49], collective communication interfaces [1,50], and collective orchestration tasks [46]. In this work, we cover the abstraction of a *distributed collective process (DCP)*, inspired by aggregate processes [20,21,48], which consists of a model for concurrent collective tasks running and spreading on dynamic domains of devices. We provide an abstract model of the abstraction on event structures, and discuss its implementation on the eXchange Calculus (XC) [9], a language, inspired by field calculi [49], for programming homogeneous systems of neighbour-interacting devices. Then, we discuss how the DCP abstraction can support multiple patterns of collective behaviour and self-organisation.

The paper is organised as follows. Section 2 provides context, related work, and motivation. Section 3 reviews the basics of the XC language. Section 4 provides the contribution. Section 5 discusses features and applications of the approach, and provides a proof-of-concept implementation. Section 6 summarises results and points out directions for future work.

2   Context, Related Work, and Motivation

This work lies in the context of models and languages for programming collective behaviour [15,17,23]. Indeed, achieving the desired collective behaviour is an engineering goal for different domains and applications:

- *Swarm robotics.* Multiple robots may be tasked to move and act as a collective to explore an unknown environment [37], to search and rescue victims for humanitarian aid after disasters [5], to map a crop field for the presence of weeds [3], to transport objects exceeding [26], etc.
- *The IoT.* The *things* should coordinate to promote application-level goals (e.g., by gathering and processing relevant data) while making efficient use of resources. For instance, the nodes could support the aggregation of machine learning models [47], or collaborate to measure the collective status of the network to support various activities from environment sensing [35] to remote attestation of system integrity [4].
- *Hybrid Collective Intelligence (CI).* Socio-technical systems involving humans and computing devices could be programmed as "social machines" [30] executing coordinated tasks [46], or promoting the emergence of collective knowledge [27].
- *Computing ecosystems.* Modern infrastructures spanning the edge–fog–cloud layers can be considered as collective systems. The computing nodes should

exchange and process information to create suitable topologies and structures [33,45] and coordinate task allocation [38], resiliently.

This problem is at the heart of several related research threads. The field of *coordination* [24,42] addresses it by governing interaction; *collective adaptive systems* engineering [23] investigates means for collective adaptation in large populations of agents; *spatial computing* [13] leverages spatial abstractions to guide behaviour and perform computation; *macroprogramming* [18,40] takes a programming language-perspective to expressing macroscopic behaviour; *multi-agent systems* programming [14] considers autonomy, cognitive, and organisational concerns; and so on.

In this work, we consider a language-based software engineering perspective [29]. In other words, we seek for abstractions supporting expressing collective behaviour. Examples of abstractions proposed in previous research include:

- *ensembles* [41]: dynamic composites of devices, e.g., formed by attribute-based formation rules;
- *computational fields* [36,49]: maps from devices to values, used to capture collective inputs, and collective outputs;
- *aggregate computations* [49]: functions mapping input computational fields to output computational fields, implicitly handling coordination;
- *aggregate processes* [10,11,20,21]: dynamic *aggregate computations* [49] on evolving domains of devices;
- *collective communication interfaces* [50]: abstractions able to flexibly express the targets of communications actions, e.g., via attributes [1,41];
- *collective-based tasks* [46]: abstractions keeping track of the lifecycle and state of tasks assigned to collectives.

In particular, we consider *collective systems*, namely largely homogeneous collections of devices or agents. Each device can be thought of as a resource that provides capabilities and provides access to a local context that depends on its situation on the environment and possibly its state. For instance, in a smart city, fixed smart lights may be located nearby streets, smart cameras may support monitoring of facilities, smart vehicles may move around to gather city-wide infrastructural data, etc. Since we would like to avoid bottlenecks and single-points-of-failure, we avoid centralisations and opt for a fully decentralised approach: a device can generally interact only within its local context, which may include a portion of the environment and other nearby devices. If our goal is to exploit the distributed, pervasive computer made of an entire collection of situated devices, an idea could be to run *collaborative* tasks involving subsets of devices—to exploit their resources, capabilities, and contexts. Since a process may not know beforehand the resources/capabilities it needs and the relevant contexts, it may embed the logic to look for them, i.e., to spread over the collective system until its proper set of supporting devices have been identified. Moreover, the requirements of the process may change over time, dynamically self-adapting to various environmental conditions and changing goals. Within a process that concurrently spans a collection of devices, local computations may be scheduled and information may flow around in order to support collective activities [15,53] such as collective perception [28], collective decision-making [16], collective movement [39], etc. So, if the collective that sustains the process decides that more resources are needed, the process may spread to a larger set of devices; conversely, if the collective task has been completed, the devices may quit the process, eventually making it vanish. This is, informally, our idea of a *distributed collective processes (DCP)*, i.e., a *process* (i.e., a running program or task) which is *collective* (i.e., a joint activity carried out by largely homogeneous entities) and *distributed* (i.e., concurrently active on distinct networked devices), whereby the collective task and the underlying ensemble can mutually affect each other, and ensemble formation is driven by decentralised device-to-device interaction.

In the following, we explain a formal framework (Sect. 3) particularly suitable to study and implement this DCP abstraction; then, we formalise a language construct (Sect. 4) to effectively *program* such DCP; and finally discuss features and applications enabled by our abstraction implementation (Sect. 5).

3   Background: The eXchange Calculus

We consider the *eXchange Calculus (XC)* [9] as the formal framework for modelling, reasoning about, and implementing DCPs. In this section, we first present the system and execution model (Sect. 3.1), providing an operational view of the kinds of systems we target, and then describe the basic constructs of XC that we leverage in this work (Sect. 3.2).

3.1   System Model

The target system that we would like to program can be modelled as a collection of *nodes*, able to interact with the environment through *sensors* and *actuators*, and able to communicate with *neighbours* by exchanging messages. We assume that each node runs in asynchronous *sense–compute–act rounds*, where

1. *sense*: the node queries sensors for getting up-to-date environmental values, and gathers recent messages from neighbours (which may expire after some time)—all this information is what we call as the node's *context*;
2. *compute*: the node evaluates the common control program, mapping the context (i.e., inputs from sensors and neighbours) to an output describing the actions to perform (i.e., actuations and communications);
3. *act*: the node executes the actions as dictated by the program, possibly resulting into environment change or message delivery to neighbours.

This kind of loop is used to ensure that the context is continuously assessed (at discrete times), and the reactions are also computed and performed continuously. This model has shown to be particularly useful to specify self-organising and collective adaptive behaviours, especially for long-running coordination tasks [49].

The semantic of a system execution can be expressed as an event structure (see Fig. 1), where events ϵ denote whole sense–compute–act rounds, and arrows

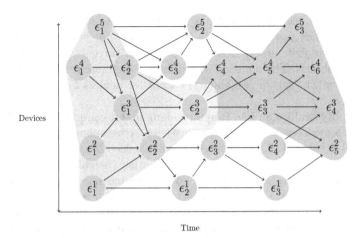

Devices

Time

Fig. 1. Example of an event structure modelling a distributed system execution. Nodes labelled by ϵ_k^δ denote the k-th round of device δ. The yellow background highlights a reference event, from which its past (green) and future (blue) are identified through the causal relationship implied by the arrows denoting neighbour events. (Color figure online)

between events denote that certain source events have provided inputs (i.e., messages) to target events. In particular, if event ϵ' is connected with an arrow to ϵ, we say that ϵ' is a *neighbour* of ϵ, denoted $\epsilon' \rightsquigarrow \epsilon$. We denote with $N(\epsilon)$ the set of all *neighbours* of ϵ, and with $d(\epsilon)$ the device where event ϵ happens, i.e., where it is executed.

Programming the systems described in this section thus means defining the control rules that specify how the context at each event is mapped to the messages to be sent to neighbour events.

3.2 XC Key Data Type: Neighbouring Values

In XC we distinguish two types of values. The *Local* values ℓ include classic atomic and structured types A such as int, float, string or list. The neighbouring values (*nvalues*) are instead maps $\underline{w}$ from device identifiers δ_i to corresponding local values ℓ_i, with an additional local value ℓ that acts as a *default*:

$$\underline{w} = \ell[\delta_1 \mapsto \ell_1, \dots, \delta_n \mapsto \ell_n]$$

A nvalue specifies a (set of) values received from or sent to neighbours: received values are gathered into nvalues, then can be locally processed, and the final resulting nvalue can be interpreted as messages to be sent back to neighbours. The devices with an associated entry in the nvalue are thus typically a (small) subset of all devices, namely those that are close-enough to the current device, and which are of course working correctly.

The default is used when a value is not available for some neighbour δ', e.g., because δ' has just been switched on and has not yet produced a value, or because it has just moved close enough to the current device δ to become one of its neighbours. The notation above should therefore read as "the nvalue $\underline{w}$ is ℓ everywhere (i.e., for all neighbours) except for devices $\delta_1, \ldots, \delta_n$ which have values $\ell_1, \ldots, \ell_n$.

To exemplify nvalues, in Fig. 1, upon waking up for computation ϵ_2^3, device δ_3 may process a nvalue $\underline{w} = 0[\delta_4 \mapsto 1, \delta_3 \mapsto 2, \delta_2 \mapsto 3]$, corresponding to the messages carrying scalar values 1, 2, and 3 received when asleep from δ_4, δ_3 (i.e., *itself* at the previous round), and δ_2. The entries for all other (neighbour) devices default to 0. After the computation, δ_2 may send out the messages represented by the nvalue $\underline{w}' = 0[\delta_4 \mapsto 5, \delta_3 \mapsto 6]$; so that 5 is sent to δ_4, 6 is sent to δ_3, and 0 is sent to every other device, such as a newly-connected device. For convenience, we may use the notation $\underline{w}(\delta')$ for the local value (specific or default) associated with δ' by $\underline{w}$.

Note that a local value ℓ can be naturally converted to a nvalue $\ell[]$ where it is the default value for every device. Except for clarity, thus local values and nvalues can be treated uniformly. Functions on local values are implicitly lifted to nvalues, by applying them on the maps' content pointwise. For example, if $\underline{w}_1$ assigns value 2 to δ_3 and $\underline{w}_2$ assigns default value 1 to δ_3, then $\underline{w}_3 = \underline{w}_1 \cdot \underline{w}_2$ shall assign value $2 \cdot 1 = 2$ to δ_3.

A fundamental operation on nvalues is provided by the built-in function $\mathtt{nfold}(f : (A, B) \to A, \underline{w} : \underline{B}, \ell : A) : A$. As suggested by the name, the function folds over a nvalue $\underline{w}$, i.e., starting from a base local value ℓ it repeatedly applies function f to neighbours' values in $\underline{w}$, excluding the value for the current device. For instance, if δ_2 with set of neighbours $\{\delta_1, \delta_3, \delta_4\}$ performs a $\mathtt{nfold}$ operation $\mathtt{nfold}(*, \underline{w}, 1)$, the output will be $1 \cdot \underline{w}(\delta_1) \cdot \underline{w}(\delta_3) \cdot \underline{w}(\delta_4)$. Note that, as nvalues are *unordered maps*, it is sensible to assume that f is associative and commutative.

Two built-in operations on nvalues act on the value associated with the current (self) device:

- $\mathtt{self}(\underline{w} : \underline{A}) : A$ returns the local value $\underline{w}(\delta)$ in $\underline{w}$ for the self device δ
- $\mathtt{updateSelf}(\underline{w} : \underline{A}, \ell : A) : \underline{A}$ returns a nvalue where the value for the self device δ is set to ℓ.

There are several other fundamental built-in operators in XC, such as $\mathtt{exchange}$ and $\mathtt{mux}$, which are however not necessary for understanding the rest of this paper. Please refer to [9] for their detailed, formal description.

4   Distributed Collective Processes in XC

In this section, we present an implementation of DCPs in XC. First, we characterise the implementation in terms of an abstract notation and formulas on event structures (Sect. 4.1). Then, we provide a formalisation of DCPs in terms of the big-step operational semantics for a new XC construct (Sect. 4.2), that can be used to actually *program* DCPs.

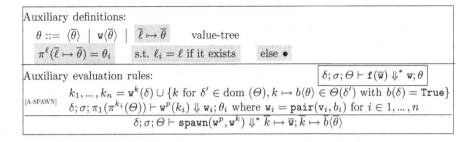

Fig. 2. Device (big-step) operational semantics of FXC

4.1 Modelling on Event Structures

In this discussion, we refer to an event structure as the one depicted in Fig. 1. A *distributed collective process (DCP)* P is a computation with given programmed behaviour. A single DCP can be run in multiple *process instances* P_i, each associated to a unique *process identifier (PID)* i, which we assume also embeds construction parameters for the process instance. New instances of an aggregate process P are spawned through a *generation field* G_P, producing a set of identifiers $G(\epsilon) = \{i \dots\}$ in each event ϵ, of process instances that need to be created in that event ϵ (which we call *initiator* for P_i). For each process instance P_i, we use the Boolean predicate $\pi_{P_i}(\epsilon)$ to denote whether such instance is being executed at event ϵ (either being initiated by ϵ, or through propagation from previous events). Each process instance P_i, if active in an event ϵ (i.e., $\pi_{P_i}(\epsilon) = \top$), locally computes both an *output* $O_{P_i}(\epsilon)$ (returned to the process caller) and a *status* $s_{P_i}(\epsilon)$, which is an nvalue mapping the device d of each neighbour event $\epsilon \in N$ to a **bool** value.

A process instance P_i which is active in an event ϵ *potentially* propagates the process to any event ϵ' of which ϵ is a neighbour ($\epsilon \rightsquigarrow \epsilon'$) depending on the value of $s_{P_i}(\epsilon)$. In formulas:

$$\pi_{P_i}(\epsilon) = \begin{cases} \top & \text{if } i \in G_P(\epsilon) \\ \top & \text{if } \exists \epsilon' \rightsquigarrow \epsilon. \ \pi_{P_i}(\epsilon') \wedge s_{P_i}(\epsilon')(d(\epsilon)) = \top \\ \bot & \text{otherwise.} \end{cases}$$

The XC defines a built-in construct $spawn_{XC}(P, G_P)$ that runs independent instances of a field computation P, where new instances are locally generated according to *generation field* G_P as explained above. The output of a $spawn_{XC}(P, G_P)$ expression in an event ϵ is the set of pairs $\{(i, O_{P_i}(\epsilon)), \dots\}$ for which $\pi_{P_i}(\epsilon) = \top$.

4.2 Formalisation

The $spawn_{XC}$ construct, defined mathematically in the previous Sect. 4.1, embeds naturally in XC as a built-in function, derived by converting the classical spawn construct [20] into XC. As a built-in in XC, **spawn** assumes the same type as the classical spawn construct in field calculus: $\forall \alpha_k, \alpha_v.((\alpha_k) \rightarrow$ $\mathtt{pair}[\alpha_v, \mathtt{bool}], \mathtt{set}[\alpha_k]) \rightarrow \mathtt{map}[\alpha_k, \alpha_v]$. However, in XC every type allows nvalues, which translates into practical differences.

Figure 2 presents the semantics of the spawn built-in, relative to the XC semantics presented in [9], which we do not include for brevity. As in [32], the overbar notation indicates a (possibly empty) sequence of elements, and multiple overbars are expanded together, e.g., $\overline{x} \mapsto \overline{y}$ is short for $x_1 \mapsto y_1, ..., x_n \mapsto y_n$ $(n \geq 0)$. The semantics is given by the auxiliary evaluation judgement for built-ins $\delta; \sigma; \Theta \vdash \mathtt{b}(\overline{\mathtt{w}}) \Downarrow^* \mathtt{w}; \theta$, to be read as "expression $\mathtt{b}(\overline{\mathtt{w}})$ evaluates to nvalue $\mathtt{w}$ and value-tree θ on device δ with respect to sensor values σ and value-tree environment Θ", where:

- θ is an ordered tree with nvalues on some nodes, representing messages to be sent to neighbours by tracking necessary nvalues and stack frames produced while evaluating $\mathtt{b}(\overline{\mathtt{w}})$;
- Θ collects the most recent value-trees received by neighbours of δ, as a map $\delta_1 \mapsto \theta_1, ..., \delta_n \mapsto \theta_n$ $(n \geq 0)$ from device identifiers to value-trees.

In order to introduce the spawn construct, it is necessary to extend the auxiliary definition of value-trees (highlighted in grey), to also allow for maps from local literals ℓ (identifiers of the running processes) to their corresponding value-trees. Then, rule [A-SPAWN] can be written by naturally porting the similar rule in [20], while using the fact that the Boolean returned by the process is an nvalue, and thus can be different for different neighbours. In this rule, a list of *process keys* $\overline{k}$ is computed by adjoining *(i)* the keys $\mathtt{w}^k(\delta)$ currently present in the second argument $\mathtt{w}^k$ of spawn for the current device δ; *(ii)* the keys that any neighbour δ' broadcast in their last message $\Theta(\delta')$, provided that the corresponding Boolean value b returned was true for the current device $b(\delta) = \mathtt{True}$ (thus, demanding process expansion to δ). To realise "multiple alignment", for each key k_i, the process $\mathtt{w}^p$ is applied to k_i with respect to the part of the value-tree environment $\pi_1(\pi^{k_i}(\Theta))$ that corresponds to key k_i, producing $\mathtt{w}_i; \theta_i$ as a result. Finally, the construct concludes returning the maps $\overline{k} \mapsto \overline{\mathtt{w}}; \overline{k} \mapsto \overline{\theta}$ mapping process keys to their evaluation result.

5   Discussion and Proof-of-Concept

In this section, we discuss the proposed abstraction (Sect. 5.1), the characteristics of the proposed programming model for DCPs (Sect. 5.2), then provide examples of applications (Sect. 5.3), and provide a proof-of-concept implementation of a wave-like propagation of a DCP (Sect. 5.4).

5.1   The DCP Abstraction

The crucial problem that we investigate in this paper revolves around the definition of collaborative activities carried out by *dynamic* collections of devices (a.k.a. *ensembles* [41]). We call these *DCPs* since they are defined by a common control program that regulates the behaviour of a largely homogeneous set of devices.

In particular, a device may participate *concurrently* to multiple collective processes, or to multiple ensembles. How participation to multiple DCPs relates to local resource usage (cf. resource-constrained devices) is abstracted away and may be dealt both programmatically (e.g., through a status computed depending on the resource availability perceived through a sensor) or automatically at the virtual machine level (e.g., by runtime checks). Furthermore, notice that, in any single round, a device executes the computation associated to all the currently joined DCPs. That is, in the basic model, the number of processes joined by a device has no effect whatsoever on the number of rounds, which follow a given scheduling policy. Therefore, the participation to several processes may in principle increase the duration of rounds significantly, possibly slowing down the reactivity of a device; so, real-world implementations have also to consider these aspects. Associating different scheduling policies to different processes is however possible, but requires an extension to the basic execution model, e.g., along the lines of [44].

We define as the *domain* of a DCP the set of the nodes that are currently running it. We define as the *shape* of a DCP the spatiotemporal region that is identified by the spatiotemporal locations of the nodes belonging to the domain of the DCP. Often, DCPs are *transient*, i.e., they have a limited lifetime: they start to exist at some time, and they dissolve once no more nodes run them.

In this work, we are mainly concerned with studying how to create and manipulate these DCPs. The supporting formal framework and implementation is described in Sect. 4. In summary, the developer has the following mechanisms for defining systems of DCPs:

- *generation logic*: the need for collective activities can be encoded in a rule for generating new instances of DCPs;
- *identity logic*: the logic used to identify DCPs can be used to distinguish between them and hence to regulate their domains (e.g., for controlling the granularity of teams);
- *internal logic*: this logic defines a collective computation (scoped within the domain of a single DCP) promoting decentralised decision-making, e.g., in terms of typical self-organisation patterns (collection, propagation, leader election, evaporation, etc.);
- *shape control logic*: it is possible to specify rules for the local expansion of the domains of DCPs (e.g., to gather more participants), typically also leveraging results from the internal computation itself—the XC implementation provides an especially flexible way to specify this, as different neighbours can receive different information;
- *termination logic*: this logic, strictly related to shape control, enables to specify how individual agents may leave a DCP instance as well as how an entire DCP may be terminated;
- *input logic*: existing DCPs may also be controlled be specifying "external inputs" provided as explicit arguments or closed over a lambda closure—an example is *meta-control logic*, based on inspecting the (results of) multiple DCPs to take decisions about their evolution.

In the following, we discuss features and examples of use of the abstraction.

5.2 Features of the Abstraction and Programming Model

Progressive and Live Construction of Ensembles (cf. Self-organisation, Self-healing, etc.). The DCPs have a *dynamic* domain, that evolves progressively to include more or less devices. The devices at the border of the DCP can choose to expand it to (a subset of) their neighbours and the neighbours themselves can opt in or out. Moreover, since evaluation of the program is repeated over time, the border is *live*, meaning that membership can be always re-evaluated, in order to consider the up-to-date context. Conversely, members that are no longer interested in participating in the collective task, or that have completed the tasks associated to their role, can leave the process by returning `False[]` in the spawn routine, or even start process termination patterns as those investigated in [11].

Flexible Control of Collective Process Shape and State. The shape and state of a DCP can be regulated flexibly, by leveraging different kinds of mechanisms. For instance, the state and shape of a process can be controlled at a collective level, as a result of a collective consensus or decision-making activity. As an alternative, the leader or owner of the DCP may centralise some of the decision-making: for instance, it may gather statistics from its members (using adaptive collection algorithms [8]), and use locally-computed policies to decide whether to let more members join (sharing the local decision with a resilient broadcast algorithm [49]). Between fully centralised and fully decentralised settings, there are intermediate solutions based e.g. on a partitioning of the DCP into sub-groups using partitioning mechanisms that can be applied at the aggregate programming level [2,19]. The state can be used, for instance, to denote different *phases* of a collective task [22], hence it is important that all the members of the DCP eventually become aware of the up-to-date situation. Regarding shape control, further flexibility is provided by XC, thanks to differentiated messages to neighbours: this feature could be used to essentially control the direction of process propagation (e.g., by filtering, random selective choice, or any other ad-hoc mechanisms).

Support for Privacy-preserving Collective Computations. The possibility in XC to send differentiated messages to neighbours (unlike classical field calculi [49]), especially when supported infrastructurally through point-to-point communication channels, can also promote *privacy* in collective computations. This way, devices that are unrelated to certain tasks, are not exposed to the information that those tasks are being carried out.

5.3 Examples

Given its features, the DCP abstraction could turn useful to program several kinds of higher-level distributed computing abstractions and tasks such as, for instance, the following.

Modelling of Teams or Ensembles of Agents [41]. A DCP can represent, through its very domain, the set of agents that belong to a certain team or ensemble. It can spread around the system to gather and (re-)evaluate a membership condition, to effectively recruit agents into different organisational structures [31]. Two main mechanisms regulate the joining of devices into DCPs: the propagation of PIDs to neighbours (i.e., an *internal* control of the process border), and the possibility to *leave* a process by a device that received a PID, which would not propagate the process further (i.e., an *external* control of the process border). The former mechanism is directly supported by our XC implementation, through the notion of *differentiated messages* to neighbours, enabled by nvalues. Concurrent participation to multiple teams is directly supported by the fact that a single device can participate in an arbitrary number of DCPs. As participation to multiple DCPs leads to increased resource requirements (in both computation time and message size), the programmer has to take into account performance issues when designing the generation and propagation logic of concurrent DCPs. However, the fully asynchronous and resilient nature of XC implies that some additional slack can be used on top of resource bounds posed by the architecture, as longer round execution or message exchange time (or even a device crash) can be handled seamlessly by the XC programming model. Last but not least, the activity within a DCP can be used to support the coordination *within* the ensemble it represents, e.g., through gossip or information spreading algorithms, whose scope is limited to the domain of the DCP; therefore, it may be useful also for *privacy-preserving* computations.

Space-based Coordination (e.g., Spatiotemporal Tuples [22]). A DCP could also be attached to a spatial location—to implemented *spatially-attached processes*. This could be used to support space-based coordination, or to implement coordination models like *spatiotemporal tuples* [22], whereby tuples and tuple operations can be emitted to reside at or query a particular spatial location. To implement the spatiotemporal tuples model, an DCP instance can be used to represent a single out (writing), rd (reading), and in (retrieval) operation—see Fig. 3 for a visual example. A tuple is denoted by its out process: it exists as long as its DCP is alive in some device. Creating tuples that reside at a fixed spatial location/area (e.g., as described by geodetic coordinates) or that remain attached to a particular mobile device is straightforward. In the former case, the DCP membership condition is just that the device's current location is inside or close by the provided spatial location. In the latter case, the DCP membership condition is just that the device's current distance to the DCP source device (which may be computed by a simple gradient) is within a certain threshold. We may call these *node-attached processes*: as a node moves, a DCP attached to it can follow through, to support collective contextual services; for instance, a node may recruit other nodes and resources for mobile tasks.

Creation of Adaptive System Structures to Support Communication and Coordination. The ability of DCPs to capture both the formation evolution and the collective activity of a group of devices within a pervasive computing system can

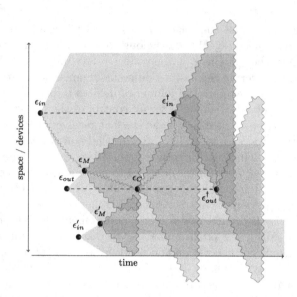

Fig. 3. Graphics of interacting DCPs modelling spatiotemoral tuple operations. Each DCP is denoted as a trapezoid-like shape that springs out at a certain event (a round by a single device). Notation: ϵ_{in} and ϵ_{out} mean that the event generates a process modelling an in (retrieval) and out (writing) tuple operation, respectively; ϵ_M means that a matching out tuple for an in operation has been found; ϵ_C means that the out tuple process has reached consensus about the in process to serve; the † superscript denotes a termination event, starting a process to close an existing process.

be leveraged to create resilient structures supporting non-local or system-wide coordination. For instance, this can be used to implement messaging channels in a peer-to-peer network of situated neighbour-interacting devices (e.g., in a smart city) [20]: the channel consists only of the devices between the source and the destination of a message, hence avoiding expensive gossip or flooding processes that would (i) consume resources of possibly all the devices in the system, and (ii) exacerbate privacy and security issues. As another example, consider the *Self-organising Coordination Regions (SCR)* pattern [19]: it is a mechanism to control the level of decentralisation in systems to flexibly support situated tasks, based on (i) decentralised leader election [43]; (ii) creation of areas around the leaders to basically partition the overall system into manageable regions [51]; and (iii) supporting intra-region and inter-region coordination e.g. by means of *information flows* [52]. Now, traditional solutions based on field calculi [19] do not easily allow for the partitions to *overlap*: this, instead, could be desired for fault-tolerance, flexibility, and improved interaction between adjacent regions, and it turns out to be easily implementable using DCPs.

Modelling of Epidemic Processes [25]. Finally, DCP also represent a tool for studying how to relate computation, coordination, and epidemic processes. By the ability of programmatically controlling how processes spread, possibly using conditions that depend on the collective computation carried out by the current ensemble, it is possible to model complex diffusion dynamics. In future work, it would be interesting to explore how XC programs leveraging DCPs could promote network-based and agent-based simulation models for epidemic spread, e.g. such as those reviewed in [34].

5.4   Proof-of-Concept Implementation

As a proof-of-concept of the techniques described in this paper, we have implemented a simple use case exploiting the FCPP simulator [7,12], which has been extended to support the XC and, in particular, the $spawn_{XC}$ built-in construct described above. The implemented use case is a network of devices where, at some point in time, a source device δ_{FROM} sends a message through a DCP to reach a destination device δ_{TO}. For simplicity, we considered devices to be stationary in the simulation, thus inducing a fixed network topology (although the proof-of-concept program could be run with dynamic topologies as well). Round durations are not identical (they can vary by 10% from base value).

We implement a *spherical* propagation, where the message originating in δ_{FROM} spreads radially in 3D trying to reach δ_{TO}. The process function executed by each process node implements the following logic:

1. if the self device δ is δ_{TO} just return a *false* nvalue $F[]$ (no propagation, since destination has been reached);
2. if it is the first round that δ executes the process, and the neighbours it knows (i.e., that have propagated the process to δ) are $\delta_1, \dots, \delta_k$, it propagates it to itself and to its *new neighbours* (that are not yet in the process) by returning an nvalue $T[\delta \mapsto T, \delta_1 \mapsto F, \dots]$;
3. finally, at the second round δ exits itself the process by returning a *false* nvalue $F[]$.

The following snippet of FCPP code shows the core of the simple function described above:

```
1        if (dest)
2            fdwav = field<bool>(false);
3        else if (rnd == 1) {
4            fdwav = field<bool>(false);
5            fdwav = mod_self(CALL, fdwav, true);
6            fdwav = mod_other(CALL, fdwav, true);
7        } else
8            fdwav = field<bool>(false);
```

Note that: flag `dest` is true only on device δ_{TO}; `fdwav` if the field that determines process propagation; a call to `field < bool > (false)` constructs a constant field of Booleans set to `false`; and a call to `mod_self` (resp. `mod_other`) sets the value in a field for the current device (resp. its known neighbours).

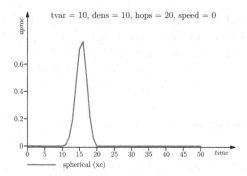

Fig. 4. Average number of active processes over time for the single-process use case.

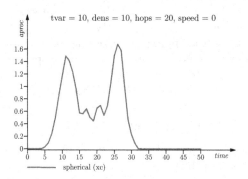

Fig. 5. Average number of active processes over time for the multi-process use case.

We exploit FCPP to simulate a first use case where only one process is generated. The simulation shows that the process propagates *as a wave* starting from δ_{FROM} outwards. Immediately after the wave front goes beyond a device, the device itself exits the process thus releasing potentially precious resources for other computations. Figure 4 shows the average number of active processes (*aproc*) within the network of devices in one specific execution of the use case (which took a time interval $[1, 50]$). For the first 10 sec, the average is 0, since no process has been created yet. After the process is created by δ_{FROM}, it propagates until it reaches its destination, and then quickly vanishes.

In a second use case, we let 10 different devices generate a new process at each round with probability 5%, in the time interval $[1, 25]$. Figure 5 shows that the average number of active processes *aproc* grows from 0 (at time 0) up to slightly more than 1.6 (just after 25), and then quickly drops again down to 0. Given that more than 10 processes are generated during the use case, the average number of active processes is kept low by the fact that the nodes exploit *spawn*$_{XC}$ to immediately exit processes after entering and propagating them.

6   Conclusion

In this paper, we have covered the abstraction of a *distributed collective process (DCP)*, which supports the definition of the collective adaptive behaviour of pervasive collections of neighbour-interacting devices working in sense–compute–interact rounds. In particular, DCPs model decentralised collective tasks that also move, spread, and retract over the collective system in which they are spawned. We have discussed the abstraction, analysed it in the general framework of event structures, and implemented it in the *eXchange Calculus (XC)*, a minimal core language particularly suitable for implementing DCPs, for its *Neighbouring Value* data structure, that enables fine-tuned control of what data gets shared with neighbours. Finally, we have discussed its features and applicability, and have shown a proof of concept implementation of a wave-propagation algorithm—which may be used for model resource-efficient information flows.

In future work, we would like to further study DCPs by a dynamical perspective, and possibly explore its ability to model and simulate epidemic processes. Further, we would like to implement in XC a library of reusable functions capturing common patterns of DCPs usage, to streamline pervasive and collective computing application development.

References

1. Abd Alrahman, Y., De Nicola, R., Loreti, M.: Programming interactions in collective adaptive systems by relying on attribute-based communication. Sci. Comput. Programm. **192**, 102428 (2020). https://doi.org/10.1016/j.scico.2020.102428
2. Aguzzi, G., Audrito, G., Casadei, R., Damiani, F., Torta, G., Viroli, M.: A field-based computing approach to sensing-driven clustering in robot swarms. Swarm Intell. **17**(1), 27–62 (2023). https://doi.org/10.1007/s11721-022-00215-y
3. Albani, D., IJsselmuiden, J., Haken, R., Trianni, V.: Monitoring and mapping with robot swarms for agricultural applications. In: 14th IEEE International Conference on Advanced Video and Signal Based Surveillance, AVSS 2017, Lecce, Italy, 29 August - 1 September 2017, pp. 1–6. IEEE Computer Society (2017). https://doi.org/10.1109/AVSS.2017.8078478
4. Ambrosin, M., Conti, M., Lazzeretti, R., Rabbani, M.M., Ranise, S.: Collective remote attestation at the internet of things scale: state-of-the-art and future challenges. IEEE Commun. Surv. Tutorials **22**(4), 2447–2461 (2020). https://doi.org/10.1109/COMST.2020.3008879
5. Arnold, R., Jablonski, J., Abruzzo, B., Mezzacappa, E.: Heterogeneous UAV multi-role swarming behaviors for search and rescue. In: Rogova, G., McGeorge, N.M., Ruvinsky, A., Fouse, S., Freiman, M.D. (eds.) IEEE Conference on Cognitive and Computational Aspects of Situation Management, CogSIMA 2020, Victoria, BC, Canada, 24–29 August 2020, pp. 122–128. IEEE (2020). https://doi.org/10.1109/CogSIMA49017.2020.9215994
6. Atzori, L., Iera, A., Morabito, G.: The internet of things: a survey. Comput. Networks **54**(15), 2787–2805 (2010). https://doi.org/10.1016/j.comnet.2010.05.010

7. Audrito, G.: FCPP: an efficient and extensible field calculus framework. In: International Conference on Autonomic Computing and Self-Organizing Systems (ACSOS), pp. 153–159. IEEE (2020). https://doi.org/10.1109/ACSOS49614.2020.00037

8. Audrito, G., Casadei, R., Damiani, F., Pianini, D., Viroli, M.: Optimal resilient distributed data collection in mobile edge environments. Comput. Electr. Eng. **96**(Part), 107580 (2021). https://doi.org/10.1016/j.compeleceng.2021.107580

9. Audrito, G., Casadei, R., Damiani, F., Salvaneschi, G., Viroli, M.: Functional programming for distributed systems with XC. In: Ali, K., Vitek, J. (eds.) 36th European Conference on Object-Oriented Programming, ECOOP 2022, 6–10 June 2022, Berlin, Germany. LIPIcs, vol. 222, pp. 20:1–20:28. Schloss Dagstuhl - Leibniz-Zentrum für Informatik (2022). https://doi.org/10.4230/LIPIcs.ECOOP.2022.20

10. Audrito, G., Casadei, R., Torta, G.: Towards integration of multi-agent planning with self-organising collective processes. In: IEEE International Conference on Autonomic Computing and Self-Organizing Systems, ACSOS 2021, Companion Volume, Washington, DC, USA, 27 September - 1 October 2021, pp. 297–298. IEEE (2021). https://doi.org/10.1109/ACSOS-C52956.2021.00042

11. Audrito, G., Casadei, R., Torta, G.: On the dynamic evolution of distributed computational aggregates. In: IEEE International Conference on Autonomic Computing and Self-Organizing Systems Companion, ACSOS-C 2022, Virtual, CA, USA, 19–23 September 2022, pp. 37–42. IEEE (2022). https://doi.org/10.1109/ACSOSC56246.2022.00024

12. Audrito, G., Rapetta, L., Torta, G.: Extensible 3D simulation of aggregated systems with FCPP. In: ter Beek, M.H., Sirjani, M. (eds.) Coordination Models and Languages. COORDINATION 2022. IFIP Advances in Information and Communication Technology, vol. 13271, pp. 55–71. Springer, Cham (2022). https://doi.org/10.1007/978-3-031-08143-9_4

13. Beal, J., Dulman, S., Usbeck, K., Viroli, M., Correll, N.: Organizing the aggregate: languages for spatial computing. In: Formal and Practical Aspects of Domain-Specific Languages: Recent Developments, chap. 16, pp. 436–501. IGI Global (2013). https://doi.org/10.4018/978-1-4666-2092-6.ch016

14. Boissier, O., Bordini, R.H., Hubner, J., Ricci, A.: Multi-agent oriented programming: programming multi-agent systems using JaCaMo. Mit Press (2020)

15. Brambilla, M., Ferrante, E., Birattari, M., Dorigo, M.: Swarm robotics: a review from the swarm engineering perspective. Swarm Intell. **7**(1), 1–41 (2013). https://doi.org/10.1007/s11721-012-0075-2

16. Bulling, N.: A survey of multi-agent decision making. KI - Künstliche Intelligenz **28**(3), 147–158 (2014). https://doi.org/10.1007/s13218-014-0314-3

17. Casadei, R.: Artificial collective intelligence engineering: a survey of concepts and perspectives (2023). https://doi.org/10.48550/ARXIV.2304.05147. https://arxiv.org/abs/2304.05147. Accepted for Publication in the Artificial Life Journal (MIT Press)

18. Casadei, R.: Macroprogramming: Concepts, state of the art, and opportunities of macroscopic behaviour modelling. ACM Computing Surveys (2023). https://doi.org/10.1145/3579353

19. Casadei, R., Pianini, D., Viroli, M., Natali, A.: Self-organising coordination regions: a pattern for edge computing. In: Riis Nielson, H., Tuosto, E. (eds.) COORDINATION 2019. LNCS, vol. 11533, pp. 182–199. Springer, Cham (2019). https://doi.org/10.1007/978-3-030-22397-7_11

20. Casadei, R., Viroli, M., Audrito, G., Pianini, D., Damiani, F.: Aggregate processes in field calculus. In: Riis Nielson, H., Tuosto, E. (eds.) COORDINATION 2019. LNCS, vol. 11533, pp. 200–217. Springer, Cham (2019). https://doi.org/10.1007/978-3-030-22397-7_12

21. Casadei, R., Viroli, M., Audrito, G., Pianini, D., Damiani, F.: Engineering collective intelligence at the edge with aggregate processes. Eng. Appl. Artif. Intell. **97**, 104081 (2021)

22. Casadei, R., Viroli, M., Ricci, A., Audrito, G.: Tuple-based coordination in large-scale situated systems. In: Damiani, F., Dardha, O. (eds.) COORDINATION 2021. LNCS, vol. 12717, pp. 149–167. Springer, Cham (2021). https://doi.org/10.1007/978-3-030-78142-2_10

23. De Nicola, R., Jähnichen, S., Wirsing, M.: Rigorous engineering of collective adaptive systems: special section. Int. J. Softw. Tools Technol. Transfer **22**(4), 389–397 (2020). https://doi.org/10.1007/s10009-020-00565-0

24. Gelernter, D., Carriero, N.: Coordination languages and their significance. Commun. ACM **35**(2), 96–107 (1992). https://doi.org/10.1145/129630.376083

25. Giudice, N.D., Matteucci, L., Quadrini, M., Rehman, A., Loreti, M.: Sibilla: a tool for reasoning about collective systems. In: ter Beek, M.H., Sirjani, M. (eds.) Coordination Models and Languages. COORDINATION 2022. IFIP Advances in Information and Communication Technology, vol. 13271, pp. 92–98. Springer, Cham (2022). https://doi.org/10.1007/978-3-031-08143-9_6

26. Groß, R., Dorigo, M.: Towards group transport by swarms of robots. Int. J. Bio Inspired Comput. **1**(1/2), 1–13 (2009). https://doi.org/10.1504/IJBIC.2009.022770

27. Gruber, T.: Collective knowledge systems: where the social web meets the semantic web. J. Web Semant. **6**(1), 4–13 (2008). https://doi.org/10.1016/j.websem.2007.11.011

28. Gunther, H., Riebl, R., Wolf, L.C., Facchi, C.: Collective perception and decentralized congestion control in vehicular ad-hoc networks. In: 2016 IEEE Vehicular Networking Conference, VNC 2016, Columbus, OH, USA, 8–10 December 2016, pp. 1–8. IEEE (2016). https://doi.org/10.1109/VNC.2016.7835931

29. Gupta, G.: Language-based software engineering. Sci. Comput. Program. **97**, 37–40 (2015). https://doi.org/10.1016/j.scico.2014.02.010

30. Hendler, J., Berners-Lee, T.: From the semantic web to social machines: a research challenge for AI on the world wide web. Artif. Intell. **174**(2), 156–161 (2010). https://doi.org/10.1016/j.artint.2009.11.010

31. Horling, B., Lesser, V.R.: A survey of multi-agent organizational paradigms. Knowl. Eng. Rev. **19**(4), 281–316 (2004). https://doi.org/10.1017/S0269888905000317

32. Igarashi, A., Pierce, B.C., Wadler, P.: Featherweight Java: a minimal core calculus for Java and GJ. ACM Trans. Program. Lang. Syst. **23**(3), 396–450 (2001)

33. Karagiannis, V., Schulte, S.: Distributed algorithms based on proximity for self-organizing fog computing systems. Pervasive Mob. Comput. **71**, 101316 (2021). https://doi.org/10.1016/j.pmcj.2020.101316

34. Li, J., Xiang, T., He, L.: Modeling epidemic spread in transportation networks: a review. J. Traffic Transport. Eng. (English Edit.) **8**(2), 139–152 (2021). https://doi.org/10.1016/j.jtte.2020.10.003

35. Liu, C., Hua, J., Julien, C.: SCENTS: collaborative sensing in proximity iot networks. In: IEEE International Conference on Pervasive Computing and Communications Workshops, PerCom Workshops 2019, Kyoto, Japan, 11–15 March 2019, pp. 189–195. IEEE (2019). https://doi.org/10.1109/PERCOMW.2019.8730863

36. Mamei, M., Zambonelli, F.: Programming pervasive and mobile computing applications with the TOTA middleware. In: Pervasive Computing and Communications, 2004, pp. 263–273. IEEE (2004). https://doi.org/10.1109/PERCOM.2004.1276864
37. McGuire, K., Wagter, C.D., Tuyls, K., Kappen, H.J., de Croon, G.C.H.E.: Minimal navigation solution for a swarm of tiny flying robots to explore an unknown environment. Sci. Robotics 4(35), eaaw9710 (2019). https://doi.org/10.1126/scirobotics.aaw9710
38. Mohan, N., Kangasharju, J.: Edge-Fog cloud: a distributed cloud for internet of things computations. In: 2016 Cloudification of the Internet of Things, CIoT 2016, Paris, France, 23–25 November 2016, pp. 1–6. IEEE (2016). https://doi.org/10.1109/CIOT.2016.7872914
39. Navarro, I., Matía, F.: A survey of collective movement of mobile robots. Int. J. Adv. Robotic Syst. 10(1), 73 (2013). https://doi.org/10.5772/54600
40. Newton, R., Welsh, M.: Region streams: Functional macroprogramming for sensor networks. In: Workshop on Data Management for Sensor Networks, pp. 78–87 (2004). https://doi.org/10.1145/1052199.1052213
41. Nicola, R.D., Loreti, M., Pugliese, R., Tiezzi, F.: A formal approach to autonomic systems programming: the SCEL language. ACM Trans. Auton. Adapt. Syst. 9(2), 1–29 (2014). https://doi.org/10.1145/2619998
42. Papadopoulos, G.A., Arbab, F.: Coordination models and languages. Adv. Comput. 46, 329–400 (1998). https://doi.org/10.1016/S0065-2458(08)60208-9
43. Pianini, D., Casadei, R., Viroli, M.: Self-stabilising priority-based multi-leader election and network partitioning. In: IEEE International Conference on Autonomic Computing and Self-Organizing Systems, ACSOS 2022, Virtual, CA, USA, 19–23 September 2022, pp. 81–90. IEEE (2022). https://doi.org/10.1109/ACSOS55765.2022.00026
44. Pianini, D., Casadei, R., Viroli, M., Mariani, S., Zambonelli, F.: Time-fluid field-based coordination through programmable distributed schedulers. Log. Methods Comput. Sci. 17(4), 18 (2021). https://doi.org/10.46298/lmcs-17(4:13)2021
45. Pianini, D., Casadei, R., Viroli, M., Natali, A.: Partitioned integration and coordination via the self-organising coordination regions pattern. Future Gener. Comput. Syst. 114, 44–68 (2021). https://doi.org/10.1016/j.future.2020.07.032
46. Scekic, O., Schiavinotto, T., Videnov, S., Rovatsos, M., Truong, H.L., Miorandi, D., Dustdar, S.: A programming model for hybrid collaborative adaptive systems. IEEE Trans. Emerg. Top. Comput. 8(1), 6–19 (2020). https://doi.org/10.1109/TETC.2017.2702578
47. Sudharsan, B., Yadav, P., Nguyen, D., Kafunah, J., Breslin, J.G.: Ensemble methods for collective intelligence: combining ubiquitous ML models in IoT. In: 2021 IEEE International Conference on Big Data (Big Data), Orlando, FL, USA, 15–18 December 2021, pp. 1960–1963. IEEE (2021). https://doi.org/10.1109/BigData52589.2021.9671901
48. Testa, L., Audrito, G., Damiani, F., Torta, G.: Aggregate processes as distributed adaptive services for the industrial internet of things. Pervasive Mob. Comput. 85, 101658 (2022). https://doi.org/10.1016/j.pmcj.2022.101658
49. Viroli, M., Beal, J., Damiani, F., Audrito, G., Casadei, R., Pianini, D.: From distributed coordination to field calculus and aggregate computing. vol. 109 (2019). https://doi.org/10.1016/j.jlamp.2019.100486

50. Welsh, M., Mainland, G.: Programming sensor networks using abstract regions. In: Morris, R.T., Savage, S. (eds.) 1st Symposium on Networked Systems Design and Implementation (NSDI 2004), 29–31 March 2004, San Francisco, California, USA, Proceedings. pp. 29–42. USENIX (2004). http://www.usenix.org/events/nsdi04/tech/welsh.html

51. Weyns, D., Holvoet, T.: Regional synchronization for simultaneous actions in situated multi-agent systems. In: Mařík, V., Pěchouček, M., Müller, J. (eds.) CEEMAS 2003. LNCS (LNAI), vol. 2691, pp. 497–510. Springer, Heidelberg (2003). https://doi.org/10.1007/3-540-45023-8_48

52. Wolf, T.D., Holvoet, T.: Designing self-organising emergent systems based on information flows and feedback-loops. In: Proceedings of the First International Conference on Self-Adaptive and Self-Organizing Systems, SASO 2007, Boston, MA, USA, 9–11 July 2007, pp. 295–298. IEEE Computer Society (2007). https://doi.org/10.1109/SASO.2007.16

53. Wood, Z., Galton, A.: A taxonomy of collective phenomena. Appl. Ontol. 4(3–4), 267–292 (2009). https://doi.org/10.3233/ao-2009-0071

Cyber-Physical Systems

Shelley: A Framework for Model Checking Call Ordering on Hierarchical Systems

Carlos Mão de Ferro[1], Tiago Cogumbreiro[2]([✉]), and Francisco Martins[3]

[1] LASIGE, Faculdade de Ciências, Universidade de Lisboa, Lisbon, Portugal
carlos@maodeferro.pt
[2] University of Massachusetts, Boston, USA
tiago.cogumbreiro@umb.edu
[3] Faculdade de Ciências e Tecnologia, Ponta Delgada, Portugal
francisco.cc.martins@uac.pt

Abstract. This paper introduces Shelley, a novel model checking framework used to verify the order of function calls, developed in the context of Cyber-Physical Systems (CPS). Shelley infers the model directly from MicroPython code, so as to simplify the process of checking requirements expressed in a temporal logic. Applications for CPS need to reason about the end of execution to verify the reclamation/release of physical resources, so our temporal logic is stated on finite traces. Lastly, Shelley infers the behavior from code using an inter-procedural and compositional analysis, thus supporting the usual object-oriented programming techniques employed in MicroPython code. To evaluate our work, we present an experience report on an industrial application and evaluate the bounds of the validity checks (up to 12^{12} subsystems under $10\,$s on a desktop computer).

1 Introduction

This paper introduces a novel model checking framework to verify a MicroPython code base against a set of requirements stated in a temporal logic on ordered function calls. MicroPython [31] is an implementation of the Python programming language designed for microcontrollers, providing a large subset of standard Python features in a reduced memory footprint. A major challenge of applying formal methods to the development of embedded cyber-physical systems, is the gap between code and the requirements being checked [9,25,43,45,56,57]. To bridge this gap, our approach is to automatically infer the model from the code and let the user focus on stating requirements in a way that is close to the subject matter.

Our research is guided by three main goals. Firstly, *the requirements and the system's behavior should be represented as ordered actions* (which denote function calls), not as a transition system. Since the behavior being analyzed is a call-order graph, then the model and its requirements should closely mirror the given abstraction. In contrast, general-purpose model checkers express their models as state-transitions systems and the requirements are stated in terms of variables of these state-transition systems [7,12,13,27,40,52,59,66]. Additionally, model-checking approaches are usually focused on process communication, which is outside of the scope of the subject of our research.

© IFIP International Federation for Information Processing 2023
S.-S. Jongmans and A. Lopes (Eds.): COORDINATION 2023, LNCS 13908, pp. 93–114, 2023.
https://doi.org/10.1007/978-3-031-35361-1_5

Secondly, *our domain of interest is finite*, so our temporal logic must be stated on finite traces. When developing code that handles cyber-physical resources, it is crucial to reason (formally) about the release of such resources. Our model checking framework features linear temporal logic on finite traces (LTL_f) [3,18]. While it is possible to encode LTL_f in model checker that uses infinite linear temporal logic, such an encoding must be carefully implemented to avoid subtle mistakes [17]; any encoding to infinite traces should be handled automatically.

Thirdly, *code reuse is encouraged*. Since our modeling language is the code being run, then our analysis must support behavior (*i.e.*, function calls) that spans across multiple procedures (say, methods, or functions). A major feature of our model checking framework is to support a compositional interprocedural analysis that follows the usual abstraction and encapsulation techniques of MicroPython codes. Further, Shelley automatically guarantees the correct usage of each system, through function calls, according to their specifications, which reduces the number of correctness claims needed to be written for each system. The idea behind our analysis is akin to protocol conformance in the context of behavior protocols [67].

In summary, our paper makes the following contributions:

1. A domain-specific language to specify stateful systems while abstracting away the internal details of the implementation. (Sect. 3)
2. A formalization of generating a system's internal behavior and of checking its validity and decidability results. (Sect. 4.2 and Sect. 4.3)
3. A toolchain that model-checks requirements expressed by a temporal logic at different hierarchy levels, ensuring correct-by-construction software. (Sect. 4.4)
4. An evaluation of our framework: verifying the Aquamote® software written in MicroPython; assessing the performance impact of behavior checking (up to 12^{12} subsystems under 10 s on a desktop computer). (Sect. 5)

Finally, Sect. 6 discusses related work and Sect. 7 concludes the paper. Shelley is open-source and available online[1]. We provide a **demonstration video** of our tool[2] and **an artifact** [26].

2   Overview

In this section, we motivate the challenge of verifying the order of method calls in a object hierarchy, and we overview using Shelley to enforce specified behaviors. The running examples in this paper are taken from an industrial application that motivated our research: Aquamote® is a battery-operated wireless controller that switches water valves according to a scheduled irrigation plan. Following, we verify the controller software that automatically adapts its plan based on the weather forecast and sensor information yielding optimal water consumption results. Listing 2.1 shows the Shelley model of our running example, which is automatically extracted form MicroPython code.

---

[1] https://github.com/cajomferro/shelley.
[2] https://www.youtube.com/watch?v=ZiGPZRQHTWc.

Listing 2.1: Shelley specifications for our running example.

```
 1  base Valve {                                     21  AppV1 (a: Valve, b: Valve) {
 2    initial test -> open, clean;                   22    final main_1 -> {
 3    open -> close;                                 23      a.test; a.open; b.test;
 4    final close -> test;                           24      b.open; a.close; b.close;
 5    final clean -> test;}                          25    }
 6                                                   26    final main_2 -> {
 7  Sector (a: Valve, b: Valve) {                    27      a.test; a.open; b.test;
 8    initial try_open_1 -> close {                  28      b.clean; a.close;
 9      a.test; a.open; b.test; b.open;              29    }
10    }                                              30    final main_3 -> {
11    initial try_open_2 -> fail {                   31      a.test; a.clean;
12      { a.test; a.clean; } +                       32    }
13      { a.test; a.open; b.test; b.clean; a.close;} 33    initial main ->
14    }                                              34      main_1, main_2, main_3 {}
15    initial try_open -> try_open_1, try_open_2 {}  35
16    final fail -> try_open {}                      36    check (!b.open) W a.open;
17    final close -> try_open {a.close; b.close;}    37  }
18                                                   38
19    check (!b.open) W a.open;                      39  AppV2 (s: Sector) {
20  }                                                40    final main_1 -> {
                                                     41      {s.try_open; s.close;} +
                                                     42      {s.try_open; s.fail;}
                                                     43    }
                                                     44    initial main -> main_1 {}}
```

Finite Behaviors. Shelley is designed to verify finite behaviors. For applications that run on battery, it is paramount to specify the explicit release of resources, *e.g.*, turning off the WiFi before suspending. Otherwise, the programmer risks exhausting the device's battery while in suspend mode. Since reasoning about finite executions on a temporal logic based on infinite traces can lead to subtle errors [17], Shelley features LTL$_f$ and the behavior of our models are all finite. Note that Shelley can easily verify long-running applications. Indeed, there is no notion of battery in Shelley, just termination. The specification in Listing 2.1 could very well be of a control software that is connected to an electrical grid. The key point is that Shelley lets us reason about the eventual termination of a program, *e.g.*, specify and enforce that all resources are freed before halting.

Model Extraction. This paper discusses the verification of Shelley models. Our tool infers Shelley models from MicroPython code automatically. However, the discussion of the inference process and of its correctness are outside of the scope of this work. Shelley over-approximates the behavior of MicroPython programs in the following ways, *i.e.*, admits false alarms. The code of each method must be expressed as a regular expression representing any possible sequence of method calls. Shelley features sequencing, nondeterministic choice, and terminating loops (via the Kleene-star operator). Non-terminating programs and recursive calls are unsupported. Further, our tool disregards the program's internal state, *e.g.*, the arguments of method calls, the condition used to branch, and the loop bounds.

Listing 2.2: Class `Valve` and a diagram specifying its intended behavior.

```
1   class Valve:
2     def __init__(self):
3       self.control = Pin(27, Pin.OUT)
4       self.clean = Pin(28, Pin.OUT)
5       self.status = Pin(29, Pin.IN)
6
7   @op_initial
8     def test(self):
9       if self.status.value():
10        return "open"
11      else:
12        return "clean"
13
14  @op
15    def open(self):
16      self.control.on()
17      return "close"

18  @op_final
19    def close(self):
20      self.control.off()
21      return "test"
22
23  @op_final
24    def clean(self):
25      self.clean.on()
26      return "test"
```

2.1 Restricting the Behavior and Usage of Systems

As an example of a requirement, a user must test a valve before opening it, so as to minimize the chance of clogging that valve, which would render it unusable. Similarly, to conserve battery, we may want to enforce that the user must test the valve before cleaning up debris. Next, we describe code annotations we defined to achieve the ordering specified in the diagram of Listing 2.2. Our verification goal is to enforce that usages of class `Valve` follow the order specified by its code.

Listing 2.2 shows a high-level API, class `Valve`, written in MicroPython, to control programmatically a valve. Since we need precise control over resource allocation, we declare which methods can be considered safe to execute at the beginning and ending of an object's lifetime. Given that only `test` is marked as `op_initial`, then after creating an instance of `Valve` the only method that can be invoked is `test` (Lines 8 to 12). We then extract the ordering behavior based on the return values. The method `test` returns either an open or clean label, which signifies the following method that can be called. In this case, after testing, the valve can be opened or cleaned, but neither closed nor tested consecutively. When enabled, method `open` opens the valve (Lines 15 to 16); after that we can only close the valve (Lines 19 to 20). Finally, we can clean the valve from debris (Lines 24 to 25). Modifier `op_final` declares that method `close` can be the last method called, with respect to the object's lifetime; method `clean` is also marked as final. Since `open` is *not* marked as final, the valve cannot be left open, as long as the usage of the valve follows its specification.

2.2 Encapsulation Complicates Verification

We now introduce two versions of the same application, which controls two valves. The first version, called `AppV1`, invokes the valves directly. The second version, called `AppV2`, adds an extra abstraction layer `Sector` that generalizes using both valves as a whole. Our intent is to illustrate the kind of programs we are interested in and how different levels of abstraction complicate verification.

Listing 2.3: Class AppV1 and a diagram specifying the internal behavior.

```
 1  @claim("(! b.open) W a.open")
 2  class AppV1:
 3    def __init__(self):
 4      self.a=Valve();self.b=Valve()
 5
 6    @op_initial_final
 7    def main(self):
 8      match self.a.test():
 9        case "open":
10          self.a.open()
11          match self.b.test():
12            case "open":
13              self.b.open()
14              self.a.close()
15              self.b.close()
16              return ""
17            case "clean":
18              self.b.clean()
19              self.a.close()
20              print("Failed to open valves")
21              return ""
22        case "clean":
23          self.a.clean()
24          print("Failed to open valves")
25          return ""
```

Version 1. Listing 2.3 lists a program that controls two valves, along with a diagram that summarizes its internal behavior. Our program expresses two side-effects: the first represents when both valves are open; and the second is when one of the valves fails to open and must be cleaned. As an example, should we omit the call open in Line 13 and Shelley would output the following error message:

```
Error in specification: INVALID SUBSYSTEM USAGE
Counter example: a.test, a.open, b.test, a.close, >b.close<
Subsystems errors:
  * Valve 'b': test, >close< (after test, expecting open or clean)
```

Besides automatically verifying that each valve is being used according to the specification in Listing 2.2, we also want to verify temporal requirements. The claim in Line 1 of Listing 2.3 guarantees that we only open valve b after opening valve a. For instance, should we switch the calls to subsystems a and b in such a way that we try to test valve b before valve a and Shelley would output the following error message:

```
Error in specification: FAIL TO MEET REQUIREMENT
Formula: (!b.open) W a.open
Counter example: b.test, b.open, a.test, a.clean, b.close
```

Correctness claims express properties on the ordering of the internal calls to subsystems during the life cycle of that object. Such claims are of great importance for software maintenance, as Shelley checks if code changes preserve the specified internal behavior.

Version 2. In Listing 2.4, our top-level system AppV2 operates the valves via a Sector class (in irrigation jargon, a *sector* is an irrigation zone where

Listing 2.4: Classes `Sector` and `AppV2` and a diagram specifying the `Sector` internal behavior.

```
 1  @claim("(! b.open) W a.open")
 2  class Sector:
 3      def __init__(self):
 4          self.a = Valve(); self.b = Valve()
 5
 6      @op_initial
 7      def try_open(self):
 8          match self.a.test():
 9              case "open":
10                  self.a.open()
11                  match self.b.test():
12                      case "open":
13                          self.b.open()
14                          return "close"
15                      case "clean":
16                          self.b.clean(); self.a.close()
17                          return "fail"
18              case "clean":
19                  self.a.clean()
20                  return "fail"
21
22      @op_final
23      def fail(self):
24          print("Failed to open valves")
25          return "try_open"
26
27      @op_final
28      def close(self):
29          self.a.close(); self.b.close()
30          return "try_open"
31
32  class AppV2:
33      def __init__(self):
34          self.s = Sector()
35
36      @op_initial_final
37      def main(self):
38          match self.s.try_open():
39              case "close":
40                  self.s.close()
41                  return ""
42              case "fail":
43                  self.s.fail()
44                  return ""
```

several water valves are grouped together), adding an extra layer of encapsulation. Moreover, to make our code more reusable, class `Sector` abstracts trying to open both valves in method `try_open` (one side effect) and then closing both valves in method `close` (another side effect). When modeling class `Sector`, methods that produce multiple side effects must be distinguished as different operations: we write operation `try_open_1` to express the single trace in method `try_open` that returns `"close"` and we write operation `try_open_2` to express both traces of method `try_open` that return `"fail"`.

Since `Sector` exposes more methods, its behavior is more general than that of `AppV1`. We note, however, that the correctness claim of version 1 also holds in version 2 (Line 1). Deriving the internal behavior is not entirely obvious: e.g., every trace in method `try_open` that returns `"close"` must be able to precede any sequence of method `close`; similarly, every trace of method `try_open` that returns `fail` must be able to precede method `fail`.

Verifying a `Sector` is more complicated than verifying an `AppV1`, not just because the code is scattered across several methods, but because verifying the life cycle of a `Sector` entails reasoning about the internal behavior that arises from all possible usages of `Sector`, which in turn depends on the ordering constraints of each method. Therefore, as an application complexity increases vertically (by arranging systems hierarchically) and horizontally (by having more operations and more systems in each level) the code gets more and more partitioned and we rapidly lose track of the sequence of calls that represent the behavior of our program. Shelley model checks the `Sector` by deriving the internal behavior, which captures all possible internal traces that arise during the life cycle of `Sector`. To this end, Shelley must consider all possible orderings of operations and all possible internal traces that such orderings may generate.

3   The Shelley Language

Shelley's specification language precisely defines the ordering constraints of calls when arranging systems hierarchically. We have a specification per system that is usually defined in a text file with the `.shy` extension. We now describe the abstract syntax of Shelley using EBNF notation.

$$S = \textbf{base } X \; s^\star \; c^\star \; \mid \; X \; (x\colon X)^\star \; o^\star \; c^\star \qquad\qquad s = \textbf{initial? final? } y \to z^\star$$

$$o = s \; \{e\} \qquad e = \textbf{skip} \mid x.y \mid e; e \mid \{e\} + \{e\} \mid \textbf{loop } \{e\} \qquad c = \textbf{claim } \phi$$

$$\phi = a \mid \neg\phi \mid \phi_1 \wedge \phi_2 \mid \mathsf{X}\phi \mid \phi_1 \; \mathsf{U} \; \phi_2$$

A system S can either be a base or a composite system. The former is identified by keyword **base**, has a name X and a zero or more operation signatures s. Meta-variable X ranges over system names, and meta-variables y, z range over operation names distinct from system names. A composite system uses zero or more subsystems, notation $(x : X)$, with each subsystem having a unique internal identifier x and the name of its system's definition X. Finally, a composite system defines zero or more operations o, each holding a signature and an operation body e. A signature s declares an operation y and has, optionally, an initial and a final modifier; we also declare zero or more operations z that can succeed y. An operation body is a regular expression, where **skip** corresponds to ϵ, $x.y$ corresponds to a call, sequencing is represented by $e; e$, union is given by $\{e\} + \{e\}$, and the Kleene-star is denoted by **loop** $\{e\}$.

Shelley accepts correctness claims expressed in terms of a linear temporal logic on finite traces (LTL_f) [18]. A formula of LTL_f, notation ϕ, uses the familiar LTL notation. Let $\mathcal{P}$ be a set of propositional symbols (representing operations/calls) closed under the boolean connectives, where $a \in \mathcal{P}$. Formula $\mathsf{X}\phi$ says that ϕ holds in the next instant. Formula $\phi_1 \; \mathsf{U} \; \phi_2$ states that ϕ_1 holds until ϕ_2 eventually holds. Standard boolean abbreviations are used: true, false, $\vee$ (disjunction), and $\implies$ (implication). Derived formulas include: $\mathsf{F}\phi = true \; \mathsf{U} \; \phi$ stands for ϕ eventually holds; $\mathsf{G}\phi = \neg\mathsf{F}\neg\phi$ stands for ϕ hold at every step of the trace; $\phi_1 \; \mathsf{W} \; \phi_2 = (\phi_1 \; \mathsf{U} \; \phi_2) \vee \mathsf{G}\phi_1$ stands for ϕ_1 has to hold at least until ϕ_2 or ϕ_1 must remain true forever. Although LTL and LTL_f share the same syntax, their semantics differ. The same formula can have different meanings according to its interpretation on finite (LTL_f) or infinite (LTL) traces [17]. The fact that traces can be arbitrarily long but *finite* is a key characteristic of our domain of interest, as we want to verifying what happens at the end of the life cycle of each object, *e.g.*, to permit resource deallocation or protocol termination.

4   The Shelley Framework

We depict the structure of the Shelley framework in Fig. 1. In the following sections, we detail each step of the framework and we formalize external and internal behavior generation and validity. Our main theoretical result is the decidability of the checking procedure.

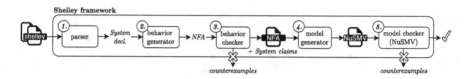

Fig. 1. The structure of the Shelley framework.

Automata Theory Background. We use standard automata theory to formalize our verification process, *e.g.*, as found in [73]. Here we briefly give the relevant background to make the reading self contained. An *NFA* is a tuple $N = (Q, \Sigma, \Delta, q_0, F)$ consisting of a finite set of states Q, a finite set of input symbols Σ called the alphabet, a transition function $\Delta \colon Q \times \Sigma \cup \{\epsilon\} \to \wp(Q)$, where $\wp(Q)$ is the power set of Q, an initial state $q_0 \in Q$, and a set of final states $F \subseteq Q$. A *DFA* is a tuple $D = (Q, \Sigma, \delta, q_0, F)$ consisting of a finite set of states Q, a finite set of input symbols Σ, a transition function $\delta \colon Q \times \Sigma \to Q$, an initial state $q_0 \in Q$, and a set of final states $F \subseteq Q$. A *word* $w = a_1 a_2 \ldots a_n$ over the alphabet Σ is accepted by an NFA N if, and only if, exists a sequence of states $r_0, r_1, \ldots, r_n$ from Q such that $r_0 = q_0$, $r_{i+1} \in \Delta(r_i, a_{i+1})$, for $i = 0, \ldots, n-1$, and $r_n \in F$. *The language of N* is the set of words accepted by N and denoted by $L(N)$. *The language of a DFA* is defined similarly. Let $f \colon \Sigma \to \Gamma^*$ be a function from one alphabet Σ to words over another alphabet Γ. An extension of function f to $\Sigma^* \to \Gamma^*$ such that $f(\epsilon) = \epsilon$ and $f(w\sigma) = f(w)f(\sigma)$, for any $w \in \Sigma^*$ and $\sigma \in \Sigma$ is called an *homomorphism*. We can extend this function to any language F by letting $f(L) = \{f(w) | w \in L\}$. When X is an automaton, we denote δ_X to be the transition function of X, Q_X denotes the states of X, and F_X denotes the final states of X.

4.1   System Declaration

The first step in our framework is to parse the Shelley language into a *system declaration* that is then used throughout the verification process. The following definition makes precise the notion of a system declaration.

Definition 1 (System declaration). *A system declaration is a tuple $S = (O, I, F, B, C, \sigma, \rho)$ where O is a set of operations a system exposes (its interface), $I \subseteq O$ is a set of initial operations, with $I \neq \emptyset$, $F \subseteq O$ is a set of final operations,*

$B \subseteq O \times O$ *is a set of operation transitions (the external system behavior),* $\sigma: \mathcal{U} \to S$ *is a function from system names to systems,* $\rho: O \to D$ *is a function from operations to DFAs over subsystems (the internal system behavior), and* C *is a set of* LTL_f *formulas (correctness claims).*

4.2 Behavior Generation

The second step in our framework concerns system's behavior generation. This section formalizes deriving the external (*vide* Definition 2) and internal (*vide* Definition 4) behaviors.

External System's Behavior. We make precise the notion of the external behavior by means of an NFA. The set of states includes an initial state q_0 and a state per operation. The transition function can be obtained by following the signature section of each operation. It contains a transition from q_0 to each state that corresponds to an initial operation, and a transition from each operation state to the succeeding operation state. An operation state is accepting whenever the corresponding operation is final.

Definition 2 (External behavior). *Let* $S = (O, I, F, B, C, \sigma, \rho)$. *The external behavior of* S, *notation* $L_{sys}(S)$, *is defined as* $L_{sys}(S) = L(N_{sys}(S))$, *where* $N_{sys}(S) = (O \cup \{q_0\}, O, \delta, q_0, F)$, *for some* q_0, *and* δ *is defined below.*

$$\delta(o_1, o_2) = \{o_2\} \text{ if } (o_1, o_2) \in B \qquad \delta(q_0, o) = \{o\} \text{ if } o \in I$$

A given system is considered a *subsystem* if it is integrated by another system. When declaring a subsystem, a unique name is assigned to it and prefixed to every usage of an operation of that subsystem. Definition 3 makes precise the notion of subsystem behavior.

Definition 3 (Subsystem behavior). *Let* $S = (O, I, F, B, C, \sigma, \rho)$. *We say that the instantiation of* S *with* u, *notation* $L_{sub}(S, u)$, *is the regular language given by the homomorphism* f *over* $L_{sys}(S)$ *where* $f(o) = u.o$, *binding the subsystem named* u *to every operation* o *of every word in* $L_{sys}(S)$.

Internal System's Behavior. Intuitively, Shelley derives the internal behavior of a system by replacing each operation-edge in the external behavior by the behavior representing each operation body. Definition 4 makes precise the notion of the internal behavior. Figure 2 is the NFA that results from applying the definition below to the Sector of Listing 2.1. We denote $X \uplus Y = X \cup Y$ where $X \cap Y = \emptyset$. For brevity, let $L_{int}(S) = L(N_{int}(S))$.

Definition 4 (Internal behavior). *Let* $S = (O, I, F, B, C, \sigma, \rho)$ *and let* $M = N_{sys}(S)$. *The internal behavior,* $L_{int}(S)$, *is defined as* $L_{int}(S) = L(N_{int}(S))$, *where* $N_{int}(S) = (Q, \Sigma, \delta, q_0, F)$ *for* $Q = Q_M \biguplus_{o \in O} Q_{\rho(o)}$, $\Sigma = \bigcup_{u \in dom(\sigma)} \Sigma_u$, Σ_u

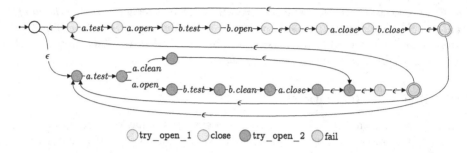

Fig. 2. Internal behavior of Sector given as a state diagram (NFA). Sink states are omitted.

is the alphabet of the DFA that recognizes $L_{sub}(\sigma(u), u)$, and δ is defined below where $q_{0,o}$ denotes the initial state of $\rho(o)$:

$$\delta(q, \epsilon) = \{q_{0,o} \mid o \in \delta_M(q, o)\} \quad \text{if } q \in Q_M$$
$$\delta(q, u.o) = \{\delta_{\rho(o')}(q, u.o)\} \text{ if } q \in Q_{\rho(o')}$$
$$\delta(q, \epsilon) = \{o\} \text{ if } q \in F_{\rho(o)}$$

4.3   Valid Behavior Checking

The third step, which concerns behavior checking, ensures that both the external and internal behaviors are valid. This section formalizes both techniques and details how Shelley reports errors in case of an invalid internal behavior.

External Behavior Validity. Shelley ensures that all operations are reachable from an initial operation in at least one usage of the system.

Definition 5 (Valid external behavior). *An operation o is valid if $o \in t$ and $t \in L_{sys}(S)$ for some trace t. A system's external behavior is valid if all of its operations are valid.*

The algorithm used in Theorem 1 ensures that all operations of a system declaration appear in at least one trace, thus disallowing erroneous cases.

Theorem 1 (Decidability of valid external behavior). *Given a system S we can decide whether S has a valid external behavior.*

Proof. Let $S = (O, I, F, B, C, \sigma, \rho)$ and let $o \in O$. We must show that it is decidable to find a trace t such that $o \in t$ and $t \in L_{sys}(S)$. Step 1: build a regular expression with all traces that contain o, using O as the alphabet. Step 2: intersect the regular language of step 1 with the regular language of $L_{sys}(S)$. Step 3: if the intersection is empty, then $o \in t$ and $t \in L_{sys}(S)$; otherwise o is invalid. The algorithm is decidable because all steps are build from decidable regular language operations.

Internal Behavior Validity. Shelley considers the internal behavior of a system valid when every subsystem being used follows its specification. The following definitions make precise the notions of usage behavior and valid internal behavior.

Definition 6 (Usage behavior). *Let $S = (O, I, F, B, C, \sigma, \rho)$. The projection of S on u, notation $\text{proj}(S, u)$, is the regular language given by the homomorphism f from $N_{\text{int}}(S)$ into $\sigma(u)$ with $f(u.o) = o$ and $f(u'.o) = \epsilon$ when $u \neq u'$.*

Definition 7 (Valid internal behavior). *Let $S = (O, I, F, B, C, \sigma, \rho)$. System S has a valid internal behavior if for all $u \in \text{dom}(\sigma)$, then $L(\text{proj}(S, u)) \subseteq L_{\text{sub}}(S, u)$.*

Theorem 2 (Decidability of valid internal behavior). *Given a system S we can decide whether S has a valid internal behavior.*

Proof. Let $S = (O, I, F, B, C, \sigma, \rho)$ and let $u \in \text{dom}(\sigma)$. We must show that $L(\text{proj}(S, u)) \subseteq L_{\text{sub}}(S, u)$ is decidable. $L(\text{proj}(S, u))$ is a regular language, since it is a homomorphism from a regular language ($N_{\text{int}}(S)$). Likewise, $L_{\text{sub}}(S, u)$ is a regular language, since it is also a homomorphism from a regular language $L_{\text{sys}}(S)$. Set inclusion between regular languages is decidable.

Error Provenance. A crucial feature of any checker is giving meaningful feedback when verification fails. When a system's internal behavior is invalid, our tool: 1) finds a trace of calls that misuse at least one subsystem (*internal trace*); 2) determines which trace of operations caused that trace of calls; 3) identifies the root-cause of the misusage. To obtain (1) (automata-)subtract the subsystem behavior from the usage behavior; Shelley identifies the *smallest* internal trace in the resulting FSM, with a breadth-first search. To obtain (2) annotate the states of the internal behavior with the operation that produced each call. To obtain (3) use the internal trace to navigate the behavior FSM, transitioning from state to state according to the sequence of calls; if after a transition, the algorithm finds itself in a non-accepting state that cannot reach any accepting state, then the call used to transition is the root-cause of the error.

4.4   Model Generation and Claim Checking

Shelley model checks an NFA against an LTL$_f$ formula to verify correctness claims. To this end, we rely on NuSMV [13]. Shelley converts an NFA into a Kripke structure, and converts an LTL$_f$ into an LTL. The NFA may represent either an external behavior or an internal behavior, but such distinction is irrelevant at this stage.

Translating from an LTL$_f$ Claim into an LTL Claim. Our implementation follows [17]. Given an LTL$_f$ formula ϕ, function $\llbracket \cdot \rrbracket$ yields an equivalent (infinite) LTL. The idea is to use a sentinel variable *end* that encodes the end of a finite trace. Let $\mathcal{P}$ represent the set of propositional symbols. Variable *end* must be distinct from all variables mentioned in ϕ, *i.e.*, *end* $\notin \mathcal{P}$. The translation must ensure that: variable *end* eventually holds, $\mathsf{F}\,end$; once *end* is true it remains true, $\mathsf{G}\,end \implies \mathsf{X}\,end$; and, no other variable in $\mathcal{P}$ becomes true after *end* is true, $\mathsf{G}\,(end \implies \bigwedge_{a\in\mathcal{P}} \neg a)$. Finally, we define $[\![\cdot]\!]$ as follows:

$$[\![a]\!] = a \qquad [\![\neg\phi]\!] = \neg[\![\phi]\!] \qquad [\![\phi_1 \wedge \phi_2]\!] = [\![\phi_1]\!] \wedge [\![\phi_2]\!] \qquad [\![\mathsf{X}\,\phi]\!] = \mathsf{X}\,([\![\phi]\!] \wedge \neg end)$$

$$[\![\phi_1 \cup \phi_2]\!] = [\![\phi_1]\!] \cup ([\![\phi_2]\!] \wedge \neg end)$$

Translating from an NFA into a NuSMV Model. We implement the word-acceptance decision procedure of an automata in NuSMV. Let NFA $N = (Q, \Sigma, \Delta, q_0, F)$. Variable `state` ranges over Q and is initialized to q_0; variable `action` ranges over Σ and represents the *next* character of the string being recognized; boolean variable `end` represents the end of the string being recognized. The key insight is to use variables `state` and `end` to represent the *current* state of automata N and variable `action` to represent the next character of the string being recognized. A NuSMV simulation should only proceed until variable `end` becomes true. While `end` $\neq$ *true* update each variable as follows. Update `action` non-deterministically from Σ. Update `state` by applying δ to the current state and the next action, *i.e.*, $\delta(\texttt{state}, \texttt{action})$. Update `end` by checking if the *upcoming* state is final; the intent is to let NuSMV non-deterministically stop if the following state is final, otherwise it should continue (and `end` be set to false). Formally, if $\delta(\texttt{state}, \texttt{action}) \in F$, then set variable `end` to any boolean non-deterministically. Otherwise set variable `end` to false. Our encoding requires a fairness constraint on variable `end`.

5 Evaluation

In Sect. 5.1 we present statistics of the Aquamote® verification, along with correctness claims and counterexamples. We assess the bounds of the validity checks of Shelley in a benchmark (Sect. 5.2), by increasing the number of levels of hierarchy (vertical), and by increasing the number of operations and calls (horizontal). To further exercise the correctness of our implementation we run Shelley against a test suite of 297 specifications, which include 33 negative tests.

Setup. Our experiments run on an 8-core Apple M1 Chip with 16GiB of RAM, and Python 3.10.5. We follow the start-up performance methodology detailed by Georges *et al.* [32], taking 11 samples of the execution time of each benchmark and discarding the first sample. Next, we compute the mean of the 10 samples with a confidence interval of 95%, using the standard normal z-statistic.

5.1 Verifying Aquamote® with Shelley

Our use case is based on the Aquamote®, a wireless controller that switches water valves according to a scheduled irrigation plan. The software consists of 9 classes, which yield 9 Shelley system declarations. Class `App` is the entry point

Table 1. Checking Aquamote® with Shelley.

System	MicroPython		Shelley					NuSMV
	LoC	Annot.	LoC	Claims	Subs.	Oper.	Calls	LoC
App	34	3	6	1	1	2	19	103
Controller	72	12	29	5	3	9	18	237
HTTP	177	12	12	1	0	10	0	–
Power	13	3	3	0	0	2	0	–
Sectors	45	7	14	1	5	4	12	152
Timer	12	2	2	0	0	1	0	–
Valve	17	3	3	0	0	2	0	–
WiFi	71	8	8	1	0	6	0	–
Wireless	84	13	30	4	2	11	21	301
TOTAL	525	63	107	13	11	47	70	793

and it uses an instance of class `Controller`. The latter encapsulates handling the success/error conditions of the communication layer (one instance of `Wireless`), decides when to operate the group of valves (one instance of `Sectors`), and decides when to suspend (one instance of `Power`). Class `Sectors` (an extension from Listing 2.4) integrates four valves (`Valve`) and one timer (`Timer`), encapsulating the behavior where the four valves are open and the four valves are shut, mediated by a timer. Class `Wireless` integrates a Wi-Fi client and an HTTP client, encapsulating both protocols within a single communication interface. The remaining classes are all base classes.

Statistics. Table 1 lists statistics for each system declaration. For instance, class `Wireless` has 90 lines of code, 13 lines are source code annotations to generate the specification, which includes 4 claims, one per line. Our MicroPython extension automatically generates a `Wireless` specification of 30 lines of Shelley code. Shelley then generates the external and internal behaviors from the specification, checks the validity of both behaviors, and, finally, generates a NuSMV model with 301 lines of code that corresponds to the internal specification. For each system we report information about 1) MicroPython source code: lines of code (LoC) and number of Shelley annotations (Annot.); 2) Shelley: lines of code and number of correctness claims (Claims), subsystems (Subs.), system operations (Oper.) and calls (Calls); and 3) NuSMV model: lines of code. The NuSMV model is only generated for systems with claims. We present the verification time in Fig. 3.

Checking Requirements. We illustrate how claims can be used to enforce strict temporal properties that relate more than one subsystem. We discuss an example of a requirement that is checked using a temporal claim taken from the specification of Sectors: after turning a valve on, a timer must be waited upon, and exactly after that, the valve must be turned off. The claim shown below applies this requirement to the four valves:

```
check G ((v1.on -> X (t.wait & (X (v1.off)))) & (v2.on -> X (t.wait & (X (v2.off))))
    & (v3.on -> X (t.wait & (X (v3.off)))) & (v4.on -> X (t.wait & (X (v4.off)))));
```

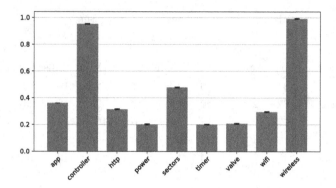

Fig. 3. Mean verification time in seconds for each specification, which includes generating the FSMs for the external and internal behaviors, the validity checks, generating the NuSMV model, and invoking NuSMV. Total verification time for all systems is 3.99 s.

The specification of Timer states that method `wait` can be invoked without restrictions. However, our temporal claim constraints the timer when it is used after a valve is turned on. Calling `t.wait` twice in between valve activation results in the following error message:

```
Error in specification: FAIL TO MEET REQUIREMENT
Formula: G ((v1.on -> X (t.wait & (X (v1.off)))) & (v2.on -> X (t.wait & (X (v2.off))))
   & (v3.on -> X (t.wait & (X (v3.off)))) & (v4.on -> X (t.wait & (X (v4.off)))))
Counter example:  v2.on, t.wait, v2.off, v1.on, >t.wait, t.wait<, v1.off
```

We further note that the temporal claim disallows opening more than one valve at the same time, which is crucial in the Aquamote® use case given that in many cases the water pressure is insufficient.

5.2 Performance Impact of Behavior Checking

In this section, we measure the performance of behavior generation (*cf.* Sect. 4.2) and valid behavior checking (*cf.* Sect. 4.3). In this experiment, the models have no claims, so the claim checking algorithm does not run.

Experiment A. We evaluate the effect of increasing the number of hierarchy levels in terms of time, by ranging from 1 to 12 levels. Level 1 instantiates twelve base systems. Every subsequent level instantiates twelve systems of the level below, *e.g.*, the system in level 5 instantiates twelve systems of level 4.

Discussion. In Fig. 4a, we see that the verification time grows logarithmically. The verification takes ~1.5 s per level and each level grows exponentially in the number of systems. Shelley verifies a total of 12^{12} (~2^{43}) systems (approximately 9 trillion system) under 10 s. Since every system has exactly one operation, this is also equivalent to checking a specification with 9 trillion operations. The benchmarks show that the vertical growth follows a logarithmic increase, which contrasts with the exponential increase of the horizontal growth.

Experiment B. We explore the limits of increasing the number of operations that can be verified under 10 s of time, as shown in Fig. 4c. We define different systems with an increasing number of operations. Figure 4b shows the impact of varying the number of operations between 1 and 81, in increments of 10.

Experiment C. We explore the limits of increasing the number of operations, and, separately, the number of calls, that can be verified under 10 s of time, as shown in Fig. 4c. We define different systems with an increasing number of calls. Every system has exactly one operation and one subsystem. Figure 4c shows the impact of varying the number of calls between 1 and 311, in increments of 10.

Discussion of Experiments B and C. Adding calls has a smaller impact in the verification time than adding operations. For instance, checking 71 operations takes ~4, 5 s while checking the same number of calls takes less than 1 s. These results highlight the importance of encapsulation to achieve compositional verification. For instance, checking a single system that integrates a total of 71 calls takes ~9 s (Fig. 4b), versus verifying a system with 12^2 subsystems that integrates a total of 144 calls takes less than 2 s (Fig. 4a).

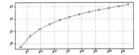 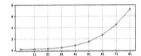 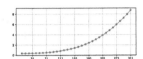

(a) Experiment A: versus total number of subsystems (log-log scale). We increase the number of hierarchy levels in terms of time, by ranging from 1 to 12 levels, where subsequent level instantiates twelve systems of the level below.

(b) Experiment B: versus number of operations (linear scale). We define different systems with an increasing number of operations ranging between 1 and 81, in increments of 10.

(c) Experiment C: versus number of calls per operation (linear scale). We define different systems with an increasing number of calls ranging between 1 and 311, in increments of 10. Every system has exactly one operation and one subsystem.

Fig. 4. Measuring the behavior checking time, in seconds.

6   Related Work

Many model checkers address concurrency problems focusing on process communication and internal state-change, rather than on ordering constraints. This includes well-known tools such as SPIN [40], MCLR2 [35], UPPAAL [52], NuSMV [13], LTSA [55], and TLA+ [49]. Java PathFinder [33] and the Bandera Tool Set [38], for Java, and JKind [27], for Lustre, are examples of model checkers targeting general-purpose programming languages [27,33,38] but again they focus on concurrency rather than ensuring specific requirements about the behavior of a program. Assume-guarantee reasoning [58,68] specifies requirements in terms of an internal state and pre-/post-conditions, and overcomes the problem of state explosion with compositional verification [10,64]. This technique has been used by different modeling tools [1,53,55]. The Gamma Statechart Composition Framework [60] offers a modeling language to compose Statecharts [37,69], which can then be model-checked. Statecharts have been applied in many different contexts, including object-oriented languages [14] and verified using process calculi as well [70]. VeriSolid [59,63] applies formal methods to verify smart contracts specified as transition-systems, and includes a visualization tool.

Typestates [77] refine the concept of type with information about which operations can be used in a particular context. Multiple authors apply typestates to object-oriented programming [2,8,11,16,24,28,29,44,48,61,62,78]. Plaid is a programming language designed from the ground up to explore typestates [2,8,28,78]. The main challenges being tackled include object aliasing, linearity, and access permission. Some authors are applying typestates to general-purpose programming languages [4,11,19,24,44,48,61,81]. Shelley explores a similar notion but from a model checking perspective; moreover typestates are based on state-change, rather than on call ordering constraints.

Type systems allow for the verification of a fix set of properties that are guaranteed by the type discipline itself. Type-and-effect systems [34,47,65,75, 76,79] and permissive interfaces [39] are concerned with checking that a program respects a certain effect discipline. Sequential effect systems [79] reason about the program order.

Session types [15,20,41,42,50,51,82], a form of behavioral type, encode the data flow in a conversation between two or more parties [20,51,82] and focus on reasoning about the data flow in a conversation between two or more parties. Session types have been also explored for object-oriented languages [23,30,71, 72,80]. Similar to Shelley, session types express ordered operations, but it is not possible to compose parties hierarchically and achieve a modular verification.

Behavior protocols [46,54,66,67] have been used to verify software components. They can describe stateful component systems, be automatically checked for behavior validity (known as protocol conformance) [54], and model-checked at different levels [46,66] but lack any form of component hierarchy, as this formalism was envisioned to describe peer-to-peer and client-server architectures.

Finally, the following are programming languages that can be verified for correctness, but lack the notion of hierarchy of events that we explore in this paper. P [22] is a domain-specific programming language to specify a system as a collection of interacting state machines that asynchronously communicate with each other using events. ModP [21] extends P with a notion of compositionality expressed as an actor system. Rebeca [74] follows similar principles and focus on implementations details. JavaBIP [9] is a framework that uses annotations directly on Java code in order to coordinate existing concurrent software components. Synchronous reactive languages [5,6,36] share a focus with Shelley on ordered event systems.

7   Conclusion

In this paper, we introduce Shelley, a domain-specific model checker where the models represent ordered actions and the requirements are LTL_f formulas. We formalize the process of obtaining the internal behavior from a Shelley model, as well as a decision procedure to check its validity with respect to the given ordering constraints, which we prove to be decidable. Further, we present a translation from a model's behavior into an off-the-shelf model checker. We assess our approach on an industrial case study, which includes detailed statistics of our specification, *e.g.*, 107 lines of Shelley generate 793 lines of NuSMV, verified in less than 4 s. Finally, we evaluate the performance of our integration checker on three scenarios and show that Shelley can check 12^{12} subsystems under 10 s, highlighting the importance of our modular verification.

Acknowledgements. This material is based upon work supported by the National Science Foundation under Grant No. 2204986. This work was supported by FCT through PhD scholarship SFRH/BD/131418/2017, and the LASIGE Research Unit, ref. UIDB/00408/2020 and ref. UIDP/00408/2020.

Data Availability Statement. The artifact is available in the Zenodo repository: doi:10.5281/zenodo.7884206

References

1. Abrial, J.R.: Modeling in Event-B: System and Software Engineering, 1st edn. Cambridge University Press, Cambridge (2010)
2. Aldrich, J., Sunshine, J., Saini, D., Sparks, Z.: Typestate-oriented programming. In: OOPSLA, New York, NY, USA, pp. 1015–1022. ACM (2009). https://doi.org/10.1145/1639950.1640073
3. Bauer, A., Leucker, M., Schallhart, C.: Comparing ltl semantics for runtime verification. J. Log. Comput. **20**(3), 651–674 (2010)
4. Beckman, N.E., Kim, D., Aldrich, J.: An empirical study of object protocols in the wild. In: Mezini, M. (ed.) ECOOP 2011. LNCS, vol. 6813, pp. 2–26. Springer, Heidelberg (2011). https://doi.org/10.1007/978-3-642-22655-7_2
5. Benveniste, A., Le Guernic, P., Jacquemot, C.: Synchronous Programming with Events and Relations: the SIGNAL Language and Its Semantics. Sci. Comput. Program. **16**(2), 103–149 (1991). https://doi.org/10.1016/0167-6423(91)90001-E
6. Berry, G., Cosserat, L.: The ESTEREL synchronous programming language and its mathematical semantics. In: Brookes, S.D., Roscoe, A.W., Winskel, G. (eds.) CONCURRENCY 1984. LNCS, vol. 197, pp. 389–448. Springer, Heidelberg (1985). https://doi.org/10.1007/3-540-15670-4_19
7. Beyer, D., Keremoglu, M.E.: CPACHECKER: a tool for configurable software verification. In: Gopalakrishnan, G., Qadeer, S. (eds.) CAV 2011. LNCS, vol. 6806, pp. 184–190. Springer, Heidelberg (2011). https://doi.org/10.1007/978-3-642-22110-1_16
8. Bierhoff, K., Aldrich, J.: Modular typestate checking of aliased objects. In: Gabriel, R.P., Bacon, D.F., Lopes, C.V., Jr., G.L.S. (eds.) OOPSLA. pp. 301–320. ACM (2007). https://doi.org/10.1145/1297027.1297050

9. Bliudze, S., Mavridou, A., Szymanek, R., Zolotukhina, A.: Exogenous coordination of concurrent software components with Javabip. Softw. Pract. Exp. **47**(11), 1801–1836 (2017). https://doi.org/10.1002/spe.2495

10. Bourbouh, H., et al.: Integrating formal verification and assurance: an inspection rover case study. In: Dutle, A., Moscato, M.M., Titolo, L., Muñoz, C.A., Perez, I. (eds.) NFM 2021. LNCS, vol. 12673, pp. 53–71. Springer, Cham (2021). https://doi.org/10.1007/978-3-030-76384-8_4

11. Bravetti, M., et al.: Behavioural types for memory and method safety in a core object-oriented language. In: Oliveira, B.C.S. (ed.) APLAS 2020. LNCS, vol. 12470, pp. 105–124. Springer, Cham (2020). https://doi.org/10.1007/978-3-030-64437-6_6

12. Bunte, O., et al.: The mCRL2 toolset for analysing concurrent systems. In: Vojnar, T., Zhang, L. (eds.) TACAS 2019. LNCS, vol. 11428, pp. 21–39. Springer, Cham (2019). https://doi.org/10.1007/978-3-030-17465-1_2

13. Cimatti, A., et al.: NuSMV 2: an OpenSource tool for symbolic model checking. In: Brinksma, E., Larsen, K.G. (eds.) CAV 2002. LNCS, vol. 2404, pp. 359–364. Springer, Heidelberg (2002). https://doi.org/10.1007/3-540-45657-0_29

14. Coleman, D., Hayes, F., Bear, S.: Introducing Objectcharts or How to Use Statecharts in Object-Oriented Design. IEEE Trans. Software Eng. **18**(1), 9–18 (1992). https://doi.org/10.1109/32.120312

15. Coppo, M., Dezani-Ciancaglini, M., Padovani, L., Yoshida, N.: A gentle introduction to multiparty asynchronous session types. In: Bernardo, M., Johnsen, E.B. (eds.) SFM 2015. LNCS, vol. 9104, pp. 146–178. Springer, Cham (2015). https://doi.org/10.1007/978-3-319-18941-3_4

16. Dai, Z., Mao, X., Lei, Y., Qi, Y., Wang, R., Gu, B.: Compositional mining of multiple object API protocols through state abstraction. Sci. World J. (2013). https://doi.org/10.1155/2013/171647

17. De Giacomo, G., De Masellis, R., Montali, M.: Reasoning on LTL on finite traces: insensitivity to infiniteness. In: AAAI, pp. 1027–1033. AAAI Press (2014)

18. De Giacomo, G., Vardi, M.Y.: Linear temporal logic and linear dynamic logic on finite traces. In: IJCAI, pp. 854–860. AAAI Press (2013)

19. DeLIne, R., Fahndrich, M.: The fugue protocol checker: Is your software baroque? Tech. report MSR-TR-2004-07, January 2004. https://www.microsoft.com/en-us/research/publication/the-fugue-protocol-checker-is-your-software-baroque/

20. Deniélou, P.-M., Yoshida, N.: Multiparty session types meet communicating automata. In: Seidl, H. (ed.) ESOP 2012. LNCS, vol. 7211, pp. 194–213. Springer, Heidelberg (2012). https://doi.org/10.1007/978-3-642-28869-2_10

21. Desai, A., Phanishayee, A., Qadeer, S., Seshia, S.A.: Compositional programming and testing of dynamic distributed systems. Proc. ACM Program. Lang. **2**(OOPSLA) (2018). https://doi.org/10.1145/3276529

22. Desai, A., et al.: P: Safe Asynchronous Event-driven Programming. In: PLDI, pp. 321–332. ACM (2013)

23. Dezani-Ciancaglini, M., Mostrous, D., Yoshida, N., Drossopoulou, S.: Session types for object-oriented languages. In: Thomas, D. (ed.) ECOOP 2006. LNCS, vol. 4067, pp. 328–352. Springer, Heidelberg (2006). https://doi.org/10.1007/11785477_20

24. Duarte, J., Ravara, A.: Retrofitting typestates into rust. In: Vasconcellos, C.D., Roggia, K.G., Bousfield, P., Collereii, V., Fernandes, J.P., Pereira, M. (eds.) SBLP, pp. 83–91. ACM (2021). https://doi.org/10.1145/3475061.3475082

25. Dutle, A., et al.: From requirements to autonomous flight: an overview of the monitoring ICAROUS project. In: Luckcuck, M., Farrell, M. (eds.) FMAS. EPTCS, vol. 329, pp. 23–30 (2020). https://doi.org/10.4204/EPTCS.329.3

26. de Ferro, C.M., Cogumbreiro, T., Martins, F.: Shelley: a framework for model checking call ordering on hierarchical systems, May 2023. https://doi.org/10.5281/zenodo.7884206
27. Gacek, A., Backes, J., Whalen, M., Wagner, L., Ghassabani, E.: The JKIND model checker. In: Chockler, H., Weissenbacher, G. (eds.) CAV 2018. LNCS, vol. 10982, pp. 20–27. Springer, Cham (2018). https://doi.org/10.1007/978-3-319-96142-2_3
28. Garcia, R., Tanter, E., Wolff, R., Aldrich, J.: Foundations of typestate-oriented programming. ACM Trans. Program. Lang. Syst. 36(4) (2014). https://doi.org/10.1145/2629609
29. Gay, S.J., Gesbert, N., Ravara, A., Vasconcelos, V.T.: Modular session types for objects. Log. Methods Comput. Sci. 11(4) (2015). https://doi.org/10.2168/LMCS-11(4:12)2015
30. Gay, S.J., Vasconcelos, V.T., Ravara, A., Gesbert, N., Caldeira, A.Z.: Modular session types for distributed object-oriented programming. In: Hermenegildo, M.V., Palsberg, J. (eds.) POPL, pp. 299–312. ACM (2010). https://doi.org/10.1145/1706299.1706335
31. George, D.: MicroPython (2022). https://micropython.org
32. Georges, A., Buytaert, D., Eeckhout, L.: Statistically rigorous java performance evaluation. In: OOPSLA, pp. 57–76. ACM (2007)
33. Giannakopoulou, D., Păsăreanu, C.S.: Interface generation and compositional verification in JavaPathfinder. In: Chechik, M., Wirsing, M. (eds.) FASE 2009. LNCS, vol. 5503, pp. 94–108. Springer, Heidelberg (2009). https://doi.org/10.1007/978-3-642-00593-0_7
34. Gordon, C.S.: Polymorphic iterable sequential effect systems. ACM Trans. Program. Lang. Syst. 43(1) (2021). https://doi.org/10.1145/3450272
35. Groote, J.F., Keiren, J.J.A., Luttik, B., de Vink, E.P., Willemse, T.A.C.: Modelling and analysing software in mCRL2. In: Arbab, F., Jongmans, S.-S. (eds.) FACS 2019. LNCS, vol. 12018, pp. 25–48. Springer, Cham (2020). https://doi.org/10.1007/978-3-030-40914-2_2
36. Halbwachs, N., Caspi, P., Raymond, P., Pilaud, D.: The synchronous data flow programming language LUSTRE. Proc. IEEE 79(9), 1305–1320 (1991)
37. Harel, D.: Statecharts: a visual formalism for complex systems. Sci. Comput. Program. 8(3), 231–274 (1987). https://doi.org/10.1016/0167-6423(87)90035-9
38. Hatcliff, J., Dwyer, M.: Using the Bandera tool set to model-check properties of concurrent Java software. In: Larsen, K.G., Nielsen, M. (eds.) CONCUR 2001. LNCS, vol. 2154, pp. 39–58. Springer, Heidelberg (2001). https://doi.org/10.1007/3-540-44685-0_5
39. Henzinger, T.A., Jhala, R., Majumdar, R.: Permissive interfaces. In: ESEC/FSE. p. 31–40. ACM (2005). https://doi.org/10.1145/1081706.1081713
40. Holzmann, G.J.: The model checker SPIN. IEEE Trans. Softw. Eng. 23(5), 279–295 (1997). https://doi.org/10.1109/32.588521
41. Honda, K., Vasconcelos, V.T., Kubo, M.: Language primitives and type discipline for structured communication-based programming. In: Hankin, C. (ed.) ESOP 1998. LNCS, vol. 1381, pp. 122–138. Springer, Heidelberg (1998). https://doi.org/10.1007/BFb0053567
42. Honda, K., Yoshida, N., Carbone, M.: Multiparty asynchronous session types. J. ACM 63(1), 9:1-9:67 (2016). https://doi.org/10.1145/2827695
43. Jacklin, S.A.: Survey of verification and validation techniques for small satellite software development. Technical report (2015)

44. Jakobsen, M., Ravier, A., Dardha, O.: Papaya: global typestate analysis of aliased objects. In: Veltri, N., Benton, N., Ghilezan, S. (eds.) PPDP, pp. 19:1–19:13. ACM (2021). https://doi.org/10.1145/3479394.3479414

45. Katis, A., Mavridou, A., Giannakopoulou, D., Pressburger, T., Schumann, J.: Capture, analyze, diagnose: Realizability checking of requirements in FRET. In: Shoham, S., Vizel, Y. (eds.) CAV. LNCS, vol. 13372, pp. 490–504. Springer (2022). https://doi.org/10.1007/978-3-031-13188-2_24

46. Kofron, J.: Checking software component behavior using behavior protocols and spin. In: Proceedings of SAC, pp. 1513–1517. ACM (2007). https://doi.org/10.1145/1244002.1244326

47. Koskinen, E., Terauchi, T.: Local temporal reasoning. In: CSL-LICS. ACM (2014). https://doi.org/10.1145/2603088.2603138

48. Kouzapas, D., Dardha, O., Perera, R., Gay, S.J.: Typechecking protocols with mungo and stmungo: a session type toolchain for java. Sci. Comput. Program. **155**, 52–75 (2018). https://doi.org/10.1016/j.scico.2017.10.006

49. Lamport, L.: Who builds a house without drawing blueprints? Commun. ACM **58**(4), 38–41 (2015). https://doi.org/10.1145/2736348

50. Lange, J., Tuosto, E., Yoshida, N.: From communicating machines to graphical choreographies. In: POPL, pp. 221–232. ACM (2015). https://doi.org/10.1145/2676726.2676964

51. Lange, J., Yoshida, N.: Verifying asynchronous interactions via communicating session automata. In: Dillig, I., Tasiran, S. (eds.) CAV 2019. LNCS, vol. 11561, pp. 97–117. Springer, Cham (2019). https://doi.org/10.1007/978-3-030-25540-4_6

52. Larsen, K.G., Pettersson, P., Yi, W.: UPPAAL in a nutshell. Int. J. Softw. Tools Technol. Transf. **1**(1–2), 134–152 (1997). https://doi.org/10.1007/s100090050010

53. Liu, J., Backes, J.D., Cofer, D., Gacek, A.: From design contracts to component requirements verification. In: Rayadurgam, S., Tkachuk, O. (eds.) NFM 2016. LNCS, vol. 9690, pp. 373–387. Springer, Cham (2016). https://doi.org/10.1007/978-3-319-40648-0_28

54. Mach, M., Plásil, F., Kofron, J.: Behavior protocol verification: fighting state explosion. Int. J. Comput. Inf. Sci. **6**(1), 22–30 (2005)

55. Magee, J., Kramer, J.: Concurrency: State Models and Java Programs. Wiley, 2 edn. (2006)

56. Mavridou, A., Bourbouh, H., Garoche, P., Giannakopoulou, D., Pressburger, T., Schumann, J.: Bridging the gap between requirements and simulink model analysis. In: Sabetzadeh, M., et al. (eds.) REFSQ. CEUR Workshop Proceedings, vol. 2584. CEUR-WS.org (2020)

57. Mavridou, A., et al.: The ten lockheed martin cyber-physical challenges: formalized, analyzed, and explained. In: Breaux, T.D., Zisman, A., Fricker, S., Glinz, M. (eds.) RE, pp. 300–310. IEEE (2020). https://doi.org/10.1109/RE48521.2020.00040

58. Mavridou, A., Katis, A., Giannakopoulou, D., Kooi, D., Pressburger, T., Whalen, M.W.: From partial to global assume-guarantee contracts: compositional realizability analysis in FRET. In: Huisman, M., Păsăreanu, C., Zhan, N. (eds.) FM 2021. LNCS, vol. 13047, pp. 503–523. Springer, Cham (2021). https://doi.org/10.1007/978-3-030-90870-6_27

59. Mavridou, A., Laszka, A., Stachtiari, E., Dubey, A.: Verisolid: Correct-by-design smart contracts for ethereum. CoRR abs/1901.01292 (2019). http://arxiv.org/abs/1901.01292

60. Molnár, V., Graics, B., Vörös, A., Majzik, I., Varró, D.: The Gamma statechart composition framework: design, verification and code generation for component-based reactive systems. In: ICSE, pp. 113–116. ACM (2018). https://doi.org/10.1145/3183440.3183489

61. Mota, J., Giunti, M., Ravara, A.: Java Typestate checker. In: Damiani, F., Dardha, O. (eds.) COORDINATION 2021. LNCS, vol. 12717, pp. 121–133. Springer, Cham (2021). https://doi.org/10.1007/978-3-030-78142-2_8

62. Naeem, N.A., Lhoták, O.: Typestate-like analysis of multiple interacting objects. In: Harris, G.E. (ed.) OOPSLA, pp. 347–366. ACM (2008). https://doi.org/10.1145/1449764.1449792

63. Nelaturu, K., Mavridou, A., Veneris, A.G., Laszka, A.: Verified development and deployment of multiple interacting smart contracts with VeriSolid. In: ICBC, pp. 1–9. IEEE (2020). https://doi.org/10.1109/ICBC48266.2020.9169428

64. Nguyen, T.K., Sun, J., Liu, Y., Dong, J.S.: A model checking framework for hierarchical systems. In: ASE, pp. 633–636. IEEE (2011). https://doi.org/10.1109/ASE.2011.6100143

65. Nielson, F., Nielson, H.R.: Type and effect systems. In: Olderog, E.-R., Steffen, B. (eds.) Correct System Design. LNCS, vol. 1710, pp. 114–136. Springer, Heidelberg (1999). https://doi.org/10.1007/3-540-48092-7_6

66. Parízek, P., Plasil, F., Kofron, J.: Model checking of software components: combining java pathfinder and behavior protocol model checker. In: Proceedings of SEW, pp. 133–141. IEEE (2006). https://doi.org/10.1109/SEW.2006.23

67. Plasil, F., Visnovsky, S.: Behavior protocols for software components. IEEE Trans. Software Eng. **28**(11), 1056–1076 (2002). https://doi.org/10.1109/TSE.2002.1049404

68. Pnueli, A.: In Transition From Global to Modular Temporal Reasoning about Programs. In: Apt, K.R. (ed.) LMCS. NATO ASI Series, vol. 13, pp. 123–144. Springer, Heidelberg (1984). https://doi.org/10.1007/978-3-642-82453-1_5

69. Pnueli, A., Shalev, M.: What is in a step: on the semantics of statecharts. In: Ito, T., Meyer, A.R. (eds.) TACS 1991. LNCS, vol. 526, pp. 244–264. Springer, Heidelberg (1991). https://doi.org/10.1007/3-540-54415-1_49

70. Roscoe, A.W., Wu, Z.: Verifying statemate statecharts using CSP and FDR. In: Liu, Z., He, J. (eds.) ICFEM 2006. LNCS, vol. 4260, pp. 324–341. Springer, Heidelberg (2006). https://doi.org/10.1007/11901433_18

71. Scalas, A., Dardha, O., Hu, R., Yoshida, N.: A linear decomposition of multiparty sessions for safe distributed programming. In: Müller, P. (ed.) ECOOP. LIPIcs, vol. 74, pp. 24:1–24:31. Schloss Dagstuhl - Leibniz-Zentrum für Informatik (2017). https://doi.org/10.4230/LIPIcs.ECOOP.2017.24

72. Scalas, A., Yoshida, N.: Lightweight session programming in scala. In: Krishnamurthi, S., Lerner, B.S. (eds.) ECOOP. LIPIcs, vol. 56, pp. 21:1–21:28. Schloss Dagstuhl - Leibniz-Zentrum für Informatik (2016). https://doi.org/10.4230/LIPIcs.ECOOP.2016.21

73. Sipser, M.: Introduction to the Theory of Computation, 1st edn.. International Thomson Publishing (1996)

74. Sirjani, M., Jaghoori, M.M.: Ten years of analyzing actors: Rebeca experience. In: Agha, G., Danvy, O., Meseguer, J. (eds.) Formal Modeling: Actors, Open Systems, Biological Systems. LNCS, vol. 7000, pp. 20–56. Springer, Heidelberg (2011). https://doi.org/10.1007/978-3-642-24933-4_3

75. Skalka, C.: Trace effects and object orientation. In: PPDP, pp. 139–150. ACM (2005). https://doi.org/10.1145/1069774.1069787

76. Skalka, C., Smith, S., Van Horn, D.: Types and trace effects of higher order programs. J. Funct. Program. **18**(2), 179–249 (2008). https://doi.org/10.1017/S0956796807006466
77. Strom, R.E., Yemini, S.: Typestate: a programming language concept for enhancing software reliability. IEEE Trans. Softw. Eng. **12**(1), 157–171 (1986). https://doi.org/10.1109/TSE.1986.6312929
78. Sunshine, J., Naden, K., Stork, S., Aldrich, J., Tanter, É.: First-class state change in plaid. In: Lopes, C.V., Fisher, K. (eds.) OOPSLA, pp. 713–732. ACM (2011). https://doi.org/10.1145/2048066.2048122
79. Tate, R.: The sequential semantics of producer effect systems. In: POPL, pp. 15–26. ACM (2013). https://doi.org/10.1145/2429069.2429074
80. Vasconcelos, V.T.: Sessions, from types to programming languages. Bull. EATCS **103**, 53–73 (2011)
81. Voinea, A.L., Dardha, O., Gay, S.J.: Typechecking Java protocols with [ST]Mungo. In: Gotsman, A., Sokolova, A. (eds.) FORTE 2020. LNCS, vol. 12136, pp. 208–224. Springer, Cham (2020). https://doi.org/10.1007/978-3-030-50086-3_12
82. Zeng, H., Kurz, A., Tuosto, E.: Interface automata for choreographies. Electron. Proc. Theor. Comput. Sci. **304**, 1–19 (2019). https://doi.org/10.4204/eptcs.304.1

STARK: A Software Tool for the Analysis of Robustness in the unKnown Environment

Valentina Castiglioni[1]([envelope]) [ID], Michele Loreti[2] [ID], and Simone Tini[3] [ID]

[1] Reykjavik University, Reykjavik, Iceland
vale.castiglioni@gmail.com
[2] University of Camerino, Camerino, Italy
[3] University of Insubria, Como, Italy

Abstract. Cyber-Physical Systems (CPSs) are characterised by the interaction of various agents operating under highly changing and, sometimes, unpredictable environmental conditions. It is therefore fundamental to verify whether these systems are *robust against perturbations*, i.e., whether systems are able to function correctly even in perturbed circumstances. In this paper we present the *Software Tool for the Analysis of Robustness in the unKnown environment* (STARK), our Java tool for the specification, analysis and testing of robustness properties of CPSs. STARK includes: (i) a specification language for systems behaviour, perturbations, distances on systems behaviours, and properties of those distances; (ii) a module for the simulation of system behaviours and their perturbed versions; (iii) a module for the evaluation of distances between behaviours; (iv) a statistical model checker for formulae in the *Robustness Temporal Logic* (*RobTL*), a temporal logic for the specification and verification of properties on the evolution of *distances* between the behaviours of CPSs, and thus also of robustness properties.

1 Introduction

Cyber-Physical Systems (CPSs) are characterised by the interaction of various agents operating under highly changing and, sometimes, unpredictable environmental conditions. For instance, the dynamic physical environmental processes can only be approximated in order to become computationally tractable; some agents may appear, disappear, or become temporarily unavailable, thus causing faults or conflicts; sensors may introduce measurement errors; etc. This means that the behaviour of the agents in a CPS is subject to uncertainty and perturbations. On top of that, there is a class of security threats which is unique to CPSs, namely cyber-physical attacks: for instance, an attacker can induce a series of perturbations in the sensed data in order to entail unexpected, hazardous, behaviour of the system.

It is therefore fundamental to verify whether a CPS is *robust against perturbations*, i.e., whether the system is able to function correctly even in the presence of perturbations. Although there is lack of agreement on the "correct" mathematical formalisation of robustness (see, e.g., [9,21,23,24]), this notion is usually presented as a *measure* of the capability of a system to tolerate perturbations in the environmental conditions and still fulfil its tasks. In other words, robustness can be specified, in general, as a temporal property of distances between the nominal and the perturbed behaviours of a system. To this purpose, we have recently proposed the *Robustness Temporal Logic* (*RobTL*) [4]

© IFIP International Federation for Information Processing 2023
S.-S. Jongmans and A. Lopes (Eds.): COORDINATION 2023, LNCS 13908, pp. 115–132, 2023.
https://doi.org/10.1007/978-3-031-35361-1_6

to capture robustness properties: RobTL is the first temporal logic for the specification and analysis of *distances* between the behaviours of CPSs over a finite time horizon.

In this paper we pursue our quest for a formal framework allowing us to specify and analyse distances between behaviours of systems operating in the presence of uncertainties, by presenting the *Software Tool for the Analysis of Robustness in the unKnown environment* (STARK), available at https://github.com/quasylab/jspear[1]. STARK is a Java tool for the specification, analysis and testing of robustness properties of CPSs that is based on the *evolution sequence* model from [3] for the representation of systems behaviour, and on RobTL for the specification of distances, perturbations, and properties. Briefly, evolution sequences are countable sequences of probability measures over a set of application-relevant data, each representing the interaction of the agents with the environment at a given time step. Then, atomic propositions in RobTL are defined by means of two simple languages: one to specify the effect of *perturbations* over an evolution sequence, and one to specify *distance expressions* between an evolution sequence and its perturbed version.

Specifically, STARK consists of a front-end and a Java library, and includes:

- A specification language for the system (agents, environment, and their interaction), for perturbations, for distance expressions, and for RobTL formulae;
- A module for the simulation of systems behaviours and their perturbed versions;
- A module for the evaluation of distances between behaviours;
- A statistical model checker for RobTL formulae.

We remark that since the simulation of system behaviours and the evaluation of distances are based on statistical inference, the evaluation of RobTL formulae is based on a three-valued semantics that takes possible statistical errors into account.

To showcase the various features of the tool, we apply it to a case-study in the analysis of CPSs proposed in [18]: we consider two unmanned ground vehicles that are moving along a straight path, in line, and have to autonomously set their acceleration in order to avoid collision with a static obstacle. Moreover, the second vehicle needs also to avoid collisions with the first one. We model both cyber-physical attacks and equipment malfunctioning in terms of perturbations in sensed data, and we study the robustness of the vehicles against the attacks and malfunctioning.

2   The Model

We consider systems consisting of a set of *agents* and an *environment*, whose interaction produces changes on a shared *data space* $\mathcal{D}$, containing the values assumed by *variables*, representing: (i) physical quantities, (ii) sensors, (iii) actuators, and (iv) internal variables of the agents. We call *system configuration* the triple consisting of the set of internal states of the agents, the set of functions constituting the environment, and the current state of the data space, called *data state* and represented by a mapping d from variables to values. At each step, the agents and the environment induce some changes on the data state providing thus a new data state at the next step. Those modifications are also subject to

---

[1] The tool has been also published on *Software Heritage* with ID swh:1:dir:98532d8c770f9d115 c692e932869c446417d8b34.

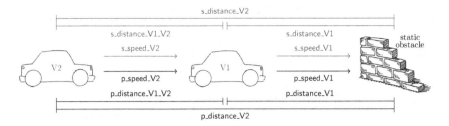

Fig. 1. The two agents and their variables: in black we report the main physical (real) data, in blue the sensed data by V1, and in red those by V2. See Table 1 for the complete list of variables.

the presence of uncertainties, meaning that it is not always possible to determine exactly the values assumed by data at the next step. Hence, following [3], we model the changes induced at each step as a probability measure on the attainable data states. The behaviour of the system is then entirely expressed by its *evolution sequence*, i.e., the sequence of probability measures over the data states obtained at each step. In other words, the evolution sequence is the discrete-time version of the cylinder of *all possible trajectories* of the system. In this paper we do not focus on how evolution sequences are generated: we simply assume a Markov kernel governing the evolution of the system, and the evolution sequence is the *Markov process* generated by it. We refer the interested reader to [3] for the details on the specification of the agents and the environment, and on the semantic mapping allowing for deriving the Markov kernel at hand.

Definition 1 (Evolution sequence, [3]). *Given a data space $\mathcal{D}$, let $\mathcal{B}_{\mathcal{D}}$ denote the Borel σ-algebra over $\mathcal{D}$, and let $\Pi(\mathcal{D}, \mathcal{B}_{\mathcal{D}})$ be the set of probability measures (henceforth simply called* distributions*) over the space $(\mathcal{D}, \mathcal{B}_{\mathcal{D}})$.*

Assume a Markov kernel step: $\mathcal{D} \to \Pi(\mathcal{D}, \mathcal{B}_{\mathcal{D}})$ *generating the behaviour of a system* s *having μ as initial distribution. Then, the* evolution sequence *of* s *is a countable sequence $\mathcal{S}_{\mu} = \mathcal{S}_{\mu}^0, \mathcal{S}_{\mu}^1, \dots$ of distributions in $\Pi(\mathcal{D}, \mathcal{B}_{\mathcal{D}})$ such that, for all $\mathbb{D} \in \mathcal{B}_{\mathcal{D}}$:*

$$\mathcal{S}_{\mu}^0(\mathbb{D}) = \mu(\mathbb{D}) \qquad \mathcal{S}_{\mu}^{i+1}(\mathbb{D}) = \int_{\mathcal{D}} \text{step}(\mathbf{d})(\mathbb{D}) \, \eth \, \mathcal{S}_{\mu}^i(\mathbf{d}).$$

2.1 Case Study: Unmanned Ground Vehicles

We present the case study that will allow us to showcase the features of our tool. We consider two unmanned ground vehicles, agents V1 and V2, that have to autonomously set their acceleration in order to avoid collisions with a static obstacle and with each other. This example was originally proposed, with a single vehicle, in [18]. We remark that our aim is not to specify a complex real-world scenario, but rather to illustrate an application of the tool. Hence, we model the system in a simplified setting: we consider the agents and the obstacle as one-dimensional objects (as done in, e.g., [6,27]), we assume that the two agents are identical, that they can move only along one direction, proceeding in line, and we consider simple versions of their control units.

Figure 1 illustrates our setting for the system: Vx is at p_distance_Vx m from the obstacle and moves towards it at a speed of p_speed_Vx m/s. Then, the distance between

Table 1. The variables, $x \in \{1, 2\}$.

Name	Domain	Role
p_speed_Vx	[0, MAX_SPEED]	physical speed of Vx (m/s)
s_speed_Vx	[0, MAX_SPEED]	sensor detecting the value of p_speed_Vx
p_distance_Vx	[0, INIT_DISTANCE_Vx]	distance of Vx from the obstacle (m)
s_distance_Vx	[0, INIT_DISTANCE_Vx]	sensor detecting the value of p_distance_Vx
accel_Vx	$\{A, N, -B\}$	actuator for acceleration (m/s^2), with $A, B > 0, N = 0$
timer_Vx	[0, TIMER]	countdown for checks by the controller of Vx
braking_dist_Vx	[0, INIT_DISTANCE_Vx]	space required by Vx to stop if accel_Vx $= -B$
required_dist_Vx	[0, INIT_DISTANCE_Vx]	braking_dist_Vx plus SAFETY_DISTANCE
safety_gap_Vx	[0, INIT_DISTANCE_Vx]	p_distance_Vx - required_dist_Vx
brake_light_Vx	$\{0, 1\}$	actuator for brake lights of Vx ($1 =$ ON)
p_distance_V1_V2	[0, INIT_DISTANCE_V1_V2]	distance of V2 from V1 (m)
s_distance_V1_V2	[0, INIT_DISTANCE_V1_V2]	sensor detecting the value of p_distance_V1_V2
safety_gap_V1_V2	[0, INIT_DISTANCE_V1_V2]	p_distance_V1_V2 - required_dist_V2
crashed_Vx	$\{0, 1\}$	gets 1 if a collision occurred
warning_Vx	$\{0, 1\}$	message from IDS_Vx ($1 =$ DANGER)

the two vehicles is p_distance_V1_V2 m. These values are detected by the controllers of V1 and V2 through sensors s_distance_Vx, s_speed_Vx, and s_distance_V1_V2, respectively. For simplicity, we assume that the values detected by sensors coincide with the physical ones, i.e., that there are no measurements errors. We will introduce noise and tampering on sensors later on, by means of *perturbations*. The vehicles can either accelerate or brake. In the former case, a vehicle has a positive acceleration, A m/s^2. In the latter case, the vehicle has a negative acceleration, whose absolute value corresponds to B m/s^2. When Vx brakes, the brake lights are switched on, as expressed by actuator brake_light_Vx. The controller of Vx, for $x \in \{1, 2\}$, checks regularly whether Vx can safely accelerate or if it has to brake, and sets the acceleration actuator accel_Vx accordingly. The decision is taken by the controller on the basis of both the speed of Vx and its distance from the obstacle, or (for V2) from the preceding vehicle. V2 brakes also when the lights of V1 are on. The decision between accelerating or braking is taken by the controller every TIMER seconds: variable timer_Vx is initially set to TIMER and the controller is woken up whenever it reaches zero. The speed can never be negative, and when the speed becomes zero then the actuator accel_Vx is set to N = 0.

The variables are listed in Table 1. Besides the variables associated to physical quantities, actuators and sensors described above, we use: (i) braking_dist_Vx for the space required to stop Vx if it starts to brake immediately; (ii) required_dist_Vx for braking_dist_Vx incremented by constant SAFETY_DISTANCE; (iii) safety_gap_Vx for the difference between p_distance_Vx and required_dist_Vx, and safety_gap_V1_V2 for that between p_distance_V1_V2 and required_dist_V2: if a safety gap is negative, the vehicles are at risk of a collision; (iv) crashed_Vx to signal if Vx collided either against the obstacle or the other vehicle.

Each controller is paired with an intrusion detection system IDS_Vx, whose task is to detect odd or hazardous behaviours. In case of anomalies, IDS_Vx uses variable warning_Vx to raise a warning message and induce the controller to react. Specifically, IDS_Vx checks whether the physical distances are large enough to guarantee a safe behaviour, expressed as p_distance_V1 > 2 · TIMER · SAFETY_DISTANCE and p_distance_V1_V2 > 2 · TIMER · SAFETY_DISTANCE; if this is not the case and Vx has a positive acceleration, the warning is raised, and Vx is required to decelerate.

3   The Robustness Temporal Logic

The *Robustness Temporal Logic* (*RobTL*) has been introduced in [4] as the first logic allowing one to express temporal properties of distances over systems behaviours. It is the core of our tool for the specification and analysis of robustness properties of CPSs against uncertainties and perturbations. This is made possible by using atomic propositions of the form $\Delta(\mathtt{exp}, \mathtt{p}) \bowtie \eta$ to evaluate the distance specified by an expression exp at a given time step between a given evolution sequence and its perturbed version, obtained by some perturbation p, and to compare it with the threshold η. Then, we combine atomic propositions with classic Boolean and temporal operators, in order to extend these evaluations to the entire evolution sequences.

Hence, there are three main components constituting RobTL formulae: 1. A language Exp to specify *distance expressions*; 2. A language P to specify *perturbations*; 3. Classic Boolean and temporal operators to specify requirements on the *evolution of distances in time*. In this section we give only a bird's-eye view on these components. We refer the interested reader to [4] for a detailed presentation of RobTL.

Distance Expressions. We use expressions in Exp to define distances over evolution sequences. The idea is to introduce a *distance over distributions on data states* measuring their differences with respect to a *given target*, and then use the operators of the logic to extend it to the evolution sequences, while possibly taking into account *different objectives and perturbations over time*. Following [3], to capture a particular task, we use a *penalty function* $\rho\colon \mathcal{D} \to [0,1]$, i.e., a function that assigns to each data state **d** a penalty in $[0,1]$ expressing how far the values of the parameters related to the considered task in **d** are from their desired ones. Then we use ρ to obtain a *distance on data states*, i.e., the 1-bounded *hemimetric* m_ρ defined for all $\mathbf{d}_1, \mathbf{d}_2 \in \mathcal{D}$ by:

$$m_\rho(\mathbf{d}_1, \mathbf{d}_2) = \max\{\rho(\mathbf{d}_2) - \rho(\mathbf{d}_1), 0\}.$$

Note that $m_\rho(\mathbf{d}_1, \mathbf{d}_2)$ expresses how much $\mathbf{d}_2$ is *worse* than $\mathbf{d}_1$ according to ρ. Then, we need to lift the hemimetric m_ρ to a hemimetric over $\Pi(\mathcal{D}, \mathcal{B}_\mathcal{D})$. To this end, we make use of the *Wasserstein lifting* [25]: for any two distributions μ, ν on $(\mathcal{D}, \mathcal{B}_\mathcal{D})$, the Wasserstein lifting of m_ρ to a distance between μ and ν is defined by

$$\mathbf{W}(m_\rho)(\mu, \nu) = \inf_{\mathfrak{w} \in \mathfrak{W}(\mu, \nu)} \int_{\mathcal{D} \times \mathcal{D}} m_\rho(\mathbf{d}, \mathbf{d}') \, \eth \, \mathfrak{w}(\mathbf{d}, \mathbf{d}')$$

where $\mathfrak{W}(\mu, \nu)$ is the set of the couplings of μ and ν, namely the set of joint distributions $\mathfrak{w}$ over the product space $(\mathcal{D} \times \mathcal{D}, \mathcal{B}(\mathcal{D} \times \mathcal{D}))$ having μ and ν as left and right marginal, respectively, i.e., $\mathfrak{w}(\mathbb{D} \times \mathcal{D}) = \mu(\mathbb{D})$ and $\mathfrak{w}(\mathcal{D} \times \mathbb{D}) = \nu(\mathbb{D})$, for all $\mathbb{D} \in \mathcal{B}(\mathcal{D})$.

Definition 2 (Distance expressions). *Expressions in* Exp *are defined as follows:*

$$\text{exp} ::= \ <^\rho \ | \ >^\rho \ | \ \text{F}^I \, \text{exp} \ | \ \text{G}^I \, \text{exp} \ | \ \text{exp} \, \text{U}^I \, \text{exp} \ |$$

$$\text{min}(\text{exp}, \text{exp}) \ | \ \text{max}(\text{exp}, \text{exp}) \ | \ \sum_{k \in K} w_k \cdot \text{exp}_k \ | \ \sigma(\text{exp}, \bowtie \zeta)$$

where ρ ranges over penalty functions, I is an interval, K is a finite set of indexes, $w_k \in (0,1]$ for each $k \in K$, $\sum_{k \in K} w_k = 1$, and $\zeta \in [0,1]$.

Distance expressions are evaluated over a pair of evolution sequences and a time step: given two evolution sequences $\mathcal{S}_1, \mathcal{S}_2$ and a time step τ, the evaluation of expressions in the triple $\mathcal{S}_1, \mathcal{S}_2, \tau$ is given by function $[\![\cdot]\!]^\tau_{\mathcal{S}_1,\mathcal{S}_2} : \text{Exp} \rightarrow [0,1]$ which is defined inductively over expressions. It bases on two atomic expressions, $<^\rho$ and $>^\rho$, where ρ is a penalty function, as follows:

$$[\![<^\rho]\!]^\tau_{\mathcal{S}_1,\mathcal{S}_2} = \mathbf{W}(m_\rho)(\mathcal{S}_1^\tau, \mathcal{S}_2^\tau) \qquad [\![>^\rho]\!]^\tau_{\mathcal{S}_1,\mathcal{S}_2} = \mathbf{W}(m_\rho)(\mathcal{S}_2^\tau, \mathcal{S}_1^\tau).$$

Then we provide three *temporal expression* operators, namely F^I, G^I and U^I, allowing for the evaluation of minimal and maximal distances over time: their semantics follows from that of the corresponding (bounded) temporal operators (resp., eventually, always, and until) by associating existential quantifications with minima, and universal quantifications with maxima. The min, max and convex combination $\sum_K w_k$ operators are as expected. The *comparison operator* $\sigma(\text{exp}, \bowtie \zeta)$ returns a value in $\{0,1\}$ used to establish whether the evaluation of exp is in relation $\bowtie$ with the threshold ζ. Summarising, by means of expressions we can measure the differences between evolution sequences with respect to various tasks (penalty functions) and temporal constraints.

Perturbations. A perturbation is the effect of unpredictable events, that can be repeated or different in time, on the current state of the system. In [4], a perturbation is therefore modelled as a time-dependent function that maps a data state into a distribution over data states. Specifically, a perturbation p is a list of mappings in which the i-th element describes the effects of p at time i, and that is specified in the following language:

Definition 3 (Perturbations). *Perturbations in* P *are defined as follows:*

$$\text{p} ::= \ \text{nil} \ | \ \text{f}@\tau \ | \ \text{p}_1 \, ; \text{p}_2 \ | \ \text{p}^n$$

where p ranges over P, *n and τ are finite natural numbers, and:*

- *nil is the perturbation with no effects, i.e., at each time step it behaves like the identity function* $\text{id}: \mathcal{D} \rightarrow \Pi(\mathcal{D}, \mathcal{B}_\mathcal{D})$ *such that* $\text{id}(\mathbf{d}) = \delta_\mathbf{d}$ *for all $\mathbf{d} \in \mathcal{D}$, with $\delta_\mathbf{d}$ the Dirac distribution defined by $\delta_\mathbf{d}(\mathbb{D}) = 1$ if $\mathbf{d} \in \mathbb{D}$ and $\delta_\mathbf{d}(\mathbb{D}) = 0$ otherwise;*
- *$\text{f}@\tau$ is an atomic perturbation, i.e., a function* $\text{f}: \mathcal{D} \rightarrow \Pi(\mathcal{D}, \mathcal{B}_\mathcal{D})$ *such that the mapping $\mathbf{d} \mapsto \text{f}(\mathbf{d})(\mathbb{D})$ is $\mathcal{B}_\mathcal{D}$-measurable for all $\mathbb{D} \in \mathcal{B}_\mathcal{D}$, and that is applied after τ time steps from the current instant;*
- *$\text{p}_1 \, ; \text{p}_2$ is a sequential perturbation, i.e., perturbation p_2 is applied at the time step subsequent to the (final) application of p_1;*

– p^n *is an* iterated perturbation, *i.e., perturbation* p *is applied for a total of n times.*

The semantics of perturbations is then defined by means of two auxiliary functions: effect(p), that describes the effect of p at the current step, and next(p), that identifies the perturbation that will be applied at the next step. These two functions are defined inductively over the structure of p. Due to space limitations, we omit their formal definition, and refer the interested reader to [4]. We make use of effect and next to define the mapping $\langle\!\langle \cdot \rangle\!\rangle : P \to (\mathcal{D} \times \mathbb{N} \to \Pi(\mathcal{D}, \mathcal{B}_{\mathcal{D}}))$ such that, for all $d \in \mathcal{D}$ and $i \in \mathbb{N}$:

$$\langle\!\langle p \rangle\!\rangle(d, i) = \mathsf{effect}(\mathsf{next}^i(p))(d),$$

where $\mathsf{next}^0(p) = p$ and $\mathsf{next}^i(p) = \mathsf{next}(\mathsf{next}^{i-1}(p))$, for all $i > 0$.

Now we can define the perturbation of an evolution sequence.

Definition 4 (Perturbation of an evolution sequence). *Given an evolution sequence* $\mathcal{S}_\mu$*, with* μ *as initial distribution, and a perturbation* p*, we define the perturbation of* $\mathcal{S}_\mu$ *via* p *as the evolution sequence* $\mathcal{S}_\mu^p$ *obtained as follows:*

$$\mathcal{S}_\mu^{p,0}(\mathbb{D}) = \int_{\mathcal{D}} \langle\!\langle p \rangle\!\rangle(d, 0)(\mathbb{D}) \, \eth \, \mu(d)$$

$$\mathcal{S}_\mu^{p,i+1}(\mathbb{D}) = \int_{\mathcal{D}} \left(\int_{\mathcal{D}} \langle\!\langle p \rangle\!\rangle(d', i+1)(\mathbb{D}) \, \eth \, \mathsf{step}(d)(d') \right) \eth \, \mathcal{S}_\mu^{p,i}(d),$$

where function step *is the Markov kernel that generates* $\mathcal{S}_\mu$*.*

Remark 1. Functions effect and next are such that, for each $i \in \mathbb{N}$, $\langle\!\langle p \rangle\!\rangle(d, i)$ is either the Dirac distribution over d, or the distribution $\mathtt{f}(d)$ induced by an atomic perturbation with function $\mathtt{f}$. In both cases, the mapping $d \mapsto \langle\!\langle p \rangle\!\rangle(d, i)(\mathbb{D})$ is guaranteed to be $\mathcal{B}_{\mathcal{D}}$-measurable for all $\mathbb{D} \in \mathcal{B}_{\mathcal{D}}$. Hence, the integrals in Definition 4 are well defined (see also [4, Proposition 4.7]).

RobTL Formulae. We use formulae in RobTL for the specification and analysis of distances between nominal and perturbed evolution sequences over a finite time horizon, henceforth denoted by $\mathfrak{h}$. The idea is that by combining atomic propositions with temporal operators, we can apply (possibly) different distance expressions and perturbations at different time steps, thus allowing for the analysis of systems behaviour in complex scenarios.

Definition 5 (RobTL). *RobTL consists in the set of formulae* L *defined by:*

$$\varphi ::= \top \mid \Delta(\mathsf{exp}, p) \bowtie \eta \mid \neg\varphi \mid \varphi \wedge \varphi \mid \varphi \, \mathcal{U}^I \varphi$$

where φ *ranges over* L*,* exp *ranges over expressions in* Exp*,* p *ranges over perturbations in* P*,* $\bowtie \in \{<, \leq, \geq, >\}$*,* $\eta \in [0, 1]$*, and* $I \subseteq [0, \mathfrak{h}]$ *is a bounded time interval.*

Formulae are evaluated in an evolution sequence and a time instant. Notice that, due to the presence of uncertainties and probability, the procedures that we use to 1. simulate the evolution sequences and the effects of perturbations, and 2. evaluate distance expressions, are based on statistical inference.

Hence, the presence of statistical errors has to be taken into account also when checking the satisfaction of RobTL formulae. Consequently, our model checker will assign a three-valued semantics to formulae by adding the truth value *unknown* ($\mathbb{U}$) to the classic true ($\top$) and false ($\bot$). Intuitively, unknown is generated by the comparison between the distance and the chosen threshold in atomic propositions: if the threshold η does not lie in the confidence interval of the evaluation of the distance, then the formula will evaluate to $\top$ or $\bot$ according to whether the relation $\bowtie \eta$ holds or not. Conversely, if η belongs to the confidence interval, then the atomic proposition evaluates to $\mathbb{U}$, since the validity of the relation $\bowtie \eta$ may depend on the particular samples obtained in the simulation. Starting from atomic propositions, the three-valued semantics is extended to the Boolean and temporal operators in the standard way [13,26]. We assign a three-valued semantics to RobTL formulae via the satisfaction function $\Omega_S : \mathsf{L} \times [0, \mathfrak{h}] \to \{\top, \mathbb{U}, \bot\}$, defined inductively on the structure of RobTL formulae. Specifically, on atomic propositions Ω_S is defined as follows:

$$\Omega_S(\Delta(\exp, \mathsf{p}) \bowtie \eta, \tau) = \begin{cases} \mathbb{U} & \text{if } \eta \in \mathsf{CI}_{\exp} \\ \top & \text{if } [\![\exp]\!]^\tau_{S, S_{|\mathsf{p}, \tau}} \bowtie \eta \\ \bot & \text{otherwise,} \end{cases}$$

where $\mathsf{CI}_{\exp}$ is the confidence interval on the evaluation of $[\![\exp]\!]^\tau_{S, S_{|\mathsf{p}, \tau}}$ with respect to the chosen coverage probability, and $S_{|\mathsf{p}, \tau}$ is the evolution sequence obtained by applying the perturbation p to S at time τ:

$$(S_{|\mathsf{p}, \tau})^t = \begin{cases} S^t & \text{if } t < \tau, \\ S^{\mathsf{p}, t-\tau}_{S^\tau} & \text{if } t \geq \tau. \end{cases}$$

Hence, for the first $\tau - 1$ steps $S_{|\mathsf{p}, \tau}$ is identical to S. At time τ the perturbation p is applied, and the distributions in $S_{|\mathsf{p}, \tau}$ are thus given by the perturbation via p of the evolution sequence having S^τ as initial distribution (cf. Definition 4).

Examples. We now provide a few examples of the use of RobTL for the specification of robustness properties of the two vehicles from Sect. 2.1.

Example 1 (Cyber-physical attacks). In this example, we use RobTL to express robustness properties against cyber-physical attacks modelled by perturbations. Let us consider an attack on the speed sensor of V2 that consists in diminishing the detected value of the speed, according to a chosen probabilistic offset. This attack aims at inducing sudden accelerations of the vehicle, thus increasing the risk of a collision with V1. Hence, we say that the system is robust against the attack if it can limit the risk of a collision between the two vehicles. Firstly, we model the attack by means of the perturbation $\mathsf{p}_{\mathtt{ItSlow}} = \mathsf{id}@0 ; (\mathsf{p}_{\mathtt{slow}})^{150}$, where $\mathsf{p}_{\mathtt{slow}} = \mathsf{slow}@(\mathsf{TIMER} - 1)$. Perturbation $\mathsf{p}_{\mathtt{ItSlow}}$ has no effect on the initial step ($\mathsf{id}@0$), then we apply function slow every TIMER steps ($\mathsf{slow}@(\mathsf{TIMER} - 1)$), for a total of 150 times. The choice of skipping the initial step, and applying the perturbation only every TIMER steps, is related to the frequency at which the controller checks the value of the speed sensor. (We recall that perturbations are lists of effects to be applied starting from the current step, which is identified with 0. So @(TIMER − 1) is a list of length TIMER.) An application of slow to a data state d is given by the following system of equations:

$$v \sim U(0, \mathsf{MAX\_OFFSET})$$
$$\mathsf{fake\_speed} = \min\{\mathsf{MAX\_SPEED}, d(\mathsf{p\_speed\_V2}) - v \cdot d(\mathsf{p\_speed\_V2})\}$$
$$\mathsf{fake\_bd} = \frac{\mathsf{fake\_speed}^2 + (A + B)(A \cdot \mathsf{TIMER}^2 + 2 \cdot \mathsf{fake\_speed} \cdot \mathsf{TIMER})}{2 \cdot B}$$
$$d(\mathsf{s\_speed\_V2}) = \mathsf{fake\_speed}$$
$$d(\mathsf{safety\_gap\_V1\_V2}) = d(\mathsf{p\_distance\_V1\_V2}) - (\mathsf{fake\_bd} + \mathsf{SAFETY\_DISTANCE}).$$

As a consequence, we have $d(\mathsf{s\_speed\_V2}) < d(\mathsf{p\_speed\_V2})$ and an augmented value for $d(\mathsf{safety\_gap\_V1\_V2})$ (the nominal one is computed by using $d(\mathsf{braking\_dist\_V2})$ instead of fake_bd). This tricks the controller of V2 into accelerating (or idling) when it should brake. Hence, attack $\mathsf{p_{ItSlow}}$ affects the distance between the two vehicles and, thus, the variation in time of variable p_distance_V1_V2. To measure the effects of $\mathsf{p_{ItSlow}}$ on the system, we evaluate the probability of a collision to occur upon its application. To this end, we can make use of the penalty function

$$\rho_{\mathsf{crash}}(\mathbf{d}) = \begin{cases} 0 & \text{if } \mathbf{d}(\mathsf{p\_distance\_V1\_V2}) > 0, \\ 1 & \text{otherwise}, \end{cases}$$

and of the distance expression $\mathsf{exp_{crash}} = G^{[t_1, t_2]} <_{\rho_{crash}}$ to quantify the maximal probability of a collision along the time interval $[t_1, t_2]$, where the time bounds t_1, t_2 are chosen according to the other system's parameters. Then, we express the robustness of the system against attack $\mathsf{p_{ItSlow}}$ via the RobTL formula

$$\varphi_{\mathsf{slow}} = \square^H \Delta(\mathsf{exp_{crash}}, \mathsf{p_{ItSlow}}) \leq \eta_{\mathsf{slow}}$$

where $H = [0, \mathfrak{h}]$, with $\mathfrak{h}$ the chosen time horizon, and the threshold η_{slow} represents the maximum acceptable risk of collision.

Similarly, we can model an attack aimed at inducing sudden decelerations of V1 by means of perturbation $\mathsf{p_{ItFast}} = \mathsf{id}@0 ; (\mathsf{p_{fast}})^{150}$ where $\mathsf{p_{fast}} = \mathsf{fast}@(\mathsf{TIMER}-1)$, and function fast differs from slow only for the use of variables of V1, and for sign of the offset $v \cdot d(\mathsf{p\_speed\_V1})$, which is added to p_speed_V1.

We can also combine the perturbations above to model an attack on both vehicles: $\mathsf{p_{comb}} = \mathsf{id}@0 ; \left(\mathsf{p_{fast}^3} ; \mathsf{p_{slow}^3}\right)^{50}$. We can then exploit RobTL to combine various requirements on the behaviour with respect to different attacks, and test elaborate guarantees on the system. For instance, we use the formula φ_{crash} below to test whether it is sufficient for the two vehicles to be robust each against their own attack, to ensure the robustness of the entire system against a combined attack:

$$\varphi_{\mathsf{fast}} = \square^H \Delta(\mathsf{exp_{crash}}, \mathsf{p_{ItFast}}) \leq \eta_{\mathsf{fast}} \qquad \varphi_{\mathsf{comb}} = \square^H \Delta(\mathsf{exp_{crash}}, \mathsf{p_{comb}}) \leq \eta_{\mathsf{comb}}$$
$$\varphi_{\mathsf{crash}} = \varphi_{\mathsf{fast}} \wedge \varphi_{\mathsf{slow}} \implies \varphi_{\mathsf{comb}}.$$

Example 2 (Collision severity). In this example, we use RobTL to express robustness against severity of collisions. Assume that, due to some malfunction, the sensors used by V2 over-approximate the distances from both V1 and the static obstacle. This may cause sudden accelerations of V2 and, possibly, a collision. Hence, we want to analyse the severity of potential collisions induced by sensor malfunction. Intuitively, the severity depends on the speed of V2 at collision instant. Hence, we say that the system is robust against sensor malfunction if it can limit the severity of collisions.

Perturbation $p_{\texttt{ItDistSens}} = \texttt{id}@0\,;\,(p_{\texttt{distSens}})^n$ allows us to model this malfunction, where $p_{\texttt{distSens}}$ is the perturbation $\texttt{distSens}@(\texttt{TIMER}-1)$, and function $\texttt{distSens}$ applied to a data state $\mathbf{d}$ has the effect given by the following system of equations:

$$offset \sim U(0, \texttt{MAX\_DISTANCE\_OFFSET})$$
$$\mathbf{d}(\texttt{s\_distance\_V1\_V2}) = \mathbf{d}(\texttt{p\_distance\_V1\_V2})(1 + offset)$$
$$\mathbf{d}(\texttt{s\_distance\_V2}) = \mathbf{d}(\texttt{p\_distance\_V2})(1 + offset)$$
$$\mathbf{d}(\texttt{safety\_gap\_V1\_V2}) = \mathbf{d}(\texttt{p\_distance\_V1\_V2})(1 + offset) - \mathbf{d}(\texttt{required\_dist\_V2})$$
$$\mathbf{d}(\texttt{safety\_gap\_V2}) = \mathbf{d}(\texttt{p\_distance\_V1\_V2})(1 + offset) - \mathbf{d}(\texttt{required\_dist\_V2})$$

By sensing distances greater than the real ones and reading augmented values for both safety_gap_V1_V2 and safety_gap_V2, the controller of V2 may opt for accelerating instead of braking. A collision may follow, whose severity can be quantified by the penalty function

$$\rho_{\texttt{crash\_speed}}(\mathbf{d}) = \begin{cases} \frac{\mathbf{d}(\texttt{p\_speed\_V2})}{\texttt{MAX\_SPEED}} & \text{if } \mathbf{d}(\texttt{crashed\_V2}) = 0 \text{ and} \\ & \min(\mathbf{d}(\texttt{p\_distance\_V1\_V2}), \mathbf{d}(\texttt{p\_distance\_V2})) \leq 0 \\ 0 & \text{otherwise.} \end{cases}$$

Here, $\mathbf{d}(\texttt{crashed\_V2}) = 0$ if and only if there was no crash in the past. In that case, it holds that $\min(\mathbf{d}(\texttt{p\_distance\_V1\_V2}), \mathbf{d}(\texttt{p\_distance\_V2})) \leq 0$ if a collision occurred at the current time step. Then, when a collision occurs, $\rho_{\texttt{crash\_speed}}$ returns a value in [0,1] expressing the severity of it, whose computation depends on the speed of V2: severity is expressed as the ratio of the speed at the moment of impact, and the maximal speed. The distance expression $\texttt{exp}_{\texttt{crash\_speed}} = \texttt{G}^{[t_1,t_2]} <_{\rho_{\texttt{crash\_speed}}}$ allows us to capture the max given by $\rho_{\texttt{crash\_speed}}$ in a suitable interval of time. Then, we express the robustness of the system against sensors' malfunction via the RobTL formula

$$\varphi_{\texttt{crash\_speed}} = \square^H \Delta(\texttt{exp}_{\texttt{crash\_speed}}, p_{\texttt{ItDistSens}}) \leq \eta_{\texttt{crash\_speed}}$$

where the threshold $\eta_{\texttt{crash\_speed}}$ represents the maximum acceptable collision severity.

4   The STARK Tool

In this section, we provide an overview of the tool *Software Tool for the Analysis of Robustness in the unKnown environment* (STARK). STARK, developed in Java, is a tool supporting specification, analysis and testing of robustness properties of CPSs. A detailed description of STARK together with a video describing the basic features of our tool is available at http://quasylab.unicam.it/stark/. STARK consists of five modules, *Models*, *Simulation*, *Statistical Model-Checker*, *Specification* and *Front-end*, that are briefly described below.

Models. This module provides interfaces and classes that can be used to describe the computational model and the resulting evolution sequence outlined in Sect. 2, and RobTL formulae discussed in Sect. 3. Below, we provide a short overview of the available interfaces and classes.

A system is described by the interface SystemState, that provides the methods used by the simulator and the model checker described later in this section. The interface is implemented by the class ControlledSystem that describes a system composed by:

- a DataState, modelling a *data state*;
- a DataStateFunction, describing how the *environment* affects a data state; and
- a Controller, describing the behaviour of the agents in the system.

To describe the behaviour of a system, the class EvolutionSequence is used. This consists of a sequence of samplings containing at the position i the set of configurations that are reachable after i-steps of computation. Efficient mechanisms have been implemented to generate the elements in an EvolutionSequence only on demand.

To model perturbations (see Definition 3) the interface Perturbation is available. A perturbation can be applied to a SystemState to obtain a PerturbedSystem. Similarly, the same perturbation can be applied to an EvolutionSequence to obtain an instance of class PerturbedEvolutionSequence.

Moreover, to measure the *distance* between two EvolutionSequences, the interface DistanceExpression is available. This is implemented, following the classic *pattern expression*, to mimic the structure of Definition 2. Similarly, to represent the formulae in Definition 5, the interface RobustnessFormula is used.

Simulation. This module contains all the interfaces and classes used to generate an EvolutionSequence (or a PerturbedEvolutionSequence), starting from a SystemState. Specifically, we rely on the class SampleSet, that allows us to manage sets of (sampled) system configurations.

We also provide classes to evaluate *penalty functions* from a evolution sequence and to collect statistical information. The classes rely on *The Apache Commons Mathematics*[2]. The simulation process can be performed following either a *sequential* or a *multithreading* approach. In the second case *Java Concurrency API* and *stream oriented* computations are used to take advantage of the *parallelism* of the hosting architecture.

Statistical Model-Checker. This module provides the classes that can be used to check if a given RobustnessFormula is satisfied or not by an EvolutionSequence. Two mechanisms can be used to *measure* the satisfaction of a formula: one based on the classic Boolean semantics, the other based on a *three-valued* semantics. Both the approaches, based on the pattern *visitor* [11], evaluate the satisfaction of the formula by inspecting its syntax structure.

---

[2] https://commons.apache.org/proper/commons-math/.

Specification. The STARK Specification Language (SSL) is a domain specific language that permits defining system behaviour and properties. This module provides the classes that can be used to load a SSL model from a file. A SSL *model* consists of:

- a set of *global variables*;
- a set of *components*;
- an *environment*;
- a set of *properties*.

Global variables are used to represent value in the data state that are not associated with a specific component and that are not under the direct control of a controller. In our examples these are[3]:

```
const SAFETY_DISTANCE = 200;
const TIMER = 5;
const MAX_SPEED = 40;

global variables {
    real p_speed_V1 range [0, MAX_SPEED] = 25;
    real p_speed_V2 range [0, MAX_SPEED] = 25;
    ...
}
```

A *component* identifies an agent in the system. It consists of a set of *local variables* and a *controller*. In our running example we have a component for each of the two vehicles, with the following structure:

```
component Vehicle1 {
    variables {
        real s_speed_V1 range [0, MAX_SPEED] = 25;
        real s_distance_V1 range [0, INIT_DISTANCE_V1] = 10000;
        ...
    }
    controller {
        state Ctrl {
            if (s_speed_V1 > 0) {
                if (safety_gap_V1 > 0) {
                    accel_V1' = A;
                    timer_V1' = TIMER;
                    brake_light_V1' = 0;
                    exec Accelerate_V1;
                } else {
                    accel_V1' = - B;
                    timer_V1' = TIMER;
                    brake_light_V1' = 1;
                    exec Decelerate_V1;
            } else {
                accel_V1' = N;
                timer_V1' = TIMER;
                exec Stop_V1;
            }
        }
        state IDS {
            ...
        }
```

---

[3] Due to a lack of space only a small code snippet is provided. Complete specification is available at http://quasylab.unicam.it/stark/.

```
    . . .
  }
  init    Ctrl  ||  IDS
}
component  Vehicle2  {
  . . .
}
```

The *environment* consists of a set of equations describing how variables are changed after one step:

```
environment  {
    timer_V1' = timer_V1 −1;
    timer_V2' = timer_V2 −1;
    p_speed_V1' = p_speed_V1+accel_V1 ;
    . . .
}
```

Front-end. In this module all the classes for the user interaction are provided. First of all, a set of utility classes are provided to read/write data in different formats, such as CSV. These classes can be used to perform some analysis on the behaviour of a CPS even if we do not have information on its specification. Indeed, we can collect the observations on the data of the system into a CSV file, build the *observed* evolution sequence from it, and then use the tool (in particular the module for the evaluation of distances) to compare this observed behaviour with an ideal one, or to compare various observed evolution sequences. This means that we can measure the impact of real world uncertainties and perturbations on the behaviour of the system, without having to specify them, i.e., without assuming any information on which data will be manipulated by them, and on how and when such manipulations occur. A *command line interpreter* is also provided to interact with the STARK modules and permits performing all the analyses outlined above. This interpreter can be either used interactively or in a *batch mode* to execute saved scripts.

5   The Tool in Action

We now apply STARK to carry out the analysis on our case study discussed in Sect. 3.

Example 3 (Cyber-physical attacks, continued). Consider the formulae φ_{slow} and φ_{comb} from Example 1. In Fig. 2 we depict their three-valued evaluations in various situations, using the identifications $\top = 1$, $\mathbb{U} = 0$, and $\bot = -1$. The plots in the upper part of the figure report the evaluations of φ_{slow}, while those in the lower part are related to φ_{comb}. We focus only on φ_{slow}, as the analysis for φ_{comb} is similar, with the following parameters: $\mathfrak{h} = 450$, $t_1 = 350$, $t_2 = 450$, $\eta_{\text{slow}} = 0.1$. Hence, we test whether, when applying the attack at any step $\tau \in [0, 450]$, the maximum probability of a collision, computed between steps $\tau + 350$ and $\tau + 450$, is at most 0.1. We used the following parameters: both vehicles start with an initial speed of 25.0 m/s, with V1 at a distance of 10000 m from the obstacle, and V2 at a distance of 5000 m from V1; A= 1.0 m/s^2, B= 2.0 m/s^2, TIMER= 5, MAX_SPEED= 40 m/s, and SAFETY_DISTANCE= 200 m. In each plot, we report the evaluations with respect to

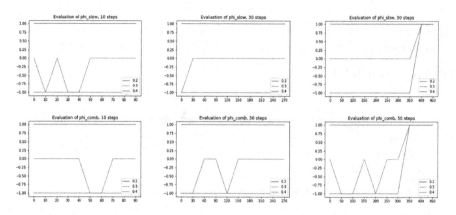

Fig. 2. Evaluations of formulae $\varphi_{\texttt{slow}}$ (top) and $\varphi_{\texttt{comb}}$ every 10, 30, and 50 steps, and with respect to different offsets (MAX_OFFSET $\in \{0.2, 0.3, 0.4\}$).

three different instances of the parameter MAX_OFFSET, namely 0.2, 0.3, and 0.4, used by the perturbations to set the random offset on speed sensors readings. The system is robust against the attacks using MAX_OFFSET= 0.2, and not robust against those using MAX_OFFSET= 0.4 (we postpone the discussion on the evaluation after step 375). In the case of MAX_OFFSET= 0.3 the formulae evaluate to $\mathbb{U}$, since the threshold $\eta_{\texttt{slow}}$ is included in the 95% confidence intervals on the computation of distances. Although the evaluation gives (mostly) unknown, the intuition is that the system is not robust in this case. In fact, by comparing the plots, we notice that there are certain time steps, like 0, at which the evaluation changes when working with different simulations of the perturbed evolution sequence. This means that the value of $\eta_{\texttt{slow}}$ (and $\eta_{\texttt{comb}}$) is in an ε-neighbourhood of the lower bound of the confidence interval, for an ε close to 0. Hence, a tiny variation in the confidence interval is sufficient to change the evaluation between $\mathbb{U}$ and $\bot$. The plots have been obtained by considering 10 evaluations of the formula, taken, respectively, every 10, 30, and 50 steps, thus giving us a general idea of the potential impact of the attack on the behaviour of the system, at different moments in time. Notice that, if the attack is applied after step 400, then the formula evaluates to $\top$ regardless of the value of the offset. Actually, this holds whenever the attack is applied after step 374. The reason becomes clear when simulating the nominal behaviour of the system: at step 375 variable p_speed_V2 assumes value 0. Clearly, the attack has no effect on a stationary vehicle. Similarly, $\texttt{p}_{\texttt{comb}}$ has no effect whenever applied after step 350. The temporal discrepancy is due to the fact that in $\texttt{p}_{\texttt{comb}}$ the attack on V2 is delayed by that on V1 that takes 15 steps to be completed (and has no side effects as V1 becomes stationary at step 260). At that point V2 is already too close to V1 to be tricked by the attack.

Example 4 (Collision severity, continued). Consider the formula $\varphi_{\texttt{crash\_speed}}$ from Example 2. In Fig. 3 we depict its three-valued evaluation in various situations, using again the identifications $\top = 1$, $\mathbb{U} = 0$, and $\bot = -1$. As in Example 3, the plots have been obtained by considering 10 evaluations of the formula, taken, respectively, every

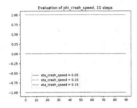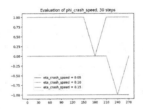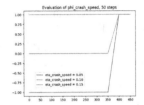

Fig. 3. Evaluations of formulae $\varphi_{\text{crash\_speed}}$ every 10, 30, and 50 steps, and with respect to different thresholds $\eta_{\text{crash\_speed}} \in \{0.05, 0.1, 0.15\}$.

10, 30, and 50 steps. The plots report the evaluations of the formula with the following parameters: $\mathfrak{h} = 450$, $t_1 = 10$, $t_2 = 400$. Hence, we test whether a malfunction on distance sensors originating at any step $\tau \in [0, 450]$ gives rise to a maximum severity of a collision, computed between steps $\tau + 10$ and $\tau + 400$, of at most $\eta_{\text{crash\_speed}}$. We used the same parameters for the initial speeds, distances and acceleration rates as in Example 3. In Fig. 3, we report the evaluations with respect to three different instances of $\eta_{\text{crash\_speed}}$, namely 0.05, 0.1, and 0.15. If the attack is applied after step 350, then the formula evaluates to $\top$, the reason being that in all simulations of the nominal behaviour of the system, after step 350 V2 is very close to V1 and also the corrupted value of the distance is enough low to induce the controller to keep braking. The system is robust against the malfunction using $\eta_{\text{crash\_speed}} = 0.15$, and not robust against that using $\eta_{\text{crash\_speed}} = 0.05$. In the case of $\eta_{\text{crash\_speed}} = 0.1$ the formulae (mostly) evaluate to $\mathbb{U}$, since the threshold on the severity is included in the 95% confidence intervals that we considered on the evaluation of the distances.

6   Concluding Remarks

We have presented STARK, a Java-based tool for the analysis of robustness properties of CPSs operating in the presence of uncertainties and perturbations. The core of STARK is constituted by the evolution sequence model for system behaviour, and the logic RobTL for the specification of temporal properties over distances between evolution sequences, and thus of requirements on system's robustness.

In the literature, we can find several proposals of tools and techniques for robustness testing for systems with a finite/discrete state space (see [16] for a survey). However, evolution sequences (that can be either obtained through the simulation module in STARK, or via direct measurements on the real system) are defined over a *continuous* state space, in order to avoid the introduction of arbitrary simplifying assumptions on the behaviour of the environment. This means that in STARK we can capture even the slightest modification on behaviour that is induced by the uncertainties.

Moreover, an evolution sequence is a discrete-time version of the cylinder of *all possible trajectories* of the system, which means that when we check RobTL properties, we do it by taking into account all possible system behaviours. This is a clear distinction with existing model checking tools, in which properties are tested on a single trajectory of the system (see [1, 15, 22]). It will be interesting to see how this feature will impact the future development of STARK. In fact, we plan to investigate the synthesis of predictive monitors [5] for RobTL specifications, and to add to STARK a module for the verification of robustness properties at run-time. Clearly, although the monitor attached to the system can observe only a single trajectory at run-time, it will need to take into account all possible future behaviours, and thus the evolution sequence, to make its predictions and take decisions. For completeness, we recall that several useful tools for monitoring (spatio-)temporal properties of CPSs have been proposed in classic run-time monitoring (i.e., without predictions) literature (see [2] for a survey). Those tools are based on temporal logics like, e.g., STL [7], MTL [14], or SSTL [26], that specify properties of a single trajectory of the system at a time.

We also plan to apply our framework to the analysis of biological networks. Some quantitative extensions of temporal logics have already been proposed in that setting (e.g. [8, 19, 20]) to capture the notion of robustness from [12] or similar proposals [17]. It would be interesting to see whether the use of RobTL and evolution sequences, and thus of STARK, can lead to new results.

At this stage in its development, STARK is meant to be used in the testing phase of a system. We leave as future work an investigation of its employment in the design phase. We will also study a possible integration of STARK with SCENIC [10], a domain-specific scenario description language that has been recently introduced for the design of Machine Learning-based CPSs. SCENIC allows us to synthetically generate data for training the system against rare events that are quite difficult to obtain from collections of real-world data. It is a probabilistic programming language for the specification of scenes, i.e., configurations of objects and their spatio-temporal features, and scenarios, i.e., a distribution over scenes and the behaviour of the agents operating in them over time. We remark that requirements over system behaviour in SCENIC are specified in MTL, and are therefore tested on a single trajectory of the system at a time.

Acknowledgements. This work has been supported by the project *"Programs in the wild: Uncertainties, adaptabiLiTy and veRificatiON"* (ULTRON) of the Icelandic Research Fund (grant No. 228376-051).

Data Availability Statement. The artifact is available in the Software Heritage repository: swh:1:dir:98532d8c770f9d115c692e932869c446417d8b34

References

1. Baier, C.: Probabilistic model checking. In: Esparza, J., Grumberg, O., Sickert, S. (eds.) Dependable Software Systems Engineering, NATO Science for Peace and Security Series - D: Information and Communication Security, vol. 45, pp. 1–23. IOS Press (2016). https://doi.org/10.3233/978-1-61499-627-9-1
2. Bartocci, E., et al.: Specification-based monitoring of cyber-physical systems: a survey on theory, tools and applications. In: Bartocci, E., Falcone, Y. (eds.) Lectures on Runtime Verification. LNCS, vol. 10457, pp. 135–175. Springer, Cham (2018). https://doi.org/10.1007/978-3-319-75632-5_5
3. Castiglioni, V., Loreti, M., Tini, S.: How adaptive and reliable is your program? In: Peters, K., Willemse, T.A.C. (eds.) FORTE 2021. LNCS, vol. 12719, pp. 60–79. Springer, Cham (2021). https://doi.org/10.1007/978-3-030-78089-0_4

4. Castiglioni, V., Loreti, M., Tini, S.: RobTL: a temporal logic for the robustness of cyber-physical systems. CoRR abs/2212.11158 (2022). 10.48550/arXiv. 2212.11158

5. Chen, X., Sankaranarayanan, S.: Model predictive real-time monitoring of linear systems. In: Proceedings of RTSS 2017, pp. 297–306. IEEE Computer Society (2017). https://doi.org/10.1109/RTSS.2017.00035

6. Chong, S., Lanotte, R., Merro, M., Tini, S., Xiang, J.: Quantitative robustness analysis of sensor attacks on cyber-physical systems. In: 26th ACM International Conference on Hybrid Systems: Computation and Control (2023)

7. Donzé, A., Maler, O.: Robust satisfaction of temporal logic over real-valued signals. In: Chatterjee, K., Henzinger, T.A. (eds.) FORMATS 2010. LNCS, vol. 6246, pp. 92–106. Springer, Heidelberg (2010). https://doi.org/10.1007/978-3-642-15297-9_9

8. Fages, F., Rizk, A.: On temporal logic constraint solving for analyzing numerical data time series. Theor. Comput. Sci. **408**(1), 55–65 (2008). https://doi.org/10.1016/j.tcs.2008.07.004

9. Fränzle, M., Kapinski, J., Prabhakar, P.: Robustness in cyber-physical systems. Dagstuhl Reports **6**(9), 29–45 (2016). https://doi.org/10.4230/DagRep.6.9.29

10. Fremont, D.J., et al.: Scenic: a language for scenario specification and data generation. Mach. Learn. (2022). https://doi.org/10.1007/s10994-021-06120-5

11. Gamma, E., Helm, R., Johnson, R., Vlissides, J.M.: Design patterns: elements of reusable object-oriented software. Addison-Wesley Professional, 1 edn. (1994)

12. Kitano, H.: Towards a theory of biological robustness. Mol. Syst. Biol. **3**(1), 137 (2007). https://doi.org/10.1038/msb4100179

13. Kleene, S.C.: Introduction to Metamathematics. Princeton, NJ, USA: North Holland (1952). https://doi.org/10.2307/2268620

14. Koymans, R.: Specifying real-time properties with metric temporal logic. Real Time Syst. **2**(4), 255–299 (1990). https://doi.org/10.1007/BF01995674

15. Kwiatkowska, M., Norman, G., Parker, D.: Stochastic model checking. In: Bernardo, M., Hillston, J. (eds.) SFM 2007. LNCS, vol. 4486, pp. 220–270. Springer, Heidelberg (2007). https://doi.org/10.1007/978-3-540-72522-0_6

16. Micskei, Z., Madeira, H., Avritzer, A., Majzik, I., Vieira, M., Antunes, N.: Robustness testing techniques and tools. In: Wolter, K., Avritzer, A., Vieira, M., van Moorsel, A. (eds.) Resilience Assessment and Evaluation of Computing Systems. Springer, Berlin, Heidelberg (2012). https://doi.org/10.1007/978-3-642-29032-9_16

17. Nasti, L., Gori, R., Milazzo, P.: Formalizing a notion of concentration robustness for biochemical networks. In: Mazzara, M., Ober, I., Salaün, G. (eds.) STAF 2018. LNCS, vol. 11176, pp. 81–97. Springer, Cham (2018). https://doi.org/10.1007/978-3-030-04771-9_8

18. Platzer, A.: Logical Foundations of Cyber-Physical Systems. Springer (2018). https://doi.org/10.1007/978-3-319-63588-0

19. Rizk, A., Batt, G., Fages, F., Soliman, S.: A general computational method for robustness analysis with applications to synthetic gene networks. Bioinform. **25**(12), 169–178 (2009). https://doi.org/10.1093/bioinformatics/btp200

20. Rizk, A., Batt, G., Fages, F., Soliman, S.: Continuous valuations of temporal logic specifications with applications to parameter optimization and robustness measures. Theor. Comput. Sci. **412**(26), 2827–2839 (2011). https://doi.org/10.1016/j.tcs.2010.05.008

21. Rungger, M., Tabuada, P.: A notion of robustness for cyber-physical systems. IEEE Trans. Autom. Control **61**(8), 2108–2123 (2016)

22. Sen, K., Viswanathan, M., Agha, G.: On statistical model checking of stochastic systems. In: Etessami, K., Rajamani, S.K. (eds.) CAV 2005. LNCS, vol. 3576, pp. 266–280. Springer, Heidelberg (2005). https://doi.org/10.1007/11513988_26

23. Shahrokni, A., Feldt, R.: A systematic review of software robustness. Inf. Softw. Technol. **55**(1), 1–17 (2013). https://doi.org/10.1016/j.infsof.2012.06.002

24. Sontag, E.D.: Input to State Stability: Basic Concepts and Results, pp. 163–220. Springer, Heidelberg (2008). https://doi.org/10.1007/978-3-540-77653-6_3
25. Vaserstein, L.N.: Markovian processes on countable space product describing large systems of automata. Probl. Peredachi Inf. **5**(3), 64–72 (1969)
26. Vissat, L.L., Loreti, M., Nenzi, L., Hillston, J., Marion, G.: Analysis of spatio-temporal properties of stochastic systems using TSTL. ACM Trans. Model. Comput. Simul. **29**(4), 1–24 (2019). https://doi.org/10.1145/3326168
27. Xiang, J., Fulton, N., Chong, S.: Relational analysis of sensor attacks on cyber-physical systems. In: 34th IEEE Computer Security Foundations Symposium, CSF 2021, Dubrovnik, Croatia, 21–25 June 2021, pp. 1–16. IEEE (2021). https://doi.org/10.1109/CSF51468.2021.00035

Verification and Testing

RSC to the ReSCu: Automated Verification of Systems of Communicating Automata

Loïc Desgeorges and Loïc Germerie Guizouarn$^{(\boxtimes)}$

Université Côte d'Azur, CNRS, I3S, Sophia Antipolis, France
{loic.desgeorges,loic.germerie-guizouarn}@univ-cotedazur.fr

Abstract. We present ReSCu, a model-checking tool for RSC (Realisable with Synchronous Communication) systems of communicating automata. Communicating automata are a formalism used to model communication protocols: each participant is represented by a finite state automaton, whose transitions are labelled by sending and receiving actions. In the general case, such automata exchanging messages asynchronously via FIFO or bag buffers are Turing-powerful, therefore most safety verification problems are undecidable. In RSC systems, the reception of a message may happen right after its send action. A lot of verification problems, e.g. reachability of a control state, are decidable for RSC systems. ReSCu checks whether a system is RSC, allowing to observe that a significant portion of protocols from the literature is RSC. This tool can also perform verification of safety properties for those systems, and is competitive in terms of time compared to non–RSC specific tools.

1 Introduction

Ensuring safety of communication protocols is admittedly a very important task. Systems of communicating automata (CA for short) are one of the formalisms modelling such protocols: each participant of the communication is represented by a finite state automaton, the transitions of which are labelled with actions, either to send or receive messages. Model-checking a system consists in verifying that it satisfies safety properties, e.g. whether an undesired configuration of control states is reachable. In this model, communications are asynchronous: messages are sent to unbounded buffers, waiting there to be received. The sender may immediately proceed with its subsequent actions. The main semantics for buffers are FIFO, for First In First Out, and bag. FIFO buffers behave like queues, messages are received in the same order as they were sent, whereas bag buffers allow receptions of messages in any order. Systems may be equipped with different structures of buffers named *communication architecture*. The most common ones being peer-to-peer, where there is one buffer per direction between

This work has been supported by the French government, through the EUR DS4H Investments in the Future project managed by the National Research Agency (ANR) with the reference number ANR-17-EURE-0004.

S.-S. Jongmans and A. Lopes (Eds.): COORDINATION 2023, LNCS 13908, pp. 135–143, 2023.
https://doi.org/10.1007/978-3-031-35361-1_7

each pair of participants, and mailbox, were each participant receives its messages from a single buffer.

From its asynchrony, comes a limitation of this model: buffers can encode the tape of a Turing Machine and therefore, deciding the reachability of a configuration of control states is undecidable [8]. Different strategies arose to circumvent this difficulty, the main ones being using semi-algorithms for verification, and restricting systems to classes in which verification problems become decidable.

The latter approach is the one we used in [13] and developed in [12]. Intuitively, a system is Realisable with Synchronous Communication (RSC for short) if all its executions can be reorganised to mimic a synchronous behaviour, where send and receive actions of the same message happen at the same time. Reachability of a regular set of configurations was shown to be decidable for RSC systems. Membership to the class of RSC systems is decidable as well, allowing to select the protocols on which the reachability algorithms can be used.

We present ReSCu (for **Re**alisable with **S**ynchronous **C**ommunication), a model-checking tool for RSC systems of CA. This tool can answer whether a given system is RSC or not, and whether a specified bad configuration is reachable. ReSCu works on systems with any communication architecture (not restricted to peer-to-peer or mailbox) and either with bag or FIFO buffers.

Outline. After a discussion about related works, we will begin with some intuition about CA in Sect. 2. In Sect. 3, we present the tool itself, how it is implemented and how it can be used. Before concluding (Sect. 5), we will present some results and benchmarks we obtained with our tool in Sect. 4.

Related Works. The closest tool to ReSCu is McScM [15]. It takes a description of a system and a set of bad configurations (defined as QDDs [5]), and checks whether a bad configuration is reachable. This tool implements various model-checking approaches, based on abstract interpretation. It is not limited to systems of a specific class. Contrary to ReSCu, most of these approaches are semi-algorithms and need a time-out to be set arbitrarily. However, the strength of McScM is the multiplicity of model-checking engines it provides, increasing the likelihood of a conclusive result for any system. We use its description language as a way to input systems in ReSCu.

The notion of *stability*, introduced in [4], is close to RSC. A system is k-stable if its behaviour with any bound $k' > k$ is equivalent (with several notions of equivalence possible) to its behaviour with a bound k. Model-checking can be performed with bounded buffers for stable systems. Stability was shown to be undecidable for FIFO systems in [3], but decidable with bag buffers (for a specific notion of equivalence) [2]. The authors of [2,3] developed STABC: a tool using semi-algorithms to check k-stability of systems. Contrary to ReSCu, it does not perform verification of safety properties, but provides only membership results.

Lange and Yoshida proposed another tool: KMC [20], for k Multiparty Compatibility. It checks whether a system could have been obtained by projection of a global type, relying on the theory of Multiparty Session Types [16] (another

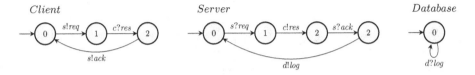

Fig. 1. Protocol from Example 1

way to model distributed systems). If a system is k-MC, various safety properties are ensured, and it is not necessary to specify them as it is for McScM or ReSCu.

2   Communicating Automata

We begin with a small example of protocol, borrowed from [3].

Example 1 (Communication protocol). We will consider a generic client/server protocol, enhanced with a database logging activity. In this protocol, the client may send a request to the server, and when it receives a result for this request, it sends an acknowledgement back to the server. The server waits for a request, and upon receiving it, it sends a result to the client. After that, it waits for an acknowledgement from the client and sends a logging message to the database. Those behaviours can be repeated indefinitely.   □

Figure 1 is a graphical representation of the system of CA modelling the protocol from Example 1. Each participant is represented by an automaton, which can change states by executing the actions labelling its transitions. An action $i!v$ means that message v is sent in buffer i, and $i?v$ that v is received from buffer i. In this system each participant receives all its messages in a single FIFO buffer (mailbox). Informally, a *configuration* is the product of the control states of each participant, paired with the content of the buffers. A configuration is *reachable* if a sequence of actions of the system can lead to it. We focus on safety properties that can be expressed as a regular language of 'bad' configurations of a system. We say that such a safety property is satisfied if no configuration of the language is reachable in the system.

Example 2 (Safety specifications). In Example 1, the configuration where the server is in state 1, and the client in state 0 is a bad configuration: it means those two participants are not at the same step of the protocol any more. Both the server and the client are not ready to receive the messages they are about to send each other. In this tiny example, it is easy to see that such a configuration is not reachable, but on bigger systems an automatic verification may be useful to ensure such properties. Another example: a set of bad configurations is formed by the ones where the server is in state 0, and the first message in buffer s is not *req*, preventing any further reception to happen for this participant (indeed, remember we use FIFO buffers, only the first message of a buffer may be received).   □

```
scm client_server_database :          automaton client:
                                      initial: 0
nb_channels = 3;                      state 0:
parameters: int req; int res;         to 1: when true, 0 ! req;
int log; int ack;                     state 1:
                                      to 2: when true, 1 ? res;
automaton server:                     state 2:
initial: 0                            to 0: when true, 0 ! ack;
state 0:
to 1: when true, 0 ? req;             bad_states:
state 1:                              (automaton client: in 0: true
to 2: when true, 1 ! res;              automaton server: in 1: true)
state 2:
to 3: when true, 0 ? ack;             (automaton server: in 0: true with
state 3:                               (log|res|ack).(req|res|log|ack)^*.#.
to 0: when true, 2 ! log;              (req|res|log|ack)^*.#.
                                       (req|res|log|ack)^*)
automaton database:
initial: 0
state 0:
to 0: when true, 2 ? log;
```

Fig. 2. SCM representation of Example 1

Intuitively, a system of CA is RSC if send actions and their respective reception can happen at the same time: there is no need for another action to be performed between sending a message and receiving it. The work in [12] provides formal definitions of CA and RSC systems, as well as algorithms for deciding membership to the class of RSC systems and reachability of a configuration.

3   ReSCu

ReSCu is a tool using the properties of RSC systems to perform model-checking. It is an OCaml implementation of the algorithms in [12]. While working on this implementation, we discovered a bug in the membership algorithm; we provide in [11] the fixed algorithms, generalised to take into account bag buffers. ReSCu provides a command line interface that takes a file describing a system of CA and its safety specifications, and outputs whether this system is RSC, and whether a bad configuration is reachable or not. If a bad configuration is reachable, ReSCu can display the execution leading to the safety counterexample. Similarly, if non-RSC executions are possible, one of them may be displayed. This tool is available at [10].

SCM Description Language. We chose, as an input format, the SCM language used in [15]. This allowed to rely on the parser that was already available thanks to the developers of McScM, and to compare easily ReSCu with this tool. Figure 2 shows the SCM description of the system in Example 1. The set of messages is declared after the keyword **parameters**, and the number of buffers after the keyword **nb_channels** ('channel' is the name used for buffers in SCM). An automaton is declared as a list of states, each of them containing a (possibly empty) list of transitions. SCM allows specification of model features we did not take

Protocol	$\|\mathbb{P}\|$	S	T	RSC	t_{rsc}	k-MC	t_{kmc}
SMTP [17,22]	2	64	108	Yes	17	Yes	34
HTTP [18,22]	2	12	48	Yes	17	Yes	28
Elevator [6]	3	13	23	No	7	Yes	41
Commit protocol [6]	4	12	12	Yes	4	Yes	15
Travel agency [22]	3	17	20	Yes	8	Yes	15
SH [22]	3	22	30	Yes	18	Yes	33

(a) Comparison with KMC

Protocol	$\|\mathbb{P}\|$	S	T	RSC	t_{rsc}	k	t_{stabc}
Estelle specification [19]	2	7	9	No	5	max	82,625
FTP transfer [7]	3	20	17	Yes	6	4	89,465
SQL server [23]	4	33	38	Yes	13	3	90,553
SSH [21]	4	27	28	Yes	7	2	43,855
Bug report repository [14]	4	11	11	Yes	4	max	134,796
Restaurant service [1]	3	16	16	No	5	2	52,793

(b) Comparison with STABC, using FIFO buffers and 'strong equivalence'. *max* means the arbitrary limit for k, set at 10, was reached.

Table 1. Membership results of ReSCu compared with KMC and STABC. $\|\mathbb{P}\|$ is the number of participants, S the number of states, and T the number of transitions. t_{rsc}, t_{kmc} and t_{stabc} denote the time (in ms) of computation of ReSCu, KMC and STABC.

into consideration, hence the 'when true' in the transitions, or the types of each message. Bad configurations are declared after the keyword 'bad_states', each one of them being a list of control states and an optional regular expression describing buffer contents. The bad states of this listing correspond to the ones in Example 2.

Usage. The command line utility allows to check both membership and safety of a system: rescu -isrsc <system> checks whether the system described in the SCM file <system> is RSC, and rescu -mc <system> checks that no bad configuration is reachable. The two options can be combined in one call to ReSCu. Option -bag specifies that all buffers should be considered as bag buffers. In this case bad specifications including a description of the buffer contents are not accepted. For convenience while testing, we included a feature allowing to output a DOT representation of an SCM file. A video demonstrating the use of ReSCu is available at [9].

Implementation Choices. McScM was designed as a framework, allowing addition of model-checking engines as modules. We opted for a stand-alone tool as the interface with McScM is way more involved than what is required for RSC algorithms. In addition, McScM is no longer maintained, and in its current state it is not possible to compile it with a modern version of OCaml.

4 Results

We used ReSCu on the set of examples provided with McScM, and we ported examples of systems available with STABC [3] and KMC [20]. This allowed to test our tool on a lot of systems, some of which modelling actual protocols.

Proportion of RSC Systems in the Wild. We used ReSCu to check the existence of RSC systems among examples from the literature. Using FIFO buffers, 30% of the systems from [15], 60% of those from [20] and 38% of those from [3] are RSC. Using bag buffers, the results are respectively 12%, 41% and 11%. These figures are to be interpreted carefully however, as the examples coming from KMC and STABC are not all random examples. Examples of systems from KMC are CSA, for *communicating session automata*, which is a class of systems where there cannot be sending and receiving transitions leaving the same state. Some systems where even (slightly) modified to become CSA. To provide a more realistic overview of the importance of RSC systems in the literature, we show in Table 1 some membership results for interesting protocols that were featured in [20] and [3]. It shows a comparison of the results of ReSCu on one hand, and the results we reproduced with their respective tools on the other hand. The k value provided by STABC is a buffer bound that may be applied to the system without restricting its behaviour. An extended version of those tables is available in [11].

Performance of our Tool. We ran both our tool and McScM on several RSC examples from McScM, KMC and STABC, and compared the model-checking time. For the ported examples, we had to design some specifications, as the tools those systems came from focused only on membership to a class. The bad configurations we added are similar to the second one of Fig. 2: they enforce that, for a specific control state of a participant, no configuration where the first message of the buffer cannot be received is reached. For reference, we ran our testing on a laptop with an Intel Core i5-8250U CPU at 1.60 GHz, equipped with 16 Gb of RAM.

Protocol	ReSCu	absint	armc	cegar	lart
ring	**137**	(19,708)	T_{max}	382	1,928
NonRegular	**4**	60	T_{max}	13	10
pop3	**33**	719	2,143	6,759	T_{max}
Nested	**4**	5	11	320	2045
con_disc_reg	4	(21)	7	9	**4**
tcp_error*	**4**	(107)	26	66	10
http-fsm	**7**	44	T_{max}	T_{max}	T_{max}
smtp	**84**	236	241	174	173
FTP	51	**29**	54	61	82
SSH	207	574	368	**188**	910

Table 2. Model-checking time (in ms) of ReSCu and McScM. Figures in brackets correspond to inconclusive verification.

Table 2 presents the times of computation of the different algorithms, averaged over 3 runs. The shortest time for each protocol is highlighted. The three horizontal sections of the table correspond to the origin of the examples: McScM, KMC and STABC, in that order. The runs that reached the time limit of 2 minutes are marked T_{max}. The columns for `cegar` and `lart` present the best time of the four variants of these algorithms.

As an example, we detail the results for a protocol: `ring`, a token passing protocol in a ring with four peers. The first algorithm, `absint`, did not provide a conclusive answer, and ran for about 19 s. The second one, `armc`, reached the time limit we set at 2 min without finishing. The next algorithms have four variants each, and even if `cegar` is the fastest in this example, one of its variant times out. Two of the variants of `lart` time out as well.

The protocol `tcp_error`* is a simplified version of TCP, intentionally modified to be erroneous. It is not RSC, but we included it as ReSCu can still find one of its bad configurations. Even though ReSCu cannot certify that a non-RSC protocol is safe, it can still help finding bugs quickly.

The rightmost column in Tables 1a and 1b gives an overview of the performance of the membership algorithm, compared to KMC and STABC respectively. Note that KMC checks the safety of a protocol, while knowing if a given system is RSC merely allows to know if our model-checking algorithm is suitable for it.

5 Conclusion

We presented ReSCu, a tool relying on the properties of RSC systems of communicating automata to verify safety of communication protocols. Through extensive testing and comparison with other tools, ReSCu proved to be performant, and allowed to notice that a significant portion of actual protocols from the literature are indeed RSC.

This tool has some limitations however: some systems are not RSC, and ReSCu cannot certify safety of those. Another drawback is that while other tools can check various safety properties taking only the description of the protocol, we need the users to define correctly the safety properties they want to check. While our current setting allows for some flexibility, generating bad configurations automatically for properties like unspecified reception, or progress (see [12]), could be an interesting improvement of ReSCu, and is left as future work.

Acknowledgements. We would like to thank all the COORDINATION reviewers for their comments that greatly improved the present paper.

Data Availability Statement. The artifact is available in the Software Heritage repository: swh:1:dir:a9fb15adfc33656029d9d84d34ec34c129ebfc34.

References

1. van der Aalst, W.M.P., Mooij, A.J., Stahl, C., Wolf, K.: Service interaction: patterns, formalization, and analysis. In: Bernardo, M., Padovani, L., Zavattaro, G. (eds.) SFM 2009. LNCS, vol. 5569, pp. 42–88. Springer, Heidelberg (2009). https://doi.org/10.1007/978-3-642-01918-0_2

2. Akroun, L., Salaün, G.: Automated verification of automata communicating via FIFO and bag buffers. Formal Methods Syst. Des. **52**(3), 260–276 (2017). https://doi.org/10.1007/s10703-017-0285-8

3. Akroun, L., Salaün, G., Ye, L.: Automated analysis of asynchronously communicating systems. In: Bošnački, D., Wijs, A. (eds.) SPIN 2016. LNCS, vol. 9641, pp. 1–18. Springer, Cham (2016). https://doi.org/10.1007/978-3-319-32582-8_1

4. Basu, S., Bultan, T.: Automatic verification of interactions in asynchronous systems with unbounded buffers. In: ACM/IEEE International Conference on Automated Software Engineering, ASE, pp. 743–754. ACM (2014). https://doi.org/10.1145/2642937.2643016

5. Boigelot, B., Godefroid, P.: Symbolic verification of communication protocols with infinite state spaces using QDDs. In: Alur, R., Henzinger, T.A. (eds.) CAV 1996. LNCS, vol. 1102, pp. 1–12. Springer, Heidelberg (1996). https://doi.org/10.1007/3-540-61474-5_53

6. Bouajjani, A., Enea, C., Ji, K., Qadeer, S.: On the completeness of verifying message passing programs under bounded asynchrony. In: Chockler, H., Weissenbacher, G. (eds.) CAV 2018. LNCS, vol. 10982, pp. 372–391. Springer, Cham (2018). https://doi.org/10.1007/978-3-319-96142-2_23

7. Bracciali, A., Brogi, A., Canal, C: A formal approach to component adaptation. In: J. Syst. Softw. **74**(1), pp. 45–54 (2005)

8. Brand, D., Zafiropulo, P.: On communicating finite-state machines. ACM **30**(2), 323–342 (1983). https://doi.org/10.1145/322374.322380

9. Desgeorges, L., Germerie Guizouarn, L.: Demonstration video of ReSCu. https://seafile.celazur.fr/f/bfa8e1380ce540f5bddb/?dl=1

10. Desge orges, L., Germerie Guizouarn, L.: ReSCu archive. https://archive.softwareheritage.org/browse/origin/directory/?originhttps://src.koda.cnrs.fr/loic.germerie.guizouarn/rescu

11. Desgeorges, L., Germerie Guizouarn, L.: RSC to the ReSCu: Automated Verification of Systems of Communicating Automata. https://hal.science/hal-04090204. Long version (2023)

12. Di Giusto, C., Germerie Guizouarn, L., Lozes, É.: Multiparty half-duplex systems and synchronous communications. J. Logic. Algebraic Methods Program. **131**, 100843. ISSN: 2352–2208 (2023). https://doi.org/10.1016/j.jlamp.2022.100843

13. Di Giusto, C., Germerie Guizouarn, L., Lozes, É.: Towards generalised half-duplex systems. In: 14th Interaction and Concurrency Experience, ICE, Proceedings EPTCS, vol. 347, pp. 22–37 (2021) https://doi.org/10.4204/EPTCS.347.2

14. Gössler, G., Salaün, G.: Realizability of choreographies for services interacting asynchronously. In: Arbab, F., Ölveczky, P.C. (eds.) FACS 2011. LNCS, vol. 7253, pp. 151–167. Springer, Heidelberg (2012). https://doi.org/10.1007/978-3-642-35743-5_10

15. Heußner, A., Le Gall, T., Sutre, G.: McScM: a general framework for the verification of communicating machines. In: Flanagan, C., König, B. (eds.) TACAS 2012. LNCS, vol. 7214, pp. 478–484. Springer, Heidelberg (2012). https://doi.org/10.1007/978-3-642-28756-5_34

16. Honda, K., Yoshida, N., Carbone, M.: Multiparty asynchronous session types. In: 35th ACM SIGPLAN-SIGACT Symposium on Principles of Programming Languages, POPL, Proceedings. ACM, pp. 273–284 (2008). https://doi.org/10.1145/1328438.1328472

17. Hu, R.: Distributed programming using Java APIs generated from session types. In: Behavioural Types: From Theory to Tools River Publishers, pp. 287–308 (2017)

18. Hu, R., Yoshida, N.: Hybrid session verification through endpoint API generation. In: Stevens, P., Wasowski, A. (eds.) FASE 2016. LNCS, vol. 9633, pp. 401–418. Springer, Heidelberg (2016). https://doi.org/10.1007/978-3-662-49665-7_24

19. Jéron, T., Claude Jard, C.: Testing for unboundedness of & #xC;fo channels. In: Theoretical Computer Science **113**(1), pp. 93–117 (1993)

20. Lange, J., Yoshida, N.: Verifying asynchronous interactions via communicating session automata. In: Dillig, I., Tasiran, S. (eds.) CAV 2019. LNCS, vol. 11561, pp. 97–117. Springer, Cham (2019). https://doi.org/10.1007/978-3-030-25540-4_6

21. Martín, J.A., Pimentel, E.: Contracts for security adaptation. In: J. Logic Algebraic Program. 80(3), pp. 154–179 (2011)

22. Neykova, R., Hu, R., Yoshida, N., Abdeljallal, F.: A session type provider: compile-time API generation of distributed protocols with refinements in F#. In: 27th International Conference on Compiler Construction, CC, Proceedings, pp. 128–138. ACM (2018) https://doi.org/10.1145/3178372.3179495

23. Poizat, P., Salaün, G.: Adaptation of open component-based systems. In: Bonsangue, M.M., Johnsen, E.B. (eds.) FMOODS 2007. LNCS, vol. 4468, pp. 141–156. Springer, Heidelberg (2007). https://doi.org/10.1007/978-3-540-72952-5_9

Reasoning About Choreographic Programs

Luís Cruz-Filipe[ID], Eva Graversen$^{(\boxtimes)}$[ID], Fabrizio Montesi[ID],
and Marco Peressotti[ID]

Department of Mathematics and Computer Science, University of Southern Denmark,
Odense, Denmark
efgraversen@imada.sdu.dk

Abstract. Choreographic programming is a paradigm where a concurrent or distributed system is developed in a top-down fashion. Programs, called choreographies, detail the desired interactions between processes, and can be compiled to distributed implementations based on message passing. Choreographic languages usually guarantee deadlock-freedom and provide an operational correspondence between choreographies and their compiled implementations, but until now little work has been done on verifying other properties.

This paper presents a Hoare-style logic for reasoning about the behaviour of choreographies, and illustrate its usage in representative examples. We show that this logic is sound and complete, and discuss decidability of its judgements. Using existing results from choreographic programming, we show that any functional correctness property proven for a choreography also holds for its compiled implementation.

1 Introduction

Programming communicating systems is hard, because of the challenge of ensuring that separate communication actions (like sending or receiving a message) executed by independent programs match each other correctly at runtime [21].

In the paradigm of *choreographic programming* [26], this challenge is tackled by providing high-level abstractions that allow programmers to express the desired flow of communications safely from a 'global' viewpoint [6,8,9,13,17, 18,20,23,27]. In a choreography program, or *choreography*, communication is expressed in some variation of the communication term from security protocol notation, Alice -> Bob: M, which reads "Alice communicates the message M to Bob" [29]. These terms can be composed in structured choreographies using common programming language constructs. Then, a compiler can automatically generate an executable distributed implementation [6,13,16], as depicted in Fig. 1.

So far, research on choreographic programming has mostly focused on improving the expressivity of choreographic programming languages, their implementation, and the formalisation of general properties about compilation. Theory of choreographic programming typically comes with proofs of correctness of the accompanying compilation procedure. A hallmark result is *deadlock-freedom by design*: since mismatched communication actions cannot be syntactically expressed in choreographies, the compiled code cannot incur deadlocks [6].

ⓒ IFIP International Federation for Information Processing 2023
S.-S. Jongmans and A. Lopes (Eds.): COORDINATION 2023, LNCS 13908, pp. 144–162, 2023.
https://doi.org/10.1007/978-3-031-35361-1_8

Choreography with n participants

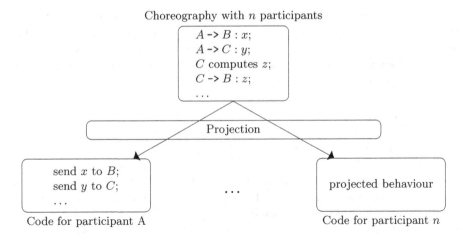

Fig. 1. Choreographic programming: the communication and computation behaviour of a system is defined in a choreography, which is then projected (compiled) to deadlock-free distributed code (adapted from [17]).

By contrast, little research has been done on general methods for proving functional correctness properties about choreographies. Yet choreographies codify distributed protocols, and reasoning about the effect that these protocols have on the states of participants is usually important.

This Work. In this work, we present a Hoare logic for reasoning about choreographies. Hoare logic [2,19] is a common way of reasoning about programs. A Hoare assertion is a triple, $\{\varphi\}P\{\psi\}$, where φ and ψ are formulas (respectively called the *precondition* and *postcondition*) and P is a program. This triple states that if P is executed from a state that satisfies φ and terminates, then the final state satisfies ψ. We develop a Hoare logic where programs are choreographies and formulas can talk about the states of multiple processes jointly.

Our framework is based on well-studied theories of choreographic programming [10,27], in particular on properties that have been formalised in Coq [11,12]. This helps with the generality and elegance of our development. For example, we leverage the property of confluence in metatheoretical proofs, and we rely on the compiler correctness results proven previously to transfer properties proven with our logic to distributed implementations compiled from choreographies.

Contribution. We define a Hoare logic for reasoning about choreographic programs expressed in standard ways, thanks to a modular design parametrised on the language of state formulas. We prove that our logic has the expected properties of a Hoare logic (soundness and partial completeness), and illustrate how it can be used to prove important properties of specific protocols encoded as choreographies.

Structure. We review the choreographic language from [10] in Sect. 2. In Sect. 3 we describe our logic and prove its soundness. Section 4 introduces weakest liberal preconditions, and uses them to show completeness and decidability results. Section 5 discusses additional related work. Illustrative examples are included throughout the text.

2   Language

In this section we recall the choreographic language from [10], which we will be reasoning about. This language models systems of independent processes (networks), which interact by means of synchronous communication. Each process is uniquely identified by a name, which is known by all other processes in the network, and can store values locally in memory referenced by variables. The set of variable names is assumed to be the same for all processes. The set of all processes is denoted by $\mathcal{P}$.

There are two kinds of messages that can be exchanged: *values* are results of evaluating *expressions* locally; and *selection labels* are special constants used to implement agreement on choices about alternative distributed behaviour.

The actual sets of expressions and labels are left unspecified, but we make some assumptions. *Labels* are taken from a (small) finite set. *Expressions* are freely generated from a (typed) signature $\varXi$ and the set of process variables. Expressions that evaluate to a Boolean value are also called Boolean expressions.

2.1   Syntax

Formally, the syntax of choreographies is defined by the grammar

$$C ::= I; C \mid \text{if p}.b \text{ then } C_1 \text{ else } C_2 \mid X \mid \lceil \vec{\mathsf{q}}, X \rfloor C \mid \mathbf{0}$$
$$I ::= \mathsf{p}.x := e \mid \mathsf{p}.e \rightarrow \mathsf{q}.x \mid \mathsf{p} \rightarrow \mathsf{q}[\mathsf{L}]$$

where C is a choreography, I is an instruction, p and q are processes names, e is an expression, v is a value, x is a variable, b is a Boolean expression, L is a selection label, and X is a procedure name.

Choreographies can be built as: an instruction I followed by a choreography; alternative composition of two choreographies C_1 and C_2; procedure calls; or the terminated choreography $\mathbf{0}$. There are two terms for procedure calls, corresponding to: (a) a procedure that has yet to be entered by any processes (X) or (b) one which has already started, annotated with the set of processes that still have to enter it ($\lceil \vec{\mathsf{q}}, X \rfloor C$).

There are three types of instructions: local assignment ($\mathsf{p}.x := e$), where p evaluates expression e and stores the result in its local variable x; value communication, where p evaluates e and sends the result to q, who stores it in variable x; and label selection, where p sends a label L to q (typically to communicate the result of a local choice – see below).

In a conditional, if $\mathsf{p}.b$ then C_1 else C_2, process p evaluates the expression b to decide whether the choreography should continue as C_1 or C_2. Since only p knows the result of the evaluation, the remaining processes need to be informed of how they should behave – this knowledge is typically propagated to other participants by means of label selections.[1]

Repetitive and iterative behaviour in this language is achieved by means of procedure calls. Calling a procedure X simply invokes the choreography corresponding to X, given in a separate mapping of procedure definitions $\mathscr{C}$. Since choreography execution is distributed, processes do not need to synchronise when entering a procedure. This requires a runtime term, $\lceil \vec{q}, X \rfloor C$, to denote a procedure call that only some processes have entered. This term keeps track of both the set of processes $\vec{q}$ that still need to enter X and the execution state of the choreography, C. As we show below, the semantics of choreographies allows for out-of-order execution, and consequently some processes may start executing their part of the procedure before others have entered it.

Example 1 (Diffie-Hellman). Consider the Diffie-Hellman key exchange protocol [14] which allows two parties, p and q, to establish a shared secret, s, that they can later use for symmetric encryption. To implement this protocol in our choreographic language we need only communication, local computation, and a language of expressions with modular exponentiation ($b^e \bmod m$) [16,27]. The protocol assumes that participants have a private key each (a, b) and that they share a prime number m and a primitive root modulo m, g.

$DH =$ p.$(g^a \bmod m) \rightarrow$ q.a;   p computes its public key and sends it to q

q.$(g^b \bmod m) \rightarrow$ p.b;   q computes its public key and sends it to p

p.$s := b^a \bmod m$;   p generates the shared secret

q.$s := a^b \bmod m$;   q generates the shared secret

0 $\lhd$

Example 2 (Zeros). Searching for a zero of a function is a common textbook example for program verification using Hoare-style logics [3]. In this example, we consider a version of the problem where p and q coordinate to find a zero of a function f over natural numbers: p is responsible for selecting the values to test and q for evaluating f and choosing whether to stop or continue searching. We capture this iterative protocol with the following recursive procedure.

$\mathscr{C}(Z) =$ p.$x \rightarrow$ q.x;

if q.$f(x) = 0$ then (q $\rightarrow$ p[L]; **0**)

else (q $\rightarrow$ p[R]; p.$x := 1 + x$; Z)

Then, to search the domain of f, we run the choreography p.$x := 0$; Z. $\lhd$

We define a function pn that returns the set of processes involved in an instruction or choreography. This function is defined inductively in the natural way.

---

[1] For this reason, the set of labels is often fixed to be a two-element set, one for each branch of a choice.

$$\mathsf{pn}(\mathsf{p}.x := e) = \{\mathsf{p}\} \qquad \mathsf{pn}(\mathsf{p}.e \rightarrow \mathsf{q}.x) = \mathsf{pn}(\mathsf{p} \rightarrow \mathsf{q}[\mathsf{L}]) = \{\mathsf{p},\mathsf{q}\}$$
$$\mathsf{pn}(I; C) = \mathsf{pn}(I) \cup \mathsf{pn}(C) \qquad \mathsf{pn}(\text{if } \mathsf{p}.b \text{ then } C_1 \text{ else } C_2) = \{\mathsf{p}\} \cup \mathsf{pn}(C_1) \cup \mathsf{pn}(C_2)$$
$$\mathsf{pn}(X) = \mathcal{P} \qquad \mathsf{pn}(\lceil \vec{\mathsf{q}}, X \rfloor C) = \vec{\mathsf{q}} \cup \mathsf{pn}(C)$$

For simplicity we assume that all processes are involved in all procedures; an alternative is to annotate procedure names with the set of processes they use, see [12]. This does not affect the behaviour of any processes actually involved in the procedure, and semantically only means that a process which would otherwise be considered terminated may first have to enter some number of empty procedure calls.

2.2 Semantics

The semantics of choreographies uses a notion of *state*, which maps each variable at each process to the value it currently stores. It is convenient to define a *local* state as a mapping from variables to values (representing the memory state at one process), and a *global* state as a function Σ such that $\Sigma(\mathsf{p})$ is the local state at p.

To evaluate expressions, we assume that there is an evaluation function that takes a local state as parameter, evaluates variables to their value according to the state, and proceeds homeomorphically. In other words, evaluation maps each symbol in Ξ to a function from values to values. We assume that all choreographies and functions are well-typed, in the sense that the values stored in each variable match the types expected in the expressions in which they occur. Furthermore, we assume that evaluation always terminates, and write $e \downarrow_{\Sigma(\mathsf{p})} v$ to denote that e evaluates to v according to state $\Sigma(\mathsf{p})$ (local at p).

The formal semantics of choreographies is defined by means of a labelled transition system capturing the intuitions given above, whose rules are given in Fig. 2. Transitions are labelled by transition labels, which abstract from the possible choreography actions that can be observed: communications of values ($\mathsf{p}.v \rightarrow \mathsf{q}$) and labels ($\mathsf{p} \rightarrow \mathsf{q}[\mathsf{L}]$), or internal actions ($\tau@\mathsf{p}$). The function pn is naturally extended to these.

$$\mathsf{pn}(\tau@\mathsf{p}) = \{\mathsf{p}\} \qquad \mathsf{pn}(\mathsf{p}.v \rightarrow \mathsf{q}) = \mathsf{pn}(\mathsf{p} \rightarrow \mathsf{q}[\mathsf{L}]) = \{\mathsf{p},\mathsf{q}\}$$

Rules C|ASSIGN, C|COM, C|SEL, C|THEN and C|ELSE capture the intuition behind the different choreographic primitives given earlier. The next three rules deal with procedure invocation: the procedure starts when one process decides to enter it, and all remaining processes are put on a "waiting list" (rule C|CALL); whenever a new process enters it, it is removed from the set of waiting processes (rule C|ENTER); and when the last process enters the call the set is removed (rule C|FINISH).

$$\frac{e \downarrow_{\Sigma(\mathsf{p})} v}{\langle \mathsf{p}.x := e; C, \Sigma \rangle \xrightarrow{\tau @ \mathsf{p}}_{\mathscr{C}} \langle C, \Sigma[\langle \mathsf{p}, x \rangle \mapsto v] \rangle} \; \mathrm{C|AssIGN}$$

$$\frac{e \downarrow_{\Sigma(\mathsf{p})} v}{\langle \mathsf{p}.e \to \mathsf{q}.x; C, \Sigma \rangle \xrightarrow{\mathsf{p}.v \to \mathsf{q}}_{\mathscr{C}} \langle C, \Sigma[\langle \mathsf{q}, x \rangle \mapsto v] \rangle} \; \mathrm{C|Com}$$

$$\frac{}{\langle \mathsf{p} \to \mathsf{q}[\mathrm{L}]; C, \Sigma \rangle \xrightarrow{\mathsf{p} \to \mathsf{q}[\mathrm{L}]}_{\mathscr{C}} \langle C, \Sigma \rangle} \; \mathrm{C|SEL} \qquad \frac{b \downarrow_{\Sigma(\mathsf{p})} \mathsf{true}}{\langle \mathsf{if}\, \mathsf{p}.b\, \mathsf{then}\, C_1\, \mathsf{else}\, C_2, \Sigma \rangle \xrightarrow{\tau @ \mathsf{p}}_{\mathscr{C}} \langle C_1, \Sigma \rangle} \; \mathrm{C|THEN}$$

$$\frac{b \downarrow_{\Sigma(\mathsf{p})} \mathsf{false}}{\langle \mathsf{if}\, \mathsf{p}.b\, \mathsf{then}\, C_1\, \mathsf{else}\, C_2, \Sigma \rangle \xrightarrow{\tau @ \mathsf{p}}_{\mathscr{C}} \langle C_2, \Sigma \rangle} \; \mathrm{C|ELSE}$$

$$\frac{\mathscr{C}(X) = C}{\langle X, \Sigma \rangle \xrightarrow{\tau @ \mathsf{r}}_{\mathscr{C}} \langle \lceil \mathsf{pn}(C) \setminus \mathsf{r}, X \rceil C, \Sigma \rangle} \; \mathrm{C|CALL}$$

$$\frac{\mathsf{r} \in \vec{\mathsf{q}} \quad \vec{\mathsf{q}} \setminus \mathsf{r} \neq \emptyset}{\langle \lceil \vec{\mathsf{q}}, X \rceil C, \Sigma \rangle \xrightarrow{\tau @ \mathsf{r}}_{\mathscr{C}} \langle \lceil \vec{\mathsf{q}} \setminus \mathsf{r}, X \rceil C, \Sigma \rangle} \; \mathrm{C|ENTER} \qquad \frac{}{\langle \lceil \mathsf{q}, X \rceil C, \Sigma \rangle \xrightarrow{\tau @ \mathsf{q}}_{\mathscr{C}} \langle C, \Sigma \rangle} \; \mathrm{C|FINISH}$$

$$\frac{\langle C, \Sigma \rangle \xrightarrow{\mu}_{\mathscr{C}} \langle C', \Sigma' \rangle \quad \mathsf{pn}(I) \# \mathsf{pn}(\mu)}{\langle I; C, \Sigma \rangle \xrightarrow{\mu}_{\mathscr{C}} \langle I; C', \Sigma' \rangle} \; \mathrm{C|DELAYI}$$

$$\frac{\langle C_1, \Sigma \rangle \xrightarrow{\mu}_{\mathscr{C}} \langle C_1', \Sigma' \rangle \quad \langle C_2, \Sigma \rangle \xrightarrow{\mu}_{\mathscr{C}} \langle C_2', \Sigma' \rangle \quad \mathsf{p} \notin \mathsf{pn}(\mu)}{\langle \mathsf{if}\, \mathsf{p}.b\, \mathsf{then}\, C_1\, \mathsf{else}\, C_2, \Sigma \rangle \xrightarrow{\mu}_{\mathscr{C}} \langle \mathsf{if}\, \mathsf{p}.b\, \mathsf{then}\, C_1'\, \mathsf{else}\, C_2', \Sigma' \rangle} \; \mathrm{C|DELAYC}$$

$$\frac{\langle C, \Sigma \rangle \xrightarrow{\mu}_{\mathscr{C}} \langle C', \Sigma' \rangle \quad \vec{\mathsf{q}} \# \mathsf{pn}(\mu)}{\langle \lceil \vec{\mathsf{q}}, X \rceil C, \Sigma \rangle \xrightarrow{\mu}_{\mathscr{C}} \langle \lceil \vec{\mathsf{q}}, X \rceil C', \Sigma' \rangle} \; \mathrm{C|DELAYP}$$

Fig. 2. Semantics

The last three rules deal with out-of-order execution: processes can always execute what for them is the next action, regardless of what other processes are doing. This is modelled by rules C|DELAYI, C|DELAYC and C|DELAYP, which allow execution of an action that is not syntactically the first instruction, conditional or procedure entering, respectively. The side conditions in these rules state that the processes involved in the action being executed do not participate in the actions being skipped (we write $X \# Y$ for $X \cap Y = \emptyset$). Additionally, the action being performed in C|DELAYC must be an action that can be made regardless of what p chooses.

The reflexive and transitive closure of transition is denoted by $\to_{\mathscr{C}}^*$; we omit the sequente of transition labels, as this is immaterial for the current presentation.

For our proofs we also need the concept of *head transition*, which is the transition relation defined by the first 8 rules in Fig. 2 – that is, disallowing out-of-order execution. We write $\langle C, \Sigma \rangle \overset{\mu}{\Rightarrow}_{\mathscr{C}} \langle C', \Sigma' \rangle$ to denote that C makes a head transition to C', and $\Rightarrow_{\mathscr{C}}^*$ for the reflexive and transitive closure of this relation.

3   A Hoare Calculus for Choreographies

In this section we introduce our formal calculus for proving semantic properties of choreographies based on Hoare logic. Our judgements are triples $\{\varphi\}C\{\psi\}$, interpreted as "if choreography C is executed from a state satisfying formula φ and execution terminates, then the final state satisfies formula ψ".

In this section we formally define the syntax and the semantics of this calculus, starting with the state logic – the language in which formulas φ and ψ are written.

3.1   State Logic

State logics in Hoare calculi typically express properties as "variable x stores a value v", which are easily expressible in equational logic. We follow this tradition, and define our state logic to be an extension of equational logic. In order to deal with assignments, we need to be able to update formulas in a way that corresponds to the state update in rule C|ASSIGN – but without computing values. This can be achieved by substituting the expression communicated in the original formula – but this means that expressions may suddenly refer to variables stored in different processes, so that they are no longer evaluated locally.

To deal with these issues, our state logic is parameterised on a set of expressions that is freely generated from the same signature $\varXi$, but using localised variables p.x. We denote these expressions as $\mathcal{E}$, and extend evaluation to them in the natural way.

State formulas are defined as

$$\varphi, \psi ::= (\mathcal{E} = \mathcal{X}) \mid \delta \mid \varphi \wedge \varphi \mid \neg\varphi$$

where $\mathcal{X}$ is a (logical) variable and $\delta \in \mathfrak{D}$, where $\mathfrak{D}$ is a decidable theory whose terms include the logical variables. Parameterising the language on $\mathfrak{D}$ keeps the syntax of formulas simpler, while giving the user flexibility to define additional needed formulas. This is similar to our treatment of the local language. For example, if $\mathfrak{D}$ includes $\mathcal{X} > \mathcal{X}'$, then the state logic is able to express constraints such as p.x > q.y, assuming values are integers: this can be written as p.x = $\mathcal{X} \wedge$ q.y = $\mathcal{Y} \wedge \mathcal{X} > \mathcal{Y}$. Disjunction and implication are defined as abbreviations in the usual way.

Given a state Σ, a formula φ and an assignment ρ from logical variables to values, we define $\Sigma \Vdash_\rho \varphi$, read "$\Sigma$ satisfies φ under ρ", by the rules

$$\frac{\mathcal{E} \downarrow_\Sigma \rho(\mathcal{X})}{\Sigma \Vdash_\rho \mathcal{E} = \mathcal{X}} \qquad \frac{\delta \in \mathfrak{D} \quad \varphi \text{ is true}}{\Sigma \Vdash_\rho \delta}$$

together with the usual rules for logical connectives.

As usual in Hoare logics, assignment is dealt with using substitution – for example, we expect to be able to prove something like

$$\overline{\{\varphi'\}\mathsf{p}.x := e; \mathbf{0}\{\varphi\}}$$

where φ' is obtained by φ by substituting $\mathsf{p}.x$ with e. However, simply replacing every occurrence of $\mathsf{p}.x$ with e yields in general an invalid formula (due to the different variables in choreographies and state formulas). We define the *localisation of e at p*, $L(\mathsf{p}, e)$, as the (logical) expression obtained from e by replacing every (choreography) variable x with $\mathsf{p}.x$; and the *localised substitution* $\mathcal{E}[\mathsf{q}.x := \mathsf{p}.e]$ as the expression obtained from $\mathcal{E}$ by replacing every occurrence of $\mathsf{q}.x$ with $L(\mathsf{p}, e)$. (The rule for communication uses different values for p and q.) Observe that these operations can both be defined by structural recursion on expressions. Localised substitution extends to formulas in the natural way.

Example 3. Take φ to be the formula $\mathsf{p}.x > 3$ and e to be the expression $y - z$. Replacing $\mathsf{p}.x$ with $y - z$ in φ would yield the ill-formed formula $\mathsf{p}.(y - z) > 3$. Instead, replacing $\mathsf{p}.x$ with $L(\mathsf{p}, y - z) = \mathsf{p}.y - \mathsf{p}.z$ yields the right formula $\mathsf{p}.y - \mathsf{p}.z > 3$, and the above judgement becomes

$$\overline{\{\mathsf{p}.y - \mathsf{p}.z > 3\}\mathsf{p}.x := y - z; \mathbf{0}\{\mathsf{p}.x > 3\}}$$

which is syntactically well-formed.   ◁

We now show that an expression that has been localised to p is interpreted as its original evaluation in p.

Lemma 1. *Let Σ be a state, v be a value, $\mathcal{X}$ be a logical variable and ρ be an assignment such that $\rho(\mathcal{X}) = v$. For any process p and expression e, $e \downarrow_{\Sigma(\mathsf{p})} v$ iff $\Sigma \Vdash_\rho L(\mathsf{p}, e) = \mathcal{X}$.*

Proof. Follows from induction on the structure of e.   □

We then show that doing a localised substitution in a formula is equivalent to changing the value of that variable in the environment.

Corollary 1. *Let Σ be a state, p be a process, e be an expression and v be a value such that $e \downarrow_{\Sigma(\mathsf{p})} v$. For any formula φ and assignment ρ, $\Sigma[\langle \mathsf{p}, x \rangle \mapsto v] \Vdash_\rho \varphi$ iff $\Sigma \Vdash_\rho \varphi[\mathsf{q}.x := \mathsf{p}.e]$.*

Proof. By structural induction on φ. One of the base cases is simply Lemma 1, while the other is trivially empty (since formulas in $\mathfrak{D}$ are not affected by substitution). The two inductive cases follow directly by induction hypothesis.   □

$$\frac{}{\vdash_{\mathfrak{C}} \{\varphi\}\mathbf{0}\{\varphi\}} \text{ H|NIL} \qquad \frac{\vdash_{\mathfrak{C}} \{\varphi\}C\{\varphi'\}}{\vdash_{\mathfrak{C}} \{\varphi[\mathsf{p}.x := \mathsf{p}.e]\}\mathsf{p}.x := e; C\{\varphi'\}} \text{ H|ASSIGN}$$

$$\frac{\vdash_{\mathfrak{C}} \{\varphi\}C\{\varphi'\}}{\vdash_{\mathfrak{C}} \{\varphi[\mathsf{q}.x := \mathsf{p}.e]\}\mathsf{p}.e \to \mathsf{q}.x; C\{\varphi'\}} \text{ H|COM} \qquad \frac{\vdash_{\mathfrak{C}} \{\varphi\}C\{\varphi'\}}{\vdash_{\mathfrak{C}} \{\varphi\}\mathsf{p} \to \mathsf{q}[L]; C\{\varphi'\}} \text{ H|SEL}$$

$$\frac{\vdash_{\mathfrak{C}} \{\varphi \wedge L(\mathsf{p},b) \overset{\mathcal{X}}{=} \mathsf{true}\}C_1\{\psi\} \quad \vdash_{\mathfrak{C}} \{\varphi \wedge L(\mathsf{p},b) \overset{\mathcal{X}}{=} \mathsf{false}\}C_2\{\psi\} \quad \mathcal{X} \text{ fresh}}{\vdash_{\mathfrak{C}} \{\varphi\}\mathsf{if}\,\mathsf{p}.b\,\mathsf{then}\,C_1\,\mathsf{else}\,C_2\{\psi\}} \text{ H|COND}$$

$$\frac{\mathfrak{C}(X) = \langle \varphi, \psi \rangle}{\vdash_{\mathfrak{C}} \{\varphi\}X\{\psi\}} \text{ H|CALL} \qquad \frac{\vdash_{\mathfrak{C}} \{\varphi\}C\{\psi\}}{\vdash_{\mathfrak{C}} \{\varphi\}\lceil \bar{\mathsf{q}}, X \rceil C\{\psi\}} \text{ H|CALL'}$$

$$\frac{\mathfrak{D} \models \varphi \to \varphi' \quad \vdash_{\mathfrak{C}} \{\varphi'\}C\{\psi'\} \quad \mathfrak{D} \models \psi' \to \psi}{\vdash_{\mathfrak{C}} \{\varphi\}C\{\psi\}} \text{ H|WEAK}$$

Fig. 3. Inference rules

3.2   Hoare Logic

We are now ready to introduce the rules for our calculus, which are depicted in Fig. 3. To deal with procedure definitions, we need additional information about their effect on states. This is achieved by the *procedure specification map* $\mathfrak{C}$, which maps each procedure name to a pair $\langle \varphi, \psi \rangle$ with intended meaning that the judgement $\{\varphi\}C\{\psi\}$ should hold, where C is the definition of X.

The rule for assignment H|ASSIGN has already been motivated earlier, and is similar to the rule in standard Hoare calculi for imperative programs; likewise, rules H|NIL and H|COND are also standard. The notation $L(\mathsf{p},b) \overset{\mathcal{X}}{=} \mathsf{true}$ in rule H|COND abbreviates the conjunction $L(\mathsf{p},b) = \mathcal{X} \wedge \mathcal{X} = \mathsf{true}$.

Rule H|WEAK is a weakening rule, which allows us to include reasoning in the state logic. The notation $\mathfrak{D} \models \varphi$ stands for "φ is a valid formula".

Rules H|COM and H|SEL adapt the intuitions behind those rules to our choreography actions — a communication is essentially an assignment of a variable located at a different process, while selection does not affect the state.

Rule H|CALL deals with unexpanded procedure calls by reading the corresponding judgement from the specification map, while H|CALL' reflects the fact that the current state of the expanded procedure is explicitly given and a process entering a procedure does not affect the state.

These rules only make sense if the specification map is consistent with the procedure definitions in the following sense.

Definition 1. *A procedure specification map $\mathfrak{C}$ is consistent with a set of procedure definitions $\mathscr{C}$ if $\vdash_{\mathfrak{C}} \{\mathsf{fst}(\mathfrak{C}(X))\}\mathscr{C}(X)\{\mathsf{snd}(\mathfrak{C}(X))\}$ for every X, where fst and snd are the standard projection operators for pairs.*

This notion plays a similar role to the more usual concept of "being a loop invariant" in Hoare logics for languages with while-loops, stating that $\mathsf{fst}(\mathfrak{C}(X))$ always holds whenever X is called.

Example 4 (Diffie-Hellman, functional correctness). Consider Example 1, and assume $\mathfrak{D}$ is a theory for deciding equality of arithmetic expressions with modular exponentiation. Functional correctness for the Diffie-Hellman protocol, states if p and q have the same modulus m and base g then they will share the same secret s once the protocol terminates. These pre- and postconditions are captured by the following state formulas $\varphi = (\mathsf{p}.g \overset{g}{=} \mathsf{q}.g \wedge \mathsf{p}.m \overset{M}{=} \mathsf{q}.m)$ and $\psi = \mathsf{p}.s \overset{S}{=} \mathsf{q}.s$. Thus, we can show the correctness of DH by deriving $\vdash \{\varphi\}DH\{\psi\}$:

$$
\cfrac{
\mathfrak{D} \models \varphi \to \varphi_1 \quad
\cfrac{
\cfrac{
\cfrac{
\cfrac{
\cfrac{\cfrac{}{\vdash \{\psi\}\mathbf{0}\{\psi\}}\ \text{H}|\text{Nil}}
{\vdash \{\varphi_4\}\mathsf{q}.s := a^b \bmod m; \mathbf{0}\{\psi\}}\ \text{H}|\text{Assign}}
{\vdash \{\varphi_3\}\mathsf{p}.s := b^a \bmod m; \dots\{\psi\}}\ \text{H}|\text{Assign}}
{\vdash \{\varphi_2\}\mathsf{q}.(g^b \bmod m) \to \mathsf{p}.b; \dots\{\psi\}}\ \text{H}|\text{Com}}
{\vdash \{\varphi_1\}\mathsf{p}.(g^a \bmod m) \to \mathsf{q}.a; \dots\{\psi\}}\ \text{H}|\text{Com}
}
{\vdash \{\varphi\}DH\{\psi\}}\ \text{H}|\text{Weak}
$$

where:

$$\varphi_1 = \varphi_2[\mathsf{q}.a := \mathsf{p}.g^a \bmod m]$$

$$= (\mathsf{q}.g^{q.b} \bmod \mathsf{q}.m)^{\mathsf{p}.a} \bmod \mathsf{p}.m \overset{S}{=} (\mathsf{p}.g^{p.a} \bmod \mathsf{p}.m)^{q.b} \bmod \mathsf{q}.m$$

$$\varphi_2 = \varphi_3[\mathsf{p}.b := \mathsf{q}.g^b \bmod m] = (\mathsf{q}.b^{q.b} \bmod \mathsf{q}.m)^{\mathsf{p}.a} \bmod \mathsf{p}.m \overset{S}{=} \mathsf{q}.a^{q.b} \bmod \mathsf{q}.m$$

$$\varphi_3 = \varphi_4[\mathsf{p}.s := \mathsf{p}.b^a \bmod m] = \mathsf{p}.b^{p.a} \bmod \mathsf{p}.m \overset{S}{=} \mathsf{q}.a^{q.b} \bmod \mathsf{q}.m$$

$$\varphi_4 = \psi[\mathsf{q}.s := \mathsf{q}.a^b \bmod m] = \mathsf{p}.s \overset{S}{=} \mathsf{q}.a^{q.b} \bmod \mathsf{q}.m \qquad \triangleleft$$

We can now show that this calculus is sound, in the sense that it only derives valid judgements. Given confluence of the transition system for the semantics of choreographies [12], it suffices to show that this holds for head transitions: if execution terminates, any path of execution must lead to the same final state.

Lemma 2. *Assume that $\mathfrak{C}$ is consistent with $\mathscr{C}$ and that $\vdash_{\mathfrak{C}} \{\varphi\}C\{\psi\}$. For every state Σ and assignment ρ, if $\Sigma \Vdash_\rho \varphi$ and $\langle C, \Sigma \rangle \Rightarrow^*_{\mathscr{C}} \langle \mathbf{0}, \Sigma' \rangle$, then $\Sigma' \Vdash_\rho \psi$.*

Proof. The proof is by induction on the number of transitions from $\langle C, \Sigma \rangle$ to $\langle \mathbf{0}, \Sigma' \rangle$. Within each case, we use induction on the size of the derivation of $\vdash_{\mathfrak{C}} \{\varphi\}C\{\psi\}$. We include some representative cases.

- If the number of transitions is 0, then $C = \mathbf{0}$ and $\Sigma = \Sigma'$. The derivation of $\vdash_{\mathfrak{C}} \{\varphi\}\mathbf{0}\{\psi\}$ must then end with an application of H|Nil – which implies that $\psi = \varphi$, establishing the thesis – or of H|Weak – and the induction hypothesis together with soundness of $\mathfrak{D}$ establishes the thesis.

- Assume that $\langle C, \Sigma \rangle \xrightarrow{\tau @ \mathsf{p}}_{\mathscr{C}} \langle C', \Sigma' \rangle \to^*_{\mathscr{C}} \langle C'', \Sigma'' \rangle$ and that the first transition is derived by rule C|ASSIGN. Then C has the form $\mathsf{p}.x := e; C'$, $e \downarrow_{\Sigma(\mathsf{p})} v$, and $\Sigma' = \Sigma[\langle \mathsf{p}, x \rangle \mapsto v]$. There are two cases, depending on the last rule applied in the derivation of $\vdash_{\mathfrak{C}} \{\varphi\} C \{\psi\}$.

  If the derivation terminates with an application of H|ASSIGN, then φ is $\varphi'[\mathsf{p}.x := \mathsf{p}.e]$ for some formula φ' such that $\vdash_{\mathfrak{C}} \{\varphi'\} C' \{\psi\}$. By Corollary 1 it follows that $\Sigma' \Vdash_\rho \varphi'$, and the induction hypothesis applied to C' establishes the thesis.

  If the derivation terminates with an application of H|WEAK, then the thesis is established by the induction hypothesis over the derivation, as in the base case.

- Assume that $\langle C, \Sigma \rangle \xrightarrow{\tau @ \mathsf{p}}_{\mathscr{C}} \langle C', \Sigma' \rangle \to^*_{\mathscr{C}} \langle C'', \Sigma'' \rangle$ and that the first transition is derived by rule C|CALL. Then C has the form $X, \lceil \mathsf{pn}(C) \setminus \mathsf{r}, X \rfloor \mathscr{C}(X)$ and $\Sigma' = \Sigma$. Again there are two cases, depending on the last rule applied in the derivation of $\vdash_{\mathfrak{C}} \{\varphi\} C \{\psi\}$.

  If the derivation terminates with an application of H|CALL, then by consistency of $\mathfrak{C}$ and $\mathscr{C}$ we know that $\vdash_{\mathfrak{C}} \{\varphi\} \mathscr{C}(X) \{\psi\}$, from which we can infer (using H|CALL') that also $\vdash_{\mathfrak{C}} \{\varphi\} \lceil \mathsf{pn}(C) \setminus \mathsf{r}, X \rfloor \mathscr{C}(X) \{\psi\}$. The induction hypothesis applies to this choreography to establish the thesis.

  If the derivation terminates with an application of H|WEAK, then the thesis is established as in the previous cases.   □

Theorem 1 (Soundness). *Assume that $\mathfrak{C}$ is consistent with $\mathscr{C}$ and we have $\vdash_{\mathfrak{C}} \{\varphi\} C \{\psi\}$. For every state Σ and assignment ρ, if $\Sigma \Vdash_\rho \varphi$ and $\langle C, \Sigma \rangle \to^*_{\mathscr{C}} \langle \mathbf{0}, \Sigma' \rangle$, then $\Sigma' \Vdash_\rho \psi$.*

Proof. By the results in [12], if $\langle C, \Sigma \rangle \to^*_{\mathscr{C}} \langle \mathbf{0}, \Sigma' \rangle$ then also $\langle C, \Sigma \rangle \Rightarrow^*_{\mathscr{C}} \langle \mathbf{0}, \Sigma' \rangle$ (combining deadlock-freedom with confluence). Lemma 2 then establishes the thesis.   □

Example 5 (Zeros, functional correctness). Correctness for the program from Example 2 requires that if f has a zero, the program terminates finding it or, equivalently, that the postcondition $\psi = ((f(\mathsf{p}.x) = 0) \overset{\mathcal{Z}}{=} \mathsf{true})$ holds. Since there are no hypothesis on the initial state, we can use as a precondition ϕ any tautology (preferably one without occurrences of variables used in the program) e.g., $\varphi = (\mathsf{true} \overset{\mathcal{I}}{=} \mathsf{true})$. The following derivation shows that the procedure specification map $\mathfrak{C}(Z) = \langle \varphi, \psi \rangle$ is consistent with $\mathscr{C}$ from Example 2:

$$
\cfrac{
\cfrac{
\cfrac{
\cfrac{}{\vdash_{\mathfrak{C}} \{\psi\} \mathbf{0} \{\psi\}} \text{H|NIL}
}{\vdash_{\mathfrak{C}} \{\psi\} \mathsf{q} \to \mathsf{p}[L]; \mathbf{0} \{\psi\}} \text{H|SEL}
\quad
\cfrac{
\cfrac{
\cfrac{\mathfrak{C}(Z) = \langle \varphi, \psi \rangle}{\vdash_{\mathfrak{C}} \{\varphi\} Z \{\psi\}} \text{H|CALL}
}{\vdash_{\mathfrak{C}} \{\varphi\} \mathsf{p}.x := x + 1; Z \{\psi\}} \text{H|ASSIGN}
}{\vdash_{\mathfrak{C}} \{\varphi\} \mathsf{q} \to \mathsf{p}[R]; \ldots \{\psi\}} \text{H|SEL}
}{\cfrac{\vdash_{\mathfrak{C}} \{\varphi_2\} \text{if } \mathsf{q}.f(x) = 0 \text{ then} \ldots \text{else} \ldots \{\psi\}}{} \text{H|COND}}
}{}
$$

$$
\cfrac{
\mathfrak{D} \vDash \varphi \to \varphi_1 \qquad \vdash_{\mathfrak{C}} \{\varphi_1\} \mathsf{p}.x \to \mathsf{q}.x; \ldots \{\psi\} \;\; \text{H|COM}
}{\vdash_{\mathfrak{C}} \{\varphi\} \mathscr{C}(Z) \{\psi\}} \text{H|WEAK}
$$

where:

$$\varphi_1 = ((f(\mathsf{p}.x) = 0) \overset{\mathcal{Z}}{=} \mathsf{true} \rightarrow \psi) \wedge ((f(\mathsf{p}.x) = 0) \overset{\mathcal{Z}}{=} \mathsf{false} \rightarrow \varphi)$$

$$\varphi_2 = ((f(\mathsf{q}.x) = 0) \overset{\mathcal{Z}}{=} \mathsf{true} \rightarrow \psi) \wedge ((f(\mathsf{q}.x) = 0) \overset{\mathcal{Z}}{=} \mathsf{false} \rightarrow \varphi)$$

The same pre- and postconditions hold for the whole program:

$$\cfrac{\cfrac{\mathfrak{C}(Z) = \langle \varphi, \psi \rangle}{\vdash_{\mathfrak{C}} \{\varphi\} Z \{\psi\}} \, \mathrm{H|C{\small ALL}}}{\vdash_{\mathfrak{C}} \{\varphi\} \mathsf{p}.x := 0; Z \{\psi\}} \, \mathrm{H|A{\small SSIGN}}$$

If follows from soundness, that any terminating execution ends in a state Σ s.t., $f(x) = 0 \downarrow_{\Sigma(\mathsf{p})} \mathsf{true}$. Termination follows by observing that p scans natural numbers starting from 0 proceeding by single increments and thus, if f has any zero, p will eventually send the first of them to q which in turn will choose to terminate the search. ◁

4 Completeness of the Hoare Calculus

To establish a completeness result for our calculus, we follow standard techniques from the literature, by using a notion of *weakest liberal precondition* – the weakest assertion φ, given $\mathfrak{C}$, C and ψ, such that $\vdash_{\mathfrak{C}} \{\varphi\} C \{\psi\}$.

4.1 Weakest Liberal Preconditions

In this section we define the weakest liberal precondition operator and show that it satisfies the expected properties.

Definition 2. *Let C be a choreography, ψ be a formula and $\mathfrak{C}$ be a procedure specification map. The* weakest liberal precondition *for C and ψ under $\mathfrak{C}$, $\mathsf{wlp}_{\mathfrak{C}}(C, \psi)$, is defined as follows.*

$$\mathsf{wlp}_{\mathfrak{C}}((\mathsf{p}.x := e; C), \psi) = \mathsf{wlp}_{\mathfrak{C}}(C, \psi)[\mathsf{p}.x := \mathsf{p}.e]$$

$$\mathsf{wlp}_{\mathfrak{C}}((\mathsf{p}.e \rightarrow \mathsf{q}.x; C), \psi) = \mathsf{wlp}_{\mathfrak{C}}(C, \psi)[\mathsf{q}.x := \mathsf{p}.e]$$

$$\mathsf{wlp}_{\mathfrak{C}}((\mathsf{p} \rightarrow \mathsf{q}[L]; C), \psi) = \mathsf{wlp}_{\mathfrak{C}}(C, \psi)$$

$$\mathsf{wlp}_{\mathfrak{C}}(\mathsf{if} \, \mathsf{p}.b \, \mathsf{then} \, C_1 \, \mathsf{else} \, C_2, \psi) = (L(\mathsf{p}, b) \overset{\mathcal{X}}{=} \mathsf{true} \rightarrow \mathsf{wlp}_{\mathfrak{C}}(C_1, \psi))$$

$$\wedge \, (L(\mathsf{p}, b) \overset{\mathcal{X}}{=} \mathsf{false} \rightarrow \mathsf{wlp}_{\mathfrak{C}}(C_2, \psi))$$

$$\mathsf{wlp}_{\mathfrak{C}}(X, \psi) = \mathsf{fst}(\mathfrak{C}(X))$$

$$\mathsf{wlp}_{\mathfrak{C}}(\lceil \bar{\mathsf{q}}, X \rfloor C, \psi) = \mathsf{wlp}_{\mathfrak{C}}(C, \psi)$$

$$\mathsf{wlp}_{\mathfrak{C}}(\mathbf{0}, \psi) = \psi$$

This operator is essentially mimicking the rules from Fig. 3. In the clause for conditionals, $\mathcal{X}$ is fresh. The only potentially surprising item is the definition of $\mathsf{wlp}_{\mathfrak{C}}(X, \psi)$, which ignores the actual formula ψ: this is again due to the fact that our results require an additional condition on $\mathfrak{C}$ (namely, that the conditions given are compatible with the definition of $\mathsf{wlp}_{\mathfrak{C}}$), which indirectly ensures that ψ is also considered.

Example 6 (Diffie-Hellman, WLP). Consider the choreography DH from Example 1 and the postcondition $\psi = (\mathsf{p}.s \overset{S}{=} \mathsf{q}.s)$ from Example 4, $\mathsf{wlp}(DH, \psi)$ is the formula φ_1 from Example 4.   ◁

Definition 3. *A procedure specification map $\mathfrak{C}$ is* adequate for ψ given a set *of procedure definitions $\mathscr{C}$ if, for any procedure name X, $\mathsf{fst}(\mathfrak{C}(X))$ is logically equivalent to $\mathsf{wlp}_{\mathfrak{C}}(\mathscr{C}(X), \psi)$ and $\mathsf{snd}(\mathfrak{C}(X)) = \psi$.*

In other words, for each ψ we are interested in a mapping $\mathfrak{C}$ that, for each procedure, includes the right precondition that ensures that ψ will hold if that procedure terminates.

Example 7 (Zeros, WLP). The procedure specification map $\mathfrak{C}$ from Example 5 is adequate for the postcondition from the same example given the set of procedure definitions $\mathscr{C}$ from Example 2. In fact, $\mathsf{wlp}_{\mathfrak{C}}(\mathscr{C}(Z), f(\mathsf{p}.x) = 0 \overset{Z}{=} \mathsf{true})$ is the formula φ_1 from Example 5, which is logically equivalent to $\mathsf{fst}(\mathfrak{C}(Z))$.   ◁

The next results show that $\mathsf{wlp}_{\mathfrak{C}}(C, \psi)$ precisely characterises the set of states from which execution of C guarantees ψ.

Lemma 3. *Assume that $\mathfrak{C}$ is adequate for ψ given $\mathscr{C}$. Then, for every choreography C, $\vdash_{\mathfrak{C}} \{\mathsf{wlp}_{\mathfrak{C}}(C, \psi)\}C\{\psi\}$.*

Proof. By structural induction on C. Most cases immediately follow from the definition of $\mathsf{wlp}_{\mathfrak{C}}$ together with the induction hypothesis. We detail the only nontrivial ones.

- If C is if $\mathsf{p}.b$ then C_1 else C_2, we observe that $\vdash_{\mathfrak{C}} \{\mathsf{wlp}_{\mathfrak{C}}(C_1, \psi)\}C_1\{\psi\}$. Since

$$(\mathsf{wlp}_{\mathfrak{C}}(\text{if } \mathsf{p}.b \text{ then } C_1 \text{ else } C_2, \psi) \wedge L(\mathsf{p}, b) \overset{x}{=} \mathsf{true}) \rightarrow \mathsf{wlp}_{\mathfrak{C}}(C_1, \psi)$$

  is a valid propositional formula, we can apply rule H|WEAK to derive $\vdash_{\mathfrak{C}}$ $\{\mathsf{wlp}_{\mathfrak{C}}(\text{if } \mathsf{p}.b \text{ then } C_1 \text{ else } C_2, \psi) \wedge L(\mathsf{p}, b) \overset{x}{=} \mathsf{true}\}C_1\{\psi\}$. A similar reasoning applied to C_2 derives the other hypothesis for rule H|COND, and combining them establishes the thesis.
- If C is X, then the thesis follows from the assumption that $\mathsf{snd}(\mathfrak{C}(X)) = \psi$.   □

Corollary 2. *If $\mathfrak{C}$ is adequate for ψ given $\mathscr{C}$, then $\mathfrak{C}$ is consistent with $\mathscr{C}$.*

Corollary 3. *Assume that $\mathfrak{C}$ is adequate for ψ given $\mathscr{C}$. For every choreography C, state Σ, and assignment ρ, if $\Sigma \Vdash_{\rho} \mathsf{wlp}_{\mathfrak{C}}(C, \psi)$ and $\langle C, \Sigma \rangle \rightarrow_{\mathscr{C}}^* \langle \mathbf{0}, \Sigma' \rangle$ for some state Σ', then $\Sigma' \Vdash_{\rho} \psi$.*

Proof. By Lemma 3, $\vdash_{\mathfrak{C}} \{\mathsf{wlp}_{\mathfrak{C}}(C, \psi)\}C\{\psi\}$. By Corollary 2, $\mathfrak{C}$ is consistent with $\mathscr{C}$. The thesis then follows by Theorem 1. $\qquad\square$

Lemma 4. *Assume that $\mathfrak{C}$ is adequate for ψ given $\mathscr{C}$. Let C be a choreography, Σ and Σ' be states, and ρ be an assignment. If $\langle C, \Sigma \rangle \Rightarrow^*_{\mathscr{C}} \langle \mathbf{0}, \Sigma' \rangle$ and $\Sigma' \Vdash_{\rho} \psi$, then $\Sigma \Vdash_{\rho} \mathsf{wlp}_{\mathfrak{C}}(C, \psi)$.*

Proof. By induction on the number of transitions from C to $\mathbf{0}$. If this number is 0, then C is $\mathbf{0}$ and the thesis trivially follows. Otherwise, we detail some representative cases. We do case analysis on C to determine the first transition.

- If C is $\mathsf{p}.x := e; C''$, then $\langle C, \Sigma \rangle \xrightarrow{\tau @ \mathsf{p}}_{\mathscr{C}} \langle C'', \Sigma'' \rangle \Rightarrow^*_{\mathscr{C}} \langle \mathbf{0}, \Sigma' \rangle$, and $\Sigma'' \Vdash_{\rho}$ $\mathsf{wlp}_{\mathfrak{C}}(C'', \psi)$ by induction hypothesis. But $\Sigma'' = \Sigma[\langle \mathsf{p}, x \rangle \mapsto v]$ where $e \downarrow_{\Sigma(\mathsf{p})}$ v, hence $\Sigma \Vdash_{\rho} \mathsf{wlp}_{\mathfrak{C}}(C'', \psi)[\mathsf{p}.x := \mathsf{p}.e]$ by Corollary 1, establishing the thesis.
- If C is if $\mathsf{p}.b$ then C_1 else C_2, then there are two cases. Assume wlog that $b \downarrow_{\Sigma(\mathsf{p})}$ true. Then $\langle$if $\mathsf{p}.b$ then C_1 else $C_2, \Sigma \rangle \xrightarrow{\tau @ \mathsf{p}}_{\mathscr{C}} \langle C_1, \Sigma \rangle \Rightarrow^*_{\mathscr{C}} \langle \mathbf{0}, \Sigma' \rangle$, and $\Sigma \Vdash_{\rho}$ $\mathsf{wlp}_{\mathfrak{C}}(C_1, \psi)$ by induction hypothesis. The only nontrivial case is when $\rho(\mathcal{X}) =$ true – otherwise the antecedents of both implications in $\mathsf{wlp}_{\mathfrak{C}}(C, \psi)$ are false and the thesis trivially holds. If $\rho(\mathcal{X}) =$ true, then $\Sigma \vdash_{\rho} L(\mathsf{p}, b) = \mathcal{X}$ by Lemma 1, and again both implications in $\mathsf{wlp}_{\mathfrak{C}}(C, \psi)$ are true (the first one has true premise and conclusion, while the premise in the second one is false). The case where $b \downarrow_{\Sigma(\mathsf{p})}$ false is analogous.
- If C is X, then $\langle X, \Sigma \rangle \Rightarrow^*_{\mathscr{C}} \langle \mathscr{C}(X), \Sigma \rangle \Rightarrow^*_{\mathscr{C}} \langle \mathbf{0}, \Sigma' \rangle$ by applying rules C|CALL, C|ENTER and C|FINISH until all processes have entered X. By adequacy, $\mathsf{fst}(\mathfrak{C}(X)) = \mathsf{wlp}_{\mathfrak{C}}(\mathscr{C}(X), \psi)$, and the induction hypothesis establishes the thesis. $\qquad\square$

Corollary 4. *Assume that $\mathfrak{C}$ is adequate for ψ given $\mathscr{C}$. Let C be a choreography, Σ and Σ' be states, and ρ be an assignment. If $\langle C, \Sigma \rangle \rightarrow^*_{\mathscr{C}} \langle \mathbf{0}, \Sigma' \rangle$ and $\Sigma' \Vdash_{\rho} \psi$, then $\Sigma \Vdash_{\rho} \mathsf{wlp}_{\mathfrak{C}}(C, \psi)$.*

Proof. Combining Lemma 4 with deadlock-freedom and confluence of the semantics, as in the proof of Theorem 1. $\qquad\square$

4.2 Completeness

Combining the results in the previous section, we obtain a completeness result for our calculus.

Theorem 2 (Partial completeness). *Let C be a choreography, φ and ψ be formulas, and assume that $\mathfrak{C}$ is adequate for ψ given $\mathscr{C}$. Assume that, for all states Σ and Σ' and assignment ρ, if $\Sigma \Vdash_{\rho} \varphi$ and $\langle C, \Sigma \rangle \rightarrow^*_{\mathscr{C}} \langle \mathbf{0}, \Sigma' \rangle$, then $\Sigma' \Vdash_{\rho} \psi$. Then $\vdash_{\mathfrak{C}} \{\varphi\}C\{\psi\}$.*

Proof. Let Σ be a state such that $\langle C, \Sigma \rangle \rightarrow^*_{\mathscr{C}} \langle \mathbf{0}, \Sigma' \rangle$, implies $\Sigma' \Vdash_{\rho} \psi$. Then $\Sigma \Vdash_{\rho} \mathsf{wlp}_{\mathfrak{C}}(C, \psi)$ by Corollary 4. Since this is the case for all states Σ such that $\Sigma \Vdash_{\rho} \varphi$, it follows that $\mathfrak{D} \Vdash \varphi \rightarrow \mathsf{wlp}_{\mathfrak{C}}(C, \psi)$. But $\vdash_{\mathfrak{C}} \{\mathsf{wlp}_{\mathfrak{C}}(C, \psi)\}C\{\psi\}$ by Lemma 3, whence by H|WEAK the thesis holds. $\qquad\square$

Theorems 1 and 2 can be combined with the EPP theorem from [12], which relates the behaviour of choreographies with the behaviour of their projections, to yield results on execution of distributed implementations generated by choreographies. This means that properties of these implementations can be analysed at the choreographic level, which is arguably simple, without the need for a specialised Hoare calculus for process languages.

4.3 Decidability

Finally we establish some decidability results for the Hoare calculus. We start by pointing out that we assume $\mathfrak{D}$ is decidable; since propositional logic is decidable and evaluation converges, the judgments of the form $\mathfrak{D} \models \varphi$ that appear on the premises of rule H|WEAK are also decidable.

Lemma 5. *The judgement $\vdash_{\mathfrak{C}} \{\varphi\}C\{\psi\}$ is decidable.*

Proof. Assume that $\vdash_{\mathfrak{C}} \{\varphi\}C\{\psi\}$. By Theorem 1, for every state Σ and assignment ρ such that $\Sigma \Vdash_\rho \varphi$ it is the case that: if $\langle C, \Sigma \rangle \rightarrow^*_{\mathscr{C}} \langle 0, \Sigma' \rangle$, then $\Sigma' \Vdash_\rho \psi$. By Corollary 4, this means that $\Sigma \Vdash_\rho \mathsf{wlp}_{\mathfrak{C}}(C, \psi)$, and therefore $\mathfrak{D} \models \varphi \rightarrow \mathsf{wlp}_{\mathfrak{C}}(C, \psi)$.

Conversely, if $\mathfrak{D} \models \varphi \rightarrow \mathsf{wlp}_{\mathfrak{C}}(C, \psi)$, then for every state Σ and assignment ρ such that $\Sigma \Vdash_\rho \varphi$ it is the case that $\Sigma \Vdash_\rho \mathsf{wlp}_{\mathfrak{C}}(C, \psi)$, and therefore if $\langle C, \Sigma \rangle \rightarrow^*_{\mathscr{C}} \langle 0, \Sigma' \rangle$ it must hold that $\Sigma' \Vdash_\rho$ by Corollary 3. By Theorem 2 this means that $\vdash_{\mathfrak{C}} \{\varphi\}C\{\psi\}$.

This shows that $\vdash_{\mathfrak{C}} \{\varphi\}C\{\psi\}$ iff $\mathfrak{D} \models \varphi \rightarrow \mathsf{wlp}_{\mathfrak{C}}(C, \psi)$. Since $\mathsf{wlp}_{\mathfrak{C}}$ is computable and validity is decidable, it follows that $\vdash_{\mathfrak{C}} \{\varphi\}C\{\psi\}$ is decidable. □

Although the set of procedure names can in principle be infinite, most practical applications only use a finite subset of them.[2] In this case, consistency and adequacy also become decidable.

Corollary 5. *If the set of procedure names is finite, then consistency between a procedure specification map $\mathfrak{C}$ and a set of procedure definitions $\mathscr{C}$ is decidable.*

Lemma 6. *If the set of procedure names is finite, then adequacy of a procedure specification map for a formula and set of procedure definitions is decidable.*

Proof. Immediate from the definition. □

We end this section with a negative result: it is not possible to compute an adequate procedure specification map.

Lemma 7. *There is no algorithm that, given a set of procedure definitions $\mathscr{C}$ and a formula ψ, always returns a procedure specification map $\mathfrak{C}$ that is adequate for ψ given $\mathscr{C}$.*

---

[2] This disallows choreographies where e.g. each procedure X_i calls procedure X_{i+1}, which do not occur in practice.

Proof. Consider the formula $\psi = \bot$, which never holds. For any choreography C and satisfiable formula φ, the judgement $\{\varphi\}C\{\bot\}$ holds iff C never terminates from a state that satisfies φ.

This means that, if $\mathfrak{C}$ is adequate for $\bot$ given $\mathscr{C}$, then $\mathsf{wlp}_{\mathfrak{C}}(C, \bot)$ characterises the set of states from which execution of C diverges. In particular, C never terminates if $\mathsf{wlp}_{\mathfrak{C}}(C, \bot)$ is logically equivalent to $\top$ – which is decidable in our state logic. But Rice's Theorem implies that the class of choreographies that always diverge is undecidable, therefore $\mathfrak{C}$ cannot be computable. □

Although this result states that adequate procedure specification maps are in general not computable, there is still the possibility that they can be shown to exist always. Such a result would entail that our calculus is strongly complete. We plan to investigate this issue in future work.

5   Related Work

The work nearest to ours is [20], where the authors propose a system for functional correctness of choreographies aimed at reasoning about distributed choices. While they also propose a Hoare calculus for choreographies, there are some key differences wrt our work.

Firstly, they introduce a new choreographic language with significant differences from common practice in choreographic programming, e.g., they require every choice to involve every process regardless of their involvement in the branches in the condition. By contrast, we used an existing language with standard constructs.

Secondly, the logic used in [20] is fixed and used in the choreography language for Boolean expressions. This coupling compromises the generality of the development, because the logic and the syntax of choreographies are not standalone. Instead, we follow the standard two-layered approach for Hoare logic [2,19], and define a state logic that is parametric on both the language of expressions in the choreographies and the theory for reasoning about them.

As a consequence, our development is more readily applicable and adaptable to other existing choreographic languages.

The only other work combining choreographies and logic is Linear Compositional Choreographies (LCC) [7], a proof theory based on linear logic for reasoning about programs that modularly combine compositional choreographies [28] with processes. This was inspired by previous work on the correspondence between linear propositions and session types [5]. LCC, however, is not aimed at functional correctness: propositions represent communication behaviour rather than assertions about states.

Design-by-Contract [25] is a framework where each protocol or function is given a contract specifying its allowed input and resulting output, similar to the pre- and postconditions of Hoare logic, which has been used to reason about distributed programs from a global level. The first work in this line [4] defined a framework for specifying contracts for multiparty sessions. Being based on session types, this work more focussed on specifying properties of communicated values than ours, which lets them specify more properties than us, but also requires adding annotations to the language being reasoned about. An extension of this idea [24] describes chaperone contracts for higher-order binary sessions, which lets contracts update dynamically at runtime. Design-by-Contract has also been applied to microservices in the form of Whip [31]. Like our work, Whip is language-agnostic with regard to the local language, though it uses global contracts to reason directly on the local language; unlike our logic, Whip is designed for monitoring communications at runtime.

Another way of reasoning about session types is combining them with dependent types [30]. Like the work of [4], dependent types can be used to reason about the values being communicated, but unlike our work they are not intended to reason about pre- and postconditions.

Hoare logic has also been used to reason directly about systems of communicating processes [1,22]. This is far more complex than reasoning about choreographies, as it requires independently considering properties of each participant's protocol and how they are combined in the global system.

6   Conclusions

We have presented a novel Hoare calculus for reasoning about choreographic programs. Our logic allows for a great deal of flexibility, since it is parametric on both the local language of the choreographic language and a decidable theory defined by the user.

We have proven that the standard properties of Hoare logics hold for our language. Using the operational correspondence theorems for choreographies and their projections, we also showed that any properties that our logic can prove for a choreography also hold for the distributed implementation automatically generated from that choreography.

Our section on decidability left open the question of whether there always exists an adequate procedure specification map for any target formula, which we plan to investigate in future work. We also want to look further into the issue of how our decidability results can be used to implement interesting algorithms, e.g. for proof automation.

Our formalism only gives us guarantees for terminating execution paths, which means that we cannot infer any properties of non-terminating choreographies. However, an inspection of the proofs of soundness and completeness (in particular, Lemmas 2 and 3) shows that these results actually guarantee something stronger, namely that the invariants described in $\mathfrak{C}$ must hold whenever the choreography reaches a procedure call. We plan to use this observation as a starting point for an investigation about how our calculus can be used to assert properties of non-terminating executions of choreographies.

Acknowledgements. This work was partially supported by Villum Fonden, grant nr 29518.

References

1. Apt, K.R., Francez, N., de Roever, W.P.: A proof system for communicating sequential processes. ACM Trans. Program. Lang. Syst. **2**(3), 359–385 (1980). https://doi.org/10.1145/357103.357110
2. Apt, K.R., Olderog, E.: Fifty years of Hoare's logic. CoRR abs/1904.03917 (2019)
3. Apt, K.R., Olderog, E.-R., Boer, F.S.: Verification of sequential and concurrent programs, vol. 2. Springer (2009). https://doi.org/10.1007/978-1-84882-745-5
4. Bocchi, L., Honda, K., Tuosto, E., Yoshida, N.: A theory of design-by-contract for distributed multiparty interactions. In: Gastin, P., Laroussinie, F. (eds.) CONCUR 2010. LNCS, vol. 6269, pp. 162–176. Springer, Heidelberg (2010). https://doi.org/10.1007/978-3-642-15375-4_12
5. Caires, L., Pfenning, F.: Session types as intuitionistic linear propositions. In: Gastin, P., Laroussinie, F. (eds.) CONCUR 2010. LNCS, vol. 6269, pp. 222–236. Springer, Heidelberg (2010). https://doi.org/10.1007/978-3-642-15375-4_16
6. Carbone, M., Montesi, F.: Deadlock-freedom-by-design: multiparty asynchronous global programming. In: Giacobazzi, R., Cousot, R. (eds.) Procs. POPL, pp. 263–274. ACM (2013). https://doi.org/10.1145/2429069.2429101
7. Carbone, M., Montesi, F., Schürmann, C.: Choreographies, logically. Distributed Computing **31**(1), 51–67 (2017). https://doi.org/10.1007/s00446-017-0295-1
8. Cruz-Filipe, L., Graversen, E., Lugovic, L., Montesi, F., Peressotti, M.: Functional choreographic programming. In: Seidl, H., Liu, Z., Pasareanu, C.S. (eds.) Theoretical Aspects of Computing – ICTAC 2022. ICTAC 2022. Lecture Notes in Computer Science, vol. 13572, pp. 212–237. Springer, Cham (2022). https://doi.org/10.1007/978-3-031-17715-6_15
9. Cruz-Filipe, L., Montesi, F.: Procedural choreographic programming. In: Bouajjani, A., Silva, A. (eds.) FORTE 2017. LNCS, vol. 10321, pp. 92–107. Springer, Cham (2017). https://doi.org/10.1007/978-3-319-60225-7_7
10. Cruz-Filipe, L., Montesi, F.: A core model for choreographic programming. Theor. Comput. Sci. **802**, 38–66 (2020). https://doi.org/10.1016/j.tcs.2019.07.005
11. Cruz-Filipe, L., Montesi, F., Peressotti, M.: Certifying choreography compilation. In: Cerone, A., Ölveczky, P.C. (eds.) ICTAC 2021. LNCS, vol. 12819, pp. 115–133. Springer, Cham (2021). https://doi.org/10.1007/978-3-030-85315-0_8
12. Cruz-Filipe, L., Montesi, F., Peressotti, M.: Formalising a Turing-complete choreographic language in Coq. In: Cohen, L., Kaliszyk, C. (eds.) Procs. ITP. LIPIcs, vol. 193, pp. 1–18. Schloss Dagstuhl - Leibniz-Zentrum für Informatik (2021). https://doi.org/10.4230/LIPIcs.ITP.2021.15
13. Dalla Preda, M., Gabbrielli, M., Giallorenzo, S., Lanese, I., Mauro, J.: Dynamic choreographies: theory and implementation. Log. Methods Comput. Sci. **13**(2), 1–57 (2017). https://doi.org/10.23638/LMCS-13(2:1)2017
14. Diffie, W., Hellman, M.E.: New directions in cryptography. IEEE Trans. Inf. Theory **22**(6), 644–654 (1976). https://doi.org/10.1109/TIT.1976.1055638
15. Gastin, P., Laroussinie, F. (eds.): CONCUR 2010. LNCS, vol. 6269. Springer, Heidelberg (2010). https://doi.org/10.1007/978-3-642-15375-4
16. Giallorenzo, S., Montesi, F., Peressotti, M.: Choreographies as objects. CoRR abs/2005.09520 (2020), https://arxiv.org/abs/2005.09520
17. Giallorenzo, S., Montesi, F., Peressotti, M., Richter, D., Salvaneschi, G., Weisenburger, P.: Multiparty languages: the choreographic and multitier cases (pearl). In: Møller, A., Sridharan, M. (eds.) Proceedings ECOOP. LIPIcs, vol. 194, pp. 1–27. Schloss Dagstuhl - Leibniz-Zentrum für Informatik (2021). https://doi.org/10.4230/LIPIcs.ECOOP.2021.22

18. Hirsch, A.K., Garg, D.: Pirouette: higher-order typed functional choreographies. Proc. ACM Program. Lang. **6**(POPL), 1–27 (2022). https://doi.org/10.1145/3498684
19. Hoare, C.: An axiomatic basis for computer programming. Commun. ACM **12**(10), 576–580 (1969). https://doi.org/10.1145/363235.363259
20. Jongmans, S., van den Bos, P.: A predicate transformer for choreographies - computing preconditions in choreographic programming. In: Sergey, I. (eds.) Programming Languages and Systems. ESOP 2022. Lecture Notes in Computer Science, vol. 13240, pp. 520–547. Springer, Cham (2022). https://doi.org/10.1007/978-3-030-99336-8_19
21. Leesatapornwongsa, T., Lukman, J.F., Lu, S., Gunawi, H.S.: Taxdc: A taxonomy of non-deterministic concurrency bugs in datacenter distributed systems. In: Conte, T., Zhou, Y. (eds.) Procs. ASPLOS, pp. 517–530. ACM (2016). https://doi.org/10.1145/2872362.2872374
22. Levin, G., Gries, D.: A proof technique for communicating sequential processes. Acta Informatica **15**, 281–302 (1981). https://doi.org/10.1007/BF00289266
23. López, H.A., Nielson, F., Nielson, H.R.: Enforcing availability in failure-aware communicating systems. In: Albert, E., Lanese, I. (eds.) FORTE 2016. LNCS, vol. 9688, pp. 195–211. Springer, Cham (2016). https://doi.org/10.1007/978-3-319-39570-8_13
24. Melgratti, H.C., Padovani, L.: Chaperone contracts for higher-order sessions. Proc. ACM Program. Lang. **1**(ICFP), 1–29 (2017). https://doi.org/10.1145/3110279
25. Meyer, B.: Applying "design by contract." Computer **25**(10), 40–51 (1992). https://doi.org/10.1109/2.161279
26. Montesi, F.: Choreographic programming, Ph. D. Thesis, IT University of Copenhagen (2013)
27. Montesi, F.: Introduction to Choreographies. Cambridge University Press (2023)
28. Montesi, F., Yoshida, N.: Compositional choreographies. In: D'Argenio, P.R., Melgratti, H. (eds.) CONCUR 2013. LNCS, vol. 8052, pp. 425–439. Springer, Heidelberg (2013). https://doi.org/10.1007/978-3-642-40184-8_30
29. Needham, R.M., Schroeder, M.D.: Using encryption for authentication in large networks of computers. Commun. ACM **21**(12), 993–999 (1978). https://doi.org/10.1145/359657.359659
30. Toninho, B., Caires, L., Pfenning, F.: Dependent session types via intuitionistic linear type theory. In: Schneider-Kamp, P., Hanus, M. (eds.) Procs. PPDP, pp. 161–172. ACM (2011). https://doi.org/10.1145/2003476.2003499
31. Waye, L., Chong, S., Dimoulas, C.: Whip: higher-order contracts for modern services. Proc. ACM Program. Lang. **1**(ICFP), 1–28 (2017). https://doi.org/10.1145/3110280

Caos: A Reusable Scala Web Animator
of Operational Semantics

José Proença[1]([✉])[ID] and Luc Edixhoven[2,3][ID]

[1] CISTER, ISEP, Polytechnic Institute of Porto, Porto, Portugal
pro@isep.ipp.pt
[2] Open University, Heerlen, The Netherlands
led@ou.nl
[3] CWI, Amsterdam, The Netherlands

Abstract. This tool paper presents Caos: a methodology and a pro-gramming framework for *computer-aided design of structural operational semantics for formal models*. This framework includes a set of Scala libraries and a workflow to produce visual and interactive diagrams that animate and provide insights over the structure and the semantics of a given abstract model with operational rules.

Caos follows an approach in which theoretical foundations and a prac-tical tool are built together, as an alternative to foundations-first design ("tool justifies theory") or tool-first design ("foundations justify prac-tice"). The advantage of Caos is that the tool-under-development can immediately be used to automatically run numerous and sizeable exam-ples in order to identify subtle mistakes, unexpected outcomes, and unforeseen limitations in the foundations-under-development, as early as possible.

We share two success stories of Caos' methodology and framework in our own teaching and research context, where we analyse a simple while-language and a choreographic language, including their operational rules and the concurrent composition of such rules. We further discuss how others can include Caos in their own analysis and Scala tools.

Demo video: https://zenodo.org/record/7876060 & https://youtu.be/Xcfn3zqpubw

Hands-on tutorial: In a companion report [17, Appendix A].

1 Introduction

Designing formal methods can be hard. Typical challenges of formal-methods-related research include identifying and dealing with corner cases, discover-ing missing assumptions, finding the right abstraction level, and—of course—proving theorems (and adequately decomposing them into lemmas). Curiously, and unlike other scientific disciplines, we find that a large majority of papers writ-ten in our community primarily focuses on research *results* instead of *methods*. In contrast, this tool paper contributes to *the methodology* of designing formal methods, with special emphasis on Structural Operational Semantics (SOS): we

© IFIP International Federation for Information Processing 2023
S.-S. Jongmans and A. Lopes (Eds.): COORDINATION 2023, LNCS 13908, pp. 163–171, 2023.
https://doi.org/10.1007/978-3-031-35361-1_9

share our experiences with _computer-aided design of SOS for formal methods_ with a set of examples produced by our toolset Caos. Source code and a compilation of examples can be found at https://github.com/arcalab/caos. We hope that it may inspire colleagues both to apply our methodology and tools, and to share their own methodology-related experiences to our community's benefit.

In a nutshell, in Caos, theoretical foundations and a practical tool are built together side-by-side, from the start, as an alternative to the more typical _foundations-first design_ ("tool justifies theory") or _tool-first design_ ("foundations justify practice"). The main advantage of Caos is that the tool-under-development can immediately be used to automatically run numerous and sizeable examples in order to identify subtle mistakes, unexpected outcomes, and/or unforeseen limitations in the foundations-under-development, as early as possible. This need for validation and supporting tools in formal methods has been acknowledged, e.g., by Garavel et al. in a recent survey over formal methods in critical systems [12].

The Caos toolset is based on ReoLive,[1] which was developed as an online set of Scala & JavaScript (JS) tools to analyse Reo connectors [6]. Currently it also hosts many extensions unrelated to Reo [5,13], where common code blocks can be compiled both to JS (client) and to Java binaries (server), allowing computations to be delegated to a remote server. Consequently, it became a **monolithic** implementation with many **replicated** blocks of code for different independent extensions, and it is non-trivial to **reuse** it for different projects. Our alternative Caos toolset aims at addressing these issues, targeting the following requirements:

- **R1**: Caos should use a general programming language, facilitating adoption and supporting more complex back-ends when desired;
- **R2**: The output from Caos-supported implementation should be easy to execute and use, without requiring specific platforms or complex installations;
- **R3**: Caos should be easily reused, and Caos-supported implementations should be modular and easily extended with new analyses.

Guided by these requirements, our Caos toolset is implemented in Scala (R1), compiles to JS that generates intuitive and interactive websites (R2), and includes a simple-to-extend API that facilitates its usage and reuse by other developers (R3). By using the Caos toolset, one can produce a webpage such as the one in Fig. 1. This webpage has an input text box and a collection of widgets that depict or animate different analyses over the input program, exploiting possible operational semantics when applicable. This example will be further detailed in Sect. 2, which analyses a simple while-language (with contracts).

Caos includes dedicated support for SOS, by animating, depicting, or comparing terms that implement a `next` and an `accepting` method. It further supports building SOS for networks of interacting components, mentioned in Sect. 3.

Similar approaches to support the development of language semantics exist, such as the ones below, which do not address all of the 3 requirements above.

---

[1] https://github.com/ReoLanguage/ReoLive.

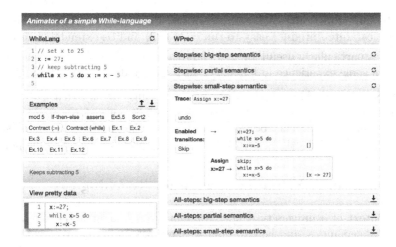

Fig. 1. Screenshot of the web interface to analyse a simple while-language, available at https://cister-labs.github.io/whilelang-scala/

The **Maude language** and toolset [3] focus on how to specify (1) a configuration (a state) using a sequence of characters, and (2) a set of possible rewrite rules capturing how configurations can be modified. It further provides a set of constructs to facilitate the creation of new syntactical notations, such as marking operators as being associative and with a given identity. Maude includes well polished model checkers and other analysis tools; other model checkers (e.g., mCRL2 [1], UPPAAL [7]) also have specification languages with an operational semantics, restricted by design to provide better model-checking support. These approaches provide a similar functionality but do not target our requirements.

Racket (and its DrRacket graphical frontend) [11] is a *Language-Oriented Programming Language*, i.e., a language meant for making languages. It is widely adopted and comes with a large collection of libraries, and includes a set of constructs that facilitate the creation of new syntactical notations, bundled as new languages, allowing multiple languages in a program to exist and to be created on the fly. Embedded in Racket, PLT Redex [10] is a domain specific language for specifying and debugging operational semantics, which receives a grammar and reduction rules and supports an interactive exploration of the terms. Arguably, Racket is a general purpose language (R1), although less adopted than Java or Scala, with extension mechanisms to support reusability (R3), and which we believe to be harder to deploy products (R2).

Some **teaching languages**, such as Pyret [16], are designed to be compiled to JavaScript and to be used when teaching introductory computing, balancing expressiveness and performance. It includes a powerful runtime to hide from the user some of the intricacies and limitations of JS, and this and similar languages include visualisation libraries to better engage students. These languages do not share the same functional goal, and do not use a general programming language (R1), but can often produce easy-to-run code (R2) and be extendable (R3).

Caos is particularly useful for users familiarised with Scala/Java, and less to users with some experience in languages such as Maude, Racket, or Pyret.

Paper Structure: This paper starts by describing our experience with Caos both in a teaching (Sect. 2) and a research (Sect. 3) context, focused on what can be produced using the toolset. Section 4 describes how the Caos toolset is structured and how it can be used by others, and Sect. 5 concludes this paper.

2   Use-Case: A While-Language for Teaching

In the context of a university course, students were taught about natural and operational semantics, and how to infer weakest preconditions. We, as teachers, used a simple while-language with integers to describe these concepts. We created a simple website **in a couple of days** using Caos, depicted in Fig. 1, improving core widgets over the period of one week. Note that we were familiarised with the tools and had some experience with writing parsers in Scala. This website was used by the students to experiment and gain better insights over the concepts.

Figure 1 illustrates the compiled output of Caos: a collection of widgets that always includes an input widget (here called WhileLang) and a list of example input programs. The other widgets are custom-made, and include: (1) *visualisation* of a string produced from the program, representing plain text, code, or a mermaid diagram (a popular Markdown-like language for diagrams);[2] and (2) *execution* given a next function that evolves the program, which can be presented either step-wise (interactive) or as a single state diagram with all reachable states. Caos also provides widgets for (3) *comparing* two program behaviours using bisimilarity or trace equivalence; and (4) *checking* for errors or warnings in a program.

Figure 1 depicts a visualisation of the source code (bottom left) and a step-wise evolution using a small-step semantics with a textual representation (right), and the remaining widgets are collapsed. These collapsed widgets use different semantics, provide a view of all steps, or calculate the weakest preconditions, and are not processed while collapsed. Students could use better understand which rules could be applied at each moment, and navigate through the state space.

3   Use-Case: Analysing Choreographies in Research

Caos can be used to illustrate research concepts using prototyping tools. We used it, for example, when investigating choreographic languages. A choreographic language describes possible sequences of interactions between agents, e.g.,

ctr→wrk1:Work ; ctr→wrk2:Work ; (wrk1→ctr:Done ∥ wrk2→ctr:Done)

---

[2] https://mermaid-js.github.io/mermaid.

captures a scenario where a controller `ctr` delegates some Work to two workers, and they reply once they are Done. Together with Guillermina Cledou and Sung-Shik Jongmans we published several choreography analyses supported by Caos-based prototypes, investigating how to detect that the behaviour of the local agents induce the global behaviour (known as realisability) using a novel underlying mathematical structure [8,9] (https://lmf.di.uminho.pt/b-pomset) and how to generate APIs that statically guarantee that the local agents follow their interaction protocol [4,14] (https://lmf.di.uminho.pt/pompset,st4mp).

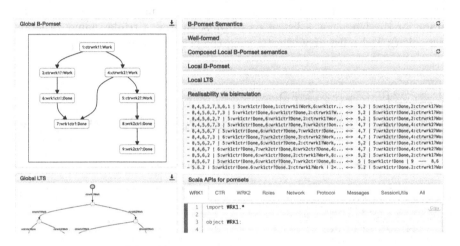

Fig. 2. Analysis of branching pomsets produced by Caos from a choreography language

An underlying mathematical structure was used to give semantics to choreographies: branching pomsets [9] (which are similar to event structures [2,15]). As shown in Fig. 2, using Caos it was possible to: (1) *visualize* the pomset structure (top left); (2) *execute* a pomset (B-Pomset Semantics) and the composition of its projections to each agent involved (Composed Local B-Pomset Semantics); (3) *check well-formedness* (Well-formed), a novel syntactic (sound but incomplete) realisability check; (4) *check realisability* using a (complete but more complex) search for a bisimulation between the global behaviour and the composed behaviour of the projections (Realisability via bisimulation); and (5) *generate Scala code* with libraries that can guarantee at compile time that local agents obey the expected protocol (bottom right). Caos provides constructors for the composition of the behaviour of the local agents and for the search for bisimulations. Setting up each of these websites **took around half a week** of work by one person. During our investigation, the Caos-supported implementation was a *crucial* mechanism to experiment with many variations of the semantics and projections of the choreography language, of the pomset structure, and of the realisability analysis, ultimately converging to the current version.

4 Caos framework

This section describes what Caos provides and how to use it to produce animators such as the ones in Sects. 2 and 3. Figure 3 depicts the structure of a typical Scala project that uses Caos. The user provides data structures for the input language with functions to parse this language and to compute analysis (Analysis.scala), and compiles a collection of widgets that use these functions using special constructors (Configuration.scala). Compiling this configuration yields a JS file used by a provided HTML file. The Configuration is an object that extends an associated class in Caos and holds: the **name** of the language and the website; the **parser** for the language; a list of **examples**, each as a triple (name, program, description); and a list of **widgets** using the provided constructors [17].

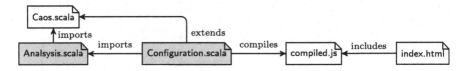

Fig. 3. Architecture of a Scala project that uses Caos

```
val Caos = project.in(file("lib/Caos"))
  .enablePlugins(ScalaJSPlugin)
  .settings(scalaVersion := "3.1.1")
val iLambda = project.in(file("."))
  .enablePlugins(ScalaJSPlugin)
  .settings(
    name := "iLambda",
    version := "0.1.0",
    scalaVersion := "3.1.1",
    scalaJSUseMainModuleInitializer := true,
    Compile/mainClass := Some("iLambda.frontend.Main"),
    Compile/fastLinkJS/scalaJSLinkerOutputDirectory:=
      baseDirectory.value / "lib" / "Caos"/
      "tool" / "js" / "gen",
    libraryDependencies += "org.typelevel" %%%
      "cats-parse" % "0.3.4" )
  .dependsOn(Caos)
                                        build.sbt
```

```
def main(args: Array[String]):Unit =
  Caos.frontend.Site.initSite[Term](MyConfig)

object MyConfig extends Configurator[Term]:
  val name = "Animator of a simple lambda calculus"
  val parser = iLambda.syntax.Parser.parseProgram
  val examples = List(
    "succ" → "(\x →x+1) 2" → "Adds 1 to 2", ...)
  val widgets = List(
    "View program"   →view(Show(_), Code("haskell")),
    "View structure" →view(Show.mermaid, Mermaid),
    "Run semantics"  →steps(e ⇒e,Semantics,Show(_),Text),
    "Build LTS"      →lts( e ⇒e,Semantics,Show(_)),
    ... )  src/main/scala/iLambda/frontend/Main.scala
```

```
enum Term:
    case Var(x:String)
    case App(e1:Term, e2:Term)
    case Lam(x:String, e:Term)
    case Val(n:Int)
    case Add(e1:Term, e2:Term)
    case If0(e1:Term, e2:Term, e3:Term)
src/main/scala/iLambda/syntax/Program.scala
```

```
object LazySemantics extends SOS[String,Term] {
  /** What are the set of possible evolutions
      (label and new state) */
  def next(t:Term): Set[(String,Term)] =
    t match {
    // Cannot evolve variables
    case Var(_)  ⇒ Set()
    // Evolve body of a lambda abstraction
    case Lam(x, e)  ⇒
      for (by, to) ← next(e) yield
        by → Lam(x, to)
    // Apply a lambda abstraction
    case App(Lam(x,e1),e2)  ⇒
      Set(s"beta-$x"  →
        Semantics.subst(e1,x,e2))
    // Evolve 1st the left of an application
    case App(e1, e2)  ⇒
      next(e1).headOption match
        case Some((s,t)) ⇒Set(s →App(t,e2))
        ...
    // Remaing cases...
  }}
src/.../iLambda/backend/LazySemantics.scala
```

Fig. 4. Snippets of code and configurations used in the iLambda project

Tool Demonstration with the iLambda Language

We provide a short demonstration on how to use Caos; an expanded version can be found in the companion report [17] and the video tutorial [18]. In this demonstration we implement a lambda-calculus language with integers (iLambda); the full source-code can be found in https://github.com/arcalab/lambda-caos.

This project requires JVM (>=1.8) and SBT (Scala Builder Tool) to compile, and a web-browser to execute. The top folder should contain the following files:

- build.sbt – is the main configuration file of the project (top-left of Fig. 4);
- project/plugins.sbt – describes the plug-in to compile to JS, in our case with addSbtPlugin("org.scala-js" % "sbt-scalajs" % "1.7.1");
- lib/Caos – includes all Caos files, as-is in its git repository; and
- src/main/scala/iLambda – includes all the source-code of our project.

Figure 4 presents 4 snippets from the iLambda project. The build.sbt configures the compilation process, including the main class to be compiled and the target folder to place the compiled JS, marked in bold. The project is compiled by the command line instruction "sbt fastLinkJS". The Program.scala defines the internal data structure, which represents our lambda terms produced by our parser in src/main/scala/iLambda/syntax/Parser. The Main.scala provides the Configuration object mentioned above, and the LazySemantics exemplifies the definition of an SOS semantics. SOS semantics are specified by extending a SOS[Act,State] class providing a function next(s:State): Set[(Act,State)] that, given a State s, returns a set of new states labelled by an Action. These instances can be animated, compared, or combined using provided widget constructors. For example, lts(e=>e,LazySemantics,Show(_)) builds the LTS, where e=>e states that the initial state is the original lambda term, LazySemantics defines the semantics, and Show(_) defines how to visualise states (which are lambda terms).

5   Conclusions and Lessons Learned

This paper follows a *computer-aided design approach for formal methods* by means of Caos, introducing its toolset and sharing experiences of its application to develop operational semantics of different systems. During the development of new structures and operational semantics, the Caos toolset provided support to quickly view, simulate, and compare different design choices. We were able to identify problems and solutions with a small investment of time in tool development. We further claim that the Caos toolset is reusable, provides intuitive outputs, and is expressive by using a general programming language. By using standard HTML and CSS, the resulting websites can be easily customisable.

Currently we consider two possible improvements. On one hand, to support a lightweight server (inspired in ReoLive [6] but using, e.g., https://http4s.org) that could be used to delegate heavier tasks, such as the usage of a model-checker. On the other hand, to support the parser development with tools such as https://

antlr.org instead of using parsing combinators. All tools are available as open-source, and we welcome any feedback, contribution, or sharing of experiences.

Acknowledgments. This work was supported by the CISTER Research Unit (UID-P/UIDB/04234/2020), financed by National Funds through FCT/MCTES (Portuguese Foundation for Science and Technology) and by project PTDC/CCI-COM/4280/2021 financed by national funds through FCT. It is also a result of the work developed under projects and Route 25 (ref. TRB/2022/00061 - C645463824-00000063) funded by the EU/Next Generation, within the Recovery and Resilience Plan (RRP); and project VALU3S (ECSEL/0016/2019 - JU grant nr. 876852) financed by national funds through FCT and European funds through the EU ECSEL JU. The JU receives support from the European Union's Horizon 2020 research and innovation programme and Austria, Sweden, Spain, Italy, France, Portugal, Ireland, Finland, Slovenia, Poland, Netherlands, Turkey - Disclaimer: This document reflects only the author's view and the Commission is not responsible for any use that may be made of the information it contains.

Data Availability Statement. The artifact is available in the Zenodo repository: doi:10.5281/zenodo.7888538

References

1. Bunte, O., et al.: The mCRL2 toolset for analysing concurrent systems. In: Vojnar, T., Zhang, L. (eds.) TACAS 2019. LNCS, vol. 11428, pp. 21–39. Springer, Cham (2019). https://doi.org/10.1007/978-3-030-17465-1_2
2. Castellani, I., Dezani-Ciancaglini, M., Giannini, P.: Event structure semantics for multiparty sessions. In: Boreale, M., Corradini, F., Loreti, M., Pugliese, R. (eds.) Models, Languages, and Tools for Concurrent and Distributed Programming. LNCS, vol. 11665, pp. 340–363. Springer, Cham (2019). https://doi.org/10.1007/978-3-030-21485-2_19
3. Clavel, M., et al.: The Maude 2.0 system. In: Nieuwenhuis, R. (ed.) RTA 2003. LNCS, vol. 2706, pp. 76–87. Springer, Heidelberg (2003). https://doi.org/10.1007/3-540-44881-0_7
4. Cledou, G., Edixhoven, L., Jongmans, S.S., Proença, J.: API generation for multiparty session types, revisited and revised using Scala 3. In: Ali, K., Vitek, J. (eds.) 36th European Conference on Object-Oriented Programming, ECOOP 2022, 6–10 June 2022, Berlin, Germany. LIPIcs, vol. 222, pp. 27:1–27:28. Schloss Dagstuhl - Leibniz-Zentrum für Informatik (2022). https://doi.org/10.4230/LIPIcs.ECOOP.2022.27
5. Cledou, G., Proença, J., Sputh, B.H.C., Verhulst, E.: Hubs for virtuosonext: online verification of real-time coordinators. Sci. Comput. Program. **203**, 102566 (2021). https://doi.org/10.1016/j.scico.2020.102566
6. Cruz, R., Proença, J.: ReoLive: Analysing Connectors in Your Browser. In: Mazzara, M., Ober, I., Salaün, G. (eds.) STAF 2018. LNCS, vol. 11176, pp. 336–350. Springer, Cham (2018). https://doi.org/10.1007/978-3-030-04771-9_25
7. David, A., Larsen, K.G., Legay, A., Mikučionis, M., Poulsen, D.B.: UPPAAL SMC tutorial. Int. J. Softw. Tools Technol. Transf. **17**(4), 397–415 (2015). https://doi.org/10.1007/s10009-014-0361-y

8. Edixhoven, L., Jongmans, S.S.: Realisability of branching pomsets. In: Tapia Tarifa, S.L., Proença, J. (eds.) FACS 2022. LNCS, vol. 13712, pp. 185–204. Springer, Cham (2022). https://doi.org/10.1007/978-3-031-20872-0_11

9. Edixhoven, L., Jongmans, S.S., Proença, J., Cledou, G.: Branching pomsets for choreographies. In: Aubert, C., Giusto, C.D., Safina, L., Scalas, A. (eds.) Proceedings 15th Interaction and Concurrency Experience, ICE 2022, Lucca, Italy, 17th June 2022. EPTCS, vol. 365, pp. 37–52 (2022). https://doi.org/10.4204/EPTCS.365.3

10. Felleisen, M., Findler, R.B., Flatt, M.: Semantics Engineering with PLT Redex. MIT Press, Cambridge (2009). http://mitpress.mit.edu/catalog/item/default.asp?ttype=2&tid=11885

11. Flatt, M.: Creating languages in racket. Commun. ACM **55**(1), 48–56 (2012). https://doi.org/10.1145/2063176.2063195

12. Garavel, H., Beek, M.H., Pol, J.: The 2020 expert survey on formal methods. In: ter Beek, M.H., Ničković, D. (eds.) FMICS 2020. LNCS, vol. 12327, pp. 3–69. Springer, Cham (2020). https://doi.org/10.1007/978-3-030-58298-2_1

13. Goncharov, S., Neves, R., Proença, J.: Implementing hybrid semantics: from functional to imperative. In: Pun, V.K.I., Stolz, V., Simao, A. (eds.) ICTAC 2020. LNCS, vol. 12545, pp. 262–282. Springer, Cham (2020). https://doi.org/10.1007/978-3-030-64276-1_14

14. Jongmans, S.S., Proença, J.: St4mp: a blueprint of multiparty session typing for multilingual programming. In: Margaria, T., Steffen, B. (eds.) ISoLA 2022. LNCS, vol. 13701, pp. 460-478. Springer, Cham (2022). https://doi.org/10.1007/978-3-031-19849-6_26

15. Nielsen, M., Plotkin, G.D., Winskel, G.: Petri nets, event structures and domains, Part I. Theor. Comput. Sci. **13**, 85–108 (1981). https://doi.org/10.1016/0304-3975(81)90112-2

16. Politz, J.G., Lerner, B.S., Porncharoenwase, S., Krishnamurthi, S.: Event loops as first-class values: a case study in pedagogic language design. Art Sci. Eng. Program. **3**(3), 11 (2019). https://doi.org/10.22152/programming-journal.org/2019/3/11

17. Proença, J., Edixhoven, L.: Caos: a reusable Scala web animator of operational semantics (extended with hands-on tutorial). CoRR abs/2304.14901 (2023). https://doi.org/10.48550/arXiv.2304.14901, https://arxiv.org/abs/2304.14901

18. Proença, J., Edixhoven, L.: Demonstration video of Caos: a reusable Scala web animator of operational semantics. CoRR, April 2023. https://doi.org/10.5281/zenodo.7876059, https://zenodo.org/record/7876059

Jot: A Jolie Framework for Testing Microservices

Saverio Giallorenzo[1,2](✉) ⓘ, Fabrizio Montesi[3] ⓘ, Marco Peressotti[3] ⓘ,
Florian Rademacher[4,5] ⓘ, and Narongrit Unwerawattana[3]

[1] Università di Bologna, Bologna, Italy
[2] INRIA, Sophia Antipolis, France
saverio.giallorenzo@gmail.com
[3] University of Southern Denmark, Odense, Denmark
{fmontesi,peressotti}@imada.sdu.dk, nau@sdu.dk
[4] Software Engineering, RWTH Aachen University, Aachen, Germany
rademacher@se-rwth.de
[5] IDiAL Institute, University of Applied Sciences and Arts Dortmund,
Dortmund, Germany

Abstract. We present JoT, a testing framework for Microservice Architectures (MSAs) based on technology agnosticism, a core principle of microservices. The main advantage of JoT is that it reduces the amount of work for a) testing for MSAs whose services use different technology stacks, b) writing tests that involve multiple services, and c) reusing tests of the same MSA under different deployment configurations or after changing some of its components (e.g., when, for performance, one reimplements a service with a different technology). In JoT, tests are orchestrators that can both consume or offer operations from/to the MSA under test. The language for writing JoT tests is Jolie, which provides constructs that support technology agnosticism and the definition of terse test behaviours. We present the methodology we envision for testing MSAs with JoT and we validate it by implementing non-trivial test scenarios taken from a reference MSA from the literature (Lakeside Mutual).

Keywords: Microservice Architectures · Testing Frameworks ·
Service-Oriented Programming

1 Introduction

The paradigm of microservices is one the modern gold standards for developing distributed applications. In this setting, a distributed application emerges as the composition of multiple services (the "microservices"). Each microservice implements a set of business capabilities, and is independently executable and deployable. Microservices interact with each other via message-passing APIs [4].

Two important factors in the diffusion of microservices are the scalability and flexibility that they support. Scaling is efficient because one can focus scaling actions precisely on those components impacted by traffic fluctuations. Flexibility is given by the usage of *technology-agnostic* APIs, which allows for using different

© IFIP International Federation for Information Processing 2023
S.-S. Jongmans and A. Lopes (Eds.): COORDINATION 2023, LNCS 13908, pp. 172–191, 2023.
https://doi.org/10.1007/978-3-031-35361-1_10

implementation technologies for different microservices without renouncing integration.

However, the good traits of microservices do not come for free. Here, we focus on one of the most prominent elements impacted by the microservices style: testing sets of microservices, or *Microservice Architectures (MSAs)*. Indeed, for unit testing, one can rely on existing frameworks tailored for and idiomatic to the general-purpose implementation technology used to develop a single microservice (e.g., Java, JavaScript, Rust, C). However, when tests cover more microservices, it can become cumbersome to specify the coordination and invocation of services developed with different technologies using a framework designed for testing the "internals" of a service.

To make a concrete example, imagine using JUnit [8] (in Java) to specify the connections to and the coordination and consumption of multiple operations of several microservices. This would not only entail the specification of (possibly complex) coordination logic in Java, but it would also mean adding, on top of the latter, the logic that encodes the data structures that microservices exchange, how connections are established and handled (including errors)—in terms of transport and application layers, etc. Besides their complexity, tests written in this way are difficult to be reused in other tests or under different deployment settings (imagine repurposing a test that uses HTTP endpoints to verb-based binary protocols).

Motivated by these observations we present JoT (Jolie Testing), a testing framework for MSAs based on technology agnosticism. Responding to its motivating points, JoT reduces the amount of work for a) testing for MSAs whose services use different technology stacks, b) writing tests that involve multiple services, and c) reusing tests of the same MSA under different deployment configurations or after changing some of its components (e.g., when, for performance, one reimplements a service with a different technology). In JoT, tests are orchestrators that can both consume or offer operations from/to the MSA under test. The language for writing JoT tests is Jolie [17], which provides constructs that support technology agnosticism [16] and the definition of terse test behaviours. One of the most relevant features introduced by JoT is the provision of Jolie annotations that users can use to structure and specify the sequence of actions that the tool needs to follow to run each test (e.g., test setup, cases, and clean up).

In Sect. 2, we discuss the methodology we envision for testing MSAs with JoT, following an example where we use JoT annotations to build a test case. In Sect. 3, we provide initial validation to JoT's approach by presenting implementations of non-trivial test scenarios taken from a reference MSA from the literature [23] (Lakeside Mutual). We draw conclusions, compare to related work, and discuss future steps in Sect. 4.

2   Methodology and Structure of Tests

To illustrate the structure of tests and the architecture of the testing framework, we start by describing the methodology we envision for building tests in JoT, i.e., the steps users should follow to define a test using the framework.

2.1 Building a Test in JoT

Following general testing practice, the first step for building a test in JoT is defining the subject under test. Our subject is an architecture of services (one or more) that can interact with each other. Considering that the subject under test are the services of an architecture, in the remainder, we use interchangeably the terms "subject under test" and "architecture under test" and use the term "service under test" to indicate a service that is part of an architecture under test (which includes the degenerate case of an architecture made of one service). For example, in the first case in Sect. 3, the architecture under test is made of two services—CustomerCore and CustomerManagement–that manage the users of an online platform.

Once we defined the subject of the test, we need to identify the cases we want to test, i.e., the functionality whose implementation we want to verify. This can range from a single invocation, e.g., calling one operation of one service, to complex behaviours that compose several operations of different services. For example, by having as the subject under test the CustomerCore-CustomerManagement architecture, we can check that users are coherently created, fetched, and modified by the two services. For instance, we can interact with CustomerCore to create a user, then we update the data related to that user via the operations provided by CustomerManagement, and then verify that the update was successful, by fetching and checking the user's information from CustomerCore.

Once we defined the subject under test and the functionality we want to test, we can proceed with the actual implementation of the JoT test and its cases.

Since a JoT test is a service itself (and an orchestrator, in particular) the information we need to provide to a JoT test coincides with the three main elements that define services in general [11]. The first two are the Application Programming Interfaces, *interfaces* for short, and the *access points* which, combined, define the public contract of the services (under test). The third element is the private, internal *behaviour* of the service, which implements the logic of each test case.

Interfaces. The interface of a service specifies what operations it offers to clients. There exist many guidelines and technologies for the description of interfaces [4]. However, we can abstract an interface as the set of labelled operations that a service promises to support. The description of the set of operations can also carry the messaging pattern (e.g., one-way, request-reply calls) of each operation and the structure of the data exchanged through each of them.

For example, one can provide them in the form of an informal list of resources that one can call, e.g., as URL addresses, and describe the shape of the in-/outbound data similarly. Alternatives include the usage of formal languages for the specification of service interfaces, such as WSDL, and the description of interfaces using metamodels [11,20] which support the generation of the same service interface under different formats (formal and informal).

Thanks to the flexibility of Jolie interfaces, JoT adopts a permissive attitude, where the minimal amount of information users need to provide regarding interfaces is: a) the list of operation labels that the test is going to use and b) the messaging pattern that characterises each operation.

For example, a minimal Jolie interface to test the "createCustomer" operation of the CustomerCore is

```
interface CustomerCoreInterface {
  requestResponse: createCustomer
}
```

In the code, we specify that the operation `createCustomer` has a request-response behaviour (from the user side, this means invoking the service on the operation and waiting for the server to answer with some response) and that the operation belongs to the `CustomerCoreInterface` interface (the latter's name is immaterial for the service under test, and it is just a reference to the interface's content within the test itself).

Interestingly, JoT provides support for specifying test invariants on the exchanged data already at the level of interfaces. Indeed, users can specify the structure of the data they expect to see in tests via Jolie types. Jolie types have a tree-shaped form, made of two components: the root of the tree, associated with a basic type (e.g., integer, string, etc.), and a set of nodes that defines the internal fields of the data structure—each node is an array with specified minimal and maximal cardinality.

For example, we can enrich `CustomerCoreInterface` with types, to both specify the kind of data we promise to provide within the test (cases)—in the request part of the `createCustomer` operation—and the shape of the data we expect the service under test to send back as the response.

For example, in the code below, we show one such interface where the request to the `createCustomer` operation needs to carry the name and surname of the user (as strings), while the operation responds with the identification number of the user (as an integer).

```
type CustomerRequest { name: string, surname: string }
type CustomerResponse { id: int }
interface CustomerCoreInterface {
  requestResponse:
    createCustomer(CustomerRequest)(CustomerResponse)
}
```

Access Points. The access point completes the public contract of a service's interface by defining where and how to contact the service, i.e., defining the stack of technologies that clients can use to interact with the service.

Specifically, the technology stack determines the media and protocols used to support the communication between a service and its clients and the format of the data that these exchange. For instance, one can decide to use SOAP and TCP/IP as a technology stack for communication and use XML to format the data.

By relying on Jolie ports, JoT makes it easy to adapt a test to the access-point specifications of a given service incarnation. For example, this allows users to write a test case that they initially want to run at the development stage, e.g., using a message broker [6] and some binary format, and then change the ports settings to test the service in production, e.g., switching the port to use TCP/IP, HTTP, and the JSON format—other examples include SOAP-based web services [17] and REST ones [16].

As we discuss below, JoT provides direct support to this level of flexibility via configuration parameters that the user can pass to the test, so that one can run the same test on different deployment settings programmatically. As an example, following the simple case made above, we can define the port to contact the `CustomerCore` service in a JoT test in the following way:

```
outputPort CustomerCore {
  location: parameters.customerCore.location
  protocol: parameters.customerCore.protocol
  interfaces: CustomerCoreInterface
}
```

Above, we define an `outputPort` called `CustomerCore`, which represents an external service that we can invoke. Through the port definition, we declare that we expect that the `CustomerCore` service implements the `CustomerCoreInterface`. Notice that the `location` and `protocol` of the port are (elements of the variable) `parameters`. We used this definition of the port to illustrate how the user can change the medium technology and endpoint definition (`location`) and the communication protocol and data format (`protocol`) by passing this information as parameters of the test instantiation.

Test Logic. The last element of the test is the definition of the actions that the test needs to enact to implement its logic.

Here, Jolie provides different ways to define the logic of the service, e.g., by allowing developers to use Java or JavaScript. We deem using these languages a viable route, e.g., if one needs to use libraries that would be difficult to expose otherwise or wants to re-use some test logic written in those languages. Notwithstanding this possibility, we envision users to mainly write JoT tests using the Jolie behaviour language. Indeed, Jolie provides a concise-yet-expressive language for behaviour specification that makes it easy to assemble even complex coordination logic, like speculative parallelism [3] and partial joins [7], which one can use to reproduce edge cases of highly-concurrent systems.

Ports make it possible to keep the logic of Jolie programs, and JoT tests, loosely coupled w.r.t. the deployment technology. For instance, let us look at a simple behaviour snippet for our example

```
createCustomer@CustomerCore ({name = "John", surname = "Doe"})(resp)
if(resp.id <= 0){
 throw (TestFailed, "Users need to have positive id numbers")
}
```

Above, we define an elementary test for the `createCustomer` operation, where we send a legit request (according to the interface we defined) and check that the response has the expected shape (verified by the Jolie type checker, given the interface definition of `createCustomer`) and that the identifier is positive. In case the test fails, we `throw` a fault, which interrupts the execution of the tests and reports to the user the failing case. Later in Sect. 3 we use the assertion library provided by JoT, which helps users in verifying the compliance of the results against the expected values even in the case of complex data structures (multi-level nested trees).

2.2 Writing a Complete Test

Before detailing the architecture of JoT, we illustrate the remaining important items that make up a JoT test. For this purpose, we show a working JoT test example by assembling the interface, port, and behaviour shown above with the remaining elements that characterise a JoT test—for brevity, we elide most of the constructs discussed above to focus on the new parts.

```
type CustomerRequest ...
interface CustomerCoreInterface { ... }

interface TestInterface {
 requestResponse:
  ///@Test
  testCreateCustomer()() throws TestFailed(string)
}

service Main(parameters: undefined){
 outputPort CustomerCore {
   location: parameters.customerCore.location
   ...
 }

 inputPort Input {
  ...
  interfaces: TestInterface
 }

 main {
  testCreateCustomer()() {
```

```
  createCustomer@CustomerCore({ name = "John", surname = "Doe" })(resp
    )
    ... }
} }
```

The salient additional parts in the example are four, described below following their top-to-bottom order of appearance in the code.

First, we have an interface, called `TestInterface`, which defines the sequence of operations the JoT framework shall run from the current test. This is done—similarly to other testing frameworks, e.g., JUnit—using comment annotations of the form `///@Annotation`. JoT currently supports five kinds of annotations: `///@BeforeAll`, `///@BeforeEach`, `///@AfterEach`, `///@AfterAll`, and `///@Test`. Respectively, these indicate operations in the body of the test that we invoke once before all test cases, before calling each test case, after we called each test case, and once after we invoked all test cases. The last annotation is to indicate test-case operations. JoT does not impose order among the operations in a given annotation category.

Second, we have a `service` (conventionally called `Main`), which is the Jolie program unit that the JoT framework instantiates to run the tests. When performing the instantiation, the framework passes the configuration parameters for the test defined by the user, which the `service` holds in the `parameters` variable (here, we leave its type `undefined`). In the example, we use the `parameters` variable to carry the information to contact the `CustomerCore` in the related `outputPort`.

Third, we have an `inputPort` (complementary inbound access points to `outputPorts`) that allows the JoT framework orchestrator to govern the operations offered by the test (`service`). Indeed, the `inputPort` publishes the `TestInterface` defined earlier.

Fourth, there is the `main` execution block, which encloses the behaviour of the test cases and the surrounding operations (before-all/each and after-all/each) of the test. In the body of the `main`, we find the test `testCreateCustomer`, which, at invocation, runs the test-case behaviour we previously commented on.

2.3   Executing JoT Tests

By design, JoT does not manage the deployment of the architecture under test. This is to let developers decide the best way to run the architecture. For example, the developer of our exemplary test could execute the service locally (using private network addresses) and later on re-use the same test logic to check the behaviour of the service in production (using public addresses). JoT achieves this flexibility via file-based configurations. Concretely, JoT configurations are JSON files that contain test parameters, such as a tested service's address or protocol. Listing 1 shows an example of a JoT configuration file. It configures the execution of the JoT test whose excerpts were shown in previous listings and which is stored in a Jolie program called "TestCustomerCore.ol" (".ol" is the extension for Jolie programs).

Listing 1. Example JoT configuration file.

```
{ "testsPath": ".",
  "params": {
    "TestCustomerCore.ol": [{
      "name": "Main",
      "params": {}
    }] } }
```

The `testsPath` element specifies the file path of the test source, relative to the configuration file. The `params` element is where users link tests to parameters. For this purpose, each member of the element is a key-value pair consisting of (i) the name of the file that contains the code of the test; (ii) an array of configuration objects. Namely, the element `name` is the name of the Jolie `service` that wraps the test code (e.g., `Main`) while the `params` node contains the parameters for the test.

To execute a test with file-based configuration, the user can save the JSON data in a "params.json" file and then launch the test with the command `jot params.json`.

When testing architectures, our suggestion is to pair JoT with widely adopted microservice deployment technologies, like Kubernetes and Docker-compose, to further automate the running of test batteries. This is the practice we follow, e.g., in Sect. 3, where the services of the architecture under test are containers, deployed through a single Docker Compose file.

JoT's source code is available on GitHub[1], and a publicly downloadable video illustrates JoT's architecture and usage [2].

3   Validation

We now show a preliminary validation of JoT by writing a pair of tests (and related test cases) drawn from the Lakeside Mutual [23] architecture[3] Briefly, Lakeside Mutual is a fictitious insurance company that provides its employees and customers with a software platform to, e.g., manage personal data and insurance policies. In total, Lakeside Mutual—in the continuation, we use the term to indicate the insurance company's software platform—consists of five backend microservices, four frontend components enabling users to operate on the data maintained by the backend microservices, and two infrastructure components for service discovery and technical administration.

---

[1] https://github.com/jolie/jot.
[2] https://drive.google.com/file/d/1VimUbh6stPQoyB_EeLJLllwLs5Vj82wX/view?usp=sharing.
[3] As retrieved at version https://github.com/Microservice-API-Patterns/Lakeside Mutual/commit/aaebc590832c9ffc064fa3a22eae20db17ab31d9

.

3.1   Tested Interaction Scenarios

We implement two testing scenarios.

Scenario 1 involves the interaction of two microservices, namely `Customer-Core` and `CustomerManagement`. The `CustomerCore` microservice provides basic capabilities to manage a customer's data. The `CustomerManagement` microservice acts as a façade for `CustomerCore` and is responsible for providing clients with a stable interface, thereby facilitating the evolution of `Customer-Core`. The testing logic for Scenario 1 covers the update of an existing insurance customer triggered by a client. Figure 1 shows the specification of the scenario as a UML sequence diagram [18].

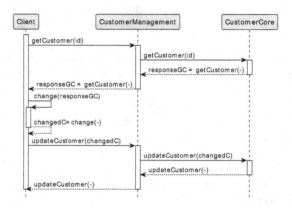

Fig. 1. Specification of tested interaction Scenario 1 as a UML sequence diagram.

In Fig. 1, the `Client` initiates the scenario by retrieving an existing customer with a given `id`, using the `CustomerManagement` operation `getCustomer`. `CustomerManagement` forwards the request to `CustomerCore` and returns the response of the latter to the `Client`. Next, the `Client` updates the received data (e.g., it can change the address of the queried customer) and calls `update-Customer` with the updated data on `CustomerManagement`. Again, `Cus-tomerManagement` forwards this call to `CustomerCore` to perform the actual update of the database.

Scenario 2 includes, on top of the services seen in Scenario 1, another microservice, i.e., `CustomerSelfService`. In this scenario, `CustomerSelf-Service` provides customers with the functionality to register themselves in the system. Scenario 2 focuses on this registration process and the correct execution of the `getCustomers` operation to find the newly registered customer. Thus, differently from Scenario 1, Scenario 2 covers a dedicated business process rather than an activity that is part of several processes. Indeed, Scenario 2 is more complex than the first one and illustrates JoT's capability to perform testing of interactions comprising more than the microservices directly accessed by the test, i.e., the test entails the correct interaction between `CustomerCore` and `CustomerManagement`. Figure 2 shows the specification of Scenario 2 as a UML sequence diagram.

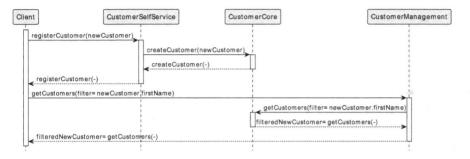

Fig. 2. Specification of tested interaction Scenario 2 as a UML sequence diagram.

In Fig. 2, a `Client` registers a new customer by calling the `register-Customer` operation of the `CustomerSelfService` with the new customer's data. `CustomerSelfService` partially acts as a façade to `CustomerCore`, to which it forwards the request for customer registration as a call to `createCustomer`. After the completion of `registerCustomer`, the `Client` continues by executing the `getCustomers` operation of `CustomerManagement`. This operation allows fetching customers via filters, e.g., via their names. This call is also forwarded to `CustomerCore`, which queries its database and performs the actual fetching.

3.2   JoT Test of Scenario 1

We move to implement Scenario 1 (cf. Fig. 1) using JoT. In the scenario, the JoT tests correspond to the `Client` components (cf. Section 3.1). We start by introducing the Jolie interfaces and access points for the test, and then we describe its logic.

Interfaces. Following the scenario specification (cf. Figure 1), the test program must invoke the `getCustomer` and `updateCustomer` operations on `CustomerManagement` to test its correct behaviour, which entails interacting with `CustomerCore`. Here, we let the test directly interact with `CustomerCore`, in the "setup" phase, to create the customer (via the `createCustomer` operation) that we want to get and update in the test case. Listing 2 shows the Jolie interfaces of the test for Scenario 1.

Listing 2. Interfaces of the test for Scenario 1.

```
 1  type CustomerProfileUpdateRequest { firstName:string,
        lastName:string, ... }
 2
 3  type CustomerResponse {
 4    customerId? :string, firstName? :string, lastName? :string,
        ...
 5  }
 6
 7  interface CustomerInformationHolder_CustomerCore {
 8    RequestResponse:
 9      createCustomer(CustomerProfileUpdateRequest)(
          CustomerResponse)
10  }
11
12  type GetCustomerRequest {
13    ids:string, fields?:string
14  }
15
16  type UpdateCustomerRequest {
17    customerId:CustomerId
18    requestDto:CustomerProfileUpdateRequest
19  }
20
21  interface CustomerInformationHolder_CustomerManagement {
22    RequestResponse:
23      getCustomer(GetCustomerRequest)(CustomerResponse),
24      updateCustomer(UpdateCustomerRequest)(CustomerResponse)
25  }
```

The CustomerInformationHolder_CustomerCore interface[4] in Lines 7–10 specifies the signature of the CustomerCore microservice's createCustomer operation used to setup the test database. The operation is a synchronous request-response operation (cf. Figure 1), and expects an instance of the CustomerProfileUpdateRequest type (cf. Line 1) as input and returns a CustomerResponse (cf. Lines 3–5) as output, whereby the most of the fields of the CustomerResponse type correspond to those of CustomerProfileUpdateRequest with optional cardinality (?)—Jolie also provides the * cardinality that means a 0-to-unbound number of elements of that type. An exception is the customerId field by which the CustomerCore microservice informs invokers of createCustomer about the unique identifier of a newly created customer.

The CustomerInformationHolder_CustomerManagement interface in Lines 21–25 specifies the getCustomer and updateCustomer operations

---

[4] Note that the prefix CustomerInformationHolder refers to the microservice API pattern Information Holder Resource conceived by the developers of Lakeside Mutual, and enabling the provisioning of domain data with integrity and quality preservation [23].

used in the test. The operation `getCustomer` expects an instance of the `Get-CustomerRequest` type (cf. Lines 12–14) to determine the identifiers of the customers to be retrieved and optionally a list of relevant fields. The operation then returns matching data in a `CustomerResponse` instance. Operation `updateCustomer` requires an instance of the type `UpdateCustomerRequest` (cf. Lines 16–19) with the customer identifier to be updated by the passed `CustomerProfileUpdateRequest` instance. As for `getCustomer`, `updateCustomer` then returns its results in the form of `CustomerResponses`.

Access Points. As mentioned, the JoT test for Scenario 1 has two output ports, `CustomerCore` and `CustomerManagement`. Listing 3 shows the expected bindings.

Listing 3. Access points of the test for Scenario 1.

```
1  outputPort customerCore {
2    location: parameters.customerCore.location
3    ...
4    interfaces: CustomerInformationHolder_CustomerCore
5  }
6
7  outputPort customerManagement {
8    location: parameters.customerManagement.location
9    ...
10   interfaces: CustomerInformationHolder_CustomerManagement
11 }
```

We specify at Lines 1–5 the output port for the `CustomerCore` microservice while at Lines 7–11 we report the output port for the `CustomerManagement` microservice. Notice that the actual binding of the ports (location, protocol) is parametric (passed through the `parameters` variable of the test).

Test Logic. Listing 4 shows the testing logic of Scenario 1. Notice that we import the same interface `CustomerInformationHolder` from different files (i.e., `customer-core.interfaces` and `customer-management.interfaces`) and we alias them (with the `as` keyword) resp. `CustomerInformationHolder_CustomerCore` and `CustomerInformationHolder_CustomerManagement`, so that we obtain a similar result as the code in Listing 2.

Listing 4. Logic of the test for Scenario 1.

```
1  // cf. Listing 2
2  from customer-core.interfaces import
       CustomerInformationHolder
3    as CustomerInformationHolder_CustomerCore
4  from customer-management.interfaces import
       CustomerInformationHolder
5    as CustomerInformationHolder_CustomerManagement
```

```
 6
 7 interface TestInterface {
 8  RequestResponse:
 9   /// @BeforeEach
10   setup(void)(void),
11   /// @Test
12   testScenario1(void)(void)
13 }
14
15 service Main {
16  outputPort customerCore { cf. Listing 3 }
17  outputPort customerManagement { cf. Listing 3 }
18  inputPort Input { ... }
19
20  main {
21   /* Setup Test */
22   [ setup()() {
23    request << { firstName = "Jane", lastName = "Doe", ... }
24    createCustomer@customerCore(request)(actual)
25    global.user_id = actual.customerId
26   } ]
27
28   /* Test Scenario 1 */
29   [ testScenario1()() {
30    // Step 1
31    getCustomer@customerManagement({ ids = global.user_id })(
     resp)
32    equals@assertions({ actual << resp.customerId, expected
     << global.user_id })()
33
34    // Step 2
35    undef(resp.customerId)
36    resp.firstName = "John2"
37    updateCustomer@customerManagement({ customerId = global.
     user_id, requestDto << resp })(resp2)
38    equals@assertions({ actual = resp2.firstName, expected =
     "John2" })()
39
40    // Step 3
41    getCustomers@customerManagement({ ids = global.user_id })
     (resp3)
42    equals@assertions({ actual = #resp3.customers, expected =
      1 })()
43   } ] } }
```

Briefly, Lines 2–5 import the types and interfaces for the CustomerCore and CustomerManagement microservices (cf. Listing 2).

Next, in Lines 7–13 we specify the TestInterface of the test. This has two operations with JoT-specific annotation. We use @BeforeEach to invoke

the setup operation before each test (here, just one). Then, we annotate with
@Test testScenario1, which will execute after all @BeforeEach (here, one)
operations.

Starting from Line 15 we find the implementation of the test, as a Jolie
service. There, we find the output ports to access CustomerCore and CustomerManagement microservices (cf. Lines 16 and 17), the input port Input that offers the test operations found in the TestInterface to the JoT
framework orchestrator. The main block encloses the implementation of the
logic of the test.

Specifically, we find at Lines 22–26 the behaviour of the setup operation,
which creates a request value with test data based on the structure of the
CustomerProfileUpdateRequest type (cf. Listing 2) and it uses the latter
in the invocation of createCustomer of CustomerCore. Since setup is
run before all tests (as per its annotation), the @Tests can assume that the
microservice's database has the test entry. The resulting identifier of the created
customer is then stored in a global field called user_id, accessible by all test
cases.

Lines 29–43 comprise the actual logic for the test operation of Scenario 1,
i.e., testScenario1. First, the operation retrieves the test customer previously
created by the setup operation. However, this call addresses the Customer-
Management rather than the CustomerCore microservice and thus verifies
whether CustomerManagement actually behaves as a façade for Customer-
Core as anticipated by Lakeside Mutual's architecture design (cf. Figure 1). In
the second step, the test operation changes the name of the test customer from
"Jane" to "John2" and issues a request to the updateCustomer operation of
the CustomerManagement microservice. The response of the latter operation
is then checked to report the new name of the customer as expected by updateCustomer after a successful update of customer data. In its final step,
testScenario1 verifies that the update is persistent by issuing a getCustomers request to the CustomerManagement microservice.

3.3   JoT Test of Scenario 2

We describe the JoT test of Scenario 2 (Fig. 2) following the same structure of
Sect. 3.2: interfaces, access points, logic.

Interfaces. Listing 5 shows the type definitions and operations of the interfaces
of the CustomerSelfService and CustomerManagement for Scenario 2
(cf. Fig. 2).

Listing 5. Interfaces of the Jolie test program for Scenario 2.

```
1  type CustomerRegistrationRequest { firstName:string,
       lastName:string, ... }
2
3  interface CustomerInformationHolder_CustomerSelfService {
4  RequestResponse:
```

```
 5 │   registerCustomer(CustomerRegistrationRequest)(
   │     CustomerResponse)
 6 │ }
 7 │
 8 │ type GetCustomersRequest {
 9 │   filter?:string, fields?:string, limit?:int, offset?:int
10 │ }
11 │
12 │ type PaginatedCustomerResponse {
13 │   filter?:string, limit?:int, offset?:int, size?:int
14 │   customers*:CustomerResponse // cf. Lines 3-5 in Listing 2
15 │ }
16 │
17 │ interface CustomerInformationHolder_CustomerManagement {
18 │   RequestResponse:
19 │     getCustomers(GetCustomersRequest)(
   │       PaginatedCustomerResponse)
20 │ }
```

The CustomerInformationHolder_CustomerSelfService interface of CustomerSelfService specifies the registerCustomer operation for the registration of new insurance customers with the Lakeside Mutual platform. It requires an instance of the CustomerRegistrationRequest type (cf. Line 1) as input and returns an instance of the CustomerResponse type (cf. Lines 3–5 in Listing 2).

The CustomerInformationHolder_CustomerManagement interface of CustomerManagement gathers the getCustomers operation (cf. Lines 17–20 in Listing 5), which lets users fetch customers based on the GetCustomersRequest type (cf. Line 10). An instance of the type determines the filter string and fields for customer matching. In case one of the fields of the record associated with a registered customer includes the filter string, the record will be part of the set of customers returned by getCustomers. The size of the set can be controlled by the limit and offset fields of GetCustomersRequest—the former prescribes the number of records in the set and the latter indicates by which offset customer matching shall start. With this mechanism, getCustomers supports paginated requests of customer records as modelled by the operation's return type PaginatedCustomerResponse (cf. Lines 12–15). An instance of the type informs the caller about the employed filter string, the prescribed limit and offset, as well as the size of the resulting record set. The set itself is comprised by the list of CustomerResponses in the customers field.

Access Points. In Scenario 2, the Client performs direct interactions with customerSelfService and customerManagement and the test has the related ports. Since it introduces no salient elements, we omit to show the access point code for brevity.

Test Logic. Listing 6 shows the test logic for Scenario 2.The imports we have at the beginning are similar to the ones included for Scenario 1, i.e., we alias `CustomerInformationHolder` for either the `CustomerManagement` and the `CustomerSelfService` resp. as `CustomerInformationHolder_Cus-tomerManagement` and `CustomerInformationHolder_CustomerSelf-Service`, so that we obtain a similar result as the code in Listing 5. In the code, we use both the Jolie value-assignment operator = and the deep-copy operator «. The first just copies the topmost element of the expression on its right. The second copies the whole structure referred by the expression on the right.

Listing 6. Logic of the Jolie test program for Scenario 2.

```
1  // cf. Listing 5
2  from customer-management.interfaces import
       CustomerInformationHolder
3    as CustomerInformationHolder_CustomerManagement
4  from customer-self-service.interfaces import
       CustomerInformationHolder
5    as CustomerInformationHolder_CustomerSelfService
6
7  interface TestInterface {
8    RequestResponse:
9     /// @Test
10    testScenario2(void)(void)
11 }
12
13 service Main {
14   outputPort customerManagement { ... }
15   outputPort customerSelfService { ... }
16   inputPort Input { ... }
17
18   main {
19    [ testScenario2()() {
20     // Step 1
21     customer << { firstName = "Homer2", lastName = "Simpson
         ", ... }
22     registerCustomer@customerSelfService(customer)(resp1 )
23     equals@assertions({ actual = resp1.firstName, expected =
         "Homer2" })()
24
25     // Step 2
26     getCustomers@customerManagement({ filter = "Homer2" })(
         resp2)
27     equals@assertions({ actual = #resp2.customers, expected
         = 1 })()
28     equals@assertions({ actual = resp2.customers.firstName,
         expected = "Homer2" })()
29    } ] }
30 }
```

Similar to Listing 2, we: (i) import the types and interfaces of the microservices involved in the scenario; (ii) define the `TestInterface`; (iii) specify the involved microservices' output ports; and (iv) define the test logic.

Focusing on the latter, Step 1 creates a test customer by invoking the `registerCustomer` operation of the `customerSelfService` microservice. At Step 2 we use `getCustomers` of `customerManagement` to fetch (and filter) the created customer, checking that there exists exactly one customer with the given name.

4   Related Work, Discussion, and Conclusion

We presented JoT, a testing framework for MSAs based on technology agnosticism. JoT tests are orchestrators that can consume or offer operations from/to the MSA under test. Since JoT adopts Jolie as the language for writing tests, it provides constructs supporting technology agnosticism and the definition of terse test behaviours. These elements facilitate the testing of MSAs with microservices based on heterogeneous technology stacks and the reuse of tests under different deployment configurations. Recent surveys and interviews with practitioners [21,22] substantiate this need, pointing out that developers urge for microservice-specific testing solutions.

We reference [21,22] for a comprehensive survey of the field, while, here, we compare with the closest proposals to ours. Gremlin [12] is a framework for MSAs that focuses on testing failure-handling by manipulating inter-service messages at the network layer. Quenum and Aknine [19] conceive an approach for the generation of executable test cases from requirements specifications, thereby focusing on acceptance tests for validating a software system's conformance with stakeholder expectations.

Hillah et al. [13] present an approach to automated functional testing based on formal specifications (of services, relations, etc.). Jayawardana et al. [15] propose a framework to produce test skeletons from business process models.

All mentioned related works concentrate on different aspects of MSA testing than JoT. In particular, they do not focus on the specification of advanced MSA tests tailored to technology agnosticism and expressed using a terse syntax, like the one provided by JoT thanks to the usage of the Jolie language. We plan to study the possible interplay between the mentioned work with JoT, e.g., for semi-automatic test generation geared towards specific traits of the architecture under test.

To improve the reliability of JoT we intend to conduct more comprehensive validation of our tool. One such validation entails more varied and complex scenarios, including synchronous and asynchronous interactions, design and architecture patterns, like Sagas for distributed transactions and Circuit Breaker for increased reliability.

In particular, looking at the design and architecture patterns, we foresee the language for test behaviours (inherited from Jolie) would play a fundamental role in helping users express complex testing logic spanning different services.

Also this aspect deserves dedicated work, i.e., how the JoT behaviour increases the productivity of testers w.r.t. existing solutions. Both empirical studies with practitioners and applying relevant software quality metrics, comparing with both existing tools for general testing (e.g., JUnit) specific to microservices (e.g., zerocode[5], Microdot[6],[7] and MounteBank[8]).

Other future endeavours regard studying the integration of JoT with MSA modelling languages like LEMMA [20] and MDSL [23], and with choreographic testing approaches [1,2,9,10]. Such an integration would allow the generation of test behaviours and coordinators in contexts where a single orchestrator is not sufficient, e.g., in decentralized, cross-organizational deployments. Furthermore, Jolie types and interfaces provide natural support for property-based testing [5], where generators randomly run tests on valid data and operations to assert relevant invariants. In this context, one could use session types [14] to specify behavioural invariants that shall hold in the system and test these in a property-based manner.

Acknowledgements. This work was partially supported by the Independent Research Fund Denmark, grant no. 0135-00219, Villum Fonden, grant no. 29518, and Innovation Fund Denmark, grant no. 9142-00001B.

Data Availability Statement

The artifact is available in the Software Heritage repository:

swh:1:dir:11bd4a17c8b8f184a5fbe50d8436719cb7de4956

References

1. Coto, A., Guanciale, R., Tuosto, E.: On testing message-passing components. In: Margaria, T., Steffen, B. (eds.) ISoLA 2020. LNCS, vol. 12476, pp. 22–38. Springer, Cham (2020). https://doi.org/10.1007/978-3-030-61362-4_2
2. Coto, A., Guanciale, R., Tuosto, E.: An abstract framework for choreographic testing. J. Log. Algebraic Methods Program. **123**, 100712 (2021)
3. Dalla Preda, M., Gabbrielli, M., Lanese, I., Mauro, J., Zavattaro, G.: Graceful interruption of request-response service interactions. In: Kappel, G., Maamar, Z., Motahari-Nezhad, H.R. (eds.) ICSOC 2011. LNCS, vol. 7084, pp. 590–600. Springer, Heidelberg (2011). https://doi.org/10.1007/978-3-642-25535-9_45
4. Dragoni, N., et al.: Microservices: yesterday, today, and tomorrow. In: Present and Ulterior Software Engineering, pp. 195–216. Springer, Cham (2017). https://doi.org/10.1007/978-3-319-67425-4_12
5. Fink, G., Bishop, M.: Property-based testing: a new approach to testing for assurance. ACM SIGSOFT Softw. Eng. Notes **22**(4), 74–80 (1997)

---

[5] https://github.com/authorjapps/zerocode.
[6] https://github.com/gigya/microdot.
[7] https://pact.io/.
[8] https://www.mbtest.org/.

6. Gabbrielli, M., Giallorenzo, S., Lanese, I., Zingaro, S.P.: A language-based approach for interoperability of iot platforms. In: 51st Hawaii International Conference on System Sciences, HICSS 2018, Hilton Waikoloa Village, Hawaii, USA, 3–6 January 2018. pp. 1–10. ScholarSpace / AIS Electronic Library (AISeL) (2018)
7. Gabbrielli, M., Giallorenzo, S., Montesi, F.: Service-oriented architectures: from design to production exploiting workflow patterns. In: Omatu, S., Bersini, H., Corchado, J.M., Rodríguez, S., Pawlewski, P., Bucciarelli, E. (eds.) Distributed Computing and Artificial Intelligence, 11th International Conference. AISC, vol. 290, pp. 131–139. Springer, Cham (2014). https://doi.org/10.1007/978-3-319-07593-8_17
8. Gamma, E., Beck, K.: Junit (2006)
9. Giallorenzo, S., Lanese, I., Russo, D.: ChIP: a choreographic integration process. In: Panetto, H., Debruyne, C., Proper, H.A., Ardagna, C.A., Roman, D., Meersman, R. (eds.) OTM 2018. LNCS, vol. 11230, pp. 22–40. Springer, Cham (2018). https://doi.org/10.1007/978-3-030-02671-4_2
10. Giallorenzo, S., Montesi, F., Peressotti, M.: Choreographies as objects. CoRR abs/2005.09520 (2020). https://arxiv.org/abs/2005.09520
11. Giallorenzo, S., Montesi, F., Peressotti, M., Rademacher, F., Sachweh, S.: Jolie and LEMMA: model-driven engineering and programming languages meet on microservices. In: Damiani, F., Dardha, O. (eds.) COORDINATION 2021. LNCS, vol. 12717, pp. 276–284. Springer, Cham (2021). https://doi.org/10.1007/978-3-030-78142-2_17
12. Heorhiadi, V., Rajagopalan, S., Jamjoom, H., Reiter, M.K., Sekar, V.: Gremlin: Systematic resilience testing of microservices. In: 2016 IEEE 36th International Conference on Distributed Computing Systems (ICDCS), pp. 57–66. IEEE (2016)
13. Hillah, L.M., et al.: Automation and intelligent scheduling of distributed system functional testing: model-based functional testing in practice. Int. J. Softw. Tools Technol. Transfer **19**, 281–308 (2017)
14. Hüttel, H., et al.: Foundations of session types and behavioural contracts. ACM Comput. Surv. (CSUR) **49**(1), 1–36 (2016)
15. Jayawardana, Y., Fernando, R., Jayawardena, G., Weerasooriya, D., Perera, I.: A full stack microservices framework with business modelling. In: 2018 18th International Conference on Advances in ICT for Emerging Regions (ICTer), pp. 78–85. IEEE (2018)
16. Montesi, F.: Process-aware web programming with Jolie. Sci. Comput. Program. **130**, 69–96 (2016)
17. Montesi, F., Guidi, C., Zavattaro, G.: Service-oriented programming with Jolie. In: Bouguettaya, A., Sheng, Q., Daniel, F. (eds) Web Services Foundations. Springer, New York (2014). https://doi.org/10.1007/978-1-4614-7518-7_4
18. OMG: OMG Unified Modeling Language (OMG UML) version 2.5.1. Standard formal/17-12-05, Object Management Group (2017)
19. Quenum, J.G., Aknine, S.: Towards executable specifications for microservices. In: 2018 IEEE International Conference on Services Computing (SCC), pp. 41–48. IEEE (2018)
20. Rademacher, F.: A language ecosystem for modeling microservice architecture, Ph. D. thesis, University of Kassel, Germany (2022). https://kobra.uni-kassel.de/handle/123456789/14176
21. Waseem, M., Liang, P., Márquez, G., Di Salle, A.: Testing microservices architecture-based applications: a systematic mapping study. In: 2020 27th Asia-Pacific Software Engineering Conference (APSEC), pp. 119–128. IEEE (2020)

22. Waseem, M., Liang, P., Shahin, M., Di Salle, A., Márquez, G.: Design, monitoring, and testing of microservices systems: the practitioners' perspective. J. Syst. Softw. **182**, 111061 (2021)
23. Zimmermann, O., Stocker, M., Lübke, D., Zdun, U., Pautasso, C.: Patterns for API design: simplifying integration with loosely coupled message exchanges. Addison-Wesley (2023)

Languages and Processes

Rollback Recovery in Session-Based Programming

Claudio Antares Mezzina[1]($^{\boxtimes}$)(ID), Francesco Tiezzi[2]($^{\boxtimes}$)(ID), and Nobuko Yoshida[3]($^{\boxtimes}$)(ID)

[1] Università degli Studi di Urbino Carlo Bo, Urbino, Italy
claudio.mezzina@uniurb.it
[2] Università degli Studi di Firenze, Florence, Italy
francesco.tiezzi@unifi.it
[3] University of Oxford, Oxford, UK
nobuko.yoshida@cs.ox.ac.uk

Abstract. To react to unforeseen circumstances or amend abnormal situations in communication-centric systems, programmers are in charge of "undoing" the interactions which led to an undesired state. To assist this task, session-based languages can be endowed with reversibility mechanisms. In this paper we propose a language enriched with programming facilities to *commit* session interactions, to *roll back* the computation to a previous commit point, and to *abort* the session. Rollbacks in our language always bring the system to previous visited states and a rollback cannot bring the system back to a point prior to the last commit. Programmers are relieved from the burden of ensuring that a rollback never restores a checkpoint imposed by a session participant different from the rollback requester. Such undesired situations are prevented at design-time (statically) by relying on a decidable *compliance* check at the type level, implemented in MAUDE. We show that the language satisfies error-freedom and progress of a session.

1 Introduction

Reversible computing [1,26] has gained interest for its application to different fields: from modelling biological/chemical phenomena [18], to simulation [29], debugging [13] and modelling fault-tolerant systems [11,19,32]. Our interest focuses on this latter application and stems from the fact that reversibility can be used to rigorously model, implement and revisit programming abstractions for reliable software systems.

Recent works [4,6,24,25,30] have studied the effect of reversibility in communication-centric scenarios, as a way to correct faulty computations by bringing

This research was funded in whole, or in part, by EPSRC EP/T006544/2, EP/K011715/1, EP/K034413/1, EP/L00058X/1, EP/N027833/2, EP/N028201/1, EP/T014709/2, EP/V000462/1, EP/X015955/1, NCSS/EPSRC VeTSS and Horizon EU TaRDIS 101093006. This work was also partially supported by the Italian MUR PRIN 2020 project NiRvAna, the Italian MUR PRIN 2017 project SEDUCE n. 2017TWRCNB, the French ANR project ANR-18-CE25-0007 DCore, the INdAM - GNCS Project "Proprietà qualitative e quantitative di sistemi reversibili" n. CUP E55F2200027001, and the project SERICS (PE00000014) under the NRRP MUR program funded by the EU - NextGenerationEU. For the purpose of Open Access, the authors have applied a CC BY public copyright licence to any Author Accepted Manuscript (AAM) version arising from this submission.

S.-S. Jongmans and A. Lopes (Eds.): COORDINATION 2023, LNCS 13908, pp. 195–213, 2023.
https://doi.org/10.1007/978-3-031-35361-1_11

back the system to a previous consistent state. In this setting, processes' behaviours are strongly disciplined by their types, prescribing the actions they have to perform within a *session*. A session consists of a structured series of message exchanges, whose flow can be controlled via conditional choices, branching and recursion. Correctness of communication is statically guaranteed by a framework based on a (session) type discipline [16]. None of the aforementioned works addresses systems in which the participants can *explicitly* abort the session, commit a computation and roll it back to a previous checkpoint. In this paper, we aim at filling this gap. We explain below the distinctive aspects of our checkpoint-based rollback recovery approach.

Linguistic Primitives to Explicitly Program Reversible Sessions. We introduce three primitives to: (i) *commit* a session, preventing undoing the interactions performed so far along the session; (ii) *roll back* a session, restoring the last saved process checkpoints; (iii) *abort* a session, to discard the session, and hence all interactions already performed in it, thus allowing another session of the same protocol to start with possible different participants. Notice that most proposals in the literature (e.g., [2–4]) only consider an abstract view, as they focus on reversible contracts (i.e., types). Instead, we focus on programming primitives at process level, and use types for guaranteeing a safe and consistent system evolution.

Asynchronous Commits. Our commit primitive does not require a session-wide synchronisation among all participants, as it is a local decision. However, its effect is on the whole session, as it affects the other session participants. This means that each participant can independently decide when to commit. Such flexibility comes at the cost of being error-prone, especially considering that the programmer has not only to deal with the usual forward executions, but also with the backward ones. Our type discipline allows for ruling out programs which may lead to these errors. The key idea of our approach is that *a session participant executing a rollback action is interested in restoring the last checkpoint he/she has committed.* For the success of the rollback recovery it is irrelevant whether the 'passive' participants go back to their own last checkpoints. Instead, if the 'active' participant is unable to restore the last checkpoint he/she has created, because it has been replaced by a checkpoint imposed by another participant, the rollback recovery is considered unsatisfactory.

In our framework, programmers are relieved from the burden of ensuring the satisfaction of rollbacks, since undesired situations are prevented at design time (statically) by relying on a *compliance* check at the type level. To this aim, we introduce cherry-pi (<u>c</u>heckpoint-based <u>r</u>ollback <u>r</u>ecovery <u>pi</u>-calculus), a variant of the session-based π-calculus [17,36] enriched with rollback recovery primitives. We present here a binary version of the calculus, which is more convenient to demonstrate the essence of our rollback recovery approach; the proposed approach can be seamlessly extended to multiparty sessions (see the companion technical report [27] available online). A key difference with respect to the standard binary type discipline is the *relaxation* of the duality requirement. The types of two session participants are not required to be dual, but they will be compared with respect to a compliance relation (as in [5]), which also takes into account the effects of commit and rollback actions. Such relaxation also involves the requirements concerning selection and branching types, and those concerning branches of conditional choices. The cherry-pi type system is used to infer types of session participants, which are then combined together for the compliance check.

Reversibility in cherry-pi is *controlled* via two specific primitives: a rollback one telling when a reverse computation has to take place, and a commit one limiting the scope of a potential reverse computation. This implies that the calculus is not fully reversible (i.e., backward computations are not always enabled), leading to have properties that are relaxed and different with respect to other reversible calculi [9, 10, 21, 30]. We prove that cherry-pi satisfies the following properties: (i) a rollback always brings back the system to a previous visited state and (ii) it is not possible to bring the computation back to a point prior to the last checkpoint, which implies that our commits have a persistent effect. Concerning soundness properties, we prove that (a) our compliance check is decidable, (b) compliance-checked cherry-pi specifications never lead to communication errors (e.g., a blocked communication where there is a receiver without the corresponding sender), and (c) compliance-checked cherry-pi specifications never activate undesirable rollbacks (according to our notion of rollback recovery mentioned above). Property (b) resembles the type safety property of session-based calculi (see, e.g., [36]), while property (c) is a new property specifically defined for cherry-pi. The technical development of property proofs turns out to be more intricate than that of standard properties of session-based calculi, due to the combined use of type and compliance checking. To demonstrate feasibility and effectiveness of our rollback recovery approach, we have concretely implemented the compliance check using the MAUDE [8] framework (the code is available at https://github.com/tiezzi/cherry-pi).

Outline. Section 2 illustrates the key idea of our rollback recovery approach; Sect. 3 introduces the cherry-pi calculus; Sect. 4 introduces typing and compliance checking; Sect. 5 presents the properties satisfied by cherry-pi; Sect. 6 concludes the paper with related and future work. Omitted rules, extension to multiparty sessions, proofs of the results, and a further example are reported on the companion technical report [27].

2   A Reversible Video on Demand Service Example

We discuss the motivations underlying our work by introducing our running example, a Video on Demand (VOD) scenario. The key idea is that a rollback requester is satisfied only if her restored checkpoint was set by herself. In Fig. 1(a), a service (S) offers to a user (U) videos with two different quality levels, namely high definition (HD) and standard definition (SD). After the *login*, U sends her video *request*, and receives the corresponding *price* and *metadata* (actors, directors, description, etc.) from S. According to this information, U selects the video quality. Then, she receives, first, a short *test* video (to check the audio and video quality in her device) and, finally, the requested *video*. If the vision of the HD test video is not satisfactory, U can roll back to her last checkpoint to possibly change the video quality, instead in the SD case U can abort the session.

Let us now add commit actions as in the run shown in Fig. 1(b). After receiving the price, U commits, while S commits after the quality selection. In this scenario, however, if U activates the rollback, she is unable to go back to the checkpoint she set with her commit action because the actual effect of rollback is to restore the checkpoint set by the commit action performed by S.

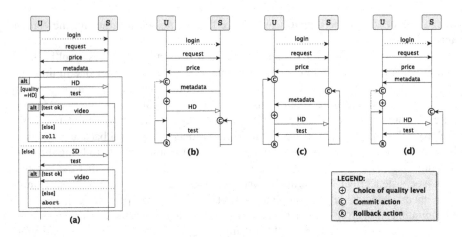

Fig. 1. VOD example: (a) a full description without commit actions; (b, d) runs with undesired rollback; (c) a run with satisfactory rollback.

In the scenario in Fig. 1(c), instead, S commits after sending the price to U. In this case, no matter who first performed the commit action, the rollback results to be satisfactory. Also if S commits later, the checkpoint of U remains unchanged, as U performed no other action between the two commits. This would not be the case if both U and S committed after the communication of the metadata, as in Fig. 1(d). If S commits before U, no rollback issue arises, but if U commits first it may happen that her internal decision is taken before S commits. In this case, U would not be able to go back to the checkpoint set by herself, and she would be unable to change the video quality.

These undesired rollbacks are caused by bad choices of commit points. We propose a compliance check that identifies these situations at design time.

3 The cherry-pi Calculus

In this section, we introduce cherry-pi, a calculus (extending that in [36]) devised for studying sessions equipped with our checkpoint-based rollback recovery mechanism.

Syntax. The syntax of the cherry-pi calculus relies on the following base sets: *shared channels* (ranged over by a), used to initiate sessions; *session channels* (ranged over by s), consisting of pairs of *endpoints* (ranged over, with a slight abuse of notation, by s, $\bar{s}$) used by the two parties to interact within an established session; *labels* (ranged over by l), used to select and offer branching choices; *values* (ranged over by v), including booleans, integers and strings (whose *sorts*, ranged over by S, are bool, int and str, respectively), which are exchanged within a session; *variables* (ranged over by x, y, z), storing values and session endpoints; *process variables* (ranged over by X), used for recursion.

Collaborations, ranged over by C, are given by the grammar in Fig. 2. The key ingredient of the calculus is the set of actions for controlling the session rollback.

$$C ::=$$ **Collaborations**
$$\bar{a}(x).P \mid a(x).P \mid C_1 \mid C_2$$ request, accept, parallel

$$P ::=$$ **Processes**
$$x!\langle e\rangle.P \mid x?(y : S).P$$ output, input
$$\mid \ x \triangleleft l.P \mid x \triangleright \{l_1 : P_1, \ldots, l_n : P_n\}$$ selection, branching
$$\mid \ \text{if } e \text{ then } P_1 \text{ else } P_2 \mid X \mid \mu X.P \mid 0$$ choice, recursion, inact
$$\mid \ \text{commit}.P \mid \text{roll} \mid \text{abort}$$ commit, roll, abort

$$e ::= \ v \mid +(e_1, e_2) \mid \wedge(e_1, e_2) \mid \ldots$$ **Expressions**

Fig. 2. cherry-pi syntax.

Actions commit, roll and abort are used, respectively, to commit a session (producing a checkpoint for each session participant), to trigger the session rollback (restoring the last committed checkpoints) or to abort the whole session. We discuss below the other constructs of the calculus, which are those typically used for session-based programming [15]. A cherry-pi collaboration is a collection of *session initiators*, i.e. terms ready to initiate sessions by synchronising on shared channels. A synchronisation of two initiators $\bar{a}(x).P$ and $a(y).Q$ causes the generation of a fresh session channel, whose endpoints replace variables x and y in order to be used by the triggered processes P and Q, respectively, for later communications. No subordinate sessions can be initiated within a running session.

When a session is started, each participant executes a *process*. Processes are built up from the empty process 0 and basic actions by means of action prefix $\_.\_$, conditional choice if e then $\_$ else $\_$, and recursion $\mu X.\_$. Actions $x!\langle e\rangle$ and $y?(z : S)$ denote output and input via session endpoints replacing x and y, respectively. These communication primitives realise the standard synchronous message passing, where messages result from the evaluation of *expressions*, which are defined by means of standard operators on boolean, integer and string values. Variables that are arguments of input actions are (statically) typed by sorts. There is no need for statically typing the variables occurring as arguments of session initiating actions, as they are always replaced by session endpoints. Notice that in cherry-pi the exchanged values cannot be endpoints, meaning that session delegation (i.e., channel-passing) is not considered. Actions $x \triangleleft l$ and $x \triangleright \{l_1 : P_1, \ldots, l_n : P_n\}$ denote selection and branching (where $l_1, \ldots, l_n$ are pairwise distinct).

Example 1. Let us consider the VOD example informally introduced in Sect. 2. The scenario described in Fig. 1(a) with commit actions placed as in Fig. 1(b) is rendered in cherry-pi as $C_{\text{US}} = \overline{login}(x). P_{\text{U}} \mid login(y). P_{\text{S}}$, where:

$$P_{\text{U}} = x!\langle v_{req}\rangle. x?(x_{price} : \text{int}). \text{commit}. x?(x_{meta} : \text{str}). \text{if } (f_{eval}(x_{price}, x_{meta}))$$
$$\text{then } x \triangleleft l_{HD}. x?(x_{testHD} : \text{str}).$$
$$(\text{if } (f_{HD}(x_{testHD})) \text{ then } x?(x_{videoHD} : \text{str}).0 \text{ else roll})$$
$$\text{else } x \triangleleft l_{SD}. x?(x_{testSD} : \text{str}).$$
$$(\text{if } (f_{SD}(x_{testSD})) \text{ then } x?(x_{videoSD} : \text{str}).0 \text{ else abort})$$

$$C ::= \bar{a}(x).P \mid a(x).P \mid C_1 \mid C_2 \mid (\nu s : C_1)\, C_2 \mid \langle P_1 \rangle \blacktriangleright P_2 \qquad \textbf{Collaborations}$$

$$P ::= r!\langle e \rangle.P \mid r?(y : S).P \mid r \triangleleft l.P \mid r \triangleright \{l_1 : P_1, \ldots, l_n : P_n\} \mid \cdots \quad \textbf{Processes}$$

Fig. 3. cherry-pi runtime syntax (the rest of processes P and expressions e are as in Fig. 2).

$$P_S = y?(y_{req} : \texttt{str}).\, y!\langle f_{price}(y_{req}) \rangle.\, y!\langle f_{meta}(y_{req}) \rangle.$$
$$y \triangleright \{\, l_{HD} : \texttt{commit.}\, y!\langle f_{testHD}(y_{req}) \rangle.\, y!\langle f_{videoHD}(y_{req}) \rangle.\, 0\ ,$$
$$l_{SD} : \texttt{commit.}\, y!\langle f_{testSD}(y_{req}) \rangle.\, y!\langle f_{videoSD}(y_{req}) \rangle.\, 0\ \}$$

Notice that expressions used for decisions and computations are abstracted by relations $f_n(\cdot)$, whose definitions are left unspecified. Considering the placement of commit actions depicted in Fig. 1(c), the cherry-pi specification of the service's process becomes:

$$y?(y_{req} : \texttt{str}).\, y!\langle f_{price}(y_{req}) \rangle.\, \texttt{commit.}\, y!\langle f_{meta}(y_{req}) \rangle.$$
$$y \triangleright \{\, l_{HD} : y!\langle f_{testHD}(y_{req}) \rangle.\, y!\langle f_{videoHD}(y_{req}) \rangle.\, 0\ ,$$
$$l_{SD} : y!\langle f_{testSD}(y_{req}) \rangle.\, y!\langle f_{videoSD}(y_{req}) \rangle.\, 0\ \}$$

Finally, considering the placement of commit actions depicted in Fig. 1(d), the cherry-pi specification of the user's process becomes:

$$x!\langle v_{req} \rangle.\, x?(x_{price} : \texttt{int}).\, x?(x_{meta} : \texttt{str}).\, \texttt{commit. if}\ (f_{eval}(x_{price}, x_{meta}))\ \texttt{then}\ \ldots$$

Semantics. The operational semantics of cherry-pi is defined for *runtime* terms, generated by the extended syntax of the calculus in Fig. 3 (new constructs are highlighted by a grey background). We use r to denote *session identifiers*, i.e. session endpoints and variables. Those runtime terms that can be also generated by the grammar in Fig. 2 are called *initial collaborations*.

At collaboration level, two constructs are introduced: $(\nu s : C_1)\, C_2$ represents a *session* along the channel s with associated starting checkpoint C_1 (corresponding to the collaboration that has initialised the session) and code C_2; $\langle P_1 \rangle \blacktriangleright P_2$ represents a *log* storing the checkpoint P_1 associated to the code P_2. At process level, the only difference is that session identifiers r are used as first argument of communicating actions. We extend the standard notion of binders to take into account $(\nu s : C_1)\, C_2$, which binds session endpoints s and $\bar{s}$ in C_2 (in this respect, it acts similarly to the restriction of π-calculus, but its scope cannot be extended in order to avoid involving processes that do not belong to the session in the rollback effect). The derived notions of bound and free names (where *names* stand for variables, process variables and session endpoints), alpha-equivalence, and substitution are standard and we assume that bound names are pairwise distinct. The semantics of the calculus is defined for *closed* terms, i.e. terms without free variables and process variables.

Not all processes allowed by the extended syntax correspond to meaningful collaborations. In a general term the processes stored in logs may not be consistent with the computation that has taken place. We get rid of such malformed terms, as we will only consider those runtime terms, called *reachable* collaborations, obtained by means of reductions from initial collaborations.

$k!\langle e\rangle.P \xrightarrow{k!\langle v\rangle} P$ $(e\downarrow v)$ [P-SND] $k?(x:S).P \xrightarrow{k?(x)} P$ [P-RCV]

$k \lhd l.P \xrightarrow{k\lhd l} P$ [P-SEL] $k \rhd \{l_1:P_1,\ldots,l_n:P_n\} \xrightarrow{k\rhd l_i} P_i$ $(1\leqslant i\leqslant n)$ [P-BRN]

if e then P_1 else $P_2 \xrightarrow{\tau} P_1$ $(e\downarrow \mathtt{true})$ [P-IFT]

commit.$P \xrightarrow{cmt} P$ [P-CMT]   roll $\xrightarrow{roll} 0$ [P-RLL]   abort $\xrightarrow{abt} 0$ [P-ABT]

Fig. 4. `cherry-pi` semantics: auxiliary labelled relation.

The operational semantics of `cherry-pi` is given in terms of a standard *structural congruence* $\equiv$ [17] and a *reduction* relation $\longmapsto$ given as the union of the *forward reduction* relation $\twoheadrightarrow$ and *backward reduction* relations $\rightsquigarrow$. The definition of the relation $\twoheadrightarrow$ over closed collaborations relies on an auxiliary labelled relation $\xrightarrow{\ell}$ over processes that specifies the actions that processes can initially perform and the continuation process obtained after each such action. Given a reduction relation $\mathcal{R}$, we will indicate with $\mathcal{R}^+$ and $\mathcal{R}^*$ respectively the *transitive* and the *reflexive-transitive* closure of $\mathcal{R}$.

The operational rules defining the auxiliary labelled relation are in Fig. 4 (omitted rules are in [27]). We use k to denote *generic session endpoints* (s or $\bar{s}$). Action label ℓ stands for either $k!\langle v\rangle$, $k?(x)$, $k \lhd l$, $k \rhd l$, *cmt*, *roll*, *abt*, or τ. The meaning of the rules is straightforward, as they just produce as labels the actions currently enabled in the process. In doing that, expressions of sending actions and conditional choices are evaluated (auxiliary function $e\downarrow v$ says that closed expression e evaluates to value v).

The operational rules defining the reduction relation $\longmapsto$ are reported in Fig. 5 (standard rules for congruence, in the forward and backward case, are omitted). We comment on salient points. Once a session is created, its initiating collaboration is stored in the session construct (rule [F-CON]). Communication, branching selection and internal conditional choices proceed as usual, without affecting logs (rules [F-COM], [F-LAB] and [F-IF]). A commit action updates the checkpoint of a session, by replacing the processes stored in the logs of the two involved parties (rule [F-CMT]). Notably, this form of commit is asynchronous as it does not require the passive participant to explicitly synchronise with the active participant by means of a primitive for accepting the commit. On the other hand, under the hood, a low-level implementation of this mechanism would synchronously update the logs of the involved parties. Conversely, a rollback action restores the processes in the two logs (rule [B-RLL]). The abort action (rule [B-ABT]), instead, kills the session and restores the collaboration stored in the session construct formed by the two initiators that have started the session; this allows the initiators to be involved in new sessions. The other rules simply extend the standard parallel, restriction rules to forward and backward relations.

Example 2. Consider the first `cherry-pi` specification of the VOD scenario given in Example 1. In the initial state C_{US} of the collaboration, U and S can synchronise in order to initialise the session, thus evolving to $C_{US}^1 = (\nu s : C_{US}) (\langle P_U[\bar{s}/x]\rangle \blacktriangleright P_U[\bar{s}/x] \mid \langle P_S[s/y]\rangle \blacktriangleright P_S[s/y])$.

$$\bar{a}(x_1).P_1 \mid a(x_2).P_2 \twoheadrightarrow (\nu s : (\bar{a}(x_1).P_1 \mid a(x_2).P_2)) \qquad \text{[F-CON]}$$
$$(\langle P_1[\bar{s}/x_1] \rangle \blacktriangleright P_1[\bar{s}/x_1] \mid \langle P_2[s/x_2] \rangle \blacktriangleright P_2[s/x_2])$$

$$\frac{P_1 \xrightarrow{\bar{k}!\langle v \rangle} P_1' \qquad P_2 \xrightarrow{k?(x)} P_2'}{\langle Q_1 \rangle \blacktriangleright P_1 \mid \langle Q_2 \rangle \blacktriangleright P_2 \twoheadrightarrow \langle Q_1 \rangle \blacktriangleright P_1' \mid \langle Q_2 \rangle \blacktriangleright P_2'[v/x]} \text{ [F-COM]} \qquad \frac{C_1 \twoheadrightarrow C_1'}{C_1 \mid C_2 \twoheadrightarrow C_1' \mid C_2} \text{ [F-PAR]}$$

$$\frac{P_1 \xrightarrow{\bar{k} \vartriangleleft l} P_1' \qquad P_2 \xrightarrow{k \vartriangleright l} P_2'}{\langle Q_1 \rangle \blacktriangleright P_1 \mid \langle Q_2 \rangle \blacktriangleright P_2 \twoheadrightarrow \langle Q_1 \rangle \blacktriangleright P_1' \mid \langle Q_2 \rangle \blacktriangleright P_2'} \text{ [F-LAB]} \qquad \frac{C_2 \twoheadrightarrow C_2' \quad \text{[F-RES]}}{(\nu s : C_1) C_2 \twoheadrightarrow (\nu s : C_1) C_2'}$$

$$\frac{P_1 \xrightarrow{cmt} P_1'}{\langle Q_1 \rangle \blacktriangleright P_1 \mid \langle Q_2 \rangle \blacktriangleright P_2 \twoheadrightarrow \langle P_1' \rangle \blacktriangleright P_1' \mid \langle P_2 \rangle \blacktriangleright P_2} \text{ [F-CMT]} \qquad \frac{P \xrightarrow{\tau} P'}{\langle Q \rangle \blacktriangleright P \twoheadrightarrow \langle Q \rangle \blacktriangleright P'} \text{ [F-IF]}$$

$$\frac{P_1 \xrightarrow{roll} P_1' \qquad \text{[B-RLL]}}{\langle Q_1 \rangle \blacktriangleright P_1 \mid \langle Q_2 \rangle \blacktriangleright P_2 \rightsquigarrow \langle Q_1 \rangle \blacktriangleright Q_1 \mid \langle Q_2 \rangle \blacktriangleright Q_2} \qquad \frac{C_1 \rightsquigarrow C_1'}{C_1 \mid C_2 \rightsquigarrow C_1' \mid C_2} \text{ [B-PAR]}$$

$$\frac{P_1 \xrightarrow{abt} P_1' \qquad \text{[B-ABT]}}{(\nu s : C)(\langle Q_1 \rangle \blacktriangleright P_1 \mid \langle Q_2 \rangle \blacktriangleright P_2) \rightsquigarrow C} \qquad \frac{C_2 \rightsquigarrow C_2'}{(\nu s : C_1) C_2 \rightsquigarrow (\nu s : C_1) C_2'} \text{ [B-RES]}$$

Fig. 5. cherry-pi semantics: forward and backward reduction relations.

Let us consider now a possible run of the session. After three reduction steps, U executes the commit action, obtaining the following runtime term:

$$C_{US}^2 = (\nu s : C_{US}) (\langle P_U' \rangle \blacktriangleright P_U' \mid \langle P_S' \rangle \blacktriangleright P_S')$$
$$P_U' = \bar{s}?(x_{meta} : \texttt{str}).\, \text{if} \left(f_{eval}(v_{price}, x_{meta}) \right) \text{then} \dots \quad P_S' = s!\langle f_{meta}(v_{req}) \rangle.\, y \rhd \{ \dots \}$$

After four further reduction steps, U chooses the HD video quality and S commits as well; the resulting runtime collaboration is as follows:

$$C_{US}^3 = (\nu s : C_{US}) (\langle P_U'' \rangle \blacktriangleright P_U'' \mid \langle P_S'' \rangle \blacktriangleright P_S'')$$
$$P_U'' = \bar{s}?(x_{testHD} : \texttt{str}).\, \text{if} \left(f_{HD}(x_{testHD}) \right) \text{then } \bar{s}?(x_{videoHD} : \texttt{str}).0 \text{ else roll}$$
$$P_S'' = s!\langle f_{testHD}(v_{req}) \rangle.\, s!\langle f_{videoHD}(v_{req}) \rangle.\, 0$$

In the next reductions, U evaluates the test video and decides to revert the session execution, resulting in $C_{US}^4 = (\nu s : C_{US}) (\langle P_U'' \rangle \blacktriangleright \text{roll} \mid \langle P_S'' \rangle \blacktriangleright s!\langle f_{videoHD}(v_{req}) \rangle.\, 0)$. The execution of the roll action restores the checkpoints P_U'' and P_S'', that is $C_{US}^4 \rightsquigarrow C_{US}^3$. After the rollback, U is not able to change the video quality as her own commit point would have permitted; in fact, it holds $C_{US}^4 \not\rightsquigarrow C_{US}^2$.

4   Rollback Safety

The operational semantics of cherry-pi provides a description of the functioning of the primitives for programming the checkpoint-based rollback recovery in a session-based language. However, as shown in Example 2, it does not guarantee high-level properties about the safe execution of the rollback. To prevent such undesired rollbacks,

$$\frac{\varnothing;\varnothing \vdash P \blacktriangleright x : T}{\bar{a}(x).P \ \blacktriangleright \ \{\bar{a} : T\}} \text{[T-REQ]} \qquad \frac{\varnothing;\varnothing \vdash P \blacktriangleright x : T}{a(x).P \ \blacktriangleright \ \{a : T\}} \text{[T-ACC]} \qquad \frac{C_1 \ \blacktriangleright \ A_1 \quad C_2 \ \blacktriangleright \ A_2}{C_1 \mid C_2 \ \blacktriangleright \ A_1 \cup A_2} \text{[T-PAR]}$$

Fig. 6. Typing system for `cherry-pi` collaborations.

we propose the use of *compliance checking*, to be performed at design time. This check is not done on the full system specification, but only at the level of session types.

Session Types and Typing. The syntax of the `cherry-pi` *session types* T is defined as follows. Type $![S].T$ represents the behaviour of first outputting a value of sort S (i.e., `bool`, `int` or `str`), then performing the actions prescribed by type T. Type $?[S].T$ is the dual one, where a value is received instead of sent. Types `end` and `err` represent inaction and faulty termination, respectively. Type $\triangleleft[l].T$ represents the behaviour that selects the label l and then behaves as T. Type $\triangleright[l_1 : T_1, \ldots, l_n : T_n]$ describes a branching behaviour: it waits for one of the n options to be selected, and behaves as type T_i if the i-th label is selected (external choice). Type $T_1 \oplus T_2$ behaves as either T_1 or T_2 (internal choice). Type $\mu t.T$ represents a recursive behaviour. Type $\mathtt{cmt}.T$ represents a commit action followed by the actions prescribed by type T. Finally, types `roll` and `abt` represent rollback and abort actions.

The `cherry-pi` type system does not perform compliance checks, but only infers the types of collaboration participants, which will be then checked together according to the compliance relation. *Typing judgements* are of the form $C \ \blacktriangleright \ A$, where A, called *type associations*, is a set of session type associations of the form $\hat{a} : T$, where $\hat{a}$ stands for either $\bar{a}$ or a. Intuitively, $C \ \blacktriangleright \ A$ indicates that from the collaboration C the type associations in A are inferred. The definition of the type system for these judgements relies on auxiliary typing judgements for processes, of the form $\Theta; \Gamma \ \vdash \ P \ \blacktriangleright \ \Delta$, where Θ, Γ and Δ, called *basis*, *sorting* and *typing* respectively, are finite partial maps from process variables to type variables, from variables to sorts, and from variables to types, respectively. Updates of basis and sorting are denoted, respectively, by $\Theta \cdot X : t$ and $\Gamma \cdot y : S$, where $X \notin dom(\Theta)$, $t \notin cod(\Theta)$ and $y \notin dom(\Gamma)$. The judgement $\Theta; \Gamma \vdash P \ \blacktriangleright \ \Delta$ stands for "under the environment $\Theta; \Gamma$, process P has typing Δ". In its own turn, the typing of processes relies on auxiliary judgments for expressions, of the form $\Gamma \vdash e \ \blacktriangleright \ S$. The axioms and rules defining the typing system for `cherry-pi` collaborations and processes are given in Figs. 6 and 7; typing rules for expressions are standard (see [27]). The type system is defined only for initial collaborations, i.e. for terms generated by the grammar in Fig. 2. Other runtime collaborations are not considered here, as no check will be performed at runtime. We comment on salient points. Typing rules at collaboration level simply collect the type associations of session initiators in the collaboration. Rules at process level instead determine the session type corresponding to each process, by mapping each process operator to the corresponding type operator. Data and expression used in communication actions are abstracted as sorts, and a conditional choice is rendered as an internal non-deterministic choice.

Compliance Checking. To check compliance between pairs of session parties, we consider *type configurations* of the form $(T, T') : \langle \tilde{T}_1 \rangle \ \blacktriangleright \ T_2 \parallel \langle \tilde{T}_3 \rangle \ \blacktriangleright \ T_4$, consisting in a pair (T, T') of session types, corresponding to the types of the parties at the initiation

$$\frac{\Gamma \vdash e \blacktriangleright S \quad \Theta;\Gamma \vdash P \blacktriangleright x:T}{\Theta;\Gamma \vdash x!\langle e\rangle.P \blacktriangleright x :![S].T} \ \text{[T-SND]} \qquad \frac{\Theta;\Gamma \cdot y : S \vdash P \blacktriangleright x:T}{\Theta;\Gamma \vdash x?(y:S).P \blacktriangleright x :?[S].T} \ \text{[T-RCV]}$$

$$\Theta;\Gamma \vdash \mathbf{0} \blacktriangleright x : \mathsf{end} \ \text{[T-INACT]} \qquad \frac{\Gamma \vdash e \blacktriangleright \mathsf{bool} \quad \Theta;\Gamma \vdash P_1 \blacktriangleright x:T_1 \quad \Theta;\Gamma \vdash P_2 \blacktriangleright x:T_2}{\Theta;\Gamma \vdash \mathsf{if}\ e\ \mathsf{then}\ P_1\ \mathsf{else}\ P_2 \blacktriangleright x : T_1 \oplus T_2} \ \text{[T-IF]}$$

$$\Gamma \cdot x : S \vdash x \blacktriangleright S \ \text{[T-VAR]}$$

$$\Theta \cdot X : t; \Gamma \vdash X \blacktriangleright t \ \text{[T-PVAR]} \qquad \frac{\Theta \cdot X : t; \Gamma \vdash P \blacktriangleright T}{\Theta;\Gamma \vdash \mu X.P \blacktriangleright \mu t.T} \ \text{[T-REC]}$$

$$\Theta;\Gamma \vdash \mathsf{roll} \blacktriangleright x : \mathtt{roll} \ \text{[T-RLL]}$$

$$\Theta;\Gamma \vdash \mathsf{abort} \blacktriangleright x : \mathtt{abt} \ \text{[T-ABT]} \qquad \frac{\Theta;\Gamma \vdash P \blacktriangleright x:T}{\Theta;\Gamma \vdash \mathsf{commit}.P \blacktriangleright x : \mathtt{cmt}.T} \ \text{[T-CMT]}$$

Fig. 7. Typing system for cherry-pi processes.

of the session, and in the parallel composition of two pairs $\langle \tilde{T}_c \rangle \blacktriangleright T$, where T is the session type of a party and $\tilde{T}_c$ is the type of the party's checkpoint. We use $\tilde{T}$ to denote either a type T, representing a checkpoint committed by the party, or $\underline{T}$, representing a checkpoint imposed by the other party. The semantics of type configurations, necessary for the definition of the compliance relation, is given in Fig. 8, where label λ stands for either $![S]$, $?[S]$, $\lhd l$, $\rhd l$, τ, cmt, roll, or abt. We comment on the relevant rules. In case of a commit action, the checkpoints of both parties are updated, and the one of the passive party (i.e., the party that has not performed the commit) is marked as 'imposed' (rule [TS-CMT]$_1$). However, if the passive party did not perform any action from its current checkpoint, this checkpoint is not overwritten by the active party (rule [TS-CMT]$_2$), as discussed in Sect. 2 (Fig. 1(c)). In case of a roll action (rule [TS-RLL]$_1$), the reduction step is performed only if the active party (i.e., the party that has performed the rollback action) has a non-imposed checkpoint; in all other situations the configuration cannot proceed with the rollback. Finally, in case of abort (rule [TS-ABT]$_1$), the configuration goes back to the initial state; this allows the type computation to proceed, in order not to affect the compliance check between the two parties.

On top of the above type semantics, we define the compliance relation, inspired by the relation in [3], and prove its decidability.

Definition 1 (Compliance). *Relation* $\dashv\vdash$ *on configurations is defined as follows:* $(T,T') : \langle \tilde{U}_1 \rangle \blacktriangleright T_1 \dashv\vdash \langle \tilde{U}_2 \rangle \blacktriangleright T_2$ *holds if for all* U_1', T_1', U_2', T_2' *such that* $(T,T') :$ $\langle \tilde{U}_1 \rangle \blacktriangleright T_1 \parallel \langle \tilde{U}_2 \rangle \blacktriangleright T_2 \longmapsto^* (T,T') : \langle \tilde{U}_1' \rangle \blacktriangleright T_1' \parallel \langle \tilde{U}_2' \rangle \blacktriangleright T_2' \not\longmapsto$ *we have that* $T_1' = T_2' = \mathsf{end}$. *Two types* T_1 *and* T_2 *are* compliant, *written* $T_1 \dashv\vdash T_2$, *if* $(T_1, T_2) : \langle T_1 \rangle \blacktriangleright T_1 \dashv\vdash \langle T_2 \rangle \blacktriangleright T_2$.

Theorem 1. *Let* T_1 *and* T_2 *be two session types, checking if* $T_1 \dashv\vdash T_2$ *holds is decidable.*

This compliance relation is used to define the notion of *rollback safety*.

Definition 2 (Rollback safety). *Let* C *be an initial collaboration, then* C *is* rollback safe *(shortened* roll-safe*) if* $C \blacktriangleright A$ *and for all pairs* $\bar{a} : T_1$ *and* $a : T_2$ *in* A *we have* $T_1 \dashv\vdash T_2$.

$$\mathtt{cmt}.T \xrightarrow{cmt} T \;\; [\text{TS-CMT}] \qquad \mathtt{roll} \xrightarrow{roll} \mathtt{end} \;\; [\text{TS-RLL}] \qquad \mathtt{abt} \xrightarrow{abt} \mathtt{end} \;\; [\text{TS-ABT}]$$

$$\frac{T_1 \xrightarrow{\tau} T_1'}{(T,T') : \langle \tilde{U}_1 \rangle \blacktriangleright T_1 \parallel \langle \tilde{U}_2 \rangle \blacktriangleright T_2 \longmapsto (T,T') : \langle \tilde{U}_1 \rangle \blacktriangleright T_1' \parallel \langle \tilde{U}_2 \rangle \blacktriangleright T_2} \;\; [\text{TS-TAU}]$$

$$\frac{T_1 \xrightarrow{![S]} T_1' \quad T_2 \xrightarrow{?[S]} T_2'}{(T,T') : \langle \tilde{U}_1 \rangle \blacktriangleright T_1 \parallel \langle \tilde{U}_2 \rangle \blacktriangleright T_2 \longmapsto (T,T') : \langle \tilde{U}_1 \rangle \blacktriangleright T_1' \parallel \langle \tilde{U}_2 \rangle \blacktriangleright T_2'} \;\; [\text{TS-COM}]$$

$$\frac{T_1 \xrightarrow{cmt} T_1' \quad \tilde{U}_2 \neq T_2}{(T,T') : \langle \tilde{U}_1 \rangle \blacktriangleright T_1 \parallel \langle \tilde{U}_2 \rangle \blacktriangleright T_2 \longmapsto (T,T') : \langle \tilde{T}_1' \rangle \blacktriangleright T_1' \parallel \langle \underline{T}_2 \rangle \blacktriangleright T_2} \;\; [\text{TS-CMT}_1]$$

$$\frac{T_1 \xrightarrow{cmt} T_1' \quad \tilde{U}_2 = T_2}{(T,T') : \langle \tilde{U}_1 \rangle \blacktriangleright T_1 \parallel \langle \tilde{U}_2 \rangle \blacktriangleright T_2 \longmapsto (T,T') : \langle \tilde{T}_1' \rangle \blacktriangleright T_1' \parallel \langle \tilde{U}_2 \rangle \blacktriangleright T_2} \;\; [\text{TS-CMT}_2]$$

$$\frac{T_1 \xrightarrow{roll} T_1'}{(T,T') : \langle U_1 \rangle \blacktriangleright T_1 \parallel \langle \tilde{U}_2 \rangle \blacktriangleright T_2 \longmapsto (T,T') : \langle U_1 \rangle \blacktriangleright U_1 \parallel \langle \tilde{U}_2 \rangle \blacktriangleright U_2} \;\; [\text{TS-RLL}_1]$$

$$\frac{T_1 \xrightarrow{roll} T_1'}{(T,T') : \langle \underline{U_1} \rangle \blacktriangleright T_1 \parallel \langle \tilde{U}_2 \rangle \blacktriangleright T_2 \longmapsto (T,T') : \langle \underline{U_1} \rangle \blacktriangleright \mathtt{err} \parallel \langle \tilde{U}_2 \rangle \blacktriangleright \mathtt{err}} \;\; [\text{TS-RLL}_2]$$

$$\frac{T_1 \xrightarrow{abt} T_1'}{(T,T') : \langle \tilde{U}_1 \rangle \blacktriangleright T_1 \parallel \langle \tilde{U}_2 \rangle \blacktriangleright T_2 \longmapsto (T,T') : \langle T \rangle \blacktriangleright T \parallel \langle T' \rangle \blacktriangleright T'} \;\; [\text{TS-ABT}_1]$$

Fig. 8. Semantics of types and type configurations (symmetric rules for configurations are omitted).

Example 3. Let us consider again the VOD example. As expected, the first `cherry-pi` collaboration defined in Example 1, corresponding to the scenario described in Fig. 1(b), is not rollback safe, because the types of the two parties are not compliant. Indeed, the session types T_U and T_S associated by the type system to the user and the service processes, respectively, are as follows:

$$T_U = ![\mathtt{str}].?[\mathtt{int}].\mathtt{cmt}.?[\mathtt{str}].(\lhd[l_{HD}].?[\mathtt{str}].(?[\mathtt{str}].\mathtt{end} \oplus \mathtt{roll})$$
$$\oplus \lhd [l_{SD}].?[\mathtt{str}].(?[\mathtt{str}].\mathtt{end} \oplus \mathtt{abt}))$$
$$T_S = ?[\mathtt{str}].![\mathtt{int}].![\mathtt{str}]. \rhd [l_{HD} : \mathtt{cmt}.![\mathtt{str}].![\mathtt{str}].\mathtt{end},$$
$$l_{SD} : \mathtt{cmt}.![\mathtt{str}].![\mathtt{str}].\mathtt{end}]$$

Thus, the resulting initial configuration is $(T_U, T_S) : \langle T_U \rangle \blacktriangleright T_U \parallel \langle T_S \rangle \blacktriangleright T_S$, which can evolve to the configuration $(T_U, T_S) : \langle \underline{T} \rangle \blacktriangleright \mathtt{roll} \parallel \langle U \rangle \blacktriangleright ![\mathtt{str}].\mathtt{end}$, with $T = ?[\mathtt{str}].(?[\mathtt{str}].\mathtt{end} \oplus \mathtt{roll})$ and $U = ![\mathtt{str}].![\mathtt{str}].\mathtt{end}$. This configuration evolves to $(T_U, T_S) : \langle \underline{T} \rangle \blacktriangleright \mathtt{err} \parallel \langle U \rangle \blacktriangleright \mathtt{err}$, which cannot further evolve and is not in a completed state (in fact, type $\mathtt{err}$ is different from $\mathtt{end}$), meaning that T_U and T_S are not compliant.

In the scenario described in Fig. 1(c), instead, the type of the server process is as follows: $T_S' = ?[\mathtt{str}].![\mathtt{int}].\mathtt{cmt}.![\mathtt{str}]. \rhd [l_{HD} :![\mathtt{str}].![\mathtt{str}].\mathtt{end}, l_{SD} :![\mathtt{str}].$

![str].end] and we have $T_{\text{U}} \dashv\!\!\mid T_{\text{S}}'$. Finally, the types of the processes depicted in Fig. 1(d) are:

$$T_{\text{U}}' = ![\text{str}].?[\text{int}].?[\text{str}].\,\text{cmt}.\,(\lhd[l_{HD}].\ldots \oplus \lhd[l_{SD}].\ldots)$$
$$T_{\text{S}}'' = ?[\text{str}].![\text{int}].![\text{str}].\,\text{cmt}. \rhd [l_{HD}:![\text{str}].![\text{str}].\,\text{end}, l_{SD}:![\text{str}].![\text{str}].\,\text{end}]$$

and we have $T_{\text{U}}' \dashv\!\!\not\mid T_{\text{S}}''$. Indeed, the corresponding initial configuration can evolve to the configuration $(T_{\text{U}}', T_{\text{S}}'') : \langle \underline{\lhd[l_{HD}].\ldots}\rangle \blacktriangleright \texttt{roll} \parallel \langle \rhd[l_{HD}:\ldots,l_{SD}:\ldots]\rangle \blacktriangleright![\text{str}].\text{end}$, which again evolves to a configuration that is not in a completed state.

MAUDE Implementation. To show the feasibility of our approach, we have implemented the semantics of type configurations in Fig. 8 in the MAUDE framework [8]. MAUDE provides an instantiation of rewriting logic [22] and it has been used to implement the semantics of several formal languages [23].

The syntax of cherry-pi types and type configurations is specified by defining algebraic data types, while transitions and reductions are rendered as rewrites and, hence, inference rules are given in terms of (conditional) rewrite rules. Since MAUDE specifications are executable, we have obtained in this way an interpreter for cherry-pi type configurations, which permits to explore the reductions arising from the initial configuration of two given session types.

Our implementation consists of two MAUDE modules. The CHERRY-TYPES-SYNTAX module provides the definition of the sorts that characterise the syntax of cherry-pi types, such as session types, selection/branching labels, type variables and type configurations. In particular, basic terms of session types are rendered as constant *operations* on the sort Type; e.g., the roll type is defined as

```
op roll : -> Type .
```

The other syntactic operators are instead defined as operations with one or more arguments; e.g., the output type takes as input a Sort and a continuation type:

```
op ![_]._ : Sort Type -> Type [frozen prec 25] .
```

To prevent undesired rewrites inside operator arguments, following the approach in [33], we have declared these operations as frozen. The prec attribute has been used to define the precedence among operators. The CHERRY-TYPES-SEMANTICS module provides *rewrite rules*, and additional operators and equations, to define the cherry-pi type semantics. For example, the operational rule [TS-SND] is rendered as follows:

```
rl [TS-Snd] : ![S].T => {![S]}T .
```

The correspondence between the operational rule and the rewrite rule is one-to-one; the only peculiarity is the fact that, since rewrites have no labels, we have made the transition label part of the resulting term. Reduction rules for type configurations are instead rendered in terms of conditional rewrite rules with rewrites in their conditions. For example, the [TS-COM] rule is rendered as:

```
crl [TS-Com] :
    init(T,T') CT1 > T1 || CT2 > T2  =>  init(T,T') CT1 > T1' || CT2 > T2'
    if T1 => {![S]}T1' /\ T2 => {?[S]}T2' .
```

Again, there is a close correspondence between the operational rule and the rewrite one.
The compliance check between two session types can be then conveniently realised
on top of the implementation described above by resorting to the MAUDE command
search. This permits indeed to explore the state space of the configurations reachable
from an initial configuration. Specifically, the compliance check between types T1 and
T2 is rendered as follows:

```
search
    init(T1,T2) ckp(T1) > T1 || ckp(T2) > T2
=>!
    init(T:Type,T':Type) CT1:CkpType > T1':Type || CT2:CkpType > T2':Type
such that T1' =/= end or T2' =/= end .
```

This command searches for all terminal states (=>!), i.e. states that cannot be rewritten
any more (see ↦ in Definition 1), and checks if at least one of the two session types
in the corresponding configurations (T1' and T2') is different from the end type.
Thus, if this search has no solution, T1 and T2 are compliant; otherwise, they are not
compliant and a violating configuration is returned.

Example 4. Let us consider the cherry-pi types defined in Example 3 for the scenario
described in Fig. 1(b). In our MAUDE implementation of the type syntax, the session
types T_U and T_S, and the corresponding initial type configuration, are rendered as follows:

```
eq Tuser = ![str]. ?[int]. cmt. ?[str].
            ((sel['hd]. ?[str]. ((?[str]. end) (+) roll))
            (+) (sel['sd]. ?[str]. ((?[str]. end) (+) abt))) .

eq Tservice = ?[str]. ![int]. ![str].
              brn[brnEl('hd, cmt. ![str]. ![str]. end);
                  brnEl('sd, cmt. ![str]. ![str]. end)] .

eq InitConfig = init(Tuser,Tservice)
                ckp(Tuser) > Tuser || ckp(Tservice) > Tservice .
```

where (+) represents the internal choice operator, sel the selection operator, brn the
branching operator, brnEl an option offered in a branching, and ckp a non-imposed
checkpoint. The compliance between the two session types can be checked by loading
the two modules of our MAUDE implementation, and executing the following command:

```
search InitConfig
    =>!
    init(T:Type,T':Type) CT1:CkpType > T1:Type || CT2:CkpType > T2:Type
such that T1 =/= end or T2 =/= end .
```

This search command returns the following solution:

```
CT1 --> ickp(?[str]. ((?[str]. end)(+)roll))
T1 --> err
CT2 --> ckp(![str]. ![str]. end)
T2 --> err
```

As explained in Example 3, the two types are not compliant. Indeed, the configuration above is a terminal state, and T1 and T2 are clearly different from end.

The scenario in Fig. 1(c) is rendered by the following implementation of the service type:

```
eq Tservice' = ?[str]. ![int]. cmt. ![str].
               brn[brnEl('hd, ![str]. ![str]. end);
               brnEl('sd, ![str]. ![str]. end)] .
```

In this case, as expected, the search command returns:

```
No solution.
```

meaning that types Tuser and Tservice' are compliant. Finally, the search command applied to the type configuration related to the scenario depicted in Fig. 1(d) returns a solution, meaning that in that case the user and service types are not compliant.

5 Properties of cherry-pi

This section presents the results regarding the properties of cherry-pi. The statement of some properties exploits labelled transitions that permit to easily distinguish the execution of commit and rollback actions from the other ones. To this end, we can instrument the reduction semantics of collaborations by means of labels of the form $cmt\ s$, $roll\ s$ and $abt\ s$, indicating the rule used to derive the reduction and the session on which such operation has been done.

Rollback Properties. We show some properties concerning the reversible behaviour of cherry-pi related to the interplay between rollback and commit primitives. The first two properties, namely Theorem 2 and Lemma 1, are an adaptation of typical properties of reversible calculi, while Lemma 2 and Lemma 3 are brand new.

The following theorem states that any reachable collaboration is also a *forward only* reachable collaboration. This means that all the states a collaboration reaches via mixed executions (also involving backward reductions) are states that we can reach from the initial configuration with just forward reductions. This assures us that if the system goes back it will reach previous visited states.

Theorem 2. *Let C_0 be an initial collaboration. If $C_0 \rightarrowtail^* C_1$ then $C_0 \twoheadrightarrow^* C_1$.*

We now show a variant of the so-called Loop Lemma [10]. In a fully reversible calculus this lemma states that each computational step, either forward or backward, can be undone. Since reversibility in cherry-pi is controlled, we have to state that if a reversible step is possible (e.g., a rollback is *enabled*) then the effects of the rollback can be undone.

Lemma 1 (Safe rollback). *Let C_1 and C_2 be reachable collaborations. If $C_1 \rightsquigarrow C_2$ then $C_2 \twoheadrightarrow^* C_1$.*

A rollback always brings the system to the last taken checkpoint. We recall that, since there may be sessions running in parallel, a collaboration may be able to do different rollbacks within different sessions. Thus, determinism only holds relative to a given session, and rollback within one session has no effect on any other parallel session.

Lemma 2 (Determinism). *Let* C *be a reachable collaboration. If* $C \overset{roll \ s}{\leadsto} C'$ *and* $C \overset{roll \ s}{\leadsto} C''$ *then* $C' \equiv C''$.

$$\frac{P_1 \xrightarrow{k!\langle v \rangle} P_1' \quad \neg P_2 \Downarrow_{k?} \quad \neg P_2 \Downarrow_{roll}}{\langle \tilde{Q}_1 \rangle \blacktriangleright P_1 \mid \langle \tilde{Q}_2 \rangle \blacktriangleright P_2 \twoheadrightarrow \mathtt{com\_error}} \text{ [E-COM1]} \qquad \frac{P_1 \xrightarrow{roll} P_1'}{\langle Q_1 \rangle \blacktriangleright P_1 \mid \langle \tilde{Q}_2 \rangle \blacktriangleright P_2 \twoheadrightarrow \mathtt{roll\_error}} \text{ [E-RLL2]}$$

Fig. 9. `cherry-pi` semantics: error reductions.

The last rollback property states that a collaboration cannot go back to a state prior to the execution of a commit action, that is commits have a persistent effect. Let us note that recursion does not affect this theorem, since at the beginning of a collaboration computation there is always a new session establishment, leading to a stack of past configurations. Hence it is never the case that from a collaboration C you can reach again C via forward steps.

Theorem 3 (Commit persistency). *Let* C *be a reachable collaboration. If* $C \overset{cmt \ s}{\twoheadrightarrow} C'$ *then there exists no* C''' *such that* $C' \twoheadrightarrow^* \overset{roll \ s}{\leadsto} C''$ *and* $C'' \twoheadrightarrow^+ C$.

Soundness Properties. The second group of properties concerns soundness guarantees. The definition of these properties requires formally characterising the errors that may occur in the execution of an unsound collaboration. We rely on error reduction (as in [7]) rather than on the usual static characterisation of errors (as, e.g., in [36]), since rollback errors cannot be easily detected statically. In particular, we extend the syntax of `cherry-pi` collaborations with the `roll_error` and `com_error` terms, denoting respectively collaborations in rollback and communication error states:

$$C :: = \ldots \mid \langle \tilde{P}_1 \rangle \blacktriangleright P_2 \mid \mathtt{roll\_error} \mid \mathtt{com\_error}$$

where $\tilde{P}$ denotes either a checkpoint P committed by the party or a checkpoint $\underline{P}$ imposed by the other party of the session. The semantics of `cherry-pi` is extended as well by the (excerpt) of error reduction rules in Fig. 9. The error semantics does not affect the normal behaviour of `cherry-pi` specifications, but it is crucial for stating our soundness theorems. Its definition is based on the notion of *barb* predicate: $P \Downarrow_\mu$ holds if there exists P' such that $P \Rightarrow P'$ and P' can perform an action μ, where μ stands for $k?, k!, k \lhd l, k \rhd l$, or $roll$ (i.e., input, output, select, branching action along session channel k, or roll action); $\Rightarrow$ is the reflexive and transitive closure of $\xrightarrow{\tau}$. The meaning of the error semantics rules is as follows. A *communication error* takes place in a collaboration when a session participant is willing to perform an output but the other participant is ready to perform neither the corresponding input nor a roll back (rule [E-COM]$_1$) or vice versa, or one participant is willing to perform a selection but the corresponding branching is not available on the other side or viceversa. Instead, a *rollback error* takes place in a collaboration when a participant is willing to perform a rollback action but her checkpoint has been imposed by the other participant ([E-RLL]$_2$). To enable this error check, the rules for commit and rollback have been modified to keep track of imposed overwriting of checkpoints. This information is not relevant for the runtime execution of processes, but it is necessary for characterising the rollback errors that our type-based approach prevents.

Besides defining the error semantics, we also need to define erroneous collaborations, based on the following notion of context: $\mathbb{C} :: = [\cdot] \mid \mathbb{C} \mid C \mid (\nu s : C) \, \mathbb{C}$.

Definition 3 (Erroneous collaborations). *A collaboration C is* communication (resp. rollback) erroneous *if* $C = \mathbb{C}[com\_error]$ *(resp.* $C = \mathbb{C}[roll\_error]$*).*

The key soundness results follow: a rollback safe collaboration never reduces to either a rollback erroneous collaboration (Theorem 4) or a communication erroneous collaboration (Theorem 5).

Theorem 4 (Rollback soundness). *If C is a roll-safe collaboration, then we have that* $C \not\rightarrowtail^* \mathbb{C}[roll\_error]$.

Theorem 5 (Communication soundness). *If C is a roll-safe collaboration, then we have that* $C \not\rightarrowtail^* \mathbb{C}[com\_error]$.

We conclude with a progress property of cherry-pi sessions: given a rollback safe collaboration that can initiate a session, each collaboration reachable from it either is able to progress on the session with a forward/backward reduction step or has correctly reached the end of the session. This result follows from Theorems 4 and 5, and from the fact that we consider binary sessions without delegation and subordinate sessions.

Theorem 6 (Session progress). *Let* $C = (\bar{a}(x_1).P_1 \mid a(x_2).P_2)$ *be a roll-safe collaboration. If* $C \rightarrowtail^* C'$ *then either* $C' \rightarrowtail C''$ *for some* C'' *or* $C' \equiv (\nu s : C)(\langle \tilde{Q_1} \rangle \bullet 0 \mid \langle \tilde{Q_2} \rangle \bullet 0)$ *for some* $\tilde{Q_1}$ *and* $\tilde{Q_2}$.

6   Conclusion and Related Work

This paper proposes rollback recovery primitives for session-based programming. These primitives come together with session typing, enabling a design time compliance check which ensures checkpoint persistency properties (Lemma 1 and Theorem 3) and session soundness (Theorems 4 and 5). Our compliance check has been implemented in MAUDE.

In the literature we can distinguish two ways of dealing with rollback: either using explicit rollbacks and implicit commits [20], or by using explicit commits and spontaneous aborts [11, 34]. Differently from these works, we have introduced a way to control reversibility by both *triggering* it and *limiting* its scope. Reversibility is triggered via an explicit rollback primitive (as in [20]), while explicit commits limit the scope of potential future reverse executions (as in [11, 34]). Differently from [11, 34], commit does not require any synchronisation, as it is a local decision. This could lead to run-time misbehaviours where a process willing to roll back to its last checkpoint reaches a point which has been imposed by another participant of the session. Our type discipline rules out such cases.

Reversibility in behavioural types has been studied in different formalisms: *contracts* [2,4], *binary session types* [24], *multiparty session types* [6,25,30,31], and *global graphs* [14,28]. In [2,4] choices can be seen as *implicit* checkpoints and the system can go back to a previous choice and try another branch. In [2] rollback is triggered non-deterministically, while in [4] it is triggered by the system only when the computation is stuck. In both works reversibility (and rollbacks) is used to achieve a relaxed variant of client-server compliance: if there exists an execution in which the client is able to terminate then the client and server are compliant. Hence, reversibility is used as a means to explore different branches if the current one leads to a deadlock. In [24] reversibility is studied in the context of binary session types. Types information is used at run-time by monitors, for binary [24] and multiparty [25] settings, to keep track of the computational history of the system. allowing to revert any computational step. where global types are enriched with computational history. There, reversibility is uncontrolled, and each computational step can be undone. In [6] global types are enriched with history information, and choices are seen as labelled checkpoints. The information about checkpoints is projected into local types. At any moment, the party who decided which branch to take in a choice may decide to revert it, forcing the entire system to go back to a point prior to the choice. Hence, rollback is confined inside choices and it is spontaneous. meaning that the former can be programmed while the latter cannot. Checkpoints are not seen as commits, and a rollback can bring the system to a state prior to several checkpoints. In [30] an *uncontrolled* reversible variant of session π-calculus is presented, while [31] studies different notions of reversibility for both binary and multiparty single sessions. In [14,28] global graphs are extended with conditions on branches. These conditions at runtime can trigger coordinated rollbacks to revert a distributed choice. Reversibility is confined into branches of a distributed choice and not all the computational steps are reversible; inputs, in fact, are irreversible unless they are inside an ongoing loop. to trigger a rollback several conditions and constraints about loops have to be satisfied. Hence, in order to trigger a rollback a runtime condition should be satisfied.

We detach from these works in several ways. Our checkpoint facility is explicit and checkpointing is not relegated to choices: the programmer can decide at any point when to commit. This is because the programmer may be interested in committing, besides choice points, a series of interactions (e.g., to make a payment irreversible). Once a commit is taken, the system cannot revert to a state prior to it. Our rollback is explicit, meaning that it is the programmer who deliberately triggers a rollback. The extension to the multiparty setting is natural and does not rely on a formalism to describe the global view of the system. Our compliance check, which is decidable, resembles those of [2–4], which are defined for different rollback recovery approaches based on implicit checkpoints.

As future work, we plan to extend our approach to deal with sessions where parties can interleave interactions performed along different sessions. This requires to deal with subordinate sessions, which may affect enclosing sessions by performing, e.g., commit actions that make some interaction of the enclosing sessions irreversible, similarly to nested transactions [35]. To tackle this issue it would be necessary to extend the notion of compliance relation to take into account possible partial commits (in case of nested sub-sessions) that could be undone at the top level if a rollback is performed. Also, the way our checkpoints are taken resembles the Communication Induced Checkpoints (CIC) approach [12]; we leave as future work a thoughtful comparison between these two mechanisms.

References

1. Aman, B., et al.: Foundations of reversible computation. In: Ulidowski, I., Lanese, I., Schultz, U.P., Ferreira, C. (eds.) RC 2020. LNCS, vol. 12070, pp. 1–40. Springer, Cham (2020). https://doi.org/10.1007/978-3-030-47361-7_1
2. Barbanera, F., Dezani-Ciancaglini, M., de'Liguoro, U.: Compliance for reversible client/server interactions. In: BEAT. EPTCS, vol. 162, pp. 35–42 (2014)
3. Barbanera, F., Dezani-Ciancaglini, M., Lanese, I., de'Liguoro, U.: Retractable contracts. In: PLACES 2015. EPTCS, vol. 203, pp. 61–72 (2016)
4. Barbanera, F., Lanese, I., de'Liguoro, U.: Retractable and speculative contracts. In: Jacquet, J.-M., Massink, M. (eds.) COORDINATION 2017. LNCS, vol. 10319, pp. 119–137. Springer, Cham (2017). https://doi.org/10.1007/978-3-319-59746-1_7
5. Barbanera, F., Lanese, I., de'Liguoro, U.: A theory of retractable and speculative contracts. Sci. Comput. Program. **167**, 25–50 (2018)
6. Castellani, I., Dezani-Ciancaglini, M., Giannini, P.: Concurrent reversible sessions. In: CONCUR. LIPIcs, vol. 85, pp. 30:1–30:17. Schloss Dagstuhl - Leibniz-Zentrum fuer Informatik (2017)
7. Chen, T., Dezani-Ciancaglini, M., Scalas, A., Yoshida, N.: On the preciseness of subtyping in session types. Logical Methods Comput. Sci. **13**(2) (2017)
8. All About Maude - A High-Performance Logical Framework. LNCS, vol. 4350. Springer, Heidelberg (2007). https://doi.org/10.1007/978-3-540-71999-1
9. Cristescu, I., Krivine, J., Varacca, D.: A Compositional Semantics for the Reversible p-Calculus. In: LICS, pp. 388–397. IEEE (2013)
10. Danos, V., Krivine, J.: Reversible communicating systems. In: Gardner, P., Yoshida, N. (eds.) CONCUR 2004. LNCS, vol. 3170, pp. 292–307. Springer, Heidelberg (2004). https://doi.org/10.1007/978-3-540-28644-8_19
11. Danos, V., Krivine, J.: Transactions in RCCS. In: Abadi, M., de Alfaro, L. (eds.) CONCUR 2005. LNCS, vol. 3653, pp. 398–412. Springer, Heidelberg (2005). https://doi.org/10.1007/11539452_31
12. Elnozahy, E.N., Alvisi, L., Wang, Y., Johnson, D.B.: A survey of rollback-recovery protocols in message-passing systems. ACM Comput. Surv. **34**(3), 375–408 (2002)
13. Engblom, J.: A review of reverse debugging. In: System, Software, SoC and Silicon Debug Conference (S4D), pp. 1–6 (Sept 2012)
14. Francalanza, A., Mezzina, C.A., Tuosto, E.: Reversible Choreographies via Monitoring in Erlang. In: Bonomi, S., Rivière, E. (eds.) DAIS 2018. LNCS, vol. 10853, pp. 75–92. Springer, Cham (2018). https://doi.org/10.1007/978-3-319-93767-0_6
15. Honda, K., Vasconcelos, V.T., Kubo, M.: Language primitives and type discipline for structured communication-based programming. In: Hankin, C. (ed.) ESOP 1998. LNCS, vol. 1381, pp. 122–138. Springer, Heidelberg (1998). https://doi.org/10.1007/BFb0053567
16. Hüttel, H., et al.: Foundations of session types and behavioural contracts. ACM Comput. Surv. **49**(1), 3:1–3:36 (2016)
17. Kouzapas, D., Yoshida, N.: Globally governed session semantics. Logical Methods Comput. Sci. **10**(4) (2014)

18. Kuhn, S., Ulidowski, I.: Local reversibility in a calculus of covalent bonding. Sci. Comput. Program. **151**, 18–47 (2018)
19. Lanese, I., Lienhardt, M., Mezzina, C.A., Schmitt, A., Stefani, J.-B.: Concurrent flexible reversibility. In: Felleisen, M., Gardner, P. (eds.) ESOP 2013. LNCS, vol. 7792, pp. 370–390. Springer, Heidelberg (2013). https://doi.org/10.1007/978-3-642-37036-6_21
20. Lanese, I., Mezzina, C.A., Schmitt, A., Stefani, J.-B.: Controlling reversibility in higher-order Pi. In: Katoen, J.-P., König, B. (eds.) CONCUR 2011. LNCS, vol. 6901, pp. 297–311. Springer, Heidelberg (2011). https://doi.org/10.1007/978-3-642-23217-6_20
21. Lanese, I., Mezzina, C.A., Stefani, J.-B.: Reversing higher-order Pi. In: Gastin, P., Laroussinie, F. (eds.) CONCUR 2010. LNCS, vol. 6269, pp. 478–493. Springer, Heidelberg (2010). https://doi.org/10.1007/978-3-642-15375-4_33
22. Meseguer, J.: Conditional rewriting logic as a unified model of concurrency. Theoret. Comput. Sci. **96**(1), 73–155 (1992)
23. Meseguer, J.: Twenty years of rewriting logic. J. Log. Algebr. Program. **81**(7–8), 721–781 (2012)
24. Mezzina, C.A., Pérez, J.A.: Reversibility in session-based concurrency: a fresh look. J. Log. Algebr. Meth. Program. **90**, 2–30 (2017)
25. Mezzina, C.A., Pérez, J.A.: Causal consistency for reversible multiparty protocols. Log. Methods Comput. Sci. 17(4) (2021)
26. Mezzina, C.A., Schlatte, R., Glück, R., Haulund, T., Hoey, J., Holm Cservenka, M., Lanese, I., Mogensen, T.Æ., Siljak, H., Schultz, U.P., Ulidowski, I.: Software and reversible systems: a survey of recent activities. In: Ulidowski, I., Lanese, I., Schultz, U.P., Ferreira, C. (eds.) RC 2020. LNCS, vol. 12070, pp. 41–59. Springer, Cham (2020). https://doi.org/10.1007/978-3-030-47361-7_2
27. Mezzina, C.A., Tiezzi, F., Yoshida, N.: Rollback Recovery in Session-based Programming. Tech. rep., DiSIA, Univ. Firenze (2023). https://github.com/tiezzi/cherry-pi/raw/main/docs/cherry-pi_TR.pdf
28. Mezzina, C.A., Tuosto, E.: Choreographies for automatic recovery. CoRR abs/1705.09525 (2017). https://arxiv.org/abs/1705.09525
29. Perumalla, K.S., Protopopescu, V.A.: Reversible simulations of elastic collisions. ACM Trans. Model. Comput. Simul. **23**(2), 12:1–12:25 (2013)
30. Tiezzi, F., Yoshida, N.: Reversible session-based pi-calculus. J. Log. Algebr. Meth. Program. **84**(5), 684–707 (2015)
31. Tiezzi, F., Yoshida, N.: Reversing single sessions. In: Devitt, S., Lanese, I. (eds.) RC 2016. LNCS, vol. 9720, pp. 52–69. Springer, Cham (2016). https://doi.org/10.1007/978-3-319-40578-0_4
32. Vassor, M., Stefani, J.-B.: Checkpoint/rollback vs causally-consistent reversibility. In: Kari, J., Ulidowski, I. (eds.) RC 2018. LNCS, vol. 11106, pp. 286–303. Springer, Cham (2018). https://doi.org/10.1007/978-3-319-99498-7_20
33. Verdejo, A., Martí-Oliet, N.: Implementing CCS in Maude 2. In: WRLA. ENTCS, vol. 71, pp. 239–257. Elsevier (2002)
34. de Vries, E., Koutavas, V., Hennessy, M.: Communicating transactions. In: Gastin, P., Laroussinie, F. (eds.) CONCUR 2010. LNCS, vol. 6269, pp. 569–583. Springer, Heidelberg (2010). https://doi.org/10.1007/978-3-642-15375-4_39
35. Weikum, G., Schek, H.J.: Concepts and applications of multilevel transactions and open nested transactions. In: Database Transaction Models for Advanced Applications, pp. 515–553. Morgan Kaufmann (1992)
36. Yoshida, N., Vasconcelos, V.T.: Language primitives and type discipline for structured communication-based programming revisited: two systems for higher-order session communication. Electr. Notes Theor. Comp. Sci. **171**(4), 73–93 (2007)

Safe Asynchronous Mixed-Choice
for Timed Interactions

Jonah Pears$^{(\boxtimes)}$ ⓘ, Laura Bocchi ⓘ, and Andy King ⓘ

University of Kent, Canterbury, UK
{jjp38,l.bocchi,a.m.king}@kent.ac.uk

Abstract. Mixed-choice has long been barred from models of asynchronous communication since it compromises key properties of communicating finite-state machines. Session types inherit this restriction, which precludes them from fully modelling timeouts – a key programming feature to handle failures. To address this deficiency, we present (binary) TimeOut Asynchronous Session Types (TOAST) as an extension to (binary) asynchronous timed session types to permit mixed-choice. TOAST deploy timing constraints to regulate the use of mixed-choice so as to preserve communication safety. We provide a new behavioural semantics for TOAST which guarantees progress in the presence of mixed-choice. Building upon TOAST, we provide a calculus featuring process timers which is capable of modelling timeouts using a **receive-after** pattern, much like Erlang, and informally illustrate the correspondence with TOAST specifications.

Keywords: Session types · Mixed-choice · Timeouts · π-calculus

1 Introduction

Mixed-choice is an inherent feature of models of communications such as communicating finite-state machines (CFSM) [11] where actions are classified as either send or receive. In this setting, a state of a machine is said to be mixed if there exist both a sending action and a receiving action from that state. When considering an asynchronous model of communication, absence of deadlocks is undecidable in general [17] but can be guaranteed in presence of three sufficient and decidable conditions: determinism, compatibility, and *absence* of mixed-states [15,17]. Intuitively, determinism means that it is not possible, from a state, to reach two different states with the same kind of action, and compatibility requires that for each send action of one machine, the rest of the system can eventually perform a complementary receive action.

This work has been partially supported by EPSRC project EP/T014512/1 (STARDUST) and the BehAPI project funded by the EU H2020 RISE under the Marie Sklodowska-Curie action (No: 778233). We thank Simon Thompson and Maurizio Murgia for their insightful comments on an early version of this work.

© IFIP International Federation for Information Processing 2023
S.-S. Jongmans and A. Lopes (Eds.): COORDINATION 2023, LNCS 13908, pp. 214–231, 2023.
https://doi.org/10.1007/978-3-031-35361-1_12

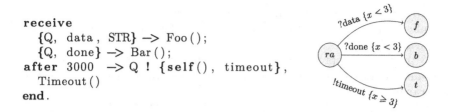

```
receive
   {Q, data, STR} -> Foo();
   {Q, done} -> Bar();
   after 3000  -> Q ! {self(), timeout},
      Timeout()
end.
```

Fig. 1. An Erlang snippet and its mixed-state machine representation

In the desire to ensure deadlock freedom, mixed-choice has been given up, even though this curtails the descriptive capabilities of CFSM and its derivatives. Despite the rapid evolution of session types, even to the point of deployment in Java [19], Python [26,28], Rust [22], F# [27] and Go [13], thus far mixed-choice has only been introduced into the synchronous binary setting [29]. In fact, the exclusion of mixed-choice pervades work on asynchronous communication which guarantee deadlock-freedom, both for communicating timed automata [8,21] and session types [6,12,18,30]. Determinism and the absence of mixed-states is baked into the very syntax of session types (the correspondence between session types and so-called safe CFSM is explained in [15]).

Timed session types [4,9,10], which extend session types with time constraints, inherit the same syntactic restrictions of session types, and hence rule out mixed-states. This is unfortunate since in the timed setting, mixed-states are a useful abstraction for timeouts. Illustrated in Fig. 1, the mixed-state CFSM (right) can be realised using a **receive-after** statement in Erlang (left). In the Erlang snippet, the process waits to receive either a 'data' or 'done' message. If neither are received within 3 s, then a timeout message is issued.

Timeouts are important for handling failure and unexpected delays, for instance, the SMTP protocol stipulates: "*An SMTP client* must *provide a timeout mechanism*" [20, Section 4.5.3.2]. Mixed-states would allow, for example, states where a server is waiting to *receive* a message from the client and, if nothing is received after a certain amount of time, *send* a notification that ends the session. Current variants of timed session types allow deadlines to be expressed but cannot, because of the absence of mixed-states, characterise (and verify) the behaviour that should follow a missed deadline, e.g., a restart or retry strategy. In this paper, we argue that time makes mixed-states more powerful (allowing timeouts to be expressed), while just adding sufficient synchonisation to ensure that mixed-states are safe in an asynchronous semantics (cannot produce deadlocks).

Contributions This work makes three orthogonal contributions to the theory of binary session types, with a focus on improving their descriptive capabilities:

- We introduce TimeOut Asynchronous (binary) Session Types (TOAST) to support timeouts. Inspired by asynchronous timed binary session types [9], TOAST shows how timing constraints provide an elegant solution for guaranteeing the safety of mixed-choice. Technically, we provide a semantics for

TOAST and a well-formedness condition. We show that well-formedness is sufficient to guarantee progress for TOAST (which may, instead, get stuck in general).

– We provide a new process calculus whose functionality extends to support programming motifs such as the widely used `receive-after` pattern of Erlang for expressing timeouts.

– We introduce timers in our process calculus to structure the counterpart of a timeout (i.e., a process that interacts with one other process displaying a timeout), as well as time-sensitive conditional statements, where the selection of a branch may be determined by timers. Time-sensitive conditional statements provide processes with knowledge that can be used to decide which branch should be followed e.g., helping understanding whether the counterpart may have timed out or not.

– We provide an informal discussion on the correspondence between TOAST and the aforementioned primitives of our new process calculus.

2   Timeout Asynchronous Session Types (TOAST)

This section presents the syntax, semantics and formation rules for Time-Out Asynchronous Session Types (TOAST), which extend asynchronous binary timed session types [9] with a well-disciplined (hence safe) form of mixed-choice.

Clocks & Constraints. We start with a few preliminary definitions borrowed from timed automata [1]. Let $\mathbb{X}$ be a finite set of clocks denoted x, y and z. A (clock) valuation ν is a map $\nu : \mathbb{X} \rightarrow \mathbb{R}_{\geqslant 0}$. The initial valuation is ν_0 where $\nu_0 = \{x \mapsto 0 \mid x \in \mathbb{X}\}$. Given a time offset $t \in \mathbb{R}_{\geqslant 0}$ and a valuation ν, $\nu + t = \{x \mapsto \nu(x) + t \mid x \in \mathbb{X}\}$. Given $\lambda \subseteq \mathbb{X}$ and ν, $\nu [\lambda \mapsto 0] = \{\text{if } (x \in \lambda) \, 0 \, \text{else } \nu(x) \mid x \in \mathbb{X}\}$. Observe $\nu [\varnothing \mapsto 0] = \nu$. $\mathbb{G}(\mathbb{X})$ denotes the set of clock constraints, where a clock constraint δ takes the form:

$$\delta ::= \mathtt{true} \mid x > t \mid x = t \mid x - y > t \mid x - y = t \mid \neg\delta \mid \delta_1 \wedge \delta_2 \qquad (1)$$

We write $\nu \models \delta$ for a constraint δ that is satisfied by the valuations of clocks within ν. We write $\downarrow \delta$ (the past of δ) for a constraint δ' such that $\nu \models \delta'$ if and only if $\exists t : \nu + t \models \delta$. For example $\downarrow (3 < x < 5) = x < 5$ and $\downarrow (x > 2) = \mathtt{true}$.

2.1   Syntax of TOAST

The syntax of TOAST (or just *types*) is given in eq. (2). A type S is a choice $\{c_i.S_i\}_{i \in I}$, recursive definition $\mu\alpha.S$, call α, or termination type `end`.

$$
\begin{aligned}
S :: &= \{c_i.S_i\}_{i \in I} \mid \mu\alpha.S \mid \alpha \mid \mathtt{end} & c :: &= \Box\, l\, \langle T \rangle \, (\delta, \lambda) \\
T :: &= (\delta, S) \mid \mathtt{Nat} \mid \mathtt{Bool} \mid \mathtt{String} \mid \mathtt{None} \mid \dots & \Box :: &= ! \mid ?
\end{aligned}
$$

$$(2)$$

Type $\{c_i.S_i\}_{i \in I}$ models a choice among options i ranging over a non-empty set I. Each option i is a selection/send action if $\Box = !$, or alternatively a branching/receive action if $\Box = ?$. An option sends (resp. receives) a label l and a message of a specified data type T is delineated by $\langle \cdot \rangle$. The send or receive action of an option is guarded by a time constraint δ. After the action, the clocks within λ are reset to 0. Data types, ranged over by T, T_i, ... can be sorts (e.g., natural, boolean), or higher order types (δ, S) to model session delegation. Only the message label is exchanged when the data type is None. Labels of the options in a choice are pairwise distinct. Recursion and terminated types are standard.

Remarks on the notation. One convention is to model the exchange of payloads as a separated action with respect to the communication of branching labels. In this paper we follow [8,31], and model them as unique actions. When irrelevant, we omit the payload, yielding a notation closer to that of timed automata.

2.2 Semantics of TOAST

We present the semantics of TOAST, building on those given in [9]; any changes are highlighted. Following [9], we define the semantics using three layers: (1) *configurations*, (2) *configurations with queues* that model asynchronous interactions, and (3) *systems* that model the parallel composition of configurations with queues. The semantics are defined over the labels ℓ given below:

$$\ell ::= \square m \mid t \mid \tau \qquad m ::= l\langle T \rangle \qquad \square ::= \; ! \mid ? \qquad (3)$$

where ℓ is either a communication, time, or silent action, and m is a message.

Configurations. A configuration $\mathbf{s}$ is a pair (ν, S). The semantics for configurations are defined by a Labelled Transition System (LTS) over configurations, the labels in eq. (3), and the rules given in Fig. 2.

$$\frac{\nu \models \delta_j \quad j \in I}{(\nu, \{\square_i l_i \langle T_i \rangle (\delta_i, \lambda_i).S_i\}_{i \in I}) \xrightarrow{\square_j l_j \langle T_j \rangle} (\nu[\lambda_j \mapsto 0], S_j)} \; [\texttt{act}]$$

$$\frac{(\nu, S[^{\mu t.S}/_t]) \xrightarrow{\ell} (\nu', S')}{(\nu, \mu t.S) \xrightarrow{\ell} (\nu', S')} \; [\texttt{unfold}] \qquad (\nu, S) \xrightarrow{t} (\nu + t, S) \quad [\texttt{tick}]$$

Fig. 2. Semantics of Configurations.

Rule [act] deviates from [9] and handles choice types. By this rule, a configuration performs one action with index $j \in I$ provided that the constraint δ_j is satisfied in the current valuation ν ($\nu \models \delta_j$). All clocks in λ_j are reset to 0 in the resulting configuration's valuation of clocks. Rule [unfold] unfolds recursive types. Rule [tick] describes time passing. A transition $\mathbf{s} \xrightarrow{t \square m} \mathbf{s}'$ indicates $\mathbf{s} \xrightarrow{t} \mathbf{s}'' \xrightarrow{\square m} \mathbf{s}'$, where $\mathbf{s}''$ is some intermediate configuration. We write $\mathbf{s} \xrightarrow{t \square m}$ if there exists $\mathbf{s}'$ such that $\mathbf{s} \xrightarrow{t \square m} \mathbf{s}'$.

$$\frac{(\nu, S) \xrightarrow{!m} (\nu', S')}{(\nu, S, M) \xrightarrow{!m} (\nu', S', M)} \; [\text{snd}] \qquad \frac{(\nu, S) \xrightarrow{?m} (\nu', S')}{(\nu, S, m; M) \xrightarrow{\tau} (\nu', S', M)} \; [\text{rcv}]$$

$$(\nu, S, M) \xrightarrow{?m} (\nu, S, M; m) \quad [\text{que}]$$

$$\frac{\begin{array}{ll} (\nu, S) \xrightarrow{t} (\nu', S) & \text{(configuration)} \\ (\nu, S) \text{ is FE} \implies (\nu', S) \text{ is FE} & \text{(persistency)} \\ \forall t' < t : (\nu + t', S, M) \xrightarrow{\tau}\!\!\!\!\!\!\!/ & \text{(urgency)} \end{array}}{(\nu, S, M) \xrightarrow{t} (\nu', S, M)} \; [\text{time}]$$

Fig. 3. Semantics of Configurations with queues.

Configurations with Queues. A configuration with queues $\mathbf{S}$ is a triple (ν, S, M) where M is a FIFO queue of messages which have been received but not yet processed. A queue takes the form $M ::= \varnothing \mid m; M$ thus is either empty, or has a message at its head. The transition $\mathbf{S} \xrightarrow{t \square m} \mathbf{S}'$ is defined analogously to $s \xrightarrow{t \square m} s'$. The semantics of configurations with queues is defined by an LTS over the labels in Eq. (3) and the rules in Fig. 3.

Rule [snd] is for sending a message. Message reception is handled by two rules: [que] inserts a message at the back of M, and [rcv] removes a message from the front of the queue. Rule [time] is for time passing which is formulated in terms of a future-enabled configuration, given in Definition 1. The second condition in the premise for rule [time] ensures the latest-enabled action is never missed by advancing the clocks. The third condition models an urgent semantics, ensuring messages are processed as they arrive. Urgency is critical for reasoning about progress.

Definition 1 (Future-enabled Configurations (FE)). *For some m, a configuration $\mathbf{s}$ (resp. a configuration with queues $\mathbf{S}$) is future-enabled (FE) if $\exists t \in \mathbb{R}_{\geqslant 0} : s \xrightarrow{t \square m} (resp. \; S \xrightarrow{t \square m}).$*

Systems. Systems are the parallel composition of two configurations with queues, written as $(\nu_1, S_1, M_1) | (\nu_2, S_2, M_2)$ or $\mathbf{S}_1 | \mathbf{S}_2$. The semantics of systems is defined by an LTS over the labels in Eq. (3) and the transition rules in Fig. 4.

Rule [com-1] handles asynchronous communication where $\mathbf{S}_1$ sends a message m via rule [snd], which arrives at the queue of $\mathbf{S}_2$ via rule [que]. Rule [com-r] is symmetric, allowing for $\mathbf{S}_2$ to be the sending party, and is omitted. Rule [par-1] allows $\mathbf{S}_1$ to process the message at the head of M_1 via [rcv]. Rule [par-r] is symmetric, allowing $\mathbf{S}_2$ to receive messages, and is omitted. By rule [wait] time passes consistently across systems.

Example 1 (Weak Persistency). In language-based approaches to timed semantics [21], time actions are always possible, even if they bring the model into a

$$\frac{S_1 \xrightarrow{!m} S_1' \quad S_2 \xrightarrow{?m} S_2'}{S_1 \mid S_2 \xrightarrow{\tau} S_1' \mid S_2'} \,[\,\texttt{com-1}\,] \qquad \frac{S_1 \xrightarrow{\tau} S_1'}{S_1 \mid S_2 \xrightarrow{\tau} S_1' \mid S_2} \,[\,\texttt{par-1}\,]$$

$$\frac{S_1 \xrightarrow{t} S_1' \quad S_2 \xrightarrow{t} S_2'}{S_1 \mid S_2 \xrightarrow{t} S_1' \mid S_2'} \,[\,\texttt{wait}\,]$$

Fig. 4. Semantics of Systems.

stuck state by preventing available actions. Execution traces are then filtered a posteriori, removing all 'bad' traces (defined on the basis of final states). In contrast, and to facilitate the reasoning on process behaviour, we adopt a process-based approach, e.g., [2,9], that only allows for actions that characterise *intended* executions of the model. Precisely, we build on the semantics in [2] for asynchronous timed automata with mixed-choice, where time actions are possible only if they do not disable: (1) the latest-enabled sending action, and (2) the latest-enabled receiving action if the queue is not empty. This ensures that time actions preserve the viability of at least one action (*weak-persistency*). In our scenario, constraint (1) is too strict. Consider type S and its dual below:

$$S = \left\{ \begin{array}{l} !\,data < String > (x < 3).S', \\ ?\,timeout(x > 4).\,\texttt{end} \end{array} \right\} \qquad \overline{S} = \left\{ \begin{array}{l} ?\,data\ < String >\ (y < 3).\overline{S'}, \\ !\,timeout\ (y > 4).\,\texttt{end} \end{array} \right\}$$

According to (1), it would never be possible for S to take the timeout branch since a time action of $t \geqslant 3$ would disable the latest-enabled send. This is reasonable in [2] because, in their general setting, there is no guarantee that a timeout will indeed be received. Unlike [2], we can rely on duality of $\overline{S}$ (introduced later in this section), which guarantees that $\overline{S}$ will send a timeout message when $y > 4$. Our new rule [time] – condition (persistency) – implements a more general constraint than (1), requiring that one latest-enabled (send or receive) action is preserved. Constraint (2) remains to implement urgency and, e.g., prevents $\overline{S}$ from sending a timeout if a message is waiting in the queue when $y < 3$.

2.3 Duality, Well-formedness, and Progress

In the untimed scenario, the composition of a binary type with its dual characterises a *protocol*, which specifies the "correct" set of interactions between a party and its co-party. The dual of a type, formally defined below, is obtained by swapping the directions (! or ?) of each interaction:

Definition 2 (Dual Types). *The dual type $\overline{S}$ of type S is defined as follows:*

$$\overline{\mu\alpha.S} = \mu\alpha.\overline{S} \qquad \overline{\alpha} = \alpha \qquad \overline{\texttt{end}} = \texttt{end} \qquad \overline{!} = ?$$
$$\overline{\left\{ \Box_i l_i \langle T_i \rangle (\delta_i, \lambda_i).S_i \right\}_{i \in I}} = \left\{ \overline{\Box_i} l_i \langle T_i \rangle (\delta_i, \lambda_i).\overline{S_i} \right\}_{i \in I} \qquad \overline{?} = !$$

Unfortunately, when annotating session types with time constraints, one may obtain protocols that are infeasible, as shown in Example 2. This is a known problem, which has been addressed by providing additional conditions or constraints on timed session types, for example compliance [3], feasibility [10], interaction enabling [8], and well-formedness [9].

Building upon [9], well-formedness is given as a set of formation rules for types. The rules check that in every reachable state (which includes every possible clock valuation) it is possible to perform the next action immediately or at some point in the future, unless the state is final. (This is formalized as the progress property in Definition 4.) By these rules, the type in Example 2 would not be well-formed. The use of mixed-choice in asynchronous communications may result in infeasible protocols or, more concretely, systems (or types) that get stuck, even if they are well-formed in the sense of [9] (discussed in Example 3).

Example 2 (Junk Types). Consider the *junk type* defined below:

$$S = !a \ (x > 3, \ \varnothing). \ \{!b \ (y = 2, \ \varnothing).\text{end}, \ ?c \ (2 < x < 5, \ \varnothing).\text{end}\}$$

Assume all clocks are 0 before a is sent. After a is sent, all clocks hold values greater than 3. The constraint on sending b is never met, and the one on receiving c may not be met. Types with unsatisfiable constraints are called *junk types* [9]. S can be amended to obtain, for example, S' or S'' below.

$$S' \ = !a \ (x > 3, \ \{y\}). \ \{!b \ (y = 2, \ \varnothing).\text{end}, \ ?c \ (2 < x < 5, \ \varnothing).\text{end}\}$$
$$S'' = !a \ (3 < x < 5, \ \varnothing). \ \{!b \ (y = 2, \ \varnothing).\text{end}, \ ?c \ (2 < x < 5, \ \varnothing).\text{end}\}$$

S' makes both options of the choice satisfiable by resetting clock y, while S'' makes at least one option (?c) always satisfiable by changing the first constraint.

Example 3 (Unsafe Mixed-choice). A mixed-choice is considered *unsafe* if actions of different directions compete to be performed (i.e., they are both viable at the same point in time). Consider system $\mathbf{S}_1|\mathbf{S}_2$, where $\mathbf{S}_1 = (\nu_0, \ S_1, \ \varnothing)$, $\mathbf{S}_2 = (\nu_0, \ S_2, \ \varnothing)$, and types S_1 and S_2 are dual as defined below:

$$S_1 = \left\{ \begin{array}{l} ? \ a(x < 5) \ .\text{end} \\ ! \ b(x = 0).S_1' \end{array} \right\} \qquad S_2 = \left\{ \begin{array}{l} ! \ a(y < 5).\text{end} \\ ? \ b(y = 0).S_2' \end{array} \right\}$$

In the system $\mathbf{S}_1|\mathbf{S}_2$ it is possible for both $\mathbf{S}_1 \xrightarrow{!b} \mathbf{S}_1'$ and $\mathbf{S}_2 \xrightarrow{!a} \mathbf{S}_2'$ to occur at the same time. In the resulting system $(\nu_0, \ S_1', \ a) \mid (\nu_0, \ \text{end}, \ b)$ neither message can be received, and S_1' may be stuck waiting for interactions from S_2' indefinitely.

Well-Formedness. In this work we extend well-formedness of [9] so that progress is guaranteed in the presence of mixed-choice. The formation rules for types are given in Fig. 5; rules differing from [9] are highlighted. Types are evaluated against judgements of the form: $A; \ \delta \vdash S$ where A is an environment containing recursive variables, and δ is a constraint over all clocks characterising the times in which state S can be reached.

$$\forall i \in I : A; \gamma_i \vdash S_i \ \wedge \ \delta_i[\lambda_i \mapsto 0] \models \gamma_i \quad \text{(feasibility)}$$
$$\forall i, j \in I : i \neq j \implies \delta_i \wedge \delta_j \models \texttt{false} \ \vee \ \square_i = \square_j \ \text{(mixed-choice)}$$
$$\forall i \in I : T_i = (\delta', S') \implies \varnothing; \gamma' \vdash S' \ \wedge \ \delta' \models \gamma' \quad \text{(delegation)}$$

$$[\texttt{choice}]$$

$$\frac{}{A; \downarrow \bigvee_{i \in I} \delta_i \vdash \{\square_i \, l_i \langle T_i \rangle \, (\delta_i, \lambda_i) \, . S_i\}_{i \in I}}$$

$$\frac{}{A; \texttt{true} \vdash \texttt{end}} \ [\texttt{end}] \qquad \frac{A, \alpha : \delta; \ \delta \vdash S}{A; \ \delta \vdash \mu\alpha.S} \ [\texttt{rec}] \qquad \frac{}{A, \alpha : \delta; \ \delta \vdash \alpha} \ [\texttt{var}]$$

Fig. 5. Well-formedness rules for types.

Rule [choice] checks well-formedness of choices with three conditions: the first and third conditions are from the branching and delegation rules in [9], respectively; the second condition is new and critical to ensure progress of mixed-choice. By using the weakest past of all constraints ($\downarrow \bigvee_{i \in I} \delta_i$) only one of the options within the choice is required to be *always* viable, for the choice to be well-formed. The first condition (feasibility) ensures that, for each option in a choice, there exists an environment γ such that the continuation S_i is well-formed, given the current constraints on clocks δ_i (updated with resets in λ_i). This ensures that in every choice, there is always at least one viable action; it would, for example, rule out the type in Example 2. The second condition (mixed-choice) requires all actions that can happen at the same time to have the same (send/receive) direction. This condition allows for types modelling timeouts, as in Example 1, and rules out scenarios as the one in Example 3. The third condition (delegation) checks for well-formedness of each delegated session with respect to their corresponding initialization constraint δ'. Rule [end] ensures termination types are *always* well-formed. Rule [rec] associates, in the environment, a variable α with an invariant δ. Rule [var] ensures recursive calls are defined.

Definition 3 (Well-formedness). *A type S is well-formed with respect to ν if there exists δ such that $\nu \models \delta$ and $\varnothing; \delta \vdash S$. A type S is well-formed if it is well-formed with respect to ν_0.*

Well-formedness, together with the urgent receive features of the semantics (rule [time] in Fig. 3) ensures that the composition of a well-formed type S with its dual $\overline{S}$ enjoys progress. A system enjoys progress if its configurations with queues can continue communicating until reaching the end of the protocol, formally:

Definition 4 (Type Progress). *A configuration with queues $\mathbf{S}$ is final if $\mathbf{S} = (\nu, \texttt{end}, \varnothing)$. A system $\mathbf{S}_1 | \mathbf{S}_2$ satisfies progress for all $\mathbf{S}'_1 | \mathbf{S}'_2$ reachable from $\mathbf{S}_1 | \mathbf{S}_2$, either:*

- *$\mathbf{S}'_1$ and $\mathbf{S}'_2$ are final, or*
- *there exists a $t \in \mathbb{R}_{\geqslant 0}$ such that $\mathbf{S}'_1 \mid \mathbf{S}'_2 \xrightarrow{t\tau}$.*

Theorem 1 (Progress of Systems). *If S is well-formed against ν_0 then $(\nu_0, \ S, \ \varnothing) \mid (\nu_0, \ \overline{S}, \ \varnothing)$ satisfies progress.*

The main result of this section is that, for a system composed of *well-formed* and dual types, any state reached is either *final*, or allows for further progress. By ensuring a system will make progress, it follows that such a system is free from communication mismatches and will not reach deadlock.

The main differences with [9] is not in the formulation of the theory (e.g., Definitions 4 and 5, and the statement of Theorem 1 are basically unchanged) but in the proofs that, now, have to check that the conditions of rule [choice] are sufficient to ensure progress of asynchronous mixed-choice. Additionally, the proof of progress in [9] relies on receive urgency. Because of mixed-choice, it is necessary to reformulate (and relax) urgency in the semantic rule [time] in Fig. 3. Despite generalising the notion of urgency the desired progress property can still be attained (see Example 1 for a discussion).

The proof of Theorem 1 proceeds by showing that system *compatibility* [9] is preserved by transitions. The formal definition of compatibility is given in Definition 5.

Definition 5 (Compatible Systems). *Let* $\mathbf{S}_1 = (\nu_1, S_1, \mathsf{M}_1)$ *and* $\mathbf{S}_2 = (\nu_2, S_2, \mathsf{M}_2)$. *System* $\mathbf{S}_1 | \mathbf{S}_2$ *is* compatible *(written* $\mathbf{S}_1 \perp \mathbf{S}_2$*) if:*

1. $\mathsf{M}_1 = \varnothing \ \vee \ \mathsf{M}_2 = \varnothing$

2. $\mathsf{M}_1 = \mathsf{M}_2 = \varnothing \implies \nu_1 = \nu_2 \ \wedge \ S_1 = \overline{S_2}$

3. $\mathsf{M}_1 = m; \mathsf{M}_1' \implies \exists \nu_1', S_1' : (\nu_1, S_1) \xrightarrow{?m} (\nu_1', S_1') \ \wedge \ (\nu_1', S_1', \mathsf{M}_1') \perp \mathbf{S}_2$

4. $\mathsf{M}_2 = m; \mathsf{M}_2' \implies \exists \nu_2', S_2' : (\nu_2, S_2) \xrightarrow{?m} (\nu_2', S_2') \ \wedge \ \mathbf{S}_1 \perp (\nu_2', S_2', \mathsf{M}_2')$

Informally, $\mathbf{S}_1 \perp \mathbf{S}_2$ if: (1) at most one of their queues is non-empty (equivalent to a half-duplex automaton), (2) if both queues are empty, then $\mathbf{S}_1$ and $\mathbf{S}_2$ have dual types and same clock valuations, and (3) and (4) a configuration is always able to receive any message that arrives in its queue.

3 A Calculus for Processes with Timeouts

We present a new calculus for timed processes which extends existing timed session calculi [8,9] with: (1) timeouts, and (2) time-sensitive conditional statements. Timeouts are defined on receive actions and may be immediately followed by sending actions, hence providing an instance of mixed-choice – which is normally not supported. Time-sensitive conditional statements (i.e., if-then-else with conditions on program clocks/timers) provide a natural counterpart to the timeout construct and enhance the expressiveness of the typing system in [9]. By counterpart, we intend a construct to be used by the process communicating with the one that sets the timeout.

Processes are defined by the grammar below. To better align processes with TOAST, send and select actions have been streamlined by each message consisting of both a label l and some message value v, which is either data or a delegated session; the same holds for receive/branch actions where q is a variable for data or delegated sessions. We assume a set of timer names $\mathbb{T}$, ranged over by x, y and z.

$$
\begin{aligned}
P, Q ::= \ & \texttt{set}\,(x)\,.P & &\mid\ X\langle \mathbf{v}; \mathbf{T}; \mathbf{R} \rangle \\
\mid\ & p \lhd lv.P & &\mid\ 0 \\
\mid\ & p \rhd \{l_i(qi) : P_i\}\ \texttt{after}\ e : Q & &\mid\ \texttt{error} \\
\mid\ & \texttt{if}\ \delta\ \texttt{then} : P\ \texttt{else}\ : Q & &\mid\ (\nu pq)P & (4) \\
\mid\ & \texttt{delay}(\delta).P & &\mid\ P \mid Q \\
\mid\ & \texttt{delay}(t).P & &\mid\ qp : h \\
\mid\ & \texttt{def}\ X(\mathbf{v}; \mathbf{T}; \mathbf{R}) = P\ \texttt{in}\ Q & h ::= & \varnothing \mid\ h \cdot lv
\end{aligned}
$$

Process $\texttt{Set}(x).P$ creates a timer x, initialises it to 0 and continues as P. If x already exists it is reset to 0. For simplicity, we assume that the timers set by each process P and Q in a parallel composition $P \mid Q$ are pair-wise disjoint.

Process $p \lhd lv.P$ is the select/send process: it selects label l and sends payload $\mathbf{v}$ to endpoint p, and continues as P. Its dual is the branch/receive process $p \rhd \{l_i(\mathbf{v}_i) : P_i\}_{i \in I}\ \texttt{after}\ e : Q$. It receives one of the labels l_i, instantiates q_i with the received payload, and continues as P_i. (Note that a similar construct has been used to model timeouts in the Temporal Process Language [7], outside of session types.) Parameter e is a linear expression over the timers and numeric constants drawn from $\mathbb{N}_{\geqslant 0} \cup \{\infty\}$. The expression e determines the duration of a timeout, after which Q is executed. Once a process with an $\texttt{after}$ branch is reached, its expression e is evaluated against the values of the timers, to derive a timeout value n where $n \in \mathbb{N}_{\geqslant 0} \cup \{\infty\}$. Setting $e = \infty$ models a blocking receive primitive that waits potentially forever for a message. Setting $e = 0$ models a non-blocking receive action. To retain expressiveness from [9] where non-blocking receive actions would trigger an exception (i.e., modelling deadlines that must not be missed) we allow Q to be $\texttt{error}$. For simplicity: (i) we write $p \rhd \{l_i(q_i) : P_i\}_{i \in I}$ when $e = \infty$; (ii) we omit the brackets in the case of a single option; (iii) for options with no payloads we omit q_i. The advantage of using an expression e to express the value of a timeout, rather than a fixed constant, is illustrated in Example 4.

Process $\texttt{if}\ \delta\ \texttt{then} : P\ \texttt{else} : Q$ is a conditional statement, except that the condition δ is on timers. Syntactically, the condition is expressed as a time constraint δ in eq. (1), but instead of clocks, defined on the timers previously set by that process. Process $\texttt{delay}(\delta).P$ models time passing for an unknown duration described by δ, and is at runtime reduced to process $\texttt{delay}(t).P$ if $\models \delta\,[\,{}^{t}/_{x}\,]$. In $\texttt{delay}(\delta).P$ we assume δ is a constraint on a single clock x. The name of the clock here is immaterial, where x is a syntactic tool used to determine the duration of a time-consuming (delay) action at run-time. In this sense, assume x is bound within $\texttt{delay}(\delta).P$. Recursive processes are defined by a process variable X and parameters $\mathbf{v}$, $\mathbf{T}$ and $\mathbf{R}$ containing *base type* values, timers and session channels, respectively. The end process is 0. The error process is $\texttt{error}$.

As standard [10,18,30], the process calculus allows parallel processes $P|Q$ and scoped processes $(\nu pq)P$ between endpoints p and q. Endpoints communicate over pairs of channels pq and qp, each with their own unbounded FIFO buffers h.[1] Within a session, p sends messages over pq and receives messages from qp (and vica versa for q). We have adopted the simplifying assumption in [9] that sessions are already instantiated. Therefore, rather than relying on reduction rules to produce correct session instantiation, we rely on a syntactic well-formedness assumption. A *well-formed process* consists of sessions of the form $(\nu pq)(P, |Q, pq : h, qp : h')$, which can be checked syntactically as in [9].

Example 4 (Parametric Timeouts). Consider the process below:

$$\texttt{delay}(z < 2).p \vartriangleright \{msg : P\} \texttt{ after } 3 : Q$$

It expresses a timeout of 3 after a delay with a duration between 0 and 2 time units (whatever this delay turns out to be). To express a timeout of 3 *despite* prior execution of a time-consuming action, we need a way to tune the timeout with the actual delay of the time-consuming action. A *parametric timeout* can model this behaviour:

$$\texttt{set}(x).\texttt{delay}(z < 2).p \vartriangleright \{msg : P\} \texttt{ after } 3 - z : Q$$

By setting the timeout as an expression, $3 - x$, with parameter x reflecting the passage of time, we allow the process to compensate for the exact delay occurred.

3.1 Process Reduction

A *timer environment* $\boldsymbol{\theta}$ is a map from a set of timer names $\mathbb{T}$ to $\mathbb{R}_{\geqslant 0}$. We define $\boldsymbol{\theta} + t = \{x \mapsto \boldsymbol{\theta}(x) + t \mid x \in \mathbb{T}\}$ and $\boldsymbol{\theta}[x \mapsto 0]$ to be the map $\boldsymbol{\theta}[x \mapsto 0](y) = $ if $(x = y)$ 0 else $\boldsymbol{\theta}(y)$.

The semantics of processes are given in Fig. 6, as a reduction relation on pairs of the form $\boldsymbol{\theta}, (P)$. The reduction relation is defined on two kinds of reduction: instantaneous communication actions $\rightharpoonup$, and time-consuming actions $\rightsquigarrow$. We write $\longrightarrow$ to denote a reduction that is either by $\rightharpoonup$ or $\rightsquigarrow$.

Rule [Set] creates a new timer x if x is undefined, and otherwise resets x to 0. Rule [IfT] selects a branch P depending on time-sensitive condition δ. The symmetric rule selects branch Q if the condition is not met, and is omitted. Rules [Recv] and [Send] are standard [24]. Rule [Det] determines the actual duration t of the delay δ (which is a constraint on a single clock). Rule [Delay] outsources time-passing to function $\Phi_t(P)$ (see Definition 6), which returns process P after the elapsing of t units of time, and updates $\boldsymbol{\theta}$ accordingly. Rules [Scope] and [ParL] are as standard and the only instant reductions, which may update $\boldsymbol{\theta}$, if any timers are introduced by [Set]. We omit the symmetric rule for [ParL]. The rule for structural congruence [Str] applies to both instantaneous and time-consuming actions. Structural equivalence of P and Q, denoted $P \equiv Q$ is as standard with the addition of rule $\texttt{delay}(0).P \equiv P$ following [9,10].

---

[1] Similar to the queues used by configurations in Sect. 2.2.

$$(\theta,\ \mathtt{set}\,(x)\,.P) \rightharpoonup (\theta[x \mapsto 0],\ P) \quad [\,\mathtt{Set}\,]$$

$$\frac{\theta \models \delta}{(\theta,\ \mathtt{if}\ \delta\ \mathtt{then}:P\ \mathtt{else}:Q) \rightharpoonup (\theta,\ P)} \quad [\,\mathtt{IfT}\,]$$

$$\frac{j \in I \quad l = l_j}{(\theta,\ p \rhd \left\{ l_i(\mathtt{v}_i):P_i \right\}_{i \in I} \mathtt{after}\ e:Q \mid qp:l\mathtt{v}\cdot h) \rightharpoonup (\theta,\ P_j\,[{}^{\mathtt{v}}\!/\!{}_{\mathtt{v}_j}] \mid qp:h)} \quad [\,\mathtt{Recv}\,]$$

$$(\theta,\ p \lhd l\mathtt{v}.P \mid pq:h) \rightharpoonup (\theta,\ P \mid pq:h\cdot l\mathtt{v}) \quad [\,\mathtt{Send}\,]$$

$$\frac{\models \delta\,[{}^t\!/\!{}_x]}{(\theta,\ \mathtt{delay}(\delta).P) \rightharpoonup (\theta,\ \mathtt{delay}(t).P)} \quad [\,\mathtt{Det}\,] \qquad (\theta,\ P) \rightsquigarrow (\theta+t,\ \Phi_t\,(P)) \quad [\,\mathtt{Delay}\,]$$

$$\frac{(\theta,\ P) \rightharpoonup (\theta',\ P')}{(\theta,\ (\nu pq)\,P) \rightharpoonup (\theta',\ (\nu pq)\,P')} \quad [\,\mathtt{Scope}\,] \qquad \frac{(\theta,\ P) \rightharpoonup (\theta',\ P')}{(\theta,\ P \mid Q) \rightharpoonup (\theta',\ P' \mid Q)} \quad [\,\mathtt{ParL}\,]$$

$$\frac{(\theta,\ Q) \rightharpoonup (\theta',\ Q')}{(\theta,\ \mathtt{def}\ X(\mathtt{v};\mathtt{T};\mathtt{R}) = P\ \mathtt{in}\ Q) \rightharpoonup (\theta',\ \mathtt{def}\ X(\mathtt{v};\mathtt{T};\mathtt{R}) = P\ \mathtt{in}\ Q')} \quad [\,\mathtt{Def}\,]$$

$$\begin{aligned}(\theta,\ \mathtt{def}\ X(\mathtt{v}';\mathtt{T}';\mathtt{R}') = P\ \mathtt{in}\ X\langle\mathtt{v};\mathtt{T};\mathtt{R}\rangle \mid Q) \rightharpoonup \\ (\theta,\ \mathtt{def}\ X(\mathtt{v}';\mathtt{T}';\mathtt{R}') = P\ \mathtt{in}\ P\,[{}^{\mathtt{v},\mathtt{T},\mathtt{R}}\!/\!{}_{\mathtt{v}',\mathtt{T}',\mathtt{R}'}] \mid Q)\end{aligned} \quad [\,\mathtt{Rec}\,]$$

$$\frac{P \equiv P' \quad (\theta,\ P') \rightharpoonup (\theta',\ Q') \quad Q \equiv Q'}{(\theta,\ P) \rightharpoonup (\theta',\ Q)} \quad [\,\mathtt{Str}\,]$$

Fig. 6. Reduction Rules for Processes

$$\mathtt{Wait}(P) = \begin{cases} \{p\} & \mathrm{if}\ P = p \rhd \left\{ l_i(b_i):P_i \right\}_{i \in I} \mathtt{after}\ e:Q \\ \mathtt{Wait}(Q)\backslash\{p,q\} & \mathrm{if}\ P = (\nu pq)\,Q \\ \mathtt{Wait}(Q) & \mathrm{if}\ P = \mathtt{def}\ X(\mathtt{v};\mathtt{T};\mathtt{R}) = P'\ \mathtt{in}\ Q \\ \mathtt{Wait}(P') \cup \mathtt{Wait}(Q) & \mathrm{if}\ P = P' \mid Q \\ \varnothing & \mathrm{otherwise} \end{cases}$$

$$\mathtt{NEQueue}(P) = \begin{cases} \{q\} & \mathrm{if}\ P = pq:h \wedge h \neq \varnothing \\ \mathtt{NEQueue}(Q)\backslash\{p,q\} & \mathrm{if}\ P = (\nu pq)\,Q \\ \mathtt{NEQueue}(Q) & \mathrm{if}\ P = \mathtt{def}\ X(\mathtt{v};\mathtt{T};\mathtt{R}) = P'\ \mathtt{in}\ Q \\ \mathtt{NEQueue}(P') \cup \mathtt{NEQueue}(Q) & \mathrm{if}\ P = P' \mid Q \\ \varnothing & \mathrm{otherwise} \end{cases}$$

Fig. 7. Definition of $\mathtt{Wait}(P)$ and $\mathtt{NEQueue}(P)$

Definition 6. *The time-passing function $\Phi_t(P)$ is a partial function on process terms, defined only for the cases below, where we use C_I as a short notation for $\{l_i(v_i) : P_i\}_{i \in I}$:*

$$\Phi_t\,(p \triangleright C_I \text{ after } e : Q) = \begin{cases} p \triangleright C_I \text{ after } e : Q & e = \infty \\ p \triangleright C_I \text{ after } e - t : Q & e \in \mathbb{R}_{\geqslant 0} \text{ and } e \geqslant t \\ \Phi_{t-e}\,(Q) & \text{otherwise} \end{cases}$$

$$\Phi_t\,(\text{delay}(t').P) = \begin{cases} \text{delay}(t' - t).P & \text{if } t' \geqslant t \\ \Phi_{t-t'}\,(P) & \text{otherwise} \end{cases}$$

$$\Phi_t\,(P_1 \mid P_2) = \Phi_t\,(P_1) \mid \Phi_t\,(P_2) \qquad \text{if } \text{Wait}(P_i) \cap \text{NEQueue}(P_j) = \varnothing, i \neq j \in \{1,2\}$$

$$\Phi_t\,(0) = 0 \qquad \Phi_t\,(\text{error}) = \text{error}$$

$$\Phi_t\,(pq : h) = pq : h \qquad \Phi_t\,((\nu pq)\,P) = (\nu pq)\,\Phi_t\,(P)$$

$$\Phi_t\,(\text{def } X(v; \text{T}; \text{R}) = P \text{ in } Q) = \text{def } X(v; \text{T}; \text{R}) = P \text{ in } \Phi_t\,(Q)$$

The first case in Definition 6 models the effect of time passing on timeouts. The second case is for time-consuming processes. The third case distributes time passing in parallel compositions and ensures that time passes for all parts of the system equally. The auxiliary functions $\text{Wait}(P)$ and $\text{NEQueue}(P)$ ensure time does not pass while a process is waiting to receive a message already in their queue, similar to rule [time] in Fig. 3 for configuration transitions. Informally, $\text{Wait}(P)$ returns the set of channels on which P is waiting to receive a message, and $\text{NEQueue}(P)$ returns the set of endpoints with a non-empty inbound queue. Full definitions are given in Fig. 7. The remaining cases allow time to pass.

Example 5. Consider the process below:

$$P = (\nu pq)\,(p \triangleright \{l_i(v_i) : P_i\}_{i \in I} \text{ after } e : Q \mid qp : \varnothing \mid Q')$$

For a time-consuming action of t to occur on P it is required that Φ_t is defined for all parallel components in P. Note that, if qp was not empty, then time could not pass since $\text{NEQueue}(P) = \text{Wait}(P) = \{p\}$. Set $t = n + 1$ so that we can observe the expiring of the timeout. The evaluation of $\Phi_t(p \triangleright \{l_i\,(v_i) : P_i\}_{i \in I} \text{ after } e : Q)$ results in the evaluation of $\Phi_1(Q)$. If $Q = 0$ (or similarly **error**, a delay, or a timeout with $n > 0$) and $\Phi_t(Q')$ is defined then time passing of t is possible and:

$$\Phi_t\,(P) = (\nu pq)(0 \mid qp : \varnothing \mid \Phi_t\,(Q'))$$

If Q is a sending process then $\Phi_t(Q)$ would be undefined, and hence $\Phi_t(P)$.

4   Expressiveness

In this section we reflect on the expressiveness of our mixed-choice extension, particularly in regard to [9], using examples to illustrate differences. Furthermore, given the increase in expressiveness, we discuss how type-checking becomes more interesting with the inclusion of **receive-after**.

4.1 Missing Deadlines

The process corresponding to $?a\ (\mathtt{true}, \varnothing).S$ is merely $p \rhd \{a : P\}$, which waits to receive a forever. By way of contrast, $?a\ (x < 3,\ \varnothing).S$, cannot receive when $x \geqslant 3$, requiring the process to take the form: $p \rhd \{a : P\}$ after $3 : Q$, where $Q = \mathtt{error}$. More generally, if an action is enabled when $x \geqslant 3$:

$$\{?a\ (x < 3,\ \varnothing).S,\ ?b\ (3 < x < 5,\ \varnothing).S'\}$$

then, amending the previous process, $Q = p \rhd \{b : P'\}$ after $2 : \mathtt{error}$.

4.2 Ping-Pong Protocol

The example in this section illustrates the usefulness of time-sensitive conditional statements. The ping-pong protocol consists of two participants exchanging messages between themselves on receipt of a message from the other [23]. One interpretation of the protocol is the following:

$$\mu\alpha.\left\{\begin{array}{l} !ping(x \leqslant 3,\ \{x\}).\left\{\begin{array}{l} ?ping(x \leqslant 3,\ \{x\}).\alpha \\ ?pong(x > 3,\ \{x\}).\alpha \end{array}\right\} \\ !pong(x > 3,\ \{x\}).\left\{\begin{array}{l} ?ping(x \leqslant 3,\ \{x\}).\alpha \\ ?pong(x > 3,\ \{x\}).\alpha \end{array}\right\} \end{array}\right\}$$

where each participant exchanges the role of sender, either sending ping early, or pong late. Without time-sensitive conditional statements, the setting in [9] only allows implementations where the choice between the 'ping' and the 'pong' branch are hard-coded. In presence of non-deterministic delays (e.g., $\mathtt{delay}(z < 6)$), the hard-coded choice can only be for the latest branch to 'expire', and the highlighted fragment of the ping-pong protocol above could be naively implemented as follows (omitting Q for simplicity):

$$\mathtt{def}\ X\,(\mathrm{v};\mathrm{t};\mathrm{r}) = P\ \mathtt{in}\ P \qquad P = \mathtt{delay}(z < 6).\ p \lhd pong.Q$$

The choice of sending ping is *always* discarded as it may be unsatisfied in *some* executions. The calculus in this paper, thanks to the time-awareness deriving from a program timer y, allows us to *potentially* honour each branch, as follows:

$$\mathtt{def}\ X\,(\mathrm{v};\mathrm{t};\mathrm{r}) = P\ \mathtt{in}\ P \qquad P = \mathtt{set}(y).\mathtt{delay}(z < 6).\,\mathtt{if}\ (y \leqslant 3)$$
$$\mathtt{then}\ : p \lhd ping.Q$$
$$\mathtt{else}\ : p \lhd pong.Q'$$

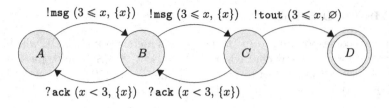

$$!msg\ (3 \leqslant x, \{x\})\quad !msg\ (3 \leqslant x, \{x\})\quad !tout\ (3 \leqslant x, \varnothing)$$

$$?ack\ (x < 3, \{x\})\quad ?ack\ (x < 3, \{x\})$$

Fig. 8. Message throttling protocol for $m = 2$.

4.3 Mixed-Choice Ping-Pong Protocol

An alternative interpretation of the ping-pong protocol can result in an implementation with mixed-choice, as shown below:

$$\mu\alpha. \left\{ \begin{array}{l} ?ping(x \leqslant 3, \{x\}).\left\{ \begin{array}{l} !pong(x \leqslant 3, \{x\}).\alpha \\ ?timeout(x > 3, \varnothing).end \end{array} \right\} \\ !pong(x > 3, \{x\}).\left\{ \begin{array}{l} ?ping(x \leqslant 3, \{x\}).\alpha \\ !timeout(x > 3, \varnothing).end \end{array} \right\} \end{array} \right\}$$

where pings are responded by pongs and vica versa. Notice that if a timely ping is not received, a pong is sent instead, which if not responded to by a ping, triggers a timeout. Similarly, once a ping has been received, a pong must be sent on time to avoid a timeout. Such a convoluted protocol can be fully implemented:

```
def X (v; t; r) = P in P
  P = set(x).p ▷ ping : set(x). if x ⩽ 3
                  then : p ◁ pong .X ⟨v′; t′; r′⟩
                  else : p ▷ timeout : 0
      after 3 − x : p ◁ pong .set(x).p ▷ pong : X ⟨v″; t″; r″⟩
                  after 3 − x : p ◁ timeout .0
```

4.4 Message Throttling

A real-world application of the previous example is *message throttling*. The rationale behind message throttling is to cull unresponsive processes, which do not keep up with the message processing tempo set by the system. This avoids a server from becoming overwhelmed by a flood of incoming messages. In such a protocol, upon receiving a message, a participant is permitted a grace period to respond before receiving another. The grace period is specified as a number of unacknowledged messages, rather than a period of time. Below we present a fully parametric implementation of this behaviour, where m is the maximum number of messages that can go unacknowledged before a timeout is issued.

$$S_0 = \mu\alpha^0.!msg(x \geqslant 3, \{x\}).S_1$$
$$S_i = \mu\alpha^i.\{?ack(x < 3, \{x\}).\alpha^{i-1},\ !msg(x \geqslant 3, \{x\}).S_{i+1}\}$$
$$S_m = \{?ack(x < 3, \{x\}).\alpha^{m-1},\ !tout(x \geqslant 3,\ \varnothing).end\}$$

which has the corresponding processes:

$$\text{def } X_0\,(\mathbf{v}_0; \mathbf{T}_0; \mathbf{R}_0) = P_0 \text{ in } p \lhd msg.P_1$$
$$\text{def } X_i\,(\mathbf{v}_i; \mathbf{T}_i; \mathbf{R}_i) = P_i \text{ in } p \rhd ack : X_{i-1}\,\langle \mathbf{v}_{i-1}; \mathbf{T}_{i-1}; \mathbf{R}_{i-1}\rangle$$
$$\text{after } 3 : p \lhd msg\,.P_{i+1}$$
$$P_m = p \rhd ack : P_{m-1}$$
$$\text{after } 3 : p \lhd tout.0$$

The system shown in Fig. 8 illustrates the system for the $m = 2$ instance. Arguably, instead of sending the message $tout$, it would also be equally valid for the system to simply reach an error state: $P_m = p \rhd ack : P_{m-1}$ after $3 :$ error.

5 Concluding Discussion

We have shown how timing constraints provide an intuitive way of integrating mixed-choice into asynchronous session types. The desire for mixed-choice has already prompted work in (untimed) synchronous session types [29]. Further afield, coordination structures have been proposed that overlap with mixed-choice, for example, fork and join [14], which permit messages within a fork (and its corresponding join) to be sent or received in any order; reminiscent of mixed-choice. Affine sessions [23,25] support exception handling by enabling an end-point to perform a subset of the interactions specified by their type, but there is no consideration of time, hence timeouts. Before session types gained traction, timed processes [5] were proposed for realising timeouts, but lacked any notion of a counterpart for timeouts.

We have integrated the notion of mixed-choice with that of time-constraints. There are many conceivable ways to realise mixed-choice using programming primitives. However, our integration with time, embodied in TOAST, offers new capabilities for modelling timeouts which sit at the heart of protocols and are a widely-used idiom in programming practice. To provide a bridge to programming languages, we provide a timed session calculus enriched with a receive-after pattern and process timers, the latter providing a natural counterpart to the former. Taken altogether, we have lifted a long-standing restriction on asynchronous session types by allowing for safe mixed-choice, through the judicious application of timing constraints.

Future work will provide type checking against TOAST for our new processes, and establish time-safety (a variant of type-safety which ensures punctuality of interactions via subject reduction) for well-typed processes. Time-safety for timed session types [9,10] (without mixed-choice) relies on a progress property called receive-liveness, which is defined on the untimed counterpart of a timed process. Receive-liveness that can be checked with existing techniques for global progress [6,16]. A progress property may seem too strong a precondition for ensuring time-safety. In untimed formulations of session types, type-safety and subject reduction do not depend on progress. Arguably, when considering time and punctuality, the distinction between progress and safety is no longer clear-cut, since deadlocks may cause violation of time constraints.

References

1. Alur, R., Dill, D.L.: A theory of timed automata. Theor. Comput. Sci. **126**, 183–235 (1994). https://doi.org/10.1016/0304-3975(94)90010-8
2. Bartoletti, M., Bocchi, L., Murgia, M.: Progress-Preserving refinements of CTA. In: CONCUR. Leibniz International Proceedings in Informatics, vol. 118, pp. 40:1–40:19. Schloss Dagstuhl-Leibniz-Zentrum fuer Informatik (2018). https://doi.org/10.4230/LIPIcs.CONCUR.2018.40
3. Bartoletti, M., Cimoli, T., Murgia, M.: Timed session types. logical methods in computer science 13(4) (2017). https://doi.org/10.23638/LMCS-13(4:25)2017
4. Bartoletti, M., Cimoli, T., Pinna, G.M.: A note on two notions of compliance. EPTCS **166**, 86–93 (2014). https://doi.org/10.4204/EPTCS.166.9
5. Berger, M., Yoshida, N.: Timed, distributed, probabilistic, typed processes. In: Shao, Z. (ed.) APLAS 2007. LNCS, vol. 4807, pp. 158–174. Springer, Heidelberg (2007). https://doi.org/10.1007/978-3-540-76637-7_11
6. Bettini, L., Coppo, M., D'Antoni, L., De Luca, M., Dezani-Ciancaglini, M., Yoshida, N.: Global progress in dynamically interleaved multiparty sessions. In: van Breugel, F., Chechik, M. (eds.) CONCUR 2008. LNCS, vol. 5201, pp. 418–433. Springer, Heidelberg (2008). https://doi.org/10.1007/978-3-540-85361-9_33
7. Bocchi, L., Lange, J., Thompson, S., Voinea, A.L.: A model of actors and grey failures. In: COORDINATION. Lecture Notes in Computer Science, vol. 13271, pp. 140–158. Springer-Verlag (2022). https://doi.org/10.1007/978-3-031-08143-9_9
8. Bocchi, L., Langue, J., Yoshida, N.: Meeting deadlines together. In: CONCUR. Leibniz International Proceedings in Informatics, vol. 42, pp. 283–296 (2015). https://doi.org/10.4230/LIPIcs.CONCUR.2015.283
9. Bocchi, L., Murgia, M., Vasconcelos, V.T., Yoshida, N.: Asynchronous timed session types: from duality to time-sensitive processes. In: ESOP. Lecture Notes in Computer Science, vol. 11423, pp. 583–610. Springer-Verlag (2019). https://doi.org/10.1007/978-3-030-17184-1_21, https://kar.kent.ac.uk/72337/
10. Bocchi, L., Yang, W., Yoshida, N.: Timed multiparty session types. In: Baldan, P., Gorla, D. (eds.) CONCUR 2014. LNCS, vol. 8704, pp. 419–434. Springer, Heidelberg (2014). https://doi.org/10.1007/978-3-662-44584-6_29
11. Brand, D., Zafiropulo, P.: On communicating finite-state machines. J. ACM **30**(2), 323–342 (1983). https://doi.org/10.1145/322374.322380
12. Carbone, M., Honda, K., Yoshida, N.: Structured interactional exceptions in session types. In: van Breugel, F., Chechik, M. (eds.) CONCUR 2008. LNCS, vol. 5201, pp. 402–417. Springer, Heidelberg (2008). https://doi.org/10.1007/978-3-540-85361-9_32
13. Castro, D., Hu, R., Jongmans, S.S., Ng, N., Yoshida, N.: Distributed programming using role-parametric session types in go: statically-typed endpoint APIs for dynamically-instantiated communication structures. In: POPL, vol. 3, pp. 1–30. ACM (2019). https://doi.org/10.1145/3290342
14. Deniélou, P.-M., Yoshida, N.: Multiparty session types meet communicating automata. In: Seidl, H. (ed.) ESOP 2012. LNCS, vol. 7211, pp. 194–213. Springer, Heidelberg (2012). https://doi.org/10.1007/978-3-642-28869-2_10
15. Deniélou, P.-M., Yoshida, N.: Multiparty compatibility in communicating automata: characterisation and synthesis of global session types. In: Fomin, F.V., Freivalds, R., Kwiatkowska, M., Peleg, D. (eds.) ICALP 2013. LNCS, vol. 7966, pp. 174–186. Springer, Heidelberg (2013). https://doi.org/10.1007/978-3-642-39212-2_18

16. Dezani-Ciancaglini, M., de'Liguoro, U., Yoshida, N.: On progress for structured communications. In: Barthe, G., Fournet, C. (eds.) TGC 2007. LNCS, vol. 4912, pp. 257–275. Springer, Heidelberg (2008). https://doi.org/10.1007/978-3-540-78663-4_18
17. Gouda, M., Manning, E., Yu, Y.: On the progress of communication between two finite state machines. Inf. Control **63**(3), 200–216 (1984). https://doi.org/10.1016/S0019-9958(84)80014-5
18. Honda, K., Yoshida, N., Carbone, M.: Multiparty asynchronous session types. In: POPL, pp. 273–284. ACM (2008). https://doi.org/10.1145/1328438.1328472
19. Hu, R., Yoshida, N., Honda, K.: Session-based distributed programming in java. In: Vitek, J. (ed.) ECOOP 2008. LNCS, vol. 5142, pp. 516–541. Springer, Heidelberg (2008). https://doi.org/10.1007/978-3-540-70592-5_22
20. Klensin, J.: SMTP, Request for Comments: 5321 (2008). https://datatracker.ietf.org/doc/html/rfc5321
21. Krcal, P., Yi, W.: Communicating timed automata: the more synchronous, the more difficult to verify. In: Ball, T., Jones, R.B. (eds.) CAV 2006. LNCS, vol. 4144, pp. 249–262. Springer, Heidelberg (2006). https://doi.org/10.1007/11817963_24
22. Lagaillardie, N., Neykova, R., Yoshida, N.: Implementing multiparty session types in rust. In: Bliudze, S., Bocchi, L. (eds.) COORDINATION 2020. LNCS, vol. 12134, pp. 127–136. Springer, Cham (2020). https://doi.org/10.1007/978-3-030-50029-0_8
23. Lagaillardie, N., Neykova, R., Yoshida, N.: Stay safe under panic: affine rust programming with multiparty session types. In: ECOOP. Leibniz International Proceedings in Informatics, Schloss Dagstuhl-Leibniz-Zentrum fuer Informatik (2022). https://doi.org/10.4230/LIPIcs.ECOOP.2022.4
24. Milner, R.: Communicating and Mobile systems - the Pi-Calculus. Cambridge University Press, Cambridge (1999)
25. Mostrous, D., Vasconcelos, V.T.: Affine Sessions. Logical Methods in Computer Science **14**(4) (2018). https://doi.org/10.23638/LMCS-14(4:14)2018
26. Neykova, R.: Session types go dynamic or how to verify your Python conversations. EPTCS 137 (2013). https://doi.org/10.4204/EPTCS.137.8
27. Neykova, R., Hu, R., Yoshida, N., Abdeljallal, F.: A session type provider: compile-time API generation of distributed protocols with refinements in F#. In: CC, pp. 128–138. ACM (2018). https://doi.org/10.1145/3178372.3179495
28. Neykova, R., Yoshida, N., Hu, R.: SPY: local verification of global protocols. In: Legay, A., Bensalem, S. (eds.) RV 2013. LNCS, vol. 8174, pp. 358–363. Springer, Heidelberg (2013). https://doi.org/10.1007/978-3-642-40787-1_25
29. Vasconcelos, V.T., Casal, F., Almeida, B., Mordido, A.: Mixed sessions. In: ESOP 2020. LNCS, vol. 12075, pp. 715–742. Springer, Cham (2020). https://doi.org/10.1007/978-3-030-44914-8_26
30. Yoshida, N., Vasconcelos, V.T.: Language primitives and type discipline for structured communication-based programming revisited: two systems for higher-order session communication. Electron. Notes Theor. Comput. Sci. **171**(4), 73–93 (2007). https://doi.org/10.1016/j.entcs.2007.02.056
31. Yoshida, N., Zhou, F., Ferreira, F.: Communicating finite state machines and an extensible toolchain for multiparty session types. In: Bampis, E., Pagourtzis, A. (eds.) FCT 2021. LNCS, vol. 12867, pp. 18–35. Springer, Cham (2021). https://doi.org/10.1007/978-3-030-86593-1_2

A Formal MDE Framework for Inter-DSL Collaboration

Salim Chehida$^{(\boxtimes)}$, Akram Idani, Mario Cortes-Cornax, and German Vega

Univ. Grenoble Alpes, CNRS, Grenoble INP, LIG, 38000 Grenoble, France
{salim.chehida,akram.idani,mario.cortes-cornax,
german.vega}@univ-grenoble-alpes.fr

Abstract. In order to master the complexity of a system at the design stage, several models have to be defined and combined together. However, when heterogeneous and independent DSLs are used to define these models, there is a need to explicitly compose their semantics. While the composition of static semantics of DSLs is straightforward, the coordination of their execution semantics is still challenging. This issue is generally called inter-DSL collaboration. In this paper, we propose a formal Model Driven Engineering (MDE) framework built on the Meeduse language workbench that we extend with the Business Process Model and Notation (BPMN). Meeduse allows to instrument DSLs with formal semantics using the B method. BPMN provides an easy-to-use notation to define the coordination of execution semantics of these DSLs. A transformation of BPMN models into Communication Sequential Process (CSP) formal language enables the possibility for animation and verification. Our approach is successfully demonstrated by modeling the collaboration of two DSLs from a real case study.

Keywords: DSL · BPMN · Model Composition · Models Collaboration · Formal Methods · B Method · CSP · Animation · Verification

1 Introduction

Domain-Specific Languages (DSLs) can be used to model different concerns of a system such as its architecture, the inherent processes, data flows or security policies. These dedicated languages permit domain experts to create models in their speciality. However, models that are built with heterogeneous DSLs must be combined together in order to favour maintenance, verification, code generation, etc. Indeed, updating a model usually leads to modifications of the other related models. Also, triggering an action in one model can induce other actions in the related models. This situation has been observed in real applications, leading to the necessity to bridge the gap between DSLs semantics and preventing inconsistencies all along a model-driven development process [12].

In this paper, we propose a novel approach, supported with a formal framework, that allows engineers to define how DSLs collaborate with each other.

© IFIP International Federation for Information Processing 2023
S.-S. Jongmans and A. Lopes (Eds.): COORDINATION 2023, LNCS 13908, pp. 232–249, 2023.
https://doi.org/10.1007/978-3-031-35361-1_13

We use Meeduse [10], the only existing language workbench (LWB) today that enables both formal reasoning (via theorem proving) and the DSL execution (via animation and model-checking). Meeduse uses the B method [1] for specifying the semantics of DSLs and ProB model checker [18] for animation and verification. It has been successfully applied to several realistic case studies [11].

However, the tool did not present any feature to deal with DSL collaboration. Hence, the goal of this work is to extend Meeduse with the capability to define, execute and verify inter-DSL collaboration. Our approach consists of three main steps:

1. In the first step, a composition metamodel is created in order to relate the semantic domains of independent DSLs, assuming that these semantics are themselves defined by means of metamodels;
2. In the second step, Meeduse is used to transform the various metamodels into formal B specifications taking benefit of the composition mechanism of the B method. The resulting specifications are then used to define the execution semantics of these metamodels via B operations;
3. The third step uses BPMN [20] to define the collaboration between the DSLs. In this model, tasks refer to B operations providing the execution workflow of the collaboration. By transforming the BPMN model into CSP (Communication Sequential Process [22]), we obtain a CSP||B [23] specification that is used for animating and verifying the so-called DSLs' collaboration.

To illustrate our approach, we apply it to a smart grid case study provided by RTE, the energy transmission company in France. The case study involves two DSLs: the first one focuses on the management of system configurations assigning to a set of applications various infrastructures. The second is dedicated to security risk assessment. The composition and the collaboration of these DSLs allow to manage configurations while dealing with security concerns.

Following the introduction, we describe a motivation scenario in Sect. 2. We present our model-based approach for inter-DSL collaboration in Sect. 3. Then, the application of our approach to the RTE case study is discussed in Sect. 4. Section 5 lists related works and finally, Sect. 6 draws the conclusions and the perspectives of this paper.

2   Case Study and Motivation

In this work, we consider a real case study inspired from [24]. To promote renewable energies, RTE aims to make extensive use of smart grid technologies and develop efficient systems that respond to *meteorological* and *security* factors. The main challenge is to deal with overcurrent in the transmission lines due to the excess energy production in the wind farms, which can create a real danger for people and goods near the transmission lines. For this purpose, a first DSL, named *CM-DSL* (Configuration Management DSL), is used for defining the system configurations to be used for responding to the environment dynamics. A second DSL, named *SRA-DSL* (Security Risk Assessment DSL), is used for security modeling and analysis. In the following sections, more details about the aforementioned DSLs are given.

2.1   Configuration Management DSL (CM-DSL)

The Configuration Management DSL (CM-DSL) describes RTE configurations by assigning applications to infrastructures. In this work, we present a simplified part of CM-DSL to illustrate the problem. Figure 1 presents a model, where three applications are defined: (1) *Fast Action* uses a simple flow chart logic and leads to the massive disconnection of wind farms from the grid; (2) *Normal* refers to predictive control algorithm in order to seek the optimal use of all levers (wind farms modulation, batteries and circuit breakers); and finally, (3) *Enhanced Forecasting* uses forecasts of the next day generation and weather (wind and sunlight) for optimisation. The model also considers three infrastructures: (1) in *Centralized RTE*, algorithms can only be run on data-center resources that communicate directly with the gateways connected to sensors or actuators for generators or batteries; (2) in *Collaborative Fog*, the execution is done in substation calculators that communicate in a peer-to-peer scheme with the other calculators; and (3) in *Hierarchical Fog-Cloud*, all calculators are available to run the applications and both data-center to substation and substation to substation communications are allowed. Combining applications and architectures a configuration can be proposed. Figure 1 presents four different ones. A configuration is also characterized by its response time (QoS in seconds) calculated using an external simulation tool. The status is decided by the software architect, which can be valid (example of AM1-IM3) or invalid (example of AM3-IM1) depending on its QoS. In the selected *AM1-IM2* configuration (framed in dotted line), the *Fast Action* application is to be deployed on *Collaborative Fog* infrastructure. Valid configurations can be used in the real operation.

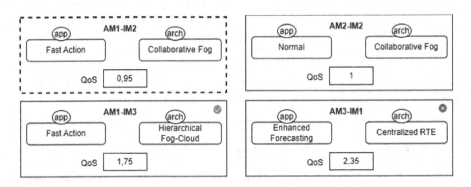

Fig. 1. A Configuration Management (CM) model showing four different configurations

2.2   Security Risk Assessment DSL (SRA-DSL)

The Security Risk Assessment DSL (SRA-DSL) refers to Attack-Defense Tree [15] for security risk assessment. A tree structure is used for specifying threats, defenses, and the combinations between them. In Fig. 2, threat nodes are represented by rectangles and defense nodes by parallelograms. The combinations between the nodes are expressed by logical operators (AND, OR, NOT) depicted by ellipses. The SRA-DSL model of Fig. 2 specifies the combination between the 8 threats (T1,T2, ...,T8) and the 5 defenses (D1,D2, ...,D5) of the RTE system. Each defense prevents a set of threats. For instance, *closing a specific breach in the network* (D2) can prevent *tampering on customer network* (T5), *denial of service* (T6), and *information disclosure* (T7). In a SRA-DSL model, it is possible to select the possible threats (framed in bold as for instance T8) on a part of the system or in a specific state of the system among the whole set of system threats. It is also possible to compute the defenses subset (framed in blue bold as for instance D4 and D5) that can counter all the selected threats. The SRA-DSL user can also set the defense *Cost* in seconds, which is the delay caused by its activation to protect the system (an example cost of D1 is 0.4 s).

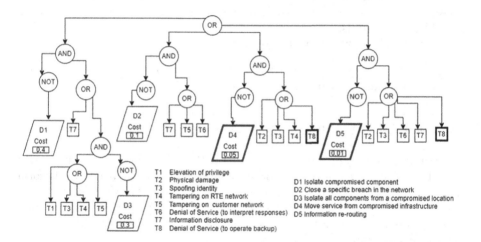

Fig. 2. The SRA model

We note that CM-DSL and SRA-DSL are independent and can be used for other applications or case studies. For example, paper [4] shows how the SRA-DSL is used for security risk assessment in Internet of Things (IoT) systems.

2.3 Collaboration and Verification Needs

CM-DSL provides the possible configurations that can meet the environmental dynamics, but it does not consider the configurations' security. On the other side, the SRA-DSL is a logic-based DSL that can be used within different security contexts. In our case study, we use SRA-DSL to identify possible threats of each configuration and to calculate the required defenses. By doing so, the response time and the validation state of the configuration can be updated based on the cost of the defenses. The integration of these two DSLs infers the need to ensure inter-DSL properties. Below, we provide some examples of properties:

- (P1) The delay caused by configuration defenses should not exceed a percentage of the configuration response time (e.g., 30%)
- (P2) At least one defense must be activated to secure a configuration.
- (P3) The response time of a configuration should not exceed a given threshold (e.g., 2 s).

In this work, we propose a new approach to manage and check the collaboration between two or more DSLs (in this case, illustrated by the CM-DSL and the SRA-DSL). We aim more precisely to:

- Highlight the links between the DSLs concepts (e.g., configuration and defenses).
- Specify the collaboration process between the DSLs actions.
- Animate interactively the collaboration process while ensuring the updates at the DSL models.
- Express and check inter-DSL properties.

In the next section, we describe the Inter-DSL approach that orchestrates the DSLs' execution collaboration.

3   Inter-DSL Collaboration: A Model-based Architecture

An overview of our approach is given in Fig. 3, divided into two main blocks: X and Y. The model-based approach is supported by the Meeduse platform for rigorous DSLs' design (block X presented in Sect. 3.1). Meeduse has been extended for modeling, animation and verification of inter-DSL collaboration (block Y presented in Sect. 3.2). Figure 3 shows the collaboration between two DSLs, but the approach can be applied for more.

3.1   Formal Model Driven DSLs

As shown in Fig. 3, we first specify the abstract syntax of each DSL using EMF-based modeling tool (Ecore, Xtext, Sirius, GMF, etc.). The DSL's concepts are represented by a metamodel. The different metaclasses are characterized by a set of attributes and operations, related by a set of associations (see examples in Fig. 4). The domain expert uses the DSL to create models (instances) that conform to the DSL metamodel.

We instrument our DSLs in Meeduse language workbench, which provides a formal framework to our approach. Meeduse produces a B machine from a given metamodel and enables the application of B method to define the execution semantics of the DSLs together with its invariant properties. The static semantics of the DSL is represented by sets, variables and typing invariants that define the structural features of the metamodel. The execution semantics of the

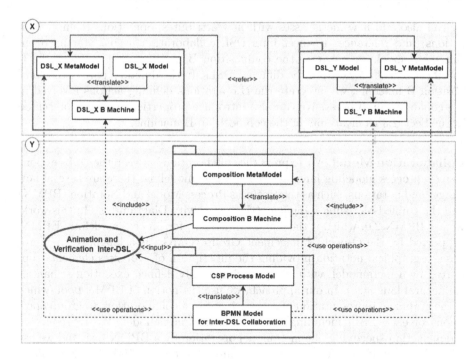

Fig. 3. Generic architecture for modeling and verification of inter-DSL collaboration

DSL is represented by operations that define the DSL actions and initialization. Meeduse is also equipped with a tool that allows to animate the execution of a model (instance of the metamodel) into the DSL B machine, by introducing the valuation of the B abstract sets and the initialization of B variables.

As mentioned earlier, the Meeduse uses ProB for the animation and verification of B specifications. In this step, each DSL can be animated separately by running its actions represented by B operations. At each animation step, the animator provides the set of operations that could be executed, which are the ones that preserve the invariants. In this work, we aim to collaboratively animate a set of DSLs by triggering actions from different DSLs while respecting the collaboration process and system properties.

3.2 Formal Model Driven Inter-DSL Collaboration

The inter-DSL collaboration is specified by a so-called "composition metamodel" and a BPMN collaboration diagram, which will then be transformed into formal specifications to be used for animation and verification.

Composition. The composition metamodel links the other DSL metamodels. It is represented by a metaclass named Composition related by composition associations to the root metaclasses of each DSL to be coordinated. In this metamodel, we can also add new metaclasses with new attributes, operations (composition actions) and references to meet inter-DSL collaboration needs. Starting from this metamodel, we generate the composition B machine that includes the B specifications obtained from the different DSLs. In the dynamic part of the composition B machine, we integrate the B operations defining actions involved in the collaboration process. We can also introduce properties like those presented in the Sect. 2.3 as invariants of the composition B machine.

Collaboration Model. We express the collaboration between the DSLs actions using a process modeling language. For process modeling, there are several languages and notations, such as the Business Process Model and Notation (BPMN) and the Unified Modeling Language (UML) Activity Diagram [21]. In this work, we use BPMN 2.0, which is the standard de-facto for process modeling. BPMN, supported by the Object Management Group (OMG), is a language that proposes a graphical notation providing the description of processes elements supported by a metamodel, without specifying a fully defined execution semantics (in natural language). In our approach, we use the notion of BPMN pool, which is the graphical representation of a participant in a collaboration, to group operations of each DSL, including the composition metamodel. We represent an atomic action specifying one metamodel operation by a BPMN task and we use expanded subprocesses to represent a grouping of tasks. BPMN sequence flows are used to represent the sequence of actions in the context of a DSL (inside the Pool), while message flows are used to represent the inter-pool communication. Gateways (exclusive or parallel) model the control flow in each DSL.

Formal Process Model. To enable the animation and verification of inter-DSL collaboration, the graphical BPMN models are mapped to a formal specification. Several works propose this transformation to process algebras languages like CSP or Calculus of Communicating Systems (CCS) [19]. In this paper, we manually transform the BPMN diagrams into CSP models. Work in progress intends to automate and validate this transformation by exploiting works like [8]. The constructor's mapping is illustrated with our use case in Sect. 4.3. From this mapping, we aim to take advantage of the ProB tool (integrated into the Meeduse platform) for the animation and verification. The ProB tool takes as input the CSP process model and the composition B machine coming from the DSLs and composition metamodels respectively. The CSP||B specification, as presented in [3], is used for animating and verifying the inter-DSL collaboration processes.

4   Application to Smart Grid System

In our approach, the *Model-driven engineer* specifies the DSLs metamodels and the BPMN models of their collaboration. Then, the metamodels and BPMN diagrams are transformed into B and CSP respectively, while integrating the system properties. Afterwards, the *operator* can animate the formal specifications while observing the respect of the properties.

In [5], we describe the different steps of our approach and its application to our case study. We also provide the different artifacts of this case study. The modeling part includes the CM-DSL and SRA-DSL metamodels, the metamodel of their composition, the models that define the instances of the metamodels, and the BPMN diagram that describes the collaboration between the DSLs. The formal specification part includes the B machines generated from the DSLs and their composition as well as the CSP model specified from the BPMN diagram.

4.1 Modeling DSLs and Their Collaboration

Metamodels. Figure 4 shows the metamodels that we propose for our case study (one per DSL, and a third one for the composition). Part A of Fig. 4 is the EMF metamodel of CM-DSL. The root class (CM) is composed of a set of applications and a set of infrastructures. Every application applies a specific optimisation algorithm that gets the production parameters and information from sensors to trigger actions such as limiting the production on wind farms or charging batteries. Infrastructures are based in RTE power stations and data-centers, connected by a private telecommunication network. A CM model is also composed of configurations, each one consists of the combination of one application and one infrastructure and it is characterized by its response time (QoS) and validation state (isValid). The CM-DSL defines the following operations : *selectConfig* selects one configuration from the list of CM configurations, *validateConfig* validates the selected configuration, and *setQoS* introduces or modifies the QoS of the selected configuration.

In part B of Fig. 4 the SRA-DSL metamodel is shown, which is composed of metaclasses for specifying the possible threats of the system and the defenses that can be deployed to protect the system. Each defense is characterised by a cost (costDef), which is the delay caused by its activation in the RTE platform. A series of metaclasses are introduced for representing the logical operators (NOT, OR, AND) combining threats and defenses. The operations of SRA-DSL are : *initSRA* selects the subset of possible threats, *selectThreat* selects a threat from the set of possible threats, *computeDefenses* calculates the subset of defenses that can block the selected threats.

Finally, part C of Fig. 4 shows the composition metamodel. Metaclass COMPOSITION is composed of the root metaclasses of the previously presented DSLs (CM-DSL and SRA-DSL). The composition has its own operations that define its execution semantics. Indeed, we introduce the notion of *Secure Configuration* that associates a set of defenses to a valid configuration (using operation *affectValidDefenses*). Furthermore, operation *approveSecureConfig* allows one to validate a Secure Configuration if it ensures risk assessment and quality of service properties.

Inter-DSL Collaboration. In our proposal, we describe the inter-DSL collaboration using a BPMN model (Fig. 5) relying on the operations of the above

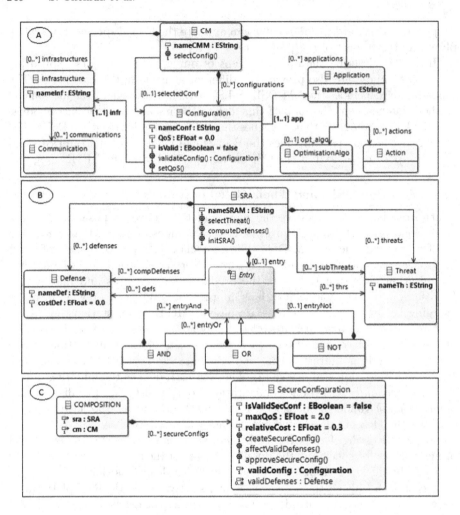

Fig. 4. DSL and composition metamodels

metamodels. We use the notion of Pool to separate the execution semantics of every DSL. The collaboration starts in pool DSLs_COMPOSITION, where it triggers via a message (named *ConfigurationRequest*) the selection and validation of a configuration at the CM-DSL level. Note that this corresponds to a functional validation, not considering yet the security aspects. Afterwards, in the composition pool, a new secure configuration is created and associated to the validated configuration. This task is triggered by the reception of message *ValidConfig*. The new secure configuration is then sent to the SRA-DSL pool in order to select possible threats of this configuration and compute the defenses that can prevent them. When receiving the defenses (message *ValidDefenses*), it is possible to approve the secure configuration after checking the global QoS and the other risk assessment properties.

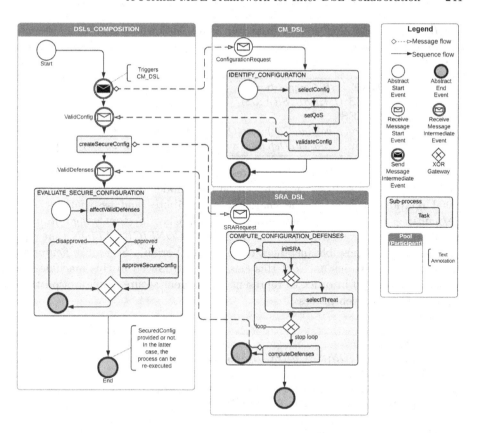

Fig. 5. BPMN collaboration model of SRA-DSL and CM-DSL

4.2   Formalization of Metamodels

While metamodels describe static semantics of DSLs, the BPMN model and the associated operations represent their execution semantics. We need on the one hand a tool to define and animate these semantics and on the other hand a way to guarantee that the security properties are preserved by the underlying behaviour. To this purpose the Meeduse framework has been extended. The tool applies the B method to formally define execution semantics of DSLs using B operations, which allows us to introduce the security properties using B invariants. From this formal specification the AtelierB prover is applied in order to guarantee the correctness of the model. In this section, we start by presenting an excerpt of the resulting B specifications, and then we discuss the CSP model that is built from our BPMN diagram.

Given a metamodel, Meeduse generates a formal B specification in which classes are defined using sets. Attributes and associations are defined using functional relations. Not all of our specifications are presented but only an example, as we rather focus on the composition metamodel. The header part of the corresponding specification is given below. This B machine includes machines

CM_DSL and *SRA_DSL* issued from our DSLs and where operations *select-Config, validateConfig, setQoS, selectThreat, computeDefenses* and *initSRA* are defined.

MACHINE *DSL_Composition*
INCLUDES *CM_DSL, SRA_DSL*
PROMOTES
  selectConfig, validateConfig, setQoS, /* from CM DSL */
  selectThreat, computeDefenses, initSRA /* from SRA DSL */

Figure 6 gives the B data structures and their typing invariants that are produced by Meeduse from the composition metamodel. Specializations of functional relations depend on the character of attributes and associations: single/multiple valuated and mandatory/optional. Class *SecureConfiguration* is transformed into an abstract set named *SECURECONFIGURATION* that represents the set of possible instances of the class. Variable *SecureConfiguration* defines the effective instances of this class. We introduced in this machine the variable *theSecConf* in order to represent the current secure configuration that is managed by a given process.

SETS
  COMPOSITION; SECURECONFIGURATION
VARIABLES
  SecureConfiguration, sra, cm, validConfig, validDefenses, secureConfigs,
  isValidSecConf, maxQoS, relativeCost, theSecConf
INVARIANT
/* Object Definition */
  SecureConfiguration $\subseteq$ *SECURECONFIGURATION* $\wedge$
/* Associations */
  sra $\in$ *COMPOSITION* $\rightarrow$ *SRA* $\wedge$
  cm $\in$ *COMPOSITION* $\rightarrow$ *CM* $\wedge$
  validConfig $\in$ *SecureConfiguration* $\rightarrow$ *Configuration* $\wedge$
  validDefenses $\in$ *SecureConfiguration* $\leftrightarrow$ *Defense* $\wedge$
  secureConfigs $\in$ *SecureConfiguration* $\nrightarrow$ *COMPOSITION* $\wedge$
/* Attributes */
  isValidSecConf $\in$ *SecureConfiguration* $\rightarrow$ **BOOL** $\wedge$
  maxQoS $\in$ *SecureConfiguration* $\rightarrow$ *REAL* $\wedge$
  relativeCost $\in$ *SecureConfiguration* $\rightarrow$ *REAL* $\wedge$
/* added variable */
  theSecConf $\in$ *SECURECONFIGURATION*

Fig. 6. B data of the composition machine

Regarding the inter-DSL properties P1, P2 and P3 introduced in Sect. 2, they are formally defined as follows. This invariant means that if a secure configuration is created (*i.e.* becomes an existing instance) and validated, then P1, P2 and P3 hold.

DEFINITIONS

$sumDefCost(sc) == \sum def . (def \in validDefenses[\{sc\}] \mid costDef(def))$

$approve(sc) ==$

   $sumDefCost(sc) + QoS(validConfig(sc)) \leq maxQoS(sc)$

   $\wedge \; sumDefCost(sc) \leq relativeCost(sc) \times QoS(validConfig(sc))$

   $\wedge \; validDefenses[\{sc\}] \neq \emptyset$

INVARIANT

   $theSecConf \in SecureConfiguration \wedge isValidSecConf(theSecConf) = \textbf{TRUE}$

   $\Rightarrow approve(theSecConf)$

The dynamic parts of the various B machines contain B operations that specify the execution semantics of our DSLs. We provide for example the specification of operation *approveSecureConfig* that is defined in the *DSL_Composition* machine:

OPERATIONS

approveSecureConfig =

   PRE

      $theSecConf \in SecureConfiguration$

      $\wedge \; isValidSecConf(theSecConf) = \textbf{FALSE}$

      $\wedge \; approve(theSecConf)$

   THEN

      $isValidSecConf(theSecConf) := \textbf{TRUE}$

   END

All our specifications have been proved correct via the AtelierB prover [6]. The latter produces Proof Obligations (POs), which correspond to theorems that require proof in order to verify the correctness and consistency of a B machine. AtelierB offers an automatic prover able to prove the majority of POs automatically, without any user interaction. This makes it easy to quickly verify large parts of the system specification, and reduces the burden on the user to manually prove each individual PO. The prover also provides interactive prover designed for handling and finalizing complex proofs, also for detecting errors in the specifications.

With AtelierB, we generated 299 POs. Most of them have been proved automatically; only 10 POs have been discharged manually using the interactive prover. The latter ones required additional information to be completed and corrected. The proof using AtelierB provides the guarantee that all the invariants of our DSLs are preserved by the formal specifications of their execution semantics and that the composition is correct with regards to these invariants and the security properties.

4.3   BPMN Formalization with a CSP Transformation

Having the B specifications, the formalization of the coordination model can be treated. Our objective is to apply the workflow of the BPMN model to the B operations issued from the machine *DSL_Composition*. To this purpose, we extend Meeduse with a transformation from BPMN into CSP, which allows us

to apply the approach of CSP||B [23]. This technique is inspired by the work of
M. Kleine [13] about the usage of CSP as a coordination language. The idea is to
coordinate (non-)atomic actions (in our case these are B operations) of a system
by a CSP-based coordination environment in a noninvasive way, meaning that
actions do not need to be modified to be coordinated. In this sense, the formal
B specifications that define the semantics of our DSLs remain unchanged. We
just layer a CSP model on top of them, to distinguish the coordination concerns
from state related properties.

In CSP, a process represents an independent entity that performs a sequence
of events, which is similar to the notion of pool in BPMN. Communication
between processes is ensured via channels, that may or not transmit data flows.
We use this notion to represent exchanged messages represented in the BPMN
model.

Accordingly, to transform the BPMN collaboration model we first transform
pools leading to independent CSP processes (Fig. 7), and then we produce a main
process (Fig. 8) to synchronize them being guided by the message exchanges
between pools. Note that by convention, processes are named in uppercase and
channels in lowercase. The used CSP constructs are:

```
Process ::= SKIP              /* terminating process */
         | ch -> Process      /* simple action prefix where ch is a channel */
         | Process ; Process  /* sequential composition */
         | Process [] Process /* external choice */
```

A channel ch may transmit data d, which is denoted as ch?d for reading data, and ch!d for writing data. Furthermore, a process can be defined
with parameters such as Process(param$_1$,...,param$_n$). Inputs, outputs and process parameters are useful in our case since the communication between pools
is done via messages that may contain some data. For example, message
ConfigurationRequest of CM_DSL enables process IDENTIFY_CONFIGURATION
without any data; on the other hand, message ValidConfig is produced by
validateConfig and received by createSecureConfig, and contains a valid
configuration. This data is represented with parameter conf. In one case it is an
input data and in the other case it is an output data.

The synchronisation of processes CM_DSL, SRA_DSL and DSLs_COMPOSITION
is done in the MAIN process (see Fig. 8). This process applies a parallel composition with channels' synchronisation, representing the exchanged messages. For
instance, processes CM_DSL and DSLs_COMPOSITION are synchronised on channels ConfigurationRequest and ValidConfig. As their starting point is channel ConfigurationRequest they are both triggered at the same time. However,
the next step of DSLs_COMPOSITION is ValidConfig?conf, which means that
DSLs_COMPOSITION is blocked until CM_DSL reaches ValidConfig!conf. This
execution conforms to the BPMN model since the coordination starts by asking
CM_DSL to provide a valid configuration and next, a secure configuration is
created from this valid configuration.

```
/* Transformation of CM_DSL Pool */
1.  CM_DSL =
2.      ConfigurationRequest → IDENTIFY_CONFIGURATION ; CM_DSL
3.  IDENTIFY_CONFIGURATION =
4.      selectConfig → setQoS → validateConfig?conf → ValidConfig!conf → SKIP
```

```
/* Transformation of SRA_DSL Pool */
5.  SRA_DSL =
6.      SRARequest → COMPUTE_CONFIGURATION_DEFENSES ; SRA_DSL
7.  COMPUTE_CONFIGURATION_DEFENSES =
8.      initSRA → SELECT_THREATS
9.      ; computeDefenses?defenses → ValidDefenses!defenses → SKIP
10. SELECT_THREATS =
11.     selectThreat → SELECT_THREATS [] SKIP
```

```
/* Transformation of DSLs_COMPOSITION Pool */
12. DSLs_COMPOSITION =
13.     ConfigurationRequest → ValidConfig?conf → createSecureConfig!conf
14.     → SRARequest → ValidDefenses?defenses
15.     → EVALUATE_SECURE_CONFIGURATION (defenses)
16.     ; DSL_COMPOSITION
17. EVALUATE_SECURE_CONFIGURATION(defenses) =
18.     affectValidDefenses!defenses → (approveSecureConfig → SKIP [] SKIP)
```

Fig. 7. Transformation of pools into CSP

```
/* Main process */
MAIN =
    CM_DSL
        [|{|ConfigurationRequest, ValidConfig|}|]
    DSLs_COMPOSITION
        [|{| SRARequest, ValidDefenses|}|]
    SRA_DSL
```

Fig. 8. Parallel synchronisation of pools

4.4   Discussion

The CSP model and the B specifications that describe the semantics of DSLs provide a formal framework that is managed by ProB and Meeduse in order to ensure the animation as well as the verification. First, Meeduse valuates the formal B specifications from the models of Figs. 1 and 2. The resulting valuations are then delivered to ProB, which allows a step-by-step animation of B operations. The execution of DSLs in Meeduse using ProB is well mastered today and has been discussed in [10]. However, the shortcoming of this approach is the absence of guidance during animation, which makes it inconvenient for DSL collaboration. In order to address this limitation, we suggest to apply the CSP∥B approach. The idea is to marry CSP and B such that the execution of a

B operation corresponds to an event that can be enabled in CSP, which provides a guidance all along the animation process. Roughly speaking, the B machine and the CSP process must synchronise on common events, that is, an operation can only happen in the combined system when it is allowed both by the B and the CSP. For more details about this technique we refer the reader to [3].

We have tested several executions of our coordination model based on our case study, leading to the creation of several secure configurations with various threats and defenses. Figure 9 shows the animation of the composition B machine presented in Sect. 4.2 guided by the CSP model of Figs. 7 and 8, using the ProB tool. In the *History* window, an example of execution scenario that creates a new secure configuration is shown. The *Enabled Operations* window lists operations that can be called at this stage and whose execution will satisfy their precondition, and therefore preserve the state invariant. The *State Properties* window provides the current value of each state variable of the composition machine. At the animation step, we can observe the insurance of system properties P1, P2 and P3 introduced in Sect. 2.3 and specified as invariants in the composition B machine in Sect. 4.2.

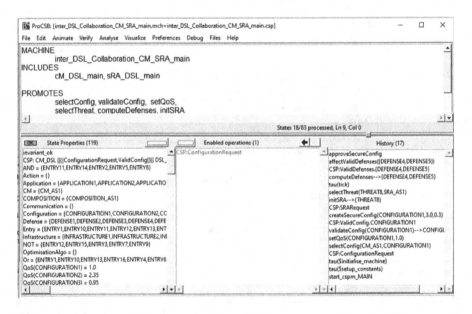

Fig. 9. ProB screenshot showing animation and verification of inter-DSL collaboration

Regarding verification, one of the advantages of B is the availability of theorem provers and model-checkers. We did not discuss in details this activity but note that all our formal specifications have been proved, which guarantees the correctness of the B models on which we built the coordination process. Indeed, our approach ensures the correctness and reliability of the resulting RTE system, which can help preventing dangerous situations that can be caused by overcurrent in the transmission lines.

5 Related Work

The problem of managing the interactions between models is not new and it has been addressed in various fields including Artificial Intelligence, Robotics, and Control Systems. In the context of Model Driven Engineering (MDE), the proposed solutions are categorized into two classes: composition and coordination approaches [16]. The composition approaches build a model specifying the structural relationships between model elements. The composition model is specified using matching operators that define the syntactic similarities between model elements and merging operators that implement rules to specify how the matched elements must be composed. The operators are provided by dedicated languages such as Epsilon [14]. The composition model can also be defined by composing the syntax of different model languages into a new language syntax expressed by a metamodel [7]. As part of the composition approaches, F. Jouault et al. [12] combine megamodeling and model weaving techniques to build an environment that ensures traceability and navigation between the DSLs models. The environment represents links between different DSL models, which provides an intuitive way to understand relationships between them. However, these composition approaches consider only the language's static syntax; they focus on traceability without taking into account execution semantics.

In coordination approaches, a new model is often built to define how the models behave and interact with each other. Dedicated languages (*e.g.* Linda [9]) have been proposed for this purpose. There also exist some coordination frameworks, such as ModHel'X [2], to automate and support the coordination process. However, the coordination is encoded using a general-purpose programming language (Java), which is not suitable for performing verification and validation. As part of the GEMOC project[2], Larsen et al. [17] propose the B-COoL language that allows specifying a coordination pattern between DSLs. The language offers concurrency and communication models representing the control-flow aspects, including the synchronisation and the causality relationships between execution functions. This is close to some CSP operators, but the missing piece is the usage of provers and model-checkers for automatic verification activities. In our work we apply well-known formal languages (B and CSP) and an established semi-formal notation (BPMN), which enables the application of widely used tools for modeling and verification.

Our approach combines the composition and coordination techniques. We build a composition metamodel that refers to the coordinated DSLs metamodels without altering their semantics and behaviors. BPMN diagram is used for expressing the coordination process between the DSLs. The DSLs metamodels and the BPMN coordination model are then transformed into a formal specification to be used for checking and validating the DSLs models coordination.

---

[2] https://gemoc.org/

6 Conclusion

This paper presented a tool-supported approach for the formal modeling and verification of inter-DSL collaboration. The approach extends the Meeduse framework by integrating a composition metamodel and BPMN model to explicitly specify inter-DSL collaboration. The formal specification generated from the models and metamodels is then used to verify the DSLs models coordination. The proposed approach was demonstrated to be effective through its successful application in a real case study.

Going forwards, the next steps include implementing and validating the transformation rules from BPMN to CSP, as well as expressing and checking properties at the workflow level. These developments will further enhance the automation and reliability of the proposed approach.

Data Availability Statement

The artifact is available in the Software Heritage repository:

swh:1:dir:c38d7336f13f438eab7212227f10fb0dbf0350c1

References

1. Abrial, J.R.: The B-book: assigning programs to meanings. Cambridge University Press (1996). https://doi.org/10.1017/CBO9780511624162
2. Boulanger, F., Hardebolle, C.: Simulation of multi-formalism models with Modhel'x. In: 2008 1st International Conference on Software Testing, Verification, and Validation, pp. 318–327 (05 2008). https://doi.org/10.1109/ICST.2008.15
3. Butler, M., Leuschel, M.: Combining CSP and B for specification and property verification. In: Fitzgerald, J., Hayes, I.J., Tarlecki, A. (eds.) FM 2005. LNCS, vol. 3582, pp. 221–236. Springer, Heidelberg (2005). https://doi.org/10.1007/11526841_16
4. Chehida, S., Baouya, A., Bozga, M., Bensalem, S.: Exploration of impactful countermeasures on IoT attacks. In: 9th Mediterranean Conference on Embedded Computing, MECO 2020, Budva, Montenegro, 8–11 June 2020, pp. 1–4. IEEE (2020). https://doi.org/10.1109/MECO49872.2020.9134200
5. Chehida, S., Idani, A., Cortes-Cornax, M., Vega, G.: GitHub artifacts. http://github.com/SalimChehida/Inter-DSL-Collaboration
6. Clearsy: Atelier B. http://www.atelierb.eu/en/
7. Emerson, M., Sztipanovits, J.: Techniques for metamodel composition. In: OOPSLA - 6th Workshop on Domain Specific Modeling (2006)
8. Flavio, C., Alberto, P., Barbara, R., Damiano, F.: An ECLIPSE Plug-in for formal verification of BPMN processes. In: 2010 Third International Conference on Communication Theory, Reliability, and Quality of Service, pp. 144–149 (2010). https://doi.org/10.1109/CTRQ.2010.32
9. Gelernter, D., Carriero, N.: Coordination languages and their significance. Commun. ACM 35(2), 97–107 (1992)

10. Idani, A.: Meeduse: a tool to build and run proved Dsls. In: Dongol, B., Troubit-syna, E. (eds.) IFM 2020. LNCS, vol. 12546, pp. 349–367. Springer, Cham (2020). https://doi.org/10.1007/978-3-030-63461-2_19

11. Idani, A., Ledru, Y., Ait Wakrime, A., Ben Ayed, R., Bon, P.: Towards a tool-based domain specific approach for railway systems modeling and validation. In: Collart-Dutilleul, S., Lecomte, T., Romanovsky, A. (eds.) RSSRail 2019. LNCS, vol. 11495, pp. 23–40. Springer, Cham (2019). https://doi.org/10.1007/978-3-030-18744-6_2

12. Jouault, F., Vanhooff, B., Bruneliere, H., Doux, G., Berbers, Y., Bezivin, J.: Inter-DSL coordination support by combining megamodeling and model weaving. In: Proceedings of the 2010 ACM Symposium on Applied Computing, pp. 2011–2018. SAC 2010, Association for Computing Machinery, New York, NY, USA (2010)

13. Kleine, M.: CSP as a coordination language. In: De Meuter, W., Roman, G.-C. (eds.) COORDINATION 2011. LNCS, vol. 6721, pp. 65–79. Springer, Heidelberg (2011). https://doi.org/10.1007/978-3-642-21464-6_5

14. Kolovos, D.S., Paige, R.F., Polack, F.A.C.: Merging models with the epsilon merging language (EML). In: Nierstrasz, O., Whittle, J., Harel, D., Reggio, G. (eds.) MODELS 2006. LNCS, vol. 4199, pp. 215–229. Springer, Heidelberg (2006). https://doi.org/10.1007/11880240_16

15. Kordy, B., Mauw, S., Radomirović, S., Schweitzer, P.: Foundations of attack–defense trees. In: Degano, P., Etalle, S., Guttman, J. (eds.) FAST 2010. LNCS, vol. 6561, pp. 80–95. Springer, Heidelberg (2011). https://doi.org/10.1007/978-3-642-19751-2_6

16. Larsen, M.E.V.: BCOol: the behavioral coordination operator language, Ph. D. thesis, University of Nice Sophia Antipolis, France (2016)

17. Larsen, M.E.V., DeAntoni, J., Combemale, B., Mallet, F.: A behavioral coordination operator language (BCOoL). In: Proceedings of the 18th International Conference on Model Driven Engineering Languages and Systems. MODELS 2015, IEEE Press (2015)

18. Leuschel, M., Butler, M.: ProB: an automated analysis toolset for the B method. Int. J. Softw. Tools Technol. Transfer 10, 185–203 (2008)

19. Milner, R.: A Calculus of Communicating Systems. Springer-Verlag, Berlin, Heidelberg (1982). https://doi.org/10.1007/3-540-10235-3

20. OMG: Business Process Model and Notation (BPMN), Version 2.0 (2011). http://www.omg.org/spec/BPMN/2.0

21. OMG: Unified modeling language™ (uml®) (2011). http://www.omg.org/spec/UML/index.htm

22. Roscoe, A.W.: The Theory and Practice of Concurrency. Prentice Hall PTR, USA (1997)

23. Schneider, S., Treharne, H.: CSP Theorems for Communicating B Machines. Form. Asp. Comput. 17(4), 390–422 (2005). https://doi.org/10.1007/s00165-005-0076-7

24. Tourchi Moghaddam, M., Rutten, E., Giraud, G.: Hierarchical control for self-adaptive IoT systems : a constraint programming-based adaptation approach. In: HICSS 2022 - Hawaii International Conference on System Sciences, pp. 1–10. Hawaii, United States (2022). http://hal.inria.fr/hal-03461137

Run-Time Changes

Legal Contracts Amending with *Stipula*

Cosimo Laneve[1(✉)] ⓘ, Alessandro Parenti[2] ⓘ, and Giovanni Sartor[2] ⓘ

[1] Department of Computer Science and Engineering, University of Bologna,
Bologna, Italy
cosimo.laneve@unibo.it
[2] Department of Legal Studies, University of Bologna, Bologna, Italy

Abstract. Legal contracts can be amended during their lifetime through the agreement of the parties or in accordance with the doctrines of force majeure and hardship. When legal contracts are defined using a programming language, amendments are made through runtime adjustments to the contract's behavior and must be expressed by means of appropriate language features. In this paper, we examine the extension of *Stipula*, a formal language for legal contracts, with *higher-order functionality* to enable the dynamic updating of contract codes. We discuss the semantics of the language when amendments either extend or override the contract's functionality. Additionally, we study two techniques for constraining amendments, one using annotations within the contract and another that allows for runtime agreements between parties.

1 Introduction

In [7] we presented *Stipula*, a domain specific language that can assist lawyers in drafting executable legal contracts, through specific software patterns. The language is based on a small set of programming primitives that have a precise correspondence with the distinctive elements of legal contracts [6]. By means of these primitives, it is possible to transfer rights (such as rights of property) from one party to another and to take advantage of escrows and securities. The benefits of coding legal contracts are evident: it enables the identification of potential inconsistencies in regulation, reducing the complexity and the ambiguity of legal texts and automatically executing legal rules.

Stipula has been designed with the principle of having an abstraction level as close as possible to traditional legal contracts, which are written in natural languages, thus easing the writing and inspecting of the codes. In this contribution we pursue on our programme addressing the need of removing or amending the effects of a contract after it has been agreed upon.

There may be several reasons for modifying a contract. For example, a contract may be declared totally or partially void by an adjudicator because its content, or the process of its formation, violates the law. More interesting are

Supported by the SERICS project (PE00000014) under the MUR National Recovery and Resilience Plan funded by the European Union – NextGenerationEU – and by the H2020 ERC Project CompuLaw (G.A. 833647).

© IFIP International Federation for Information Processing 2023
S.-S. Jongmans and A. Lopes (Eds.): COORDINATION 2023, LNCS 13908, pp. 253–270, 2023.
https://doi.org/10.1007/978-3-031-35361-1_14

the situations of *force majeure* and *hardship*, which occur when unforeseen events make performance impossible or impracticable (force majeure) or substantially upset the economic balance of the contract (hardship) [3,11]. While in the first case the party successfully invoking force majeure may be relieved, at least temporarily, from performance or may terminate the contract, in the second case the party subject to hardship may be entitled to obtain an adaptation of the contract to the changed circumstances.

The current *Stipula* contracts are immutable. Therefore, in order to model either force majeure or hardship one should anticipate when the contract is traded all the appropriate amendments for each possible circumstance. While this is easy for termination clauses (it is enough to include a transition to a final state), it is clearly impossible for generic amendments [18]. Even an attempt to do that would raise drafting costs and introduce huge complexities in the contract, thus nullifying one of the main objectives of *Stipula*, which is to have a simple and intelligible code.

To address amendments we propose an extension of *Stipula* with a higher-order mechanism. Following [20], we admit that function invocations may carry *codes* that patch the previous ones. In Sect. 4 we study the formal semantics of the resulting language, called *higher-order Stipula*. In particular, we identify and discuss two paradigmatic scenarios. A scenario where the modification affects the whole body of the contract and its code is completely changed and substituted by a new code. Another scenario is where the amendment only regards some parts of the contract while leaving the other parts still operative. This situation adds a further level of semantic complexity in that it requires to deal with the coexistence of old and new code. We give examples of the use of *higher-order Stipula* in Sect. 3 that will spot these issues.

According to the semantics defined in Sect. 4, in *higher-order Stipula* amendments are unconstrained: a party may modify the contract without the consent of all the parties involved. This is clearly at odds with the fundamental principles of contract law (i.e., *consensus ad idem*). We then explore two methods for limiting amendments. In Sect. 5 we discuss a set of static-time constraints on amendments that the parties agree when the contract is traded. The constraints allow one to implement a predicate that parses the (run-time) amendments and verifies their compliance. In Sect. 6 we study a technique that requires the agreement of the parties in correspondence of every amendment.

We end our contribution by discussing the related work in Sect. 7 and delivering our final remarks in Sect. 8.

2   From *Stipula* to *higher-order Stipula*

Higher-order Stipula is an extension of *Stipula* with higher-order functions. In this contribution, for simplicity, we extend a *lightweight* version of the language in [7] (the full language also has the *agreement clause* and *events*); this allows us to avoid discussions that are out of the scope of this paper. Additionally, since *Stipula* is not popular, we first present the lightweight language and then the extension.

Table 1. Syntax of *Stipula* (in black only) and *higher-order Stipula*

$F ::= \_ \quad | \quad$ @Q A : $\text{f}(\overline{y})[\overline{k}]\,(E)\{\,S\,\} \Rrightarrow$ @Q$'\ F \quad | \quad$ @Q A : $\text{F}(\overline{X})\{\,H\,\}\ F$

$P ::= E \rightarrow x \quad | \quad E \rightarrow \text{A} \quad | \quad E \times h \multimap h' \quad | \quad E \times h \multimap \text{A} \quad | \quad \text{if}\,(E)\,\{\,S\,\}\,\text{else}\,\{\,S\,\}$

$S ::= \_ \quad | \quad P\ S$

$E ::= v \quad | \quad V \quad | \quad E \,\text{op}\, E \quad | \quad \text{uop}\, E$

$H ::= (\text{remove}\ X)?\ (\text{add}\ X)?\ \text{run}\ X$

We use disjoint sets of names: *contract names*, ranged over by C, C', $\cdots$; names referring to digital identities, called *parties*, ranged over by A, A', $\cdots$; *function names* ranged over by f, g, $\cdots$ (in general, function names start with a small-case letter); *asset names*, ranged over by h, k, $\cdots$, to be used both as contract's assets and function's asset parameters; *non asset names*, ranged over x, y, $\cdots$, to be used both as contact's fields and function's non asset parameters. Assets and generic contract's fields are syntactically set apart since they have different semantics, similarly for functions' parameters. Names of assets, fields and parameters are generically ranged over by V. Names @Q, @Q', $\cdots$ will range over contract states. To simplify the syntax, we often use the vector notation $\overline{x}$ to denote possibly empty *sequences* of elements. With an abuse of notation, in the following sections, $\overline{x}$ will also represent the *set* containing the elements in the sequence.

The code of a *Stipula* contract is

stipula C { parties $\overline{\text{A}}$ fields $\overline{x}$ assets $\overline{h}$ init @Q F }

where C identifies the *contract name*; $\overline{\text{A}}$ are the *parties* that can invoke contract's functions, $\overline{x}$ and $\overline{h}$ are the *fields* and the *assets*, respectively, and the *initial state* is set to @Q. The contract body also includes the sequence F of functions, whose syntax is defined in Table 1 (the terms in black). It is assumed that there is no clash of names of parties, fields, assets and functions' parameters. In the following, the *declaration part* of a contract, namely the sequence parties $\overline{\text{A}}$ fields $\overline{x}$ assets $\overline{h}$ F will be ranged over by the symbols $\mathbb{D}$, $\mathbb{D}'$, $\cdots$.

First-order functions highlight who is the caller party A, the state @Q when the invocation is admitted and the name of the function. The invocation has two lists of parameters: the *formal parameters* $\overline{y}$ in brackets and the *asset parameters* $\overline{k}$ in square brackets. The *precondition* E constrains the execution of the body; the *body* $\{\,S\,\} \Rrightarrow$ @Q$'$ specifies the *statement part* S and the state @Q$'$ of the contract when the function execution terminates.

Statements S include the empty statement $\_$ and different prefixes followed by a continuation. Prefixes P use the two symbols $\rightarrow$ and $\multimap$ to differentiate operations on non-asset names and on assets, respectively. The prefix $E \rightarrow x$ updates the field or the parameter x with the value of E; $E \rightarrow \text{A}$ sends the value of E to the party A; $E \times h \multimap h'$ subtracts the value of $E \times h$ from the asset h and adds it to h', $E \times h \multimap \text{A}$ subtracts the value of $E \times h$ from the asset h and transfers it to A. (The semantics in Sect. 4 will enforce that assets never have negative values.) In the rest of the paper we will always abbreviate

Table 2. The Deposit contract with a higher-order function

```
stipula Deposit {
    parties Client, Farm
    fields cost_flour
    assets flour
    init @Standard

    @Standard Farm: send()[h]{ h → Client    h ⊸ flour } ⇒ @Standard

    @Standard Client: buy(x)[w] (w == x×cost_flour && x <= flour){
            (x/flour)×flour ⊸ Client    w ⊸ Farm
        } ⇒ @Standard

    @Standard ~ : Hardship(| X, Y, Z |){ remove X add Y run Z }
}
```

$1 \times h \multimap h'$ and $1 \times h \multimap$ A (which are very usual, indeed) into $h \multimap h'$ and $h \multimap$ A, respectively. It is worth to spot the difference between $h \to$ A and $h \multimap$ A: in the first case, the real number representing the *value* of h is sent to A, but h still retain its value; in the second case, the asset h is sent to A and h *is emptied*. We also use " ~ " to address all the parties. For instance, if the parties are A and B, then "hello" → ~ means "hello" → A   "hello" → B (the order is not relevant, according to the extensional semantics in [7]). Prefixes also include *conditionals* if (E) { S } else { S' } with the standard semantics.

Expressions. E include constant values v, which may be strings, reals, booleans, and asset values, names V, and both binary and unary operations (on reals and booleans). In particular, real numbers n are written as nonempty sequences of digits, possibly followed by "." and by a sequence of digits (*e.g.* 13 stands for 13.0). The number may be prefixed by the sign + or -. Reals come with the standard set of binary arithmetic operations (+, -, ×, /). Boolean constants are false and true; the operations on booleans are conjunction &&, disjunction ||, and negation !. Constant values of type asset represent *fungible* resources (*e.g.* digital currencies). For simplicity, fungible asset constants are assumed to be identical to *nonnegative real numbers* (assets can never assume negative values). Relational operations (<, >, <=, >=, ==) are available between any expression.

To illustrate lightweight *Stipula*, we discuss a simple contract in Table 2 (the part in black). A Client contracts with a Farm to pay flour at a given cost. The protocol is the following: Farm sends the flour (function send) and the good is stored in the flour asset: no delivery to Client is operated till he pays for it. The prefix h → Client communicates to the Client that a new amount of flour is available. The function buy takes in input a value x denoting that the Client wants to buy an amount x of flour, and an asset w representing the money he wants to spend. The function takes x kg of flour from the deposit (provided it is in – see the guard), sends the flour to the Client and updates the asset flour correspondingly – operation (x/flour)×flour ⊸ Client –; the money w is transferred to Farm.

Contract are invoked by specifying the actual identities of parties and the fields' values (at the beginning all the assets are empty) – *c.f.* the semantics in Sect. 4. We use italic fonts A, B, *Farm*, *Client*, $\cdots$, to distinguish parties' actual identities from parties formal names A, B, Farm, Client, $\cdots$. These parties' actual identities correspond to digital identities and the same identity may be given to different formal names (which are always pairwise different). Indeed, it may happen that the same party may have two roles in a legal contract. The contract will begin in the state that is specified in the init clause.

Higher-order Stipula extends the syntax of *Stipula* in Table 1 with *higher-order functions* – the red part. In particular, we use *higher-order function names* ranged over F, G, $\cdots$ (in general, function names that start with an upper-case letter). We discuss the declaration @Q A : F$(\!(X, Y, Z)\!)$ { remove X add Y run Z } that has a complete set of *(amendment) directives* H. The parameters of F are X, Y and Z: X is a sequence of function names (possibly with state and party names) that will be removed from the contract; Y is a possible empty sequence of declarations of new parties with their identities, fields and assets as well as of functions that will amend the contract – it will be instantiated by codes $\mathbb{D}$; Z is the body of F and will be instantiated by codes { S } $\Rightarrow$ @Q, where @Q may also be a new state defined in (the code that instantiates) Y. According to the syntax in Table 1, the remove and add clauses in the directives H are optional, while the run clause is mandatory. For example, the function Hardship of the Deposit contract in Table 2 represents a clause included by Client and Farm according to which a party can ask either for the amendment of the contract or for its termination. (This may be subordinated to a third party's decision – a court, an arbitrator or a mediator – assessing the existence of hardship conditions; here, for simplicity, we empower Client and Farm to perform these updates). In Sect. 3 we will study possible amendments of the Deposit contract.

We notice that our syntax has been inspired by the Delta-Oriented Programming paradigm [15]: the directives "remove" and the "add" are taken from that paradigm. Preliminary investigations show that these directives are already sufficient for specifying hardship clauses. It will be a focus for future works to test *higher-order Stipula* with the representation of more complex, context-specific contracts.

Remark 1. The syntax of (*higher-order*) *Stipula* is type-free: types have been dropped because there are no such annotations in standard legal contracts and therefore they may be initially obscure to unskilled users, such as legal practitioners. The paper [7] defines and the prototype [8] implements a type inference system that allows one to derive types of assets, fields and functions' arguments, and that can be used in the future to develop a user-friendly programming interface for *Stipula*.

3 Examples of Amendments

Because of the variety of situations, needs and dynamics involved, the contractual practice is, by nature, a very heterogeneous field. This makes it difficult, if not impossible, to create general overarching examples starting from particular cases. Here we discuss three simple examples built on the Deposit contract of Table 2, with the specific purpose of explaining the technical functioning of the *higher-order* to modify *Stipula* contracts.

The initial example is commonly found in practice, *i.e.* *hardship* cases [11], and builds a simplistic representation of contractual relationship around it. Because of a war outbreak and a sudden rise in production costs, the Farm requests to amend the contract: she requires that the payment is performed *in advance* with respect to the delivery and that half of the amount is sent immediately to her. Therefore she invokes

$$\text{Farm} \ : \ \text{Hardship}(\!| \, \varepsilon, \mathbb{D}, \{\text{"Pay\_in\_Advance"} \rightarrow \ ^{\sim} \ \text{flour} \multimap \text{Farm}\} \Rrightarrow \text{@Excp} \, |\!)$$

where ε indicates that there is no function to remove and $\mathbb{D}$ is

```
assets wallet
@Excp Client: order(x)[w] {
     w/cost_flour → Farm     0.5×w ⊸ Farm     w ⊸ wallet } ⇒ @Excp2
@Excp2 Farm: send(x)[h] (h == (2×wallet)/cost_flour){
     h ⊸ Client     wallet ⊸ Farm } ⇒ @Excp
@Excp ~ : Hardship(| X, Y |){ add X run Y }
```

That is, the code $\mathbb{D}$ is specifying a new asset and three new functions. The function order lets Client pay in advance, sends to Farm the order w/cost_flour and half of the cost 0.5 × w, the other half is stored in the new asset wallet. Once the flour is ready, it is delivered to the Client (function send) and the wallet is delivered to Farm. Notice that the third parameter (the one replacing Z in Table 2) empties the flour asset returning the amount to Farm and lets the contract transit to the *new* state @Excp. Overall, the old behaviour is suppressed in favour of the new one because it is not possible to return to the @Standard state.

After some time, the parties want to return to the old protocol. However, a new law imposes a 20% tax on flour sales. To bear the new taxation, the Farm invokes the hardship clause to increase flour price (also tax payment to the Government gets implemented). Therefore, in the state @Excp, Farm invokes Hardship(| $\mathbb{D}'$, B' |) (notice that the Hardship in @Excp has two arguments only and a different body than the one in @Standard) where

```
𝔻' = parties Government = Govern
     @Standard Client: buy(x)[w] (w == x×cost_flour && x <= flour){
          (x/flour)×flour ⊸ Client     0.2×w ⊸ Government     w ⊸ Farm
     } ⇒ @Standard
B' = { "Back_to_Standard_and_upgrade_flour_price" → ~
          cost_flour + 0.2×cost_flour → cost_flour } ⇒ @Standard
```

$\mathbb{D}'$ is extending the parties with a new one (`Government` whose id is *Govern*) and the function `buy` dispatches the 20% of the cost of every transaction to the `Government`. The old protocol is restored because the body in the last line is making the transition to the `Standard` state. However, in this case, the new function `@Standard Client:buy` is *overriding* the old one in Table 2, which will be never accessed again because its guard is the same of the new function. We observe that, in *higher-order Stipula*, parties, assets and fields names may be added by the amendment; we only constrain the new names not to clash with old ones.

Later on, `Farm` decides to accept orders only if they are above a certain quantity `lbval`. Therefore, in the state `@Standard`, she invokes `Hardship`$(\!|$ `buy`$, \mathbb{D}'', B'' |\!)$ where

```
D'' = fields lower_bound

      @Standard Client: buy(x)[w]
          (w == x×cost_flour && x <= flour && x >= lower_bound){
              (x/flour)×flour ⊸ Client   0.2×w ⊸ Government  w ⊸ Farm
          } ⇒ @Standard

B'' = { "No_order_below_lbval_anymore" → ~
        cost_flour + 0.2×cost_flour → cost_flour
        lbval → lower_bound   } ⇒ @Standard
```

In this case, the directive to execute is **remove** `buy` **add** $\mathbb{D}''$ **run** B'' that removes the function `buy` from $\mathbb{D}$ and adds the new one in $\mathbb{D}''$. We observe that the new field `lower_bound` is initialized in B''. It is also worth to notice that the invocation `Farm:Hardship`$(\!| \varepsilon, \mathbb{D}'', B'' |\!)$ would have displayed a different effect: in this last case, since the `buy` in Table 2 is still in force, the invocations of `buy` with amount lower that `lbval` would have been dispatched to the old `buy` and accepted. This is an issue because the `buy` in Table 2 does not comply with the new law about taxes.

4 Semantics

Following the presentation of Sect. 2, we first define the operational semantics of lightweight *Stipula* and then we discuss the extension. We use a *transition relation* between *configurations*, *i.e.* $\mathbb{D} \Vdash \mathtt{@Q}\,,\, \ell\,,\, \Sigma \xrightarrow{\mu} \mathbb{D}' \Vdash \mathtt{@Q}'\,,\, \ell'\,,\, \Sigma'$ where

- $\mathbb{D}$, $\mathbb{D}'$ are the declaration part of a contract (in *Stipula*, it is always $\mathbb{D} = \mathbb{D}'$, in *higher-order Stipula* $\mathbb{D}$ and $\mathbb{D}'$ may be different because of amendments, see below);
- $\mathtt{@Q}$, $\mathtt{@Q}'$ are states of $\mathbb{D}$ or $\mathbb{D}'$;
- ℓ, ℓ' called *memories*, are mappings from names (parties, fields, assets and function's parameters) to values. The values of parties are noted with italic fonts $A, A', \cdots$. These names cannot be passed as function's parameters and cannot be hard-coded into the source contracts, since they do not belong to expressions; they are initialized when the contract is instantiated or, for new parties, in the higher-order step;

Table 3. The transition relation of *Stipula* (in black only) and *higher-order Stipula*

[VALUE-SEND]
$$\frac{[\![E]\!]_\ell = v \quad \ell(\mathtt{A}) = A}{\mathbb{D} \Vdash \mathtt{@Q}, \ell, E \to \mathtt{A} \ \Sigma \xrightarrow{v \to A} \mathbb{D} \Vdash \mathtt{@Q}, \ell, \Sigma}$$

[FIELD-UPDATE]
$$\frac{[\![E]\!]_\ell = v \quad \ell' = \ell[x \mapsto v]}{\mathbb{D} \Vdash \mathtt{@Q}, \ell, E \to x \ \Sigma \longrightarrow \mathbb{D} \Vdash \mathtt{@Q}, \ell', \Sigma}$$

[ASSET-SEND]
$$\frac{\ell(\mathtt{A}) = A \quad 0 \le [\![E]\!]_\ell \le 1 \quad [\![E \times \mathtt{h}]\!]_\ell = u}{[\![\mathtt{h} - u]\!]_\ell = v \quad \ell' = \ell[\mathtt{h} \mapsto v]}{\mathbb{D} \Vdash \mathtt{@Q}, \ell, E \times \mathtt{h} \multimap \mathtt{A} \ \Sigma \xrightarrow{u \multimap A} \mathbb{D} \Vdash \mathtt{@Q}, \ell', \Sigma}$$

[ASSET-UPDATE]
$$\frac{0 \le [\![E]\!]_\ell \le 1 \quad [\![E \times \mathtt{h}]\!]_\ell = u \quad [\![\mathtt{h} - u]\!]_\ell = v}{[\![\mathtt{h}' + u]\!]_\ell = v' \quad \ell' = \ell[\mathtt{h} \mapsto v, \mathtt{h}' \mapsto v']}{\mathbb{D} \Vdash \mathtt{@Q}, \ell, E \times \mathtt{h} \multimap \mathtt{h}' \ \Sigma \longrightarrow \mathbb{D} \Vdash \mathtt{@Q}, \ell', \Sigma}$$

[COND-TRUE]
$$\frac{[\![E]\!]_\ell = \mathtt{true}}{\mathbb{D} \Vdash \mathtt{@Q}, \ell, \mathtt{if}\,(E)\,\{\,S'\,\}\,\mathtt{else}\,\{\,S'\,\}\ \Sigma \longrightarrow \mathbb{D} \Vdash \mathtt{@Q}, \ell, S\ \Sigma}$$

[COND-FALSE]
$$\frac{[\![E]\!]_\ell = \mathtt{false}}{\mathbb{D} \Vdash \mathtt{@Q}, \ell, \mathtt{if}\,(E)\,\{\,S\,\}\,\mathtt{else}\,\{\,S'\,\}\ \Sigma \longrightarrow \mathbb{D} \Vdash \mathtt{@Q}, \ell, S'\ \Sigma}$$

[STATE-CHANGE]
$$\mathbb{D} \Vdash \mathtt{@Q}, \ell, \_ \Rightarrow \mathtt{@Q}' \longrightarrow \mathbb{D} \Vdash \mathtt{@Q}', \ell, \_$$

[FUNCTION]
$$\frac{\mathtt{@Q\,A}: \mathtt{f}(\overline{y})[\overline{k}]\,(E)\{\,S\,\} \Rightarrow \mathtt{@Q}' \ \in\ \mathbb{D}[\mathtt{@Q\,A}:\mathtt{f}]_{\ell,\overline{u},\overline{v}}}{\ell(\mathtt{A}) = A \quad \ell' = \ell[\overline{y} \mapsto \overline{u}, \overline{k} \mapsto \overline{v}]}{\mathbb{D} \Vdash \mathtt{@Q}, \ell, \_ \xrightarrow{A:\mathtt{f}(\overline{u})[\overline{v}]} \mathbb{D} \Vdash \mathtt{@Q}, \ell', S \Rightarrow \mathtt{@Q}'}$$

[HO-FUNCTION]
$$\frac{\mathtt{@Q\,A}: \mathtt{F}(\!(X,Y,Z)\!)\{\,\mathtt{remove}\ X\ \mathtt{add}\ Y\ \mathtt{run}\ Z\,\} \ \in\ \mathbb{D}[\mathtt{@Q\,A}:\mathtt{F}]_{\ell,\varepsilon,\varepsilon}}{\mathbb{D}' = \mathtt{parties}\ \overline{A'} = \overline{A'}\ \mathtt{fields}\ \overline{z}\ \mathtt{assets}\ \overline{k}\ F \quad \ell(\mathtt{A}) = A \quad \ell' = \ell[\overline{k} \mapsto \overline{0}, \overline{A'} \mapsto \overline{A'}]}{\mathbb{D} \Vdash \mathtt{@Q}, \ell, \_ \xrightarrow{A:\mathtt{F}(\!(P,\mathbb{D}',B)\!)} \mathbb{D} \setminus P \lhd \mathbb{D}' \Vdash \mathtt{@Q}, \ell', B}$$

- Σ, Σ' are (possibly empty) residuals of function bodies, *i.e.* Σ is either $\_$ (idle) or a term $S \Rightarrow \mathtt{@Q}$. We assume that $\_\ S \Rightarrow \mathtt{@Q}$ is equal to $S \Rightarrow \mathtt{@Q}$;
- μ is a *label*, which is either empty, or a function call $A : \mathtt{f}(\overline{u})[\overline{v}]$, or a value send $v \to A$, or an asset transfer $v \multimap A$. Labels are used to highlight the interactions between the contract and the parties.

We also use the *evaluation function* $[\![E]\!]_\ell$ that returns the value of E in the memory ℓ. In particular:

- $[\![v]\!]_\ell = v$ for values, $[\![V]\!]_\ell = \ell(V)$ for names of assets, fields and parameters.
- let $\underline{uop}$ and $\underline{op}$ be the semantic operations corresponding to *uop* and *op*, then $[\![uop\,E]\!]_\ell = \underline{uop}\,v$, $[\![E\ op\ E']\!]_\ell = v\ \underline{op}\ v'$ with $[\![E]\!]_\ell = v$, $[\![E']\!]_\ell = v'$.

Finally, let the *selection operation* be

$$\mathbb{D}[\mathtt{@Q\,A}:\mathtt{f}]_{\ell,\overline{u},\overline{v}} = \left\{ \begin{array}{c} \mathtt{@Q\,A}: \mathtt{f}(\overline{y})[\overline{k}]\,(E)\{\,S\,\} \Rightarrow \mathtt{@Q}' \mid \mathtt{@Q\,A}: f(\overline{y})[\overline{k}]\,(E)\{\,S\,\} \Rightarrow \mathtt{@Q}' \ \mathrm{in}\ \mathbb{D} \\ \mathrm{and}\ [\![E]\!]_{\ell[\overline{y} \mapsto \overline{u}, \overline{k} \mapsto \overline{v}]} = \mathtt{true} \end{array} \right\}$$

That is, the selection $\mathbb{D}[\mathtt{@Q\,A}:\mathtt{f}]_{\ell,\overline{u},\overline{v}}$ returns a *set* of functions in $\mathbb{D}$ such that the corresponding guard E is true.

Table 3 reports the definition of the transition relation for lightweight *Stipula* (the black part); the additional rule for the higher-order functions is discussed afterwards.

Among standard rules, [ASSET-SEND] delivers part of an asset h to A. This part, named u, is removed from the asset, *c.f.* the memory of the right-hand side configuration in the conclusion. In a similar way, [ASSET-UPDATE] moves a part u of an asset h to an asset h'. For this reason, the final memory becomes $\ell[h \mapsto v, h' \mapsto v']$, where $v = \ell(h) - u$ and $v' = \ell(h') + u$. Rule [STATE-CHANGE] says that a contract changes state upon termination of the statement in the function body. The relevant rule is [FUNCTION] that defines invocations of (first-order) functions: the label of the transition specifies the party A performing the invocation and the function name f with the actual parameters. The transition may occur provided (*i*) the contract is in the state @Q that admits invocations of f from A, (*ii*) it is *idle*, and (*iii*) the code $\mathbb{D}$ contains a function @Q $A : f(\overline{y})[\overline{k}] (E)\{ S \} \Rightarrow @Q'$ such that E is true in the memory ℓ updated with the actual parameters.

A contract stipula C { parties $\overline{A}$ fields $\overline{x}$ assets $\overline{h}$ init @Q F } is triggered by executing $C(\overline{A}, \overline{u})$ that corresponds to the *initial configuration*

$$\text{parties } \overline{A} \text{ fields } \overline{x} \text{ assets } \overline{h} \quad F \Vdash @Q, [\overline{A} \mapsto \overline{A}, \overline{x} \mapsto \overline{u}, \overline{h} \mapsto \overline{0}], \_ .$$

That is, parties' names are instantiated to parties' identities, fields are initialized to values $\overline{u}$ and the initial value of assets is 0.

In *higher-order Stipula* the declaration part of a configuration has the form $\mathbb{D} \lhd \mathbb{D}_1 \lhd \cdots \lhd \mathbb{D}_n$, where $\mathbb{D}$ is the declaration of the initial contract and $\mathbb{D}_1, \cdots, \mathbb{D}_n$ is a sequence of amendments. We recall that amendments $\mathbb{D}_i$ have shape

$$\text{parties } \overline{A'} = \overline{A'} \text{ fields } \overline{z} \text{ assets } \overline{k} \quad F$$

that extends the declaration part of a contract by admitting initializations of parties' names.

Let $\mathbb{D} = \mathbb{D}_0 \lhd \cdots \lhd \mathbb{D}_n$; we let *parties*($\mathbb{D}$), *assets*($\mathbb{D}$) and *fields*($\mathbb{D}$) be the union of party names, asset names and field names defined in every $\mathbb{D}_i$, with $0 \leq i \leq n$, respectively. The sequence $\mathbb{D}_0 \lhd \cdots \lhd \mathbb{D}_n$ is defined provided that, for every $i, j \in 0..n$, $i \neq j$: *parties*($\mathbb{D}_i$) $\cap$ *parties*($\mathbb{D}_j$) $= \varnothing$ and *assets*($\mathbb{D}_i$) $\cap$ *assets*($\mathbb{D}_j$) $= \varnothing$ and *fields*($\mathbb{D}_i$) $\cap$ *fields*($\mathbb{D}_j$) $= \varnothing$. In the following, with an abuse of notation, we will use $\mathbb{D}, \mathbb{D}', \cdots$ to range over sequences $\mathbb{D}_0 \lhd \cdots \lhd \mathbb{D}_n$.

We then extend the *selection operation* to declaration parts of *higher-order Stipula* configurations ($\mathbb{D}'$ is a single amendment):

$$(\mathbb{D} \lhd \mathbb{D}')[@Q A : f]_{\ell, \overline{u}, \overline{v}} = \begin{cases} \mathbb{D}'[@Q A : f]_{\ell, \overline{u}, \overline{v}} & \text{if } \mathbb{D}'[@Q A : f]_{\ell, \overline{u}, \overline{v}} \neq \varnothing \\ \mathbb{D}[@Q A : f]_{\ell, \overline{u}, \overline{v}} & \text{otherwise} \end{cases}$$

That is, our selection returns the newest set of functions in the list of amendments whose guard E is true. When the function is higher-order, the selection returns $\mathbb{D}[@Q A : F]_{\ell, \varepsilon, \varepsilon}$ (*i.e.* fields and asset parameters are empty). Finally, let P range over *sequences* of items p that are f or F, $A : f$ or $A : F$, @Q $A : f$ or @Q $A : F$. We define $\mathbb{D} \setminus P$ by induction on the length of P:

- $\mathbb{D} \setminus \varepsilon = \mathbb{D}$;

- $\mathbb{D} \setminus p \cdot P = \mathbb{D}' \setminus P$, where $\mathbb{D}'$ is obtained from $\mathbb{D}$ by erasing (in every declaration in $\mathbb{D}$)
  - every function f, if $p = f$;
  - every function f that is invoked by A, if $p = A : f$;
  - every function f that is invoked by A in a state $@Q$, if $p = @Q\ A : f$;
  - similarly for higher-order functions.

Remark 2. The sequence P allows the programmer to be more and more selective during the remove operation $\mathbb{D} \setminus P$. However, the operation $\mathbb{D} \setminus P$ removes function at every depth in $\mathbb{D}$. We might be less demanding, extending the directives with a "surface remove" that removes the more recent function only.

Every preliminary definition is in place, we therefore comment rule [HO-FUNCTION] defining higher-order function invocations. This rule addresses higher-order functions with a complete set of directives – the other type of invocations are sub-cases of it. Once the function F has been chosen, the actual arguments P, $\mathbb{D}'$ and B' are used as follows: functions in P are removed from the declaration part $\mathbb{D}$, which is then amended with the code $\mathbb{D}'$ (provided this operation is well-defined, *c.f.* the foregoing constraint about names in $\mathbb{D}'$) and the memory ℓ is updated with the binding of party names and the initialization of new asset names to 0. We observe that new fields are not initialized: in case, the initialization must be explicitly performed in the body B (*c.f.* the third example in Sect. 3).

To illustrate the semantics, consider the Deposit contract in Table 2 where Client and Farm have identities *Client* and *Farm*, respectively, and cost_flour is assumed to be 2 (euro per kg). Let $\ell = [\text{Client} \mapsto \textit{Client}, \text{Farm} \mapsto \textit{Farm}, \text{cost\_flour} \mapsto 2, \text{flour} \mapsto 0]$, $\mathbb{D}_{\text{Dep}}$ be the declaration part of the Deposit contract and let

$$S = \text{h} \to \text{Client}\quad \text{h} \multimap \text{flour}$$
$$S' = (\text{x/flour}) \times \text{flour} \multimap \text{Client}\quad \text{w} \multimap \text{Farm}$$
$$B = \text{"Pay\_in\_Advance"} \to \ \tilde{}\quad \text{flour} \multimap \text{Farm}$$

We have the following transitions (in the rightmost column we write the rule that has been used); memories $\ell_1, \cdots, \ell_5$ are defined afterwards:

$\mathbb{D}_{\text{Dep}} \Vdash @\text{Standard}, \ell, \_$
$\xrightarrow{Farm:\text{send}()\,[10]}$

$\xrightarrow{10 \to Client}$	$\mathbb{D}_{\text{Dep}} \Vdash @\text{Standard}, \ell_1, S \Rightarrow @\text{Standard}$ [FUNCTION]
	$\mathbb{D}_{\text{Dep}} \Vdash @\text{Standard}, \ell_1, \text{h} \multimap \text{flour} \Rightarrow @\text{Standard}$ [VALUE-SEND]
$\longrightarrow$	$\mathbb{D}_{\text{Dep}} \Vdash @\text{Standard}, \ell_2, \_ \Rightarrow @\text{Standard}$ [ASSET-UPDATE]
$\longrightarrow$	$\mathbb{D}_{\text{Dep}} \Vdash @\text{Standard}, \ell_2, \_$ [STATE-CHANGE]
$\xrightarrow{Client:\text{buy}(4)\,[8]}$	$\mathbb{D}_{\text{Dep}} \Vdash @\text{Standard}, \ell_3, S'$ [FUNCTION]
$\xrightarrow{4 \multimap Client}$	$\mathbb{D}_{\text{Dep}} \Vdash @\text{Standard}, \ell_4, \text{w} \multimap \text{Farm} \Rightarrow @\text{Standard}$ [ASSET-SEND]
$\xrightarrow{8 \multimap Farm}$	$\mathbb{D}_{\text{Dep}} \Vdash @\text{Standard}, \ell_5, \_ \Rightarrow @\text{Standard}$ [ASSET-SEND]
$\longrightarrow$	$\mathbb{D}_{\text{Dep}} \Vdash @\text{Standard}, \ell_5, \_$ [STATE-CHANGE]
$\xrightarrow{Farm:\text{Hardship}(\!(\_,\mathbb{D},B)\!)}$	$\mathbb{D}_{\text{Dep}} \lhd \mathbb{D} \Vdash @\text{Standard}, \ell_5, B$ [HO-FUNCTION]

where $\mathbb{D}$ is the code of Sect. 3 and

$$\ell_1 = \ell[\mathtt{h} \mapsto 10] \qquad \ell_2 = \ell_1[\mathtt{h} \mapsto 0, \mathtt{flour} \mapsto 10] \qquad \ell_3 = \ell_2[\mathtt{x} \mapsto 4, \mathtt{w} \mapsto 8]$$
$$\ell_4 = \ell_3[\mathtt{flour} \mapsto 6] \qquad \ell_5 = \ell_4[\mathtt{w} \mapsto 0]$$

Remark 3. (*Higher-order*) *Stipula* admits a form of *nondeterminism*, called *internal* in the literature, that is problematic in juridical acts: when a party can invoke two homonymous functions. In this case the selection operator returns a set that is not a singleton and, according to [FUNCTION] and [HO-FUNCTION], the function that is executed is chosen randomly. This corresponds to those real legal contracts that contain contradictions, which are usually solved by a court. In the design of *Stipula*, we privileged the direct formalisation of normative elements as programming patterns, so to increase transparency and help in disambiguating contractual clauses. Contradictions and erroneous contracts behaviours can later be identified by means of static analysis tools developed on top of the formal semantics of the language.

5 Constraining Amendments

Up-to now *higher-order Stipula* enables parties to make any kind of amendment, which is considered too liberal by the current legal doctrines. Beside the limit represented by the counterparties' consent to amendings (which will be dealt with in Sect. 6), parties' freedom is often bound in legal system's mandatory rules (*cf.* the principle in Art. 1418 of the Italian Civil Code, the Art. 1:103 of PECL – the European Principle of Contract Law – and the Art. 1.4 of the international Unidroit Principles). For example, the legislator can impose or set limits to prices for basic commodities, employees' salary or loan interest rates. Additionally, parties themselves can decide to set constraints to their amendment power by declaring them in specific clauses.

In order to implement such possibility, we first discuss restriction that can be added at static-time. That is, when a contract is stipulated, parties agree on the type of amendments they might accept in the future. In particular, by means of a syntactic clause we are going to discuss below, we define a predicate $\mathbb{T}(\cdot)$ that takes amendments and verifies whether they comply or not with the restrictions in the clause. In this context, the rule [HO-FUNCTION] becomes (for readability sake, we rewrite the premises of [HO-FUNCTION]):

[HO-FUNCTION-SC]

$$\mathtt{@Q\,A:}\,\mathtt{F}(\!|X,Y,Z|\!)\{\,\mathtt{remove}\ X\ \mathtt{add}\ Y\ \mathtt{run}\ Z\,\} \ \in \ \mathbb{D}[\mathtt{@Q\,A}:\mathtt{F}]_{\ell,\varepsilon,\varepsilon}$$
$$\mathbb{D}' = \mathtt{parties}\ \overline{\mathtt{A}'} = \overline{A'}\ \mathtt{fields}\ \overline{\mathtt{z}}\ \mathtt{assets}\ \overline{\mathtt{k}}\ F \qquad \ell(\mathtt{A}) = A \qquad \ell' = \ell[\overline{\mathtt{k}} \mapsto \overline{0}, \overline{\mathtt{A}'} \mapsto \overline{A'}]$$
$$\mathbb{T}(\mathtt{remove}\ \mathtt{P}\ \mathtt{add}\ \mathbb{D}'\ \mathtt{run}\ B)$$

$$\rule{10cm}{0.4pt}$$

$$\mathbb{D} \Vdash \mathtt{@Q}, \ell, \_ \ \xrightarrow{A:\mathtt{F}(\!|P,\mathbb{D}',B|\!)} \ \mathbb{D} \setminus P \lhd \mathbb{D}' \Vdash \mathtt{@Q}, \ell', B$$

that enables the transition if $\mathbb{T}(\mathtt{remove}\ \mathtt{P}\ \mathtt{add}\ \mathbb{D}'\ \mathtt{run}\ B)$ is true. The predicate $\mathbb{T}(\cdot)$ is defined by the following clause

```
stipula C { parties A̅   fields x̅   assets h̅   init @Q   F   T }
```

T ::= constraints [(parties: fixed;)?   (fields: z̅ constant;)?
                      (assets: k̅ not-decrease;)?   (reachable states: @Q̅)?]

where every constraint in T may be missing (when all the constraints are empty then "constraints [ ]" is omitted and we are back to the basic syntax). The constraint "parties: fixed" specifies that amendments cannot modify the set of parties. If this constraint was present in the Deposit contract of Table 2 then the amendment $\mathbb{D}'$ of Sect. 3 would have been rejected. The constraint "fields: z̅ constant" disables updates of fields in z̅. For example, if the field rate contains the interest rate of a loan, the parties may initially decide that the rate can never be changed (loan with fixed rate). In *higher-order Stipula* this may be simply enforced by "fields: rate constant". The constraint "assets: k̅ not-decrease" protects private assets to be drained by unauthorised parties. For example, in the code of Table 2, only Client can withdraw from the asset flour. If this policy must not be changed during the contract lifetime, it is sufficient to insert the constraint "assets: flour not-decrease" that disallows amendments draining flour (on the contrary, addition of flour is always admitted; we remind that asset values sent during invocation are always nonnegative). Finally, the constraint "reachable states: Q̅" guarantees that, whatever contract update is performed, the states in Q̅ can be reached from the ending state of the amendment. This is because, for example, the corresponding functionalities cannot be disallowed forever.

Below we discuss the implementation of $\mathbb{T}$(remove P add $\mathbb{D}$ run B) that we are designing for our prototype [8], given a constraint clause in the code of the contract.

Fixed Parties. This constraint is easy to implement: it is sufficient to verify that, no term parties: A̅, with A̅ not empty, belongs to $\mathbb{D}$.

Constant Fields and Not-Decreasing Assets. The technique for assessing the constraints about fields and assets amounts to parse the amendment and spot the problematic instructions. In particular, if fields: z̅ constant and y ∈ z̅ then both $\mathbb{D}$ and B must not contain the instruction $E \to$ y. Similarly, if assets: k̅ not-decrease and k′ ∈ k̅ then $\mathbb{D}$ and B must not contain the instructions $E \times k′ \multimap$ h and $E \times k′ \multimap$ A. The predicate $\mathbb{T}(\cdot)$ uses the judgments $\overline{f} ; \overline{h} \vdash G$, where G ranges over $\mathbb{D}, B, F$, and S, which are formally defined by a type system whose key rules are in Table 4.

The rules [T-UPDATE], [T-SEND], and [T-ASSET-UPDATE] are the basic one for guaranteing fields: f̅ constant and assets: h̅ not-decrease; the other rules reduce the analysis to the components of a code. More precisely, according to [T-AMENDMENT], $\mathbb{D}, S$ @Q is correct provided that the body of every function in $\mathbb{D}$ satisfies $\mathbb{T}(\cdot)$ – premise $\overline{f} ; \overline{h} \vdash F$ – and the statement S satisfies $\mathbb{T}(\cdot)$ as well – premise $\overline{f} ; \overline{h} \vdash S$.

Table 4. Key rules for verifying constant fields and not-decreasing assets

$$
\begin{array}{ccc}
[\text{T-Update}] & [\text{T-Send}] & [\text{T-Asset-update}] \\[2pt]
\dfrac{g \notin \overline{f}}{\overline{f};\overline{h} \vdash E \to g} & \dfrac{k \notin \overline{h}}{\overline{f};\overline{h} \vdash E \times k \multimap A} & \dfrac{k \notin \overline{h}}{\overline{f};\overline{h} \vdash E \times k \multimap h'}
\end{array}
$$

$$
\begin{array}{cc}
[\text{T-Cond}] & [\text{T-Seq}] \\[2pt]
\dfrac{\overline{f};\overline{h} \vdash S \quad \overline{f};\overline{h} \vdash S'}{\overline{f};\overline{h} \vdash \texttt{if}\,(E)\,\{\,S\,\}\,\texttt{else}\,\{\,S'\,\}} & \dfrac{\overline{f};\overline{h} \vdash P \quad \overline{f};\overline{h} \vdash S}{\overline{f};\overline{h} \vdash P\ S}
\end{array}
$$

$$
\begin{array}{cc}
[\text{T-Function}] & [\text{T-Amendment}] \\[2pt]
\dfrac{\left(\overline{f};\overline{h} \vdash S\right)^{\,\texttt{@Q A: f(}\overline{y}\texttt{)}\overline{[k]}\,(E)\{\,S\,\}\Rightarrow\texttt{@Q'}\ \text{in}\ F}}{\overline{f};\overline{h} \vdash F} & \dfrac{\mathbb{D} = \texttt{parties}\ \overline{A'} = \overline{A'}\ \texttt{fields}\ \overline{x}\ \texttt{assets}\ \overline{h}\ F}{\overline{f};\overline{h} \vdash \mathbb{D}, B}
\end{array}
$$

with the side condition

$$B = \{\,S\,\} \Rightarrow \texttt{@Q} \qquad \overline{f};\overline{h} \vdash F \qquad \overline{f};\overline{h} \vdash S$$

State Reachability. In general, it is not possible to assess state reachability at static time because the values of guards of functions may depend on memories and actual parameters. That is the following technique may return *false positives* (while it never returns *false negatives*: if a state is unreachable then there is no computation ending in that state). False positives are ruled out only in the restricted case when the functions in the contract code and in the amendments are unguarded.

Following [5], we use the predicate is_in: @Q A : f @Q″ is_in $\mathbb{D}$ holds true if

- $\mathbb{D}$ is a single declaration part and there is @Q A : f$(\overline{y})\overline{[k]}$ (E){ S } ⇒ @Q′ in $\mathbb{D}$;
- or $\mathbb{D} = \mathbb{D}' \lhd \mathbb{D}''$, where $\mathbb{D}''$ is a single declaration part, and either @Q A : f$(\overline{y})\overline{[k]}$ (E){ S } ⇒ @Q′ in $\mathbb{D}'$ or @Q A : f$(\overline{y})\overline{[k]}$ (E){ S } ⇒ @Q′ in $\mathbb{D}''$.

The predicate @Q A : f @Q″ is_in $\mathbb{D}$ is false otherwise. Notice that we are considering first-order functions only.

The set of reachable states in $\mathbb{D}$ from @Q, noted $\mathbb{Q}_{@Q}$, is the least set such that

1. @Q $\in \mathbb{Q}_{@Q}$;
2. if @Q′ $\in \mathbb{Q}_{@Q}$ and @Q′ A : f @Q″ is_in $\mathbb{D}$ then @Q″ $\in \mathbb{Q}_{@Q}$.

We notice that $\mathbb{Q}_{@Q}$ is always finite and can be easily computed by a standard fixpoint technique that must be run in correspondence of every higher-order function invocation. For example, in Sect. 3, the invocation

```
Farm : Hardship(| ε, 𝔻, {"Pay_in_Advance" → ˜    flour ⊸ Farm} ⇒ @Excp |)
```

returns the declaration part $\mathbb{D}_{Dep} \lhd \mathbb{D}$ where @Standard $\notin \mathbb{Q}_{@Excp}$, while the second amendment gives a declaration part $\mathbb{D}_{Dep} \lhd \mathbb{D} \lhd \mathbb{D}'$ where @Standard $\in \mathbb{Q}_{@Standard}$.

When **reachable states:** $\overline{@Q}$ is a constraint and $\mathbb{D}$ is the current declaration part, the predicate $\mathbb{T}(\texttt{remove P add } \mathbb{D}' \texttt{ run } \{\,S\,\} \Rightarrow @Q')$ verifies that $\overline{@Q} \subseteq \mathbb{Q}_{@Q'}$ when the declaration part is $\mathbb{D} \setminus P \lhd \mathbb{D}'$.

We conclude by discussing the presence of false positives in $\mathbb{T}(\cdot)$ with an example. Consider the **Deposit** contract in Table 2 and change the final state of buy into @End (the Client can buy only one time). Then assume the presence of the constraint clause constraints [reachable states: @End] and verify the predicate $\mathbb{T}(\cdot)$ for the initial declaration part $\mathbb{D}_{\text{Dep}}$. It is easy to check that @End $\in \mathbb{Q}_{\text{@Standard}}$. However, if cost_flour has been initialized with a negative value (because of an error) then no transition buy will ever be performed because of its guard that is always false and @End will never be reached. Overcoming this issue is out of the scope of this paper. A possible technique could use the definition of $\mathbb{Q}_{\text{@Q}}$ to synthesize computations and verify the guards by means an (off-the-shelf) constraint solver technique.

6 Agreement on Amendments

The Unidroit Art. 6.2.3 states that a *contract may be supplemented, amended, or modified only by the mutual agreement of the parties.* That is, to deal with this principle, it is necessary to enforce an agreement protocol between parties in correspondence of runtime amendments. Actually, the full *Stipula* language already retains an agreement clause between parties that corresponds to the so-called "meeting of the minds": every one must accept the terms of the contract and the legal effects of the *Stipula* contract are triggered by the achievement of the agreement (see rule [AGREE] in [7]; this feature has been omitted in this contribution because we are addressing is a lightweight version of the language).

Below we propose an extension of *higher-order Stipula* with an additional agreement clause that occurs in correspondence of every amendment. To define the rule, let A ACCEPTS H IN ℓ be a predicate that takes a directive H and verifies whether it complies or not with A's policy in the memory ℓ. It is worth to notice that the predicate depends on the memory; therefore the policy of A might change in accordance with the updates. In particular, if ℓ stores a timestamp (the semantics of full *Stipula* has a global clock by which the events are modelled), then ACCEPT may change from time to time. In this context, the rule [HO-FUNCTION] becomes (we also rewrite the premises):

[HO-FUNCTION-AGREE]

$$\frac{\begin{array}{c} \text{@Q A: F}(\!|X,Y,Z|\!)\{\text{ remove } X \text{ add } Y \text{ run } Z\} \in \mathbb{D}[\text{@Q A : F}]_{\ell,\varepsilon,\varepsilon} \\ \mathbb{D}' = \text{parties } \overline{A'} = \overline{A'} \text{ fields } \overline{x} \text{ assets } \overline{h} \ F \quad \ell(A) = A \quad \ell' = \ell[\overline{h} \mapsto \overline{0}, \overline{A'} \mapsto \overline{A'}] \\ (\ell(A'') \text{ ACCEPTS remove P add } \mathbb{D}' \text{ run } B \text{ IN } \ell)^{A'' \in parties(\mathbb{D}) \,\&\&\, \ell(A'') \neq A} \end{array}}{\mathbb{D} \Vdash \text{@Q}, \ell, \_ \xrightarrow{A:F(\!|P,\mathbb{D}',B|\!)} \mathbb{D} \setminus P \lhd \mathbb{D}' \Vdash \text{@Q}, \ell', B}$$

We notice that, according to [HO-FUNCTION-AGREE], the acceptance of the directive is restricted to parties in $\mathbb{D}$: the new parties in $\mathbb{D}'$ have nothing to accept. For instance, in the first example of Sect. 3, we have the invocation

Farm : Hardship$(\!|\varepsilon, \mathbb{D}, \{\text{"Pay\_in\_Advance"} \rightarrow \tilde{\ } \quad \text{flour} \multimap \text{Farm}\} \Rightarrow \text{@Excp}|\!)$

($\mathbb{D}$ refers to the declaration part defined in Sect. 3). At this point, for the new code becoming operational and enter into force, *Client* must satisfies the predicate

Client ACCEPTS add $\mathbb{D}$ run {"Pay_in_Advance" → ˜   flour ─∘ Farm} ⇒ @Excp IN ℓ'

assuming that ℓ and ℓ' are the memories before and after the transition, respectively. (In this case we have omitted the remove directive because it is empty.)

7 Related Works

Higher-order have been widely used in programming languages to pass functions as arguments to other functions, thus allowing to easily model closures and currying (*cf.* Haskell, JavaScript, and lambdas in C++ and Java). As regards languages for legal contracts, up-to our knowledge, no-one addresses amendments of contracts. In particular, the literature reports a number of languages and frameworks that aim at transforming legal semantic rules into code, *e.g.* [9, 10,13,14]. These languages are actually specification languages, that provide attributes and clauses that naturally encode rights, obligations, prohibitions, which are not easily mapped to high-level programming languages, such as Java. *Stipula*, with its distinctive primitives and legal design patterns, aims to be intermediate between a specification language and a high-level programming language. That is, *Stipula* and its higher-order extension can be considered a *legal calculus* in the terminology of [2], similar to Orlando [1] that has been designed for modeling conveyances in property law and Catala [17] for modeling statutes and regulations clauses in the fiscal domain.

Recently, there has been increasing interest in smart contract languages because they allow to define programs that can manage and transfer assets. These programs run on distributed networks whose nodes store a common state (that also includes the programs themselves) in the form of a blockchain. Due to the immutability of information stored on a blockchain, several projects have proposed legal frameworks that target smart contracts on Ethereum [4], such as OpenLaw [22] and Lexon [16]. Amending the code of these frameworks is equivalent to upgrading Ethereum smart contracts, which is not straightforward, as once a smart contract is deployed on a blockchain, it is immutable. However, since upgrading may be necessary to fix vulnerabilities or to change smart contract business logic, designers have proposed a number of patterns for safely modifying a contract still preserving the immutability of the blockchain [12]. These pattern rely either (*i*) on decoupling the data storage from the business logic of a contract or (*ii*) on the usage of proxies. In case (*i*), the contract has been defined in such a way that the business logic is accessed by an address stored in the contract (this is similar to our requirement that a contract has an hardship function). This means that updating the business logic amounts to rewrite a new logic, store it in the blockchain at a (new) address x and use x to update the address stored in the contract. In case (*ii*), the users interact with a proxy contract rather than the original contract, whose data and functionalities are accessed by means of addresses stored in the proxy. Therefore, updating (both the state and the business logic of) the contract amounts to change the addresses stored in the proxy. Proxies are also used for implementing contract versioning: the address of the contract is actually that of a package and ad-hoc policies may direct the invocation to one version or another. When several versions do coexist (*cf.* diamond patterns [19]) and a protocol may dispatch an invocation to one version or another, we get a smart contract concept similar to our operation $\mathbb{D} \lhd \mathbb{D}'$.

Clearly, the foregoing solutions allow neither a control on whom is going to modify the contract nor an agreement between the parties. In fact, *higher-order Stipula* turns out to be at a higher level of abstraction than addresses or proxies, thus allowing reasonings about amendments that integrate well with the other features of the language. Said otherwise, *higher-order Stipula* seems more appropriate and more faithful in representing the structure of a legal contract and the procedure for amending it.

In designing *higher-order Stipula* we have been inspired by operations of Delta-Oriented Programming [15] that has been conceived for implementing software product lines. In this paradigm, deltas are codes that are attached to products and can be combined to obtain complex products starting from a core feature. Compliance and other correctness properties can be verified at static time. On the contrary, in *higher-order Stipula* amendments are not known when the contract is stipulated and every analysis must be postponed at runtime.

8   Conclusions

This paper discusses the amendments of legal contracts in *Stipula* by resorting to higher-order. Our solution handles both amendments where the contract code is completely modified and substituted as well as those where the new code has to coexist with the old one. The latter case, though, may require particular attention, especially to the conditions laid out in the new functions. A wrongly formulated condition could affect the order of codes priorities. This, in turn, could result in an unwanted function overriding or, *vice-versa*, in the persistence uptime of a function that had to be overridden.

We believe that the higher-order extension is crucial for the effective applicability of legal contracts in real-world scenarios. Specifically, it can be used (in the full *Stipula* language which also includes events) to handle new events by passing a function to be executed when an event occurs. This enables more flexible and modular event handling that can account for unforeseen circumstances at the time the contract was initiated. We are already experimenting the higher-order extension of the *Stipula* prototype (that is available on-line at [8]). The higher-order extension admits functions that input codes; these codes are compiled on-the-fly and added to the contract (the compilation also includes a type inference analysis, see [7]). In correspondence of every invocation, a selection function retrieves the right function code as specified by rule [HO-FUNCTION].

Future works on the matter shall deal with analyzing a set of more complex use-cases and to implement the policies discussed in Sects. 5 and 6. It is worth to remark that our prototype, taking inspiration from visual interfaces as in [21], is integrated with a user-friendly and easy-to-use programming interface. We hope that this additional feature will allow us to collect comments and reports of the proposal by non-expert users.

Acknowledgements. We are grateful to Silvia Crafa for the many insightful discussions about *Stipula* and Adele Veschetti for prototyping both *Stipula* and *higher-order Stipula*. We also thank the anonymous Coordination referees for the detailed suggestions that considerably improved the paper.

References

1. Basu, S., Foster, N., Grimmelmann, J.: Property conveyances as a programming language. In: Proceedings of 2019 ACM SIGPLAN International Symposium on New Ideas, New Paradigms, and Reflections on Programming and Software, Onward! 2019, pp. 128–142. Association for Computing Machinery, New York (2019)
2. Basu, S., Mohan, A., Grimmelmann, J., Foster, N.: Legal calculi. Technical report, ProLaLa 2022 ProLaLa Programming Languages and the Law (2022). https://popl22.sigplan.org/details/prolala-2022-papers/6/Legal-Calculi
3. Bortolotti, F.: Force Majeure and Hardship Clauses - Introductory note and commentary. Technical report, International Chamber of Commerce (2020)
4. Vitalik Buterin. Ethereum white paper (2013). https://github.com/ethereum/wiki/wiki/White-Paper
5. Crafa, S., Laneve, C.: Liquidity analysis in resource-aware programming. In: Proc. 18th Int. Conference, FACS 2022, vol. 13712. LNCS, pp. 205–221. Springer (2022)
6. Crafa, S., Laneve, C., Sartor, G.: Stipula: a domain specific language for legal contracts. Presented at the Int. Workshop Programming Languages and the Law, January 16, 2022
7. Crafa, S., Laneve, C., Sartor, G., Veschetti, A.: Pacta sunt servanda: legal contracts in Stipula. Science of Computer Programming, 225, January 2023
8. Crafa, S., Laneve, C., Veschetti, A.: The Higher-order Stipula Prototype, July 2022. Available on github: https://github.com/stipula-language
9. de Kruijff, J.T., Hans Weigand, H.: An introduction to commitment based smart contracts using reactionruleml. In: Proc. 12th Int. Workshop on Value Modeling and Business Ontologies (VMBO), vol. 2239, pp. 149–157. CEUR-WS.org (2018)
10. de Kruijff, J.T., Hans Weigand, H.: Introducing commitruleml for smart contracts. In: Proc. 13th Int. Workshop on Value Modeling and Business Ontologies (VMBO), vol. 2383. CEUR-WS.org (2019)
11. Fontaine, M., De Ly, F.: Drafting International Contracts. BRILL (2006)
12. Ethereum Foundation. Upgrading smart contracts (2023). https://ethereum.org/en/developers/docs/smart-contracts/upgrading
13. Frantz, C.K., Nowostawski, M.: From institutions to code: Towards automated generation of smart contracts. In: 2016 IEEE 1st International Workshops on Foundations and Applications of Self* Systems (FAS*W), pp. 210–215 (2016)

14. He, X., Qin, B., Zhu, Y., Chen, X., Liu, Y.: Spesc: a specification language for smart contracts. In: 2018 IEEE 42nd Annual Computer Software and Applications Conference (COMPSAC), vol. 01, pp. 132–137 (2018)
15. Lopez-Herrejon, R.E., Batory, D., Cook, W.: Evaluating support for features in advanced modularization technologies. In: Black, A.P. (ed.) ECOOP 2005. LNCS, vol. 3586, pp. 169–194. Springer, Heidelberg (2005). https://doi.org/10.1007/11531142_8
16. Lexon Foundation. Lexon Home Page (2019). http://www.lexon.tech
17. Merigoux, D., Chataing, N., Protzenko, J.: Catala: a programming language for the law. In: Proceedings of ACM Program. Lang., 5(ICFP), Aug 2021
18. Mik, E.: Smart contracts terminology, technical limitations and real world complexity. Law Innov. Technol. **9**, 269–300 (2017)
19. Mudge, N.: How diamond upgrades work (2022). https://dev.to/mudgen/how-diamond-upgrades-work-417j
20. Sangiorgi, D.: From p-calculus to higher-order p-calculus — and back. In: Gaudel, M.-C., Jouannaud, J.-P. (eds.) CAAP 1993. LNCS, vol. 668, pp. 151–166. Springer, Heidelberg (1993). https://doi.org/10.1007/3-540-56610-4_62
21. Weingaertner, T., Rao, R., Ettlin, J., Suter, P., Dublanc, P.: Smart contracts using blockly: Representing a purchase agreement using a graphical programming language. In: 2018 Crypto Valley Conference on Blockchain Technology (CVCBT), pp. 55–64 (2018)
22. Wright, A., Roon, D., ConsenSys AG.: OpenLaw Web Site (2019). https://www.openlaw.io

Toward Run-time Coordination
of Reconfiguration Requests in Cloud
Computing Systems

Salman Farhat[1]([✉])[iD], Simon Bliudze[1]([✉])[iD], Laurence Duchien[2]([✉])[iD],
and Olga Kouchnarenko[3]([✉])[iD]

[1] Univ. Lille, Inria, CNRS, Centrale Lille, UMR 9189 CRIStAL, 59000 Lille, France
`{Salman.Farhat,Simon.Bliudze}@inria.fr`
[2] Univ. Lille, CNRS, Inria, Centrale Lille, UMR 9189 CRIStAL, 59000 Lille, France
`Laurence.Duchien@inria.fr`
[3] Université de Franche-Comté, CNRS, Institut FEMTO-ST, 25000 Besançon, France
`Olga.Kouchnarenko@femto-st.fr`

Abstract. Cloud applications and cyber-physical systems are becoming increasingly complex, requiring frequent reconfiguration to adapt to changing needs and requirements. Existing approaches compute new valid configurations either at design time, at runtime, or both. However, these approaches can lead to significant computational or validation overheads for each reconfiguration step. We propose a component-based approach that avoids computational and validation overheads using a representation of the set of valid configurations as a variability model. More precisely, our approach leverages feature models to automatically generate, in a component-based formalism called JavaBIP, run-time variability models that respect the feature model constraints. Produced run-time variability models enable control over application reconfiguration by executing reconfiguration requests in such a manner as to ensure the (partial) validity of all reachable configurations. We evaluate our approach on a simple web application deployed on the Heroku cloud platform. Experimental results show that the overheads induced by generated run-time models on systems involving up to 300 features are negligible, demonstrating the practical interest of our approach.

Keywords: Concurrent Component-based Systems · Variability Models · Self-Configuration · Dynamic Reconfiguration

1 Introduction

Systems are increasingly required to be able to function continuously under tough circumstances, such as partial failures of subsystems, or changing user needs,

S. Bliudze was partially supported by ANR Investissments d'avenir (grant number ANR-16-IDEX-0004 ULNE)

O. Kouchnarenko was supported by the EIPHI Graduate School (grant number ANR-17-EURE-0002). This work was partially carried out while she was on a research leave at Inria Lille.

© IFIP International Federation for Information Processing 2023
S.-S. Jongmans and A. Lopes (Eds.): COORDINATION 2023, LNCS 13908, pp. 271–291, 2023.
https://doi.org/10.1007/978-3-031-35361-1_15

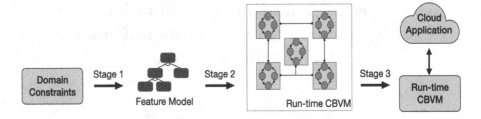

Fig. 1. Stages of the FeCo4Reco process.

while running without interruption and often unsupervised. Thus, after an initial configuration, reconfigurations are needed to keep the application compliant with the new needs and underlying platform constraints at run-time [22,30]. Reconfigurations may modify the system architecture, and also the coordination between sub-parts of the system, notably w.r.t. failure events, components requests, or new requirements needed to be fulfilled.

Let us consider cloud applications, i.e., large concurrent software systems that are further constrained by the cloud platforms they run on [22]. In this context, a system's configuration is the set of resources that host an application, as well as the set of rules that define the system's sub-parts coordination and dependencies. The initial configuration aims to meet startup system needs and is not meant to last. Thus, in response to changing user requirements, systems must be reconfigured accordingly while ensuring that platform constraints are respected. Modeling and managing the variability and reconfigurations is an active software architecture research domain [9,16,30]. Feature modeling (FM) [19,27] is a widely used approach to capture commonalities and variability across software systems that are part of a system family or a product line. Note that the problem of finding an assignment with only required constraints and XOR-groups is NP-hard [20]. Component-based systems (CBS), e.g., [13] for CBS supporting hierarchical architecture, allow building complex systems by composing components, which encapsulate data and code. In addition, some component models, e.g. Aeolus, Madeus, Concerto [12], JavaBIP [7], are executable, and allow run-time monitoring and control. We call them component-based run-time models.

Whatever the approach to developing complex systems that are able to adapt to changing needs and demands–e.g., component-/agent-based systems, autonomous computing, emergent bio-inspired systems, etc.–analyzing and planning reconfigurations requires handling some metrics based on models [23,32], and rules/policies [11,22]. While using these approaches, computing either all valid configurations at design time, an appropriate one at run-time, or both, induces computation and/or validation overheads for each reconfiguration operation. This paper presents an approach to leverage variability models for acquiring a compact representation of a set of valid configurations of a system. It aims to automatically generate a formal executable model to safely perform reconfigurations in a scalable manner. To this end, we take advantage of feature models and component-based run-time models for enforcing safe-by-construction behaviour of concurrent component-based systems through the automatic derivation of executable models from requirements and safety constraints. Our framework, joining forces of features and components for safe reconfigurations (FeCo4Reco for short) with a lightweight effort, allows applying reconfigurations in a safe manner, with no overhead of either computing or validating the new configuration while having an executable model.

The FeCo4Reco process, shown in Fig 1, consists of three stages: 1) domain constraints are specified as a feature model, 2) the feature model is automatically transformed into a run-time Component-based Variability Model (CBVM) to make it run alongside the system, 3) the generated model is used by the deployers to set up initial configurations of the system, and to automatically monitor reconfiguration requests from the environment and safely execute them at run-time.

Outline and Contributions. Section 2 presents the Heroku cloud running example used throughout the paper, and it also lists the research questions. Section 3 provides an overview of the underpinnings: feature models and component-based models. Motivated by driving the reconfiguration process without the need of pre-computing the possible configurations at design time, our *first* contribution is a component-based run-time variability model leveraging feature models and their underlying constraints.

Model transformation rules in Sect. 4, which are general enough for both feature models and component-based models, constitute the *second* contribution leading to a component-based variability model automatically generated with FeCo4Reco. Its main advantage consists of a compact encoding of all valid or partial-valid configurations, with partial-valid meaning that it can be transformed into a valid configuration by adding features. Being run-time, this model encodes reconfiguration operations while ensuring the safety property, saying that only partial-valid configurations can be reached as a result of any reconfigurations. Main properties related to reconfigurations are described in Sect. 5. Section 6 describes the implementation, and reports on experimental results on a non-trivial cloud example, with a discussion on the validity of the approach. They constitute the *third* practical contribution showing the interest of our approach in practice. Finally, Sect. 7 is dedicated to related work, and Sect. 8 concludes with future work directions.

Proofs of all the theoretical results and additional details of the experimental setup are available in the companion report [15].

2   Motivating Example

This section describes the Heroku cloud [25] to motivate our approach and to illustrate its application. Heroku offers a range of API-controlled services, including dyno types, add-ons, buildpack, and regions, which provide developers with the means to create complex applications consisting of interacting pieces. For example, a typical web application may have a web component that is responsible for handling web traffic. It may also have a queue (typically represented by

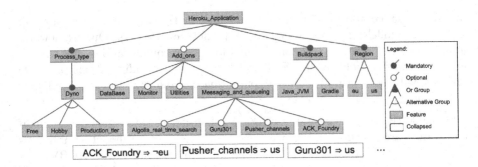

Fig. 2. Part of the Heroku cloud feature model.

an add-on on Heroku), and one or more workers that are responsible for taking some elements off of the queue and for processing them. Heroku permits building such architectures by allowing the user to configure the application using the process type, region, buildpack, and add-ons.

- Process type: All Heroku applications are launched and scaled using the container model on the Heroku platform. The Heroku containers, called Dynos, are virtualized Linux containers to run programs in isolation.
- Region: Applications on Heroku may be deployed in various geographic regions.
- Buildpack: Buildpacks convert the deployed code to an executable slug on a Dyno.
- Add-ons: Add-ons are additional services that can be attached to a Heroku application to provide extra functionalities such as data storage, monitoring, analytics, and data processing.

Figure 2 presents the Heroku cloud with services and constraints between these services. In addition to the mandatory components, optional functionalities, such as Heroku add-ons, are available. To help the developer, they are maintained by either a third-party provider or by Heroku. Add-ons are installed onto applications by using the Heroku service API interface. Furthermore, other constraints must be taken into account. For example, in Heroku, they express regional availability of services, inter-service dependencies, as well as architectural constraints. As a result, developers are expected to be Heroku experts in order to manage and control applications in a safe way while taking into account all the constraints on the context, in which the application is hosted.

Research Question – The main challenge is to allow the reconfiguration of software systems in a safe manner while avoiding additional overhead at run-time, the paper aims to address the following research question (RQ):

RQ How to enforce domain constraints during dynamic reconfiguration at low cost?

3   Background

3.1   Feature Models

Introduced for product lines, feature models are used for representing the commonality and variability of features and of relationships among them [6]. A feature f could be a software artefact such as a part of code, a component, or a requirement. In Fig. 2 for the he Heroku cloud, features, graphically represented by rectangles, are organized in a tree-like hierarchy with multiple levels of increasing detail. To express the variability of the system, feature models provide 1) a decomposition in sub-features, where a sub-feature may be mandatory (*black circle*), or optional (*unfilled circle*), 2) *XOR*-group or an *OR*-group. In a *XOR*-group, exactly one feature is selected, while in an *OR*-group, one or more features are selected, whenever the parent feature is selected. In addition, the combination of the optional and mandatory features is seen as an *AND*-group.

In the main hierarchy, cross-tree constraints can be used to describe dependencies between arbitrary features, e.g.selecting a feature *requires* the selection of another one, or that two features mutually *exclude* each other.

More precisely, let F be a set of features, and $Node$ the set of the nodes of a tree-like structure defined by the grammar of axiom $Node$:

$$Node ::= OR(Node_1, \ldots, Node_k) \mid XOR(Node_1, \ldots, Node_k)$$
$$\mid AND([\textbf{mand}]Node_1, \ldots, [\textbf{mand}]Node_k) \mid leaf$$

We denote by $\pi \subseteq Node \times Node$ the *parent* relation, i.e.a node n is a child of n' iff $\pi(n) = n'$. Let $\mu \subseteq Node \times Node$ be the reflexive and transitive closure of π^{-1}, i.e. $\mu(n)$ is the set of all descendants of $n \in Node$, including itself.

Definition 1. *A feature model FM over a set of features F is a tuple $(root, \phi, \rho, \chi)$, where $root \in Node$, $\phi : \mu(root) \to F$ is an injective function associating features to nodes, and $\rho, \chi \subseteq F \times F$ are the requires and excludes relations, respectively, with χ being symmetric.*[1]

Given a feature $f \in F$ that appears in the FM, we denote by n_f the node corresponding to f, i.e.such that $\mu(n_f) = f$. Abusing notation, we also write $\pi(f) = f'$ iff $\pi(n_f) = n_{f'}$. Given an AND-node n, for each child mandatory node n' of n, i.e.such that $n = AND(\ldots, \textbf{mand}\ n', \ldots)$, we write $mand(n')$.

Example 1. Figure 2 shows a simplified example of the Heroku cloud feature model. `Process_type`, `Region`, and `Buildback` are mandatory features, whereas `Add_ons` are optional. The `Process_type` feature can be realized by using only one of the three alternative `Dyno` sub-features `Free`, `Hobby`, and `Production_tier`. On the contrary, `Messaging_and_queuing` can be implemented using any combination of the sub-features `Algolia_real_time_search`, ..., `ACK_Foundry`. In addition, `ACK_Foundry` and `eu` are mutually exclusive, and both `Guru301` and `Pusher_channels` require `us`.

---

[1] In Fig. 2, we write $f_1 \Rightarrow f_2$ iff $\rho(f_1, f_2)$ and $f_1 \Rightarrow \neg f_2$ (equivalently $f_2 \Rightarrow \neg f_1$) iff $\chi(f_1, f_2)$.

Definition 2. *Given a feature model* $(root, \phi, \rho, \chi)$ *over* F, *its dependency graph is a directed graph* $G = (F, E)$, *where* F *is the set of features, and* $E \subseteq F \times F$ *is the set of edges representing the parent, mandatory and requires relations:*

$$E = \big\{(f_1, f_2) \mid \pi(f_1) = f_2\big\} \cup \big\{(f_1, f_2) \mid \pi(f_2) = f_1 \wedge mand(f_2)\big\} \cup \rho.$$

The FM semantics is the set of its valid configurations [28].

The following definition allows for incremental design and development of real-world systems by considering consistent and well-formed configurations, even if they are not complete.

Definition 3. *Let* $FM = (root, \phi, \rho, \chi)$ *be a feature model over a set of features* F *and let* (F, E) *be its dependency graph. A* configuration *is a set of features* $\Phi \subseteq F$. *We say that* Φ *is*

1. free from internal conflict, *if for any* $f_1, f_2 \in \Phi$, *holds* $(f_1, f_2) \notin \chi$.
2. saturated, *if, for any* $f \in \Phi$, *holds* $E(f) \subseteq \Phi$, *i.e., the dependencies for each feature in the configuration are also included in the configuration.*
3. valid, *if it is saturated, free from internal conflict, and respects structural constraints of XOR and OR nodes: exactly one (XOR) or at least one (OR) child feature selected, respectively (saturation implies the respect of AND-node constraints);*
4. partial-valid, *if there exists a valid configuration* $\Phi' \supseteq \Phi$ *and it is free from internal conflict. A partial-valid configuration may not be saturated, meaning that some of the dependencies of its features are not included in the configuration.*

Saturated partial valid configurations are more restrictive than partially valid ones, as they require all the dependencies of the selected features to be included as well. This means that when building complex systems incrementally, we can ensure that each intermediate step includes the desired features with their necessary dependencies, resulting in consistent and well-formed configurations.

Assumption 1. *We assume that all considered feature models are such that any configuration free from internal conflict is partial-valid.*

3.2   JavaBIP Component-Based Approach

A component is a software object, that encapsulates certain behaviours of a software element. The concept of component is broad and may be used for component-based software systems, microservices, service-oriented applications, and so on. For the coordination of concurrent components, we make use of JavaBIP [7], which is an open-source Java implementation of the BIP (Behaviour-Interaction-Priority) framework [4]. Given a set of *components* and a set of their

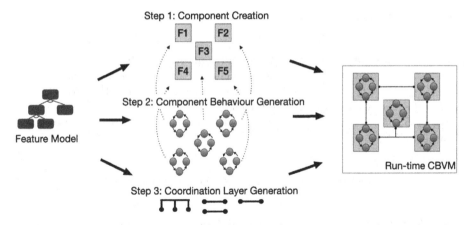

Fig. 3. The generation of the component-based variability model involves a three-step transformation process, where Steps 1, 2, and 3 correspond to Subsects. 4.1, 4.2, and 4.3, respectively.

ports, the component behaviour is defined by a finite state machine (FSM) with transitions labelled by ports. JavaBIP allows two types of ports: *enforceable* and *spontaneous*. Enforceable ports represent actions controlled by the JavaBIP engine. They can be *synchronised*, i.e.executed together atomically. Spontaneous ports represent notifications that components receive about events that happen in their environment. They cannot be synchronised with other ports. An *interaction* is a set of ports—either one or several enforceable ports, or exactly one spontaneous port. In order to define allowed interactions, JavaBIP provides *requires* and *accepts* macros associated with enforceable ports and representing causal and acceptance constraints, respectively. This allows JavaBIP to provide a coordination layer that is powerful enough to model naturally and compositionally the constraints expressed in the feature model. Detailed presentation of these macros is provided in [7]. Intuitively, the *requires* macro specifies ports required for synchronization with the given port. For example, **requires(C1.p)** = **{C2.q, C3.r, C4.s}**[2] means that port p of component C1 must be synchronized with at least one of the three ports: q, r, or s of components C2, C3 and C4, respectively. The *accepts* macro lists all ports that are allowed to synchronize with the given port, thus allowing *optional* ports. For example, **accepts(C1.p)** = **{C2.q, C3.r, C4.s, C5.t}** means that in addition to the ports listed by the *requires* macro, the port t of component C5 is *also* allowed to synchronize with p despite not being required by it. Graphically, allowed interactions are defined by *connectors*. The behaviour specification of each component along with the set of *requires* and *accepts* macros are provided to the *JavaBIP engine*. The engine orchestrates the overall execution of the whole component-based system by deciding which component transitions must be executed at each cycle. The

---

[2] We use a notation that is slightly different from that in [7] without change of meaning.

operational semantics of a JavaBIP model is defined by a labelled transition system (LTS) $L = (Q, \Sigma, \rightarrow)$, where:

- Q is the cartesian product of the sets of component states,
- Σ is the set of allowed interactions (including singleton spontaneous ports),
- $\rightarrow \subseteq Q \times \Sigma \times Q$ is the maximal set of transitions such that the projection of each $(q, e, q') \in \rightarrow$ onto any component B is either $(q_B, \emptyset, q_B)$, for some state q_B of B, or a transition $(q_B, \{p\}, q'_B)$ with q_B, q'_B and p being two states and a port of B.

A configuration q' is *reachable* from a configuration q if there exists a sequence of interactions $e_1, e_2, \ldots, e_n \in \Sigma$ such that $(q, e_1, q_1), (q_1, e_2, q_2), \ldots,$ $(q_{n-1}, e_n, q') \in \rightarrow$.

Example 2. Building on Example 1, Fig. 5 on page 11 illustrates a JavaBIP model with five components. Graphically, enforceable and spontaneous transitions are shown by solid black and dashed green lines, respectively. Ports are shown as grey boxes on the sides of the components, and five connectors linking the ports define the possible interactions. Port $activate_f$ of the `Algolia_read_time_search` component can only be fired together with port $selected_f$ of the `Messaging_and_queuing` component. As there is no transition from init state of label `selected_f` of the component `Messaging_and_queuing`, this prevents the `Algolia_read_time_search` component from entering the final state when the `Algolia_read_time_search` component is in S_f state. In this example, connector C1 is binary, while C5 defines an interaction involving five ports.

4 Design and Transformation

This section describes a set of design rules for automatically generating a run-time component-based variability model using a feature model as input. Figure 3 presents the steps for the transformation of the encoding process. The process of encoding the feature model into a component-based variability model is done recursively. The process starts with the *root* node of the feature model and generates the components and their behavior. Subsequently, the generation of the coordination layer is performed based on the feature model constraints.

4.1 From Features to Components

Let us start by establishing a mapping between features and components. Given a feature, cf. Sect. 3, it is turned into a component. Let $f \in F$ and $n_f \in Node$, s.t. $f(n_f) = f$. To associate components with the nodes of the tree-like structure of root *root* whose nodes correspond to features, we define a function $\kappa : Node \rightarrow 2^{Comp}$ by:

$$\kappa(n_f) = \begin{cases} enc(n_f), & \text{if } n_f = leaf \\ \bigcup_{i=1}^{k} \kappa(Node_i) \cup enc(n_f), & \text{if } n_f = OR(Node_1, ..., Node_k) \vee \\ & n_f = XOR(Node_1, ..., Node_k) \vee \\ & n_f = AND([opt]Node_1, ..., [opt]Node_k) \end{cases} \quad (1)$$

Defined by induction on the node type, $\kappa(root)$ returns the set of components to be generated for the $root$ node and all its descendent nodes. Then for a feature f on the n_f leaf node, $enc(n_f)$ encoding is called to generate a component of name f. For a compound feature, its encoding is called, and κ is recursively invoked on all the sub-nodes until the leafs are met.

4.2 Component Behaviour Generation

Once the set $\kappa(root)$ of components are determined, their behaviour is defined by finite
state machines (FSMs), that are automatically generated. Each FSM has finite sets
$S, T \subseteq S \times S$ of resp. states and transitions,
with specific initial and final states in S. The
corresponding FSM for a component f is generated, as illustrated in Fig. 4:

$$enc(n_f) = \text{FSM in Fig. 4} \quad (2)$$

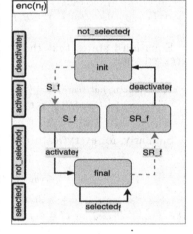

States. In the FSM associated with component f, the states generated are: initial state
init, where no feature is requested, and no
feature is activated; intermediate states S_f
and SR_f, to resp. start f or start reset f,
while dealing with requests to activate f or
deactivate f; and final a state, where feature f is activated.

Fig. 4. Feature component FSM.

Transitions. The FSM transitions are associated with either API functions, which require
a component to perform actions (enforceable transitions), or event notifications,
which allow reacting to external events from the environment (spontaneous transitions). Transitions correspond to the method invocations.

Example 3. Figure 4 illustrates a FSM for feature f, with four states in blue
and transitions among them. Transitions represented by dashed green arrows
are spontaneous. For example, a spontaneous transition is performed to go to
the intermediate state S_f when there is a reconfiguration request to activate f.

4.3 Coordination Layer Generation

Once the individual behaviour of the generated components is defined, a coordination layer between components has to be fixed. Coordination is applied

through interactions, which are sets of ports that define allowed synchroniza-
tions between components. These interactions are represented by connectors
which are the structural representations of the interactions between the ports
of the components. To construct this coordination layer, the dependency graph
G_{FM} is built by Definition 2, and then it is used to compute strongly connected
components (SCCs) to capture the set of features that are mutually dependent.

The macros for activating feature f are created based on the strongly connected component of f, denoted by SCC_f, the set of features that f depends on,
via $E(f)$, both extracted from G_{FM}, and the set of features that are mutually
exclusive with f, via $\chi(f)$. The activation macros of feature f are in Eq. 3 to 6.

Equation 3 states that firing port `activate_f` requires firing three groups
of ports at the same time: 1) `activate` ports of features in SCC_f except
f, 2) `selected` ports of features that f depends on outside SCC_f, and 3)
`not_selected` ports of features that f excludes.

$$
\begin{aligned}
requires(enc(n_f).activate_f) &\stackrel{\text{def}}{=} \{\, enc(n_{f'}).activate_{f'} \mid f' \in SCC_f \setminus \{f\}\} \\
&\cup \{\, enc(n_{f'}).selected_{f'} \mid f' \in E(f) \setminus SCC_f\} \cup \{\, enc(n_{f'}).not\_selected_{f'} \mid f' \in \chi(f)\} \,.
\end{aligned}
\tag{3}
$$

Equation 4 states that the required ports of port `activate_f` are also the
accepted ones:

$$
\begin{aligned}
accepts(enc(n_f).activate_f) &\stackrel{\text{def}}{=} \{\, enc(n_{f'}).activate_{f'} \mid f' \in SCC_f \setminus \{f\}\} \cup \\
\{\, enc(n_{f'}).selected_{f'} \mid f' \in E(f) &\setminus SCC_f\} \cup \{\, enc(n_{f'}).not\_selected_{f'} \mid f' \in \chi(f)\} \,.
\end{aligned}
\tag{4}
$$

Similarly, for every feature $f' \in E(f)$,

$$
requires(enc(n_{f'}).selected_{f'}) \stackrel{\text{def}}{=} \emptyset
$$

$$
\begin{aligned}
accepts(enc(n_{f'}).selected_{f'}) &\stackrel{\text{def}}{=} \{\, enc(n_{f''}).activate_{f''} \mid f'' \in SCC_f\} \cup \\
\{\, enc(n_{f''}).selected_{f''} \mid f'' \in E(f) \setminus \{SCC_f, f'\}\} &\cup \{\, enc(n_{f''}).not\_selected_{f''} \mid f'' \in \chi(f)\} \,.
\end{aligned}
\tag{5}
$$

For every feature $f' \in \chi(f)$,

$$
requires(enc(n_{f'}).not\_selected_{f'}) \stackrel{\text{def}}{=} \emptyset
$$

$$
\begin{aligned}
accepts(enc(n_{f'}).not\_selected_{f'}) &\stackrel{\text{def}}{=} \{\, enc(n_{f''}).activate_{f''} \mid f'' \in SCC_f\} \cup \\
\{\, enc(n_{f''}).selected_{f''} \mid f'' \in E(f) \setminus SCC_f\} &\cup \{\, enc(n_{f''}).not\_selected_{f''} \mid f'' \in \chi(f) \setminus \{f'\}\} \,.
\end{aligned}
\tag{6}
$$

Given the construction of the macros for activation, the corresponding deactivation connectors can be derived by reversing the activation process. In other
words, the process of deactivating a feature f is symmetrical to the activation
process, where the reverse operation of activation is deactivation, and *selected*
becomes *not_selected* of $E^{-1}(f)$ set extracted from the transpose graph G_{FM}^{-1}.
Notice that exclude constraints are not considered because they only affect the
activation of features, not their deactivation.

$$requires\big(enc(n_f).deactivate_f\big) \overset{\text{def}}{=} \{\, enc(n_{f'}).deactivate_{f'} \mid f' \in SCC_f \setminus \{f\}\}$$
$$\cup \{\, enc(n_{f'}).not\_selected_{f'} \mid f' \in E^{-1}(f) \setminus SCC_f \,\} \ .$$
$$accepts\big(enc(n_f).deactivate_f\big) \overset{\text{def}}{=} \{\, enc(n_{f'}).deactivate_{f'} \mid f' \in SCC_f \setminus \{f\}\}$$
$$\cup \{\, enc(n_{f'}).not\_selected_{f'} \mid f' \in E^{-1}(f) \setminus SCC_f \,\} \ . \tag{7}$$

For every feature $f' \in E^{-1}(f)$,

$$requires\big(enc(n_{f'}).not\_selected_{f'}\big) \overset{\text{def}}{=} \emptyset$$
$$accepts\big(enc(n_{f'}).not\_selected_{f'}\big) \overset{\text{def}}{=} \{\, enc(n_{f''}).deactivate_{f''} \mid f'' \in SCC_f\}$$
$$\cup \{\, enc(n_{f''}).not\_selected_{f''} \mid f'' \in E^{-1}(f) \setminus \{SCC_f, f'\}\} \ . \tag{8}$$

Example 4. Based on the feature model presented in Fig. 5, the coordination layer macros were generated. To illustrate this step, let us consider `Algolia_real_time_` search feature, which forms a singleton strongly connected component (SCC) in the dependency graph G generated from the feature model presented in Fig. 5. The SCC has only one dependency: `Messaging_and_queuing` is the parent of `Algolia_real_time_` search feature. Moreover, `Algolia_real_time_search` is not mutually exclusive with any other features in the model. Using this information, the macro for the activation of `Algolia_real_time_search` feature is created as discussed in Sect. 4.3, which is represented graphically by Connector C1. This connector synchronises `activate_f` port of `Algolia_real_time_search` component with `selected_f` port of its parent `Messaging_and_queuing` component. Intuitively, this ensures that the configuration with `Algolia_real_time_search` can be reached only when its dependencies are satisfied.

Similarly, consider the deactivation of `Messaging_and_queuing` feature, which forms a singleton strongly connected component (SCC) in the G^{-1}, and it has four dependencies with its sub-features. Using this information, the macro for the deactivation of `Messaging_and_queuing` feature is created as discussed in Sect. 4.3 which is represented graphically by Connector C5. Connector C5 synchronizes port `deactivate_f` of component `Messaging_and_queuing` with all ports `not_selected_f` of its sub-features. Intuitively, this ensures that the parent can be deactivated only when all its sub-features are in the inactive states.

After having performed all the steps, the encoding process presented in Fig. 3 terminates. Indeed, at every step, the designed rules deal with the finite sets of features, constraints, nodes, components, and connectors. It is easy to establish that the FM semantics in terms of feature configurations [28] is preserved from the FM to the run-time CBVM by applying the encoding process, as the dependency graph issued from the feature model is used.

Since the CBVM is a JavaBIP model, it inherits the operational semantics of JavaBIP [7]. Notice that all interactions among enforceable ports correspond to either the activation of features (Eqs. (3–6)) or their deactivation (Eqs. (7) and

282   S. Farhat et al.

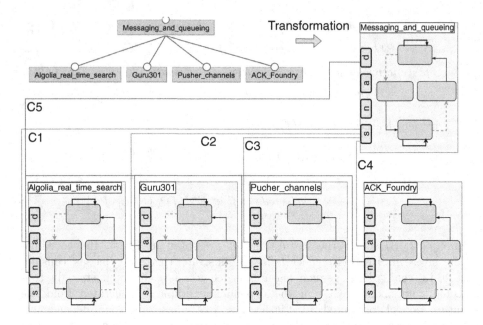

Fig. 5. Part of the generated CBVM for the Heroku cloud FM: The behaviour of all the components is the same as shown in Fig. 4. For the sake of clarity, we shorten the names of the ports to the first letter.

(8)). Requesting individual feature activation or deactivation is done through notifications on spontaneous ports.

Proposition 1. *Given a run-time CBVM, for each interaction e allowed by Eqs. (3–8), exactly one of the sets $\{f \in F \mid enc(n_f).activate_f \in e\}$ and $\{f \in F \mid enc(n_f).deactivate_f \in e\}$ is not empty. Furthermore, that set is an SCC of the dependency graph.*

In other words, given a run-time CBVM, each interaction is either a feature activation or deactivation, which involves a strongly connected component in the dependency graph.

Proof. Follows trivially from Eqs. (3–8). □

5   CBVM to Deal with Reconfigurations

By construction, the operational semantics of the run-time CBVM is represented by an LTS, whose states are implicitly described configurations with selected features, and whose transitions are labelled by interactions. Performing interactions leads to a configuration change, i.e.reconfigurations, and this section describes their properties.

Proposition 2. *Any configuration reachable in the run-time CBVM is a saturated partial-valid configuration.*

Lemma 1. *Let $\Phi \subseteq F$ be a saturated partial-valid configuration. Let C be an SCC of the dependency graph. Then either $C \subseteq \Phi$ or $C \subseteq F \setminus \Phi$.*

Proposition 3. *Let $\Phi \subset \Phi'$ be two saturated partial-valid configurations. Assume Φ is the current configuration of the run-time CBVM. Then the operation of requesting the activation of all features in $\Phi' \setminus \Phi$ is confluent and terminates in the configuration Φ'.*

Corollary 1. *For any reachable configuration in the run-time CBVM, there exists a reachable valid configuration.*

Corollary 2. *Any saturated partial-valid configuration is reachable in the run-time CBVM.*

Lemma 2. *Any synchronized activation of a set of features can be reversed by the corresponding synchronized deactivation of the same features.*

Lemma 3. *Let Φ and Φ' be two saturated partial-valid configurations. Then $\Phi \cap \Phi'$ is a saturated partial-valid configuration.*

Proposition 4. *Let Φ and Φ' be two saturated partial-valid configurations. Assume Φ is the current configuration in the run-time CBVM. Then the configuration Φ' can be reached by deactivating all and only those features in $\Phi \setminus \Phi'$, then activating all and only those features in $\Phi' \setminus \Phi$.*

Given a software architecture represented by a feature model, reconfigurations are operations applied to the architecture in response to either user requirements or external events in the system environment. The generated model is used to handle reconfiguration requests concurrently by controlling the application API through the methods associated with component transitions, as depicted in Fig. 6. The run-time CBVM provides the capability to perform reconfigurations without the need to compute a path. The coordination layer, which is built based on the dependency graph of the feature model by Definition 2, ensures that the activation or deactivation of a feature occurs in the correct order and only if it is feasible to execute. Additionally, if the interaction of activation or deactivation of a feature is not possible from the current configuration, it will not be executed thus it will be on hold until it can be executed.

Example 5. Building on Example 1, let us consider the scenario where we need to move the system from configuration $\alpha_1 = \{$Heroku_Application, Process_type, Dyno, Free, Region, us, Add_ons, Messaging_and_queuing, Guru301$\}$ to $\alpha_2 = \{$Heroku_Application, Process_type, Dyno, Free, Region, eu$\}$ by changing the region from us to eu and deactivating the Guru301 service. There are six possible reconfiguration paths, as shown in Table 1, that can be taken to move the system from configuration α_1 to α_2. The run-time CBVM can

Table 1. Possible paths for performing reconfigurations.

Path	Interaction 1	Interaction 2	Interaction 3	Validity
Path 1	Activate eu	Deactivate us	Deactivate Guru301	Invalid
Path 2	Activate eu	Deactivate Guru301	Deactivate us	Invalid
Path 3	Deactivate us	Deactivate Guru301	Activate eu	Invalid
Path 4	Deactivate us	Activate eu	Deactivate Guru301	Invalid
Path 5	Deactivate Guru301	Activate eu	Deactivate us	Invalid
Path 6	Deactivate Guru301	Deactivate us	Activate eu	Valid

Paths 1, 2 & 5 are invalid because the mutually exclusive us and eu regions are both activated at some point. Paths 3 & 4 are invalid because Guru301 requires us but us is deactivated first.

receive the reconfiguration request in any order, however, not all reconfiguration paths are valid, as certain interactions can only occur in specific states. For instance, the only interaction possible from configuration α_1 is the deactivation of Guru301 feature, as none of the other features depend on it. Once Guru301 feature is deactivated, the us region can be deactivated since it requires synchronization with the "not_selected" port of Guru301 component, which is already deactivated. Therefore, the interaction for deactivating the us region can be executed only from a state where Guru301 is not active. Finally, the activation of the eu feature can only be executed from the state where the us region is not active since the eu feature is mutually exclusive with other regions, and its activation should be synchronized with the "not_selected" ports of other regions. Hence, the interaction for activating eu can be executed only from a state where the us region is not active.

Therefore, the only safe order of interactions is to first deactivate Guru301, then deactivate us, and finally activate eu. Any other order can take the system through a not-saturated partial valid intermediate configuration.

To conclude, notice that the run-time CBVM is only generated once without computing the set of valid configurations. Furthermore, it drives the reconfiguration process in a "lazy" manner, by postponing feature (de)activation until it can be safely executed. In particular, this means that we do not have to compute the reconfiguration plan.

6   FeCo4Reco Implementation and Experiments

On the Implementation. Our model transformation process has been implemented using the ATLAS Transformation Language (ATL) [18]. ATL is a domain-specific language for specifying model-to-model transformations. Starting from a source model that conforms to a source meta-model, it allows the developer to produce a target model that conforms to a target meta-model [26]. In our approach, the generated model specification conforms to the JavaBIP meta-model [24]. The generated XML file is parsed using the DOM library in

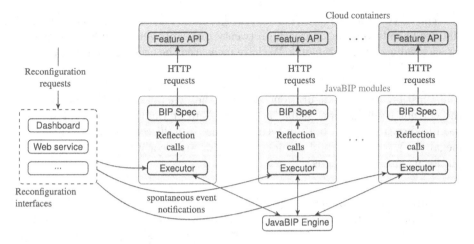

Fig. 6. Integration of the JavaBIP Run-time CBVM with a Cloud Computing System.

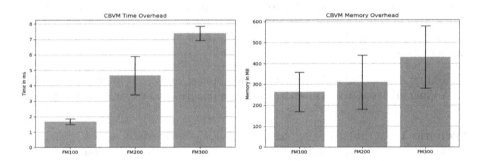

Fig. 7. Model overhead (average values for the generated FMs).

Java to generate the JavaBIP specification and the glue coordination. The reader can find our implementation on the Zenodo platform [1].

Figure 6 shows the FeCo4Reco architecture that enables stages 3 and 4 (Sect. 1). The run-time CBVM consists of BIP Specs and the coordination glue. Each BIP Spec is run by a dedicated Executor (forming a JavaBIP module), which implements the FSM semantics and notifies the JavaBIP Engine about the enabled enforceable transitions. The engine uses the coordination glue to decide which components should take which transitions and notifies them accordingly. Component transitions that represent actual reconfiguration actions issue the corresponding HTTP requests through the feature APIs. Finally, reconfiguration requests are injected into the system in the form of spontaneous event notifications (cf. Sect. 3.2). This can be done by different means depending on the requirements of the Cloud computing system. For the purposes of this paper, we have designed a dashboard application with two buttons (Activate and Deactivate) for each feature.

On the Overhead Measures. Given the number of features (100, 200, and 300) we have tested our approach on twenty randomly generated feature models for each value of this parameter. We have measured the overhead of the generated run-time CBVM over the system.

More precisely, we measured the overhead required to move the system from configuration α_1 to configuration α_2 using the generated CBVM, where α_1 is the current configuration, while α_2 is picked up at random. The CBVM overhead is shown in Fig. 7, both in terms of time (in milliseconds) and memory (in megabytes). Both time and memory overheads are clearly negligible for modern platforms and applications.

On Safe Reconfiguration. To illustrate that the reconfigurations are performed safely we deployed a simple web application onto the Heroku cloud with the run-time CBVM generated from the Heroku cloud FM (Fig. 2). The CBVM is running on a local server using Tomcat 9. It intercepts (re)-configuration requests via APIs using HTTP request methods. The CBVM acts on the received requests to control migrating the system along a valid path to the desired configuration. A simple configuration for the web application is dyno-free (free container), region (eu), and build-pack (Java JVM). Consider two reconfiguration scenarios in relation to Example 1:

1. Adding add-on `Guru301` service to the application hosted in the **us** region
2. Adding add-on `Guru301` service to the application hosted in the **eu** region

Scenario 1: In this case, the `Guru301` service is successfully added to the web application. Indeed, the web application is hosted in the **us** region. Thus, the CBVM transition for activating `Guru301` is triggered synchronously with the selection of the **us** region.

Scenario 2: In this case, the `Guru301` service is not added to the web application. Upon receiving the request, the run-time CBVM postponed the activation of `Guru301` service until the application region becomes **us**.

This experiment illustrates that, as expected, the run-time CBVM enforces safe reconfiguration of the cloud application.

7 Related Work

The last two decades have seen various forms of systems evolution. In computer science, it is often related to system architectures, where *dynamic reconfiguration* and *self-adaptation* remain very active research axes for self-adaptive systems [2, 30]. Model-based approaches and service-oriented techniques make use of models together with different artefacts, such as rules, policies, objectives, to model and to deal with system evolution, as e.g., in the framework of self-adaptive systems [30,31].

Model-based approaches to reconfiguration use system models to analyze information and calculate a reconfiguration plan/self-adaptation plan to keep the system compliant with the user expectation and context constraints. Following [21], the approaches in [22] either compute the set of all possible configurations in advance at design time or a new valid configuration at run-time. As indicated in Sect. 1, this induces computational or validation overheads, whenever a reconfiguration is needed. Indeed, when all valid configurations are precomputed at design time, they must be stored explicitly, e.g. for determining the appropriate choice at run-time. This is problematic, since the set of configurations is exponential in the number of features, or in the size of logic formulae, but particularly so for distributed systems, where a copy of the list of features or subformulae has to be stored at every node. Alternatively, at run-time, the new configuration must be computed and validated thus inducing a computational overhead. In [10] the authors advocate the re-use of variability and commonalities at run-time for autonomic computing. In FAMA [5] the engine, Autonomic Reconfigurator, uses the associated resolution to query the run-time models about necessary architectural modifications defined by conditions at design time, in order to generate a reconfiguration plan. Our proposals further leverage variability models to exploit both features and components within component-based run-time variability models.

Component-based approaches allow describing system architectures made up of components that define the life-cycle of the system parts. Connectors control the relationships between the components and establish interactions between them. Typically, Madeus and Concerto [12] define component-based models focusing on modelling and coordinating the life-cycle of interacting parts of a system. Concerto provides ports that represent the ability of a component to provide services to other components (e.g. service, piece of data) during its life cycle. Unlike Madeus, Concerto is equipped with a reconfiguration language that allows the system administrator to modify the architecture by executing reconfiguration scripts (controlling the system by inserting new reconfiguration actions).

The recent survey [2] analyses approaches, methodologies, or design patterns for managing runtime variability through software reconfigurations in Dynamic SPL for self-adaptive systems. The authors note that many existing approaches compensate between memory and time, as, e.g., [26, 29].

Our approach exploits the advantages of both features and components to generate run-time component-based variability models that ensure, by construction, safety properties through reconfigurations. In [29], FM has been extended with relative cardinalities and then used for checking temporal logic formulae, in order to support the dynamic evolution of microservices applications. Starting from an extended FM, instead of generating a whole transition system to check the reconfiguration path against propositional and temporal constraints, in the present paper, we generate a run-time CBVM for handling reconfiguration safely. However, dealing with liveness temporal properties remains a future work direction.

The novelty of our approach lies in the generation of a correct-by-construction runtime CBVM that enforces domain constraints for dynamic reconfiguration while leveraging SPL tools to capture domain variability. Unlike many works using SPL techniques and tools, our approach goes beyond employing static variability models at run-time, e.g. [14], and avoids the overhead of computing or validating new target configurations explicitly. Furthermore, our approach differs from other by-construction reconfiguration techniques, such as [29], which require computing the global LTS to derive the reconfiguration paths. Instead, we encode the feature model constraints into a JavaBIP run-time CBVM. In turn, the JavaBIP engine relies on Binary Decision Diagrams (BDDs) [3] to efficiently encode the various operational and coordination constraints of the system and to compute the possible interactions from the current CBVM state [7,17]. In particular, permanent constraints, which encode information about the behavior, glue, and data wires of the components, are encoded only once at the initialization of the JavaBIP system. The only constraints that are recomputed at each cycle are the temporary ones that encode the current states of the components. This allows us to strike the right balance between, on one hand, precomputing the global reconfiguration LTS—which involves a very long computation at the initialisation phase and potentially requires a huge amount of memory to store the result—and, on the other hand, verifying all the constraints at run-time—which eliminates the initialisation phase and the memory overhead at the cost of a run time overhead orders of magnitude larger than that observed with our approach.

8   Conclusion and Future Work

This paper describes an automated approach for enforcing by construction the safe reconfiguration behaviour of software products through the automatic derivation of executable, run-time component-based variability models (CBVMs) from feature models. The run-time CBVMs, control the application behaviour by handling reconfiguration requests and executing them so as to ensure the saturated partial validity of all reachable configurations without having to compute, nor validate them at run-time. Our approach ensures the preservation of feature model semantics and constraint consistency in the generated models as established in Sect. 5. Additionally, the feasibility and effectiveness of our approach are demonstrated through an evaluation of the overhead induced by the run-time CBVM on applications containing up to 300 features. The experimental results show the interest of our approach for handling reconfiguration requests with low overhead over the application. Furthermore, the successful integration of our approach into a real-world case scenario with the Heroku cloud demonstrates the feasibility of our approach for practical applications. Therefore, our approach provides a solution to the research question formulated in Sect. 2.

The key threat to the validity of our work lies in Assumption 1. We expect that assumption to hold for a large proportion of realistic feature models. Efficiently verifying or enforcing that assumption in the general case is hard [20].

However, we can put in place additional heuristics based on the propagation of exclusion constraints to further increase the proportion of feature models that satisfy the assumption. As a future work direction, we will explore stronger heuristics to enforce Assumption 1. Furthermore, we intend to generalise our approach to constraints among features formulated in terms of arbitrary Boolean formulas. As shown in [8], that will require extending JavaBIP with priority models. To streamline the user experience and minimise the necessity to wait for user input, we also plan to extend the feature model with default values. Additionally, we aim to incorporate temporal constraints over features, e.g.excluding the possibility of downgrading the database plan [29] and plan to investigate the analytical treatment of the space complexity of the BDDs used in our approach.

References

1. Toward run-time coordination of reconfiguration requests in cloud computing systems. Zenodo (2023). https://doi.org/10.5281/zenodo.7703952
2. Aguayo, O., Sepúlveda, S.: Variability management in dynamic software product lines for self-adaptive systems-a systematic mapping. Appl. Sci. **12**(20), 10240 (2022). https://doi.org/10.48550/arXiv.2205.08487
3. Akers, S.: Binary decision diagrams. IEEE Trans. Comput. **C-27**(6), 509–516 (1978). https://doi.org/10.1109/TC.1978.1675141
4. Basu, A., et al.: Rigorous component-based system design using the BIP framework. IEEE Softw. **28**(3), 41–48 (2011)
5. Benavides, D., Trinidad, P., Ruiz-Cortés, A., Segura, S.: FaMa. In: Capilla, R., Bosch, J., Kang, KC. (eds.) Systems and Software Variability Management. Springer, Berlin, Heidelberg (2013). https://doi.org/10.1007/978-3-642-36583-6_11
6. Berger, T., et al.: A survey of variability modeling in industrial practice. In: Proceedings of the 7th International Workshop on Variability Modelling of Software-intensive Systems, pp. 1–8 (2013)
7. Bliudze, S., Mavridou, A., Szymanek, R., Zolotukhina, A.: Exogenous coordination of concurrent software components with JavaBIP. Softw.: Pract. Exper. **47**(11), 1801–1836 (2017)
8. Bliudze, S., Sifakis, J.: Synthesizing glue operators from glue constraints for the construction of component-based systems. In: Apel, S., Jackson, E. (eds.) SC 2011. LNCS, vol. 6708, pp. 51–67. Springer, Heidelberg (2011). https://doi.org/10.1007/978-3-642-22045-6_4
9. Butting, A., Heim, R., Kautz, O., Ringert, J.O., Rumpe, B., Wortmann, A.: A classification of dynamic reconfiguration in component and connector architecture description languages. In: 4th International Workshop ModComp, vol. 1 (2017)
10. Capilla, R., Bosch, J., Trinidad, P., Ruiz-Cortés, A., Hinchey, M.: An overview of dynamic software product line architectures and techniques: observations from research and industry. J. Syst. Softw. **91**, 3–23 (2014)
11. Cetina, C., Fons, J., Pelechano, V.: Applying software product lines to build autonomic pervasive systems. In: 2008 12th International SPL Conference, pp. 117–126. IEEE (2008)

12. Chardet, M., Coullon, H., Robillard, S.: Toward safe and efficient reconfiguration with concerto. Sci. Comput. Program. **203**, 102582 (2021)
13. Crnkovic, I., Chaudron, M., Sentilles, S., Vulgarakis, A.: A classification framework for component models. Software Engineering Research and Practice in Sweden, p. 3 (2007)
14. Entekhabi, S., Karataş, A.S., Oğuztüzün, H.: Dynamic constraint satisfaction algorithm for online feature model reconfiguration. In: International Conference on Control Engineering and Information Technology (CEIT), pp. 1–7 (2018). https://doi.org/10.1109/CEIT.2018.8751750
15. Farhat, S., Bliudze, S., Duchien, L., Kouchnarenko, O.: Run-time coordination of reconfiguration requests in cloud computing systems. Research Report 9504, Inria (2023). https://inria.hal.science/hal-04085278
16. Gomaa, H., Hussein, M.: Software reconfiguration patterns for dynamic evolution of software architectures. In: Proceedings 4th Working IEEE/IFIP Conference WICSA 2004, pp. 79–88 (2004)
17. Jaber, M., Basu, A., Bliudze, S.: Symbolic implementation of connectors in BIP. In: Bonchi, F., Grohmann, D., Spoletini, P., Tuosto, E. (eds.) Proceedings 2nd Interaction and Concurrency Experience: Structured Interactions, ICE 2009, Bologna, Italy, 31st August 2009. EPTCS, vol. 12, pp. 41–55 (2009). https://doi.org/10.4204/EPTCS.12.3
18. Jouault, F., Allilaire, F., Bézivin, J., Kurtev, I.: ATL: a model transformation tool. Sci. Comput. Program. **72**(1–2), 31–39 (2008)
19. Kang, K.C., Cohen, S.G., Hess, J.A., Novak, W.E., Peterson, A.S.: Feature-oriented domain analysis (FODA) feasibility study. Carnegie-Mellon Univ Pittsburgh, PA, Software Engineering Inst, Tech. rep. (1990)
20. Kautz, O.: The complexities of the satisfiability checking problems of feature diagram sublanguages. Software and Systems Modeling, pp. 1–17 (2022)
21. Kephart, J.O.: Research challenges of autonomic computing. In: Roman, G., Griswold, W.G., Nuseibeh, B. (eds.) 27th International Conference ICSE, pp. 15–22. ACM (2005)
22. Krupitzer, C., Roth, F.M., VanSyckel, S., Schiele, G., Becker, C.: A survey on engineering approaches for self-adaptive systems. Pervasive Mob. Comput. **17**, 184–206 (2015)
23. Lascu, T.A., Mauro, J., Zavattaro, G.: A planning tool supporting the deployment of cloud applications. In: 2013 IEEE 25th International Conference on Tools with Artificial Intelligence, pp. 213–220. IEEE (2013)
24. Mavridou, A., Sifakis, J., Sztipanovits, J.: DesignBIP: A design studio for modeling and generating systems with BIP. arXiv preprint arXiv:1805.09919 (2018)
25. Middleton, N., Schneeman, R.: Heroku: up and running: effortless application deployment and scaling. "O'Reilly Media, Inc." (2013)
26. Quinton, C., Romero, D., Duchien, L.: Saloon: a platform for selecting and configuring cloud environments. Softw.: Pract. Exper. **46**(1), 55–78 (2016)
27. Schaefer, I., et al.: Software diversity: state of the art and perspectives (2012)
28. Schobbens, P., Heymans, P., Trigaux, J.: Feature diagrams: a survey and a formal semantics. In: 14th IEEE International Conference RE2006, pp. 136–145. IEEE Computer Society (2006)
29. Sousa, G., Rudametkin, W., Duchien, L.: Extending dynamic software product lines with temporal constraints. In: 2017 IEEE/ACM 12th International Symposium on Software Engineering for Adaptive and Self-Managing Systems (SEAMS), pp. 129–139. IEEE (2017)

30. Weyns, D.: Software engineering of self-adaptive systems. In: Handbook of Software Engineering, pp. 399–443. Springer, Cham (2019). https://doi.org/10.1007/978-3-030-00262-6_11

31. Yang, Z., Li, Z., Jin, Z., Chen, Y.: A systematic literature review of requirements modeling and analysis for self-adaptive systems. In: Salinesi, C., van de Weerd, I. (eds.) REFSQ 2014. LNCS, vol. 8396, pp. 55–71. Springer, Cham (2014). https://doi.org/10.1007/978-3-319-05843-6_5

32. Zhang, J., Cheng, B.H.: Model-based development of dynamically adaptive software. In: Proceedings of the 28th International Conference on Software Engineering, pp. 371–380 (2006)

Author Index

© IFIP International Federation for Information Processing 2023
S.-S. Jongmans and A. Lopes (Eds.): COORDINATION 2023, LNCS 13908, p. 293, 2023.
https://doi.org/10.1007/978-3-031-35361-1

Printed in the United States
by Baker & Taylor Publisher Services